Christ's
Subversive Body

Christ's Subversive Body

*Practices of Religious Rhetoric
in Culture and Politics*

✦

Olga V. Solovieva

NORTHWESTERN UNIVERSITY PRESS
EVANSTON, ILLINOIS

Northwestern University Press
www.nupress.northwestern.edu

Copyright © 2018 by Northwestern University Press.
Published 2018. All rights reserved.

Printed in the United States of America

10   9   8   7   6   5   4   3   2   1

ISBN 978-0-8101-3600-7 (cloth)
ISBN 978-0-8101-3599-4 (paper)
ISBN 978-0-8101-3601-4 (ebook)

In dear, grateful memory of Ludmila Viktorovna Polyakova

Library of Congress Cataloging-in-Publication data are available from the Library
of Congress.

The kingdom of God is not a matter of speech, but of power.
—Paul, 1 Corinthians 4:20

For example, by proclaiming: everything that we have said-written-done up to now wasn't really serious or strict; it was all a joke: sarcastic, even a bit ironic, parasitical, metaphorical, citational, cryptic, fictional, literary, insincere, etc.
What force they would gain by doing this!!
But will they take the risk?
—Jacques Derrida, *Limited Inc*

CONTENTS

ILLUSTRATIONS

ACKNOWLEDGMENTS

This book started at my time in the Department of Comparative Literature at Yale University. I am thankful to the department for the precious freedom of research and intellectual trust, from which I greatly profited. Yale University provided me with funding, including a John F. Enders Fellowship in summer 2003 and a John Perry Miller Fellowship in summer 2004. Further support was supplied by fellowships in the Department of Germanic Studies and in the Committee on Social Thought at the University of Chicago.

I gratefully acknowledge the support of the librarians of the Sterling Memorial Library and Divinity School Library at Yale and the Regenstein Library at the University of Chicago, who helped me with researching and compiling bibliographies in a variety of subjects. I owe a special debt to the exceptional competence and generosity of June Pachuta Farris, bibliographer for Slavic, East European, and Eurasian studies and linguistics at Regenstein Library.

The Prussian Cultural Heritage Foundation supported with a scholarship my study of the *Book of the Holy Trinity* at the Berlin State Museum of Prints and Drawings in the fall of 2009. The curators of the museum assisted with my acquisition of a microfilm and slides of the manuscript.

To my education at the University of Connecticut School of Law, supported through a Ralph Gregory Elliot Memorial Scholarship in 2010–11, I owe my introduction to American legal discourse, to the skills of legal analysis and writing, as well as the discovery of the materials of the Enfield Schools case discussed in this book.

The independent news broadcast *DemocracyNow!* taught me American political history through the best examples of investigative journalism. In my eyes, the work of Amy Goodman and her crew sets the highest standard for civil courage, integrity of research, and intellectual accountability to society. I am highly aware that without "my universities" of *DemocracyNow!* and UConn Law, the completion of this book would not have been possible.

I would also like to thank Ulrike Bergermann for sharing her expertise in sign language, Elisabeth Strowick for constructive theoretical discussions of the Pasolini chapter, Giacomo Manzoli for pointing me to *Intellettuale*, Stuart Semmel for locating Marjorie Kelly's critique of the corporation, and a stranger in black, an admirer of Kant and alchemy, whom I encountered one day in the corridor of the Classics Library at the Freie Universität Berlin and who directed me to the *Book of the Holy Trinity*. Their contributions have been reflected in the book.

I acknowledge the American Comparative Literature Association (ACLA) and the Society of Cinema and Media Studies (SCMS), which over the years have given me stimulating opportunities to develop and test the ideas of this book in conference presentations. Academic editors in several disciplines— Caroline Torra-Mattenklott and Thomas Strässle, the late Erika Greber, William Katerberg, Volker Drecoll, and Joseph Francese—courageously gave me space where I could explore the material of this book, share my conclusions, and receive constructive feedback from specialists in the subject matter.

Material from the first chapter was previously published in my articles "Epiphanius of Salamis and His Invention of Iconoclasm in the Fourth Century A.D.," *Fides et Historia* 42, no. 1 (2010): 21–46, and "Epiphanius of Salamis between Church and State: New Perspectives on the Iconoclastic Fragments," *Zeitschrift für Antikes Christentum / Journal of Ancient Christianity* 16, no. 2 (2012): 344–67.

The material of the second chapter was first presented in German at the interdisciplinary symposium "Stoffe: Theorie und Geschichte der Materialität in Künsten und Wissenschaften" at the University of Zurich in October 2003 and was subsequently published as a book chapter, "Corpus Libri als Corpus Christi: Zur prekären Transsubstantiation des alchemistischen Sprachstoffes im *Buch der Heiligen Dreifaltigkeit* (1415–1419)," in *Poetiken der Materie: Stoffe und ihre Qualitäten in Literatur, Kunst und Philosophie*, ed. Thomas Strässle and Caroline Tora-Mattenklott (Freiburg i.B.: Rombach, 2005), 145–64.

The fourth chapter was developed and partially presented in talks given at the ACLA in 2006; the School of Humanities at the University of California, Irvine in 2007; and the Franke Institute for the Humanities at the University of Chicago in 2016. Some of its material was published in "Polyphonie und Karneval: Spuren Dostoevskijs in Thomas Manns Roman *Doktor Faustus*," *Poetica* 3–4 (2005): 463–94.

The fifth chapter was developed in lectures given at the SCMS in 2005, at the 16 Beaver Artist Organization, New York, in 2005; and at the University of Virginia in 2006. Some of its material was published as "The Intellectual Embodied in His Medium, or the Cinematic Passion of Pier Paolo Pasolini," *Italian Culture* 29, no. 1 (2011): 52–68. Each of these publications brought me closer to the completion of this book. I am thankful to the editors and publishers for their permission to reuse previously published material.

The support of several individuals was pivotal to this project. Haun Saussy provided an institutional cover for the project, translated passages from ancient Greek, Latin, and other languages, recommended books, and helped with bibliographies and idiom. Without his generous and unwavering commitment, this book would not be possible, for which I owe him many thanks.

The late Helen Tartar was loyally dedicated to the publication of this book through thick and thin, all the way to her tragic death in March 2014. Her precise and painstakingly detailed editing notes to the introduction will stay with me as a tangible memorial to our shared adventure. I am grateful to my editor Michael L. Levine at the Northwestern University Press for his support of this book.

Soelve I. Curdts was the most incisive and encouraging critic of the manuscript. Her understanding of the book's theoretical framework and constructive input helped strengthen its formal presentation. To Bridget Madden of the Visual Resources Center at the University of Chicago goes the credit of preparing the illustrations.

René, Tino, and Kiki contributed with their contagious energy, inspiring curiosity about the world, and a delightful challenge to keep pace.

Haun Saussy

Why a discontinuous history of the body of Christ?

The "body of Christ" is the dominant figure of connection, centrality, continuity, and unity in Western culture. Perpetually regenerated through the enigmatic Eucharist, it makes all tables one table, joins all believers in "that mystical body . . . which is the blessed company of all faithful people" (*The Book of Common Prayer*), that is, the church, and commands the return of its wandering parts: geographically, the Holy Land in the era of the Crusades; doctrinally, the denominations that are deemed to have separated themselves from the trunk. This continuity is asserted as a fact (the community is necessarily one) and as an imperative (whatever has been broken off must be reunited). And, like every self-respecting body in a hierarchical age, the body has a head, which directs the action of its members.

Temporally, this body is thought to have a beginning (the Incarnation), a middle (the history of the church in the world), and an end (the ingathering of the faithful at the apocalypse). It is the "substantial link" among all the phenomena in the world (Leibniz),[1] the "one needful thing" (Luke 10:42).[2] Semiotically speaking, its privilege is uncontestable.

But to take the "body of Christ" as a physically, temporally, and epistemologically continuous thing is to accept the postulates of a theological cosmology that disregards the acts whereby that body has been posited as a body, and has been linked up with its replications and consequences. This book aims to narrate—discontinuously, as it may have to be—a series of shifts in the place and meaning of the "body of Christ." For at many points in the history of European civilization at which the legitimating function of that body was for one reason or another in suspense, what we might call theological entrepreneurs (or *bricoleurs*) grasped the elements of that body, reordered them, connected them differently to the lives of humans and states, and proclaimed (deviously) the newly confected body to be the same as the previous body. This operation Solovieva calls "subversion," and the persistent recourse to it, shown through the history of Western culture over the last 1,600 years, is her most important discovery.

Bricolage of this sort has long had a bad reputation. Another name for it is "heresy" (from *hairēsis*, the act of picking and choosing). Tertullian characterizes it as an evil specific to textuality:

I am the apostles' heir . . . As they ordered in their testament, as they charged their executors, as they pledged themselves, so do I possess. . . . Wherever diversity of doctrines is found, we will necessarily find adulteration of the Scriptures and their interpretation. . . . What indeed has ever been found contrary to us in our Scriptures? What have we ever inserted of our own for the sake of changing something in the Scriptures that we find inopportune, whether by excerpting, supplementing or transforming [*detractione vel adiectione vel transmutatione*] them? . . . Marcion, on the other hand, openly and notoriously used not the pen but the expunging-knife, when he murdered the Scriptures in refashioning them to suit his purpose. . . . Though I read that "there must be heresies among us," these heresies could never have arisen without the Scriptures.[3]

Though the idea of a media-based history of religion is already to be found among the fathers of the church, it is already implicitly bifurcated. The properly witnessed and transmitted "testament" that makes one an "heir to the apostles" is already, in Tertullian, menaced by a discontinuous and suspiciously confected one—a "cento" or collage, a scroll with patches and erasures. Against the advice of major voices in the Patrology, Solovieva is not afraid to try the collage model out and see where it leads.

What does a history become when it is no longer the history of an entity persisting or developing in time (the self, the state, an idea) and becomes a set of episodes of recombination? The logic and rhetoric of continuous narratives is called into question (recall the baffling moments of transition, which were really brute-force shifts in the semiotic order, in Michel Foucault's *The Order of Things*). Agency takes on a new meaning, as it is no longer the ability to accomplish what the will has already desired, but becomes a form of contextual engineering aimed at producing a desiring and willing agent; we witness, not games played to their end according to the rules, but metagames in which the moves are nothing other than changes in the rules of the game.

Resituated thus, the history and the body Solovieva narrates here are profoundly non-teleological. But that does not mean that they are aimless. The transitions she describes are prompted by an urgent sense of purpose, only their purposes are not discernible in the "before" of the act that seeks to accomplish them. We could call this the Redeemer's Paradox: "Think not that I am come to destroy the law or the prophets. I am come, not to destroy, but to fulfill" (Matt. 5:17), says the man who to all intents and purposes did destroy the Jewish law and prophets for those who would become his followers. The fact that what the pre-Jesus observer would have seen as incontestably "destroying" them is just what the post-Jesus observer claims is "fulfilling" them indicates how integral to the continuities of the "body of Christ" are the discontinuities that go into fashioning it.

And yet Solovieva's book is not a history of a religious concept or of a mode of Christian thought. It is, as it were, lined with such a history. In the publishing protocols that Borges imagined for the country of Tlön, "a book which does not contain its counterbook is considered incomplete."[4] Here the relation between this book and its implied anti-book is one of steady opposition. We are to keep the identitarian, triumphalist, Whiggish narrative in mind as we read the inventory of devices used to subvert continuity in the name of continuity.

A parallel for the work done by Solovieva here is the history of formalist literary criticism. Conventional literary criticism asks: What does the work mean? How does it measure up to the canons of quality? Formalist criticism asks: How does the work produce its meanings, and what is a meaning anyway? In what way do canons of taste or truth respond, and fail to respond, to the individuality of literary works? Formalist criticism (like its predecessor, rhetorical theory) asks a different question from thematic criticism. For formalist criticism, all signs are empty a priori, and become full or meaningful in the act of their co-inscription with other signs to make a context. This is why formalism is often denounced as nihilistic. But to be fair, formalism is intensely optimistic and pragmatic, for the meaning of the work is always in its future. "What is happening here?" asks the formalist critic. "What is about to happen?"

For many historical reasons, the fates of formalism in literary and religious studies have diverged. In a religious context, perhaps, "formalism" inescapably denotes insincerity and pedantry. But to approach religious discourse in a literary spirit means not to appreciate its aesthetic qualities—for these can be introduced without any subversion of the traditional subordination of the senses to the spirit; "The Bible as Literature" shocks nobody—but to be attentive to the constructed, the tactical, the random, and the allegorical as crucial features of religious representation. It would be taking Solovieva's painstakingly philological investigation too far off its track to assimilate her procedure to those of other critics, but for illustrative purposes I might suggest what would happen if we considered the "body of Christ" in the company of the "device" (Shklovsky), the "prosthesis" (Derrida), the "body without organs" (Deleuze), the "dispositif" (Lyotard), "biopower" (Foucault), or "bare life" (Agamben). None of these thinkers have quite the same agenda or means as Solovieva, but the enumeration of them suffices to document the transformation, in twentieth-century thought, of life into robotics as an essential mode of critique and renewal. Her enterprise should be considered as being in dialogue with theirs.

As a consequence of the constitution and temporality of the "subversive body of Christ" in parallel with its traditional counterpart, Solovieva does not particularly signal the transitions among domains such as "religion," "rhetoric," and "politics." Claims such as "religion is ultimately about power" or "literature is social hierarchy inscribed in language" have their force only by virtue of religion, power, literature, and the social being thought, preliminarily, as separate things, which is not the assumption here. The utterly hybrid and omnivorous category of "figura," that novel mode of reinterpretation that Erich Auerbach saw as defining Christianity's relation to scripture, to history and to empirical life, is one of her models.[5] The figurations—the making-into-figure—of the prior things taken as "figures for" the things to come display, as in Auerbach, an unsettlingly retroactive temporality. The staff of Aaron is a "figure for" the cross because it must be found to have a meaning consisting in its reference to an event in the life of Christ. I say "the life of Christ" advisedly, because the designation "Christ" was necessary to accomplish the reinscription; even "the life of Jesus" had to be transformed by "figura" into a figure for "the life of Christ." The meaning of a pre-Christian fact or event for pre- or non-Christians is necessarily subverted (overturned, like a judicial error) into its meaning for Christians. So too with the subversions recounted here (none of which, it must be acknowledged, left a lasting historical effect comparable to Paul's original subversion). While "figura" can assimilate any possible content—and thus opens the way to the "mixed style" that Auerbach saw as a necessary ingredient in Western literary realism[6]—it knows no meaning but its own. To read "figura" from an external standpoint requires patience and an ability to keep one's eye on the processes, not the contents, of cultural meaning-production.

It is plain to see that a discontinuous mode of writing alone enables the specific critical standpoint that is Solovieva's here. "Parataxis," in the hands of Adorno, became not a clumsy, disordered mode of writing but an articulation of the disarticulation that the knowingly alienated poet throws back to normal language in its instrumentalized, subordinated, consensual form.[7] It is the first opening of a dissensus. Or to quote Saint Paul:

> For he hath put all things under [*hypetaxen*, the verb corresponding to the noun *hypotaxis*] his feet. But when he saith all things are put under [*hypotetaktai*] him, it is manifest that he is excepted, which did put all things under him [*tou hypotaxantos*]. And when all things shall be subdued [*hypotagēi*] under him, then shall the Son also himself be subject [*hypotagēsetai*] unto him that put all things under him [*tōi hypotaxanti autōi*], that God may be all in all. (1 Cor. 15:27–28)

With daring, consistency and a certain strain of humor, Solovieva reverses Paul's culminating, hypotactical string of hypotaxes into parataxes and declines to let "all history move toward one great goal" (Joyce, *Ulysses*).

Christ's
Subversive Body

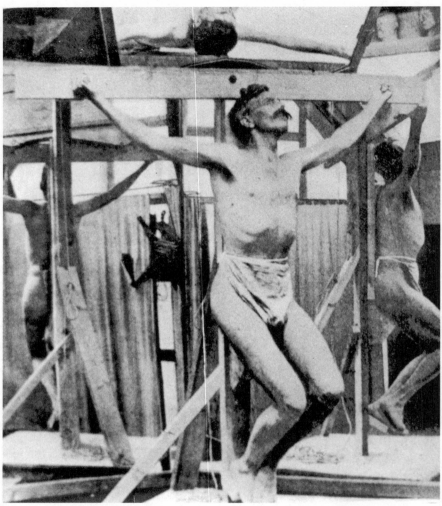

Figure 0.1. Crucifixion model, Antonio Gaudí workshop, circa 1910. Copyright ©
Expiatory Temple of the Sagrada Família.

INTRODUCTION

In the basement of the still unfinished church of the Sagrada Família in Barcelona, one can see on display a photographic image of a model posing as the crucified Christ in Antoni Gaudí's workshop. (See fig. 0.1.) A man in his thirties, draped only in a loincloth, is holding tight to two handles fixed on a horizontal plank of a wooden structure that has been elevated on a platform in imitation of the cross. His head is thrown back against the beam of wood that supports him. His face is raised toward the ceiling in evocation of the famous reproach. His feet are placed one over the other on a tiny footstand below, pointing downward at a sharp angle—an uncomfortable, trying position but also an exceptionally powerful one in its lasting command over the imagination of the world.

The imitation of Christ, this image suggests, is a matter of positionality. Anyone can assume it as did this man coiffed according to the fashion of the early twentieth century—an underpaid laborer from a construction site, or maybe an unemployed paterfamilias from the street seeking a few extra pesos. He has assumed the role, however, in compliance with Gaudí's instructions. He is there to assist the architect who explores new spatial possibilities of familiar iconography in his work on an altarpiece or a façade figure for his modern church. The model on the cross embodies this intentionality, being in a way a prosthetic extension of Gaudí himself, whom we can easily imagine guiding his model's limbs, commenting, gesturing, taking the posture himself in demonstration of his vision.

Familiar though it is, the positionality of Christ, as the photograph conveys, is still not a given but needs to be constructed and readjusted anew each time someone, like Gaudí's model, is willing to step into the role. The structure on which the man is positioned is flexible in its mechanics. The wooden beam supporting his body is not solid but assembled from several removable and interchangeable planks. Their length, thickness, and breadth are a matter of choice. The angles, proportions, and measurements of the scaffold's combined parts can easily be manipulated by bolts, screws, and clamps so as to fit a model's size exactly, but they in turn are there to shape the posture of the person on the cross.

The potential of readjustment built here into Christ's position might be merely a matter of detail, but it is often details that trigger the most radical shifts of meaning. Gaudí staged this *tableau vivant* in the course of his invention of what he called a "synthetic" geometrical form. This synthetic form was to take the simple shapes of conventional architecture (such as triangles, squares, circles, prisms, and cylinders) to a new level of spatial complexity, refashioning them into the curved surfaces of para- and hyperboloids, helicoids, and conoids—forms usually found in the world of nature. Eager to realize these more intricate spatial arrangements in the realm of culture, Gaudí relied on three-dimensional experiments with models and mirrors such as we see in the photograph.[1]

The model on the cross brings out the logic of the kind of spiraling, invertible helicoid surface that Gaudí favored in the architectural design of his church. The virtual space created through the multiple mirror reflections synthesizes four perspectives on the model's body. The front, side, and back views convey an impression of circular carousel-like movement frozen in time, while a view from above simultaneously allows for an inverted image. But this synthetic space also feeds back into the body's shape: in the straight angles of the model's joints, in the protruding triangularity of his rib cage, in the sharp contours of his face, and in the wiry elongated arms are already recognizable the sinusoid, stretched-out, curvy figures of sacred history which populate the organically formed alcoves of the Sagrada Família. Most importantly, the image shows a position that seemed to be singular and stable as polyvalent and invertible.

In its function as a construction device, the photograph of the model betrays the manmade quality of something for which ultimate, revelatory truth is claimed. Behind the vertical beam hangs a long braided rope that helps control the angle of the mirror above. The drapery surrounding the crucifix hides the artist's studio as the setting of the scene. In the curtains' folds discreetly nestles the camera whose invisible operator has fixed upon a point of view most advantageous for the sculpture. The future erasure of all traces of construction is already built into the process of construction itself.

And yet, this memory prop for Gaudí's design of Christ's body, the sculptured body on the cross as well as the body of the building that is supposed to envelop it, exposes a spatial and logical grid which, according to the architect's calculation, keys one dimension of this body to another: the positionality of the imitation of Christ relative to its symbolic, cosmic, and social context.

The photograph was taken circa 1910. In the 1907 papal encyclical "Against the Errors of the Modernists," Pope Pius X in sixty-five paragraphs had condemned and proscribed the scholarly exegesis of the scriptures for doing in the realm of biblical philology what the studio photograph shows Gaudí was doing (perhaps clandestinely) in the realm of the sacred arts— questioning the divine immutability of dogmatic truths, revealing their manmade, historically conditioned character, insisting on a modern readjustment of doctrines. The photograph was not singled out for orthodox objections, nor did it succumb to the destruction of the Sagrada Família's archive during the Spanish Civil War. It survived to become a rare testimony to the architect's planning and design of a church that insidiously subverts the traditions of sacred architecture.

In his design of Sagrada Família, commissioned not by the church but by a private patron in 1882, the architect challenged Barcelona's venerable Gothic Cathedral. Since its foundation in the fourth century, enduring the usual series of destructions, updates, and reconstructions, the see of Catalan archbishops has faithfully clung to its cornerstone, becoming an embodiment of tradition and continuity itself. Not so Sagrada Família. Whatever form of personal religious mysticism might have guided Gaudí's vision of the modern church, it is difficult to ward off the impression that his Christ's body embraces a pantheistic, if not a Darwinian universe. The vegetative elements of his church structure seem to be driven into the skies by a spontaneous outburst of élan vital dominating and taking over the familiar geometry of the Gothic, extruding the decorative-looking figures of biblical history as a mere side effect of creation.

Gaudí's photographic study for a crucifix was never sculpturally realized as a part of this architectural program, but it still suggests a useful parable about the positionality of Christ and its integration into projects of individualistic hubris. The image caught my eye because it offers a perfect visual counterpart to the logical and verbal scaffolding of the "discourse apart" studied in this book, that is, a discourse where the protean notion of Christ's body provides a particular positionality for the speaking subject, circumscribes the broader social, political, and cosmic horizon of speech, and constitutes the medium in and through which the two are interlocked; and where this notion's discursive potentiality is used in pursuit of culturally or politically subversive goals.

Positionality, Subversion, Ideological Operator: Christ's Body in Paul

This book is not a theological study in Christology. What the book offers is rather an investigation into the topos of Christ's body and the very specific rhetorical and epistemological functions that this religious notion has the potential to occupy when removed from the immediate context of ritual worship or theology and used in areas where it is least expected: in conceptualizations of the power of the state, or the materiality of a book, or the virtual space of a novel of consciousness, or in cinematic apparatus, or in a business corporation, to name just a few of its possible protean transformations.

The goal is to demonstrate through a series of concrete historical examples how the performative power associated with religious idiom and the positionality of the subject who claims to speak on behalf of the divine have been repeatedly smuggled outside the precincts of the church into the broader realm of culture and politics. The discursive, conceptual, and communicative effectiveness of a language which presumably can turn a wafer into the Eucharist, ascertain the resurrection of the dead, or accomplish the philosophical synecdoche of cosmos, humanity, and congregation under the name of Christ's body, accounts for the desire to apply it in the extra-ecclesial domains.

This book's approach to the figure of Christ (as we know it from the Christian tradition) in terms of its discursive function is not unprecedented. In his seminal article "L'Opérateur christologique" ("The Christological Operator," 1985), the French scholar of ancient Christianity René Nouailhat already outlined a program of studying the ideological functioning of Christianity by approaching the figure of Christ precisely in these terms.

On the basis of studies on the structure of Christological dogma as it was developed by theologians in the early centuries of Christian history, Nouailhat showed how certain structural elements of the discursive formation of the dogma (such as, for example, the heterogeneity of its pre-Christian religious and philosophical sources, the ambiguity implicit in Christ's divine and human natures, the paradox of triumph through defeat or life through death, and its alliance with and adoption of the universalism of Roman imperial claims) resulted in its peerless status as an "ideological operator," capable not only of meaningfully organizing religious discourse, no matter how contradictory or heterogeneous the ideas composing it, but also of grouping and regrouping participants in religious discourse, no matter how diverse, along varying political lines. Nouailhat observed:

> By this amalgam of heteroclite backgrounds, the figure of Jesus Christ manages to express contradictory practices and to bring them to concord through a certain kind of discursive practice in which the Christological concept functions as an operator of unification. The syncretic composition of the figure of Jesus Christ thus ideologically made possible the functioning of this discursive practice in social, economic, political, and culturally heterogeneous contexts and social milieux.[2]

While preserving this helpful understanding of the figure of Christ as an "ideological operator," this book at once narrows and broadens the approach suggested by Nouailhat. It narrows his approach by limiting the discursive operation under scrutiny to the type of subversive discourse developed through interpretations of the notion of Christ's body in the Pauline epistles.

However, the book does not deal with Pauline theology or ecclesiastical politics in their own right but focuses on the adaptation of the Christ-driven subversive modality of Paul's discourse in the realm of culture and politics. In this respect, this book broadens the problematic suggested by Nouailhat, which was limited to the "religious field proper" (le champ religieux) and religiously inspired social movements (including, for example, Christian fundamentalism in the United States or liberation theology in Latin America).

The Pauline type of subversion informing the concept of this book should also be further characterized at the outset. The book builds on a theoretical framework derived from the analysis of Paul's rhetoric in such methodologically different yet complementary works as Alain Badiou's *Saint Paul: The Foundation of Universalism* and Dale Martin's *The Corinthian Body*. Among the vast scholarship on Paul, these two studies were chosen deliberately because of their particular attention to the figure of Christ as an ideological operator in Nouailhat's sense and because of the special theoretical insight they allow into the subversive function of this operator.

Through the example of Paul, Badiou defined a "militant" rhetorical positionality characteristic of any revolutionary discourse that aims at a radical change in the order of things. He has called this type of discourse "antiphilosophy" and famously compared it with Lenin's strategic adaptation of Marx. This positionality is grounded in what he calls Paul's "eventual conception of Christianity,"[3] in which "everything is brought to a single point: Jesus, son of God . . . , and Christ in virtue of this, died on the cross and was resurrected. The rest, all the rest, is of no real importance" (Badiou, *Saint Paul*, 33).

Non-dialectical in its character, the Christ-event doesn't transform but disrupts the established order of things: "Resurrection suddenly comes forth *out from* the power of death, not through its negation" (Badiou, *Saint Paul*, 73). Paul's declaration of belief in Christ's resurrection mimics the founding event itself: it interrupts the previous regime of discourses, as the resurrection had disrupted the natural order of things. Badiou observed that Paul's declaration is supported solely by the force of "subjective upsurge," or "conviction." But, paradoxically, "the self-legitimating subjective declaration" (Badiou, *Saint Paul*, 61) is precisely what bestows on a fabulous event the status of truth.

The positionality of the imitation of Christ thus becomes a rhetorical positionality of intervention in the order of discourses "without wisdom of language." Badiou quotes Paul (1 Cor. 1:28): "God has chosen the things that are not [*ta mē onta*] in order to bring to nought those that are [*ta onta*]." He comments: "That the Christ-event causes nonbeings rather than beings to arise as attesting to God; that it consists in the abolition of what all previous discourses held as existing, or being, gives a measure of the ontological subversion to which Paul's antiphilosophy invites the declarant or militant" (Badiou, *Saint Paul*, 47).

Dale Martin analyzed specifically the discursive horizon of Paul's speech, the ideological context within which Paul's positionality of the imitation of Christ became subversively effective. Following in the steps of Marxist scholarship, Martin approached the Pauline discourse "*as it relates to the (usually) asymmetrical social relations of power and domination.*"[4] He sees the theological differences addressed by Paul in the First Letter to the Corinthians as reflecting a conflict among groups of different social status in the local church in Corinth. This conflict was expressed, according to Martin, in their divergent forms of the body politic.

Reading Paul's letter in terms of the ancient conceptions of the body, Martin has shown that Paul's foundation of the church was based on the rhetorically skillful displacement of an "elitist" Greco-Roman body politic, based on an open and porous notion of the body, by alternative "low-class" practices driven by popular beliefs and superstitions about the body. It was the low-class, hermetic notion of the body that Paul found institutionally more potent and construed as the body of Christ. "Paul's proposed body, the body of Christ," Martin writes, "represents the hierarchical reversal of the normal cosmic body of upper-class ideology." To demonstrate this, Martin cites a passage from Paul (1 Cor. 22–25) which he translates so as to bring out its status-minded vocabulary:

> But by much more the members of the body which are judged (supposed) to be weaker (of lower status) are actually necessary, and what we judge (or suppose) to be the less honorable of the body, to these we accord more honor, and our least beautiful (presentable) have more beauty (presentableness), whereas our beautiful parts do not need it. But God arranged the body, giving greater honor to the lesser, in order that there may be no schism in the body, but that the members may be equally concerned for one another. (Martin, *Corinthian Body*, 94)

In this famous passage Paul relies on the bodily metaphor commonly used in the Greek *homonoia* speeches (speeches of unity) for conveying a hierarchy of social values. But paradoxically, he ascribes higher status to the underappreciated organs, thus declaring the initial customary hierarchy as illusory. Martin's book is dedicated specifically to the analysis of what he calls "the disruptive hierarchy of the body of Christ," that is, to Paul's rhetorical and conceptual strategies of substituting the low-class body with its system of values for the upper-class body within one paradigm of the ancient bodily understanding of the universe.

One of these strategies, he shows, is to oppose the two different worlds: "the world of Greco-Roman rhetoric and status, with its attendant upper-class ideology," reflected in the ancient corporeal construal of "the cosmos, with its value system, epistemology, and power structures," and "a somewhat hidden world of apocalyptic reality proclaimed in the gospel of Christ, which has its own, alternative system of values and status attribution," construed as "the kingdom of God, with its very different values, revealed knowledge, and revolutionary challenge to the power hierarchy of 'this world' "—the body of Christ. These "two realms . . . constitute two different worlds of meaning, contrary axiological systems of signification, different 'texts' " (Martin, *Corinthian Body*, 177).

Martin observes that the "body of Christ in some sense 'mirrors' the values of 'this world' but in another sense counters and overturns those values. In order to speak about both worlds, Paul must use language that has currency in both realms" (Martin, *Corinthian Body*, 57). Therefore Martin relies on Mikhail Bakhtin's term "heteroglossia" to describe another subversive strategy of Paul—the deliberate polyvalence of his rhetoric, which allows the apostle not just to oppose but also to bridge the two discourses, inconspicuously overturning one system of meaning in favor of another.

For example, in Paul's claim that the Corinthians already possess "the mystery of Christ" (1 Cor. 1:6), the word "mystery" has this heteroglossic function: for a Greek it evokes the mystery cults common in the city culture of the Mediterranean, but for a Christian it carries an allusion to apocalypticism. "For Paul the apocalypticist, 'mystery' refers to the apocalyptic narrative in which the expected revelation of the heavenly Christ will overturn the structures of the world," Martin writes. "The heteroglossic nature of his rhetoric, therefore, reflects his need to inject the truth of an apocalyptic realm and its discourse into the mist and delusion of a supposedly unified and monolithic discourse of 'this world,' the world of Greco-Roman, upper-class ideology" (Martin, *Corinthian Body*, 57).

To return to Alain Badiou, the body of Christ, he argued, could become an effective tool of rupture and inversion of the established Greco-Roman social discourse only because Paul carried it out in his own body, that is, by means of his self-referential positionality of being in Christ. He postulated first in his own person the belief in Christ's resurrection. It is upon this belief alone that the universality of Christian identity has been predicated, with no more proof or support than the "subjective materiality"[5] (*matérialité subjective*) of Paul's enunciation. The logic of overturning, Paul has shown, requires a higher, divine authorization, which an author or inventor of a new discourse can claim for himself in order to cement an act of enunciation as a deed. Effective subversion, even if just on a discursive level, cannot be a matter of philosophy but only of practice.

Double-Text, Authorial Presence, Claim to Truth: Adoption of Pauline Subversion in "Discourse Apart"

Even though Martin and Badiou come to their studies of Paul from different backgrounds (one from the history of religion, focused on the heterogeneous ideas about the body politic, and one from social philosophy, focused on the formation of communities), both pay close attention to the pragmatics of Paul's rhetorical practice. Their analyses reveal the modality of Pauline discourse as performative: its locution is inseparable from its context as well as from the agent authorized to perform an utterance, that is, from the subject of enunciation. This double bondage appears to be the condition of its success (its "felicity").[6]

The performative modality of a locution always implies, according to J. L. Austin, the concomitant acts of perlocution and illocution. Martin's reading of Paul is concerned with perlocution, that is, with the conceptually subversive makeup of the discourse which outlines a new status of things. Badiou focuses on illocution, that is, on the subjective act of enunciation of belief with its claim to divine authorization which inaugurates the subversive construct as a new law in the public forum and secures its uptake.

Only in combination do Martin and Badiou expose the performativity of Pauline discourse as an integral part of its subversive scheme: Paul inaugurates, while he persuades. Inauguration accomplishes a break with the past, whereas persuasion is supposed to be based on existing consensus. Hence the paradoxical nature of his discourse: Paul often strategically postulates as already existent things that he wants to bring about. Consider his usage of the topos of unity when he writes to the Corinthians whose community is torn by schisms. He declares that *all* Corinthians are *already* in possession of *grace* and *mystery*, although to persuade the schismatics into the body of Christ and to consolidate the community via their common partaking of this body's grace and mystery is still a distant goal.[7]

The body of Christ, in regard to its performative function in Pauline discourse, is a typical "masquerader," as Austin calls performative utterances hiding among constative or descriptive sentences (Austin, *How to Do Things with Words*, 10). Often they cannot be distinguished from statements of fact, if one takes them out of context, disregards the agency of intention behind them, and deprives them of their character as event. But once these dimensions are restored, as Badiou and Martin have helped us to do, the role of Christ's body in Paul can be called "operative" in the legal sense of the word, for it fulfills the same function as the "operative" (Austin, *How to Do Things with Words*, 4) part of a legal instrument, that "which serves to effect the transaction . . . which is its main object, whereas the rest of the document merely 'recites' the circumstances in which the transaction is to be effected" (ibid., 7).

This part of a performative speech-act does not allow any psychological ambiguity or conscious deceit, for even if given in bad faith, "[its] word is [its] bond, wherein morality and modality coincide" (ibid., 10). Similarly, the divinity of the body underlying the construction of Pauline subversive discourse is a guarantee of the validity of its claim as well as of its effectiveness.

It is this performative function of Christ's body as an "ideological operator" in Paul that has been preserved in the six historical instances of subversive discourse presented in this book. These instances are the fourth-century iconoclasm of Epiphanius of Salamis; the sacramental alchemy of the pre-Reformation period in the *Book of the Holy Trinity* (1415–19); Lavater's anti-Enlightenment project; Dostoevsky's transformation of the novel; Pier Paolo Pasolini's cinema; and the theoconservative movement's reshaping of the American political system from the 1980s to the present.

In all these instances we will deal with ideologically heterogeneous and culturally and politically subversive meta-discourses, as these are organized and made effective through the notion and rhetoric of the body of Christ. What unites them into one logical set are the subversive strategies that all of them borrow from Paul but adopt in idiosyncratic ways and according to changing ideological goals and historical horizons. As Pier Paolo Pasolini once observed: "Christ would not be universal if he were not different for each different historical phase."[8]

The word "subversion" is used in this book with reference to Pauline subversion. It means not the destruction but the substitution of one system of meaning by another within a shared cultural horizon. Since this process usually implies the replacement of a stronger form of authority with a weaker one, the term "subversion" seems to be more adequate than simply "substitution" or "reversal."

What are the Pauline features which constitute the commonality of the "discourse apart" along a diachronic axis established in this book?

The notion of Christ's body, as Martin has demonstrated, allowed Paul to stay within the epistemological paradigm of his contemporaries' corporeal understanding of the cosmos, while overturning its system of values from within. Paul's construal of a Christian body on "low-class" but divinely ordained premises was intended to entail a cosmic, universal reversal of values by virtue of the ancient understanding of material linkage or continuity between the bodily microcosm and cosmic macrocosm.[9] Such an archaic microcosm/macrocosm model conducive to a correlation of different "texts" within one given cultural paradigm constitutes the basic structure of subversion in our instances of the "discourse apart."

This discourse is informed by the logic of a double text, functioning as a microcosmic model of a social discourse at large, within which salutary interventions are being undertaken *en miniature* in order to work their effects by way of analogy on the rest of society. For example, an alchemical manuscript of the pre-Reformation period, discussed later in this book, was conceived by its writers as an embodiment of the Eucharist, with its ink and parchment standing for Christ's blood and body; reading it was therefore an act of communion. In this way, apart from its content, *corpus libri*, the body of the book, fulfilled the reformatory demand for both sacraments well before any Western church had officially accepted this claim. This early endorsement of the two sacraments in effigy was supposed to work its magic on a conflicted society and help bring about the wished-for reformation of the church. The "discourse apart" is always driven by such magical logic in that it construes its medium as a microcosmic body and performs within its small scope those changes which its author wishes to bring about or to influence on a distant macrocosmic scale.[10]

Each of the instances of subversion discussed in this book, though each in its own way, relies on the Pauline positionality of the imitation of Christ in order to undertake what they define as a shift in an established system of values—to change social perceptions, or to influence constellations of power by reenacting the divine law's incarnation in the materiality proper to their own medium.

Their legitimizing reference to the body of Christ takes this body as a self-explanatory medium of divine truth, charged with moral authority and power to work correct ethical choices at times when good and evil seem nearly indistinguishable on rational premises. But their reliance on the body of Christ is also a strategy that blindly justifies their pursuit of particular societal interests in the troubled waters of discursive and semiotic loss.

The emphasis on the authorial presence is especially important here because the discourse in question does not obey any principle of aesthetic autonomy but quite deliberately oversteps it as part of its subversive scheme. In the steps of Pauline discourse, the "discourse apart" is a thought-practice, or antiphilosophy: "But it is of the essence of antiphilosophy that the subjective position figure as a decisive factor in discourse. Existential fragments, sometimes anecdotal in appearance, are elevated to the rank of guarantor of truth." What Badiou writes about Paul applies precisely to the type of discourse studied here: "For an antiphilosopher, the enunciative position is obviously part of the statement's protocol. No discourse can lay claim to truth if it does not contain an explicit answer to the question: Who speaks?"[11]

Thus the "discourse apart" usually springs from the authors' personal involvement with the issues at stake, which they usually make quite pronounced in advancing their goals. For example, Dostoevsky's concern with the reform of criminal justice was a direct result of his own imprisonment and conversion in Siberia, an experience which he made manifest in his essays and which subliminally informs his philosophical novels.

The subversive discourse we study here greatly depends on its author's direct participation and social standing; these are not impersonal forms of discourse, though they harbor positions that may be inhabited by a variety of subjects.

All instances of this discourse inherit from Paul their legal and religious performativity in that they also aim at introducing a new law in a broader sense of the word, a new structure of discourse, a new media system, a new constellation of power, and so forth. The authorial presence aims at invigorating language as well as reinforcing its effectiveness by nonverbal means: gestures, body language, objects.

For example, Epiphanius attempts to convince the emperor to introduce iconoclasm as the law of the Roman Empire by way of his own example: he destroys a textile image of Christ in a church in Palestine. His iconoclasm aims at replacing two-dimensional representations of a human Christ with three-dimensional architectural renditions of the body of Christ. But if successful, this initiative would also imply the imperial yielding of political and legal leadership to the institution of the church. The new system of representation would entail a new constellation of power.

To achieve their goals, the subversive adventurers reenact the foundational Pauline discourse but in different cultural circumstances. Herein lies the most important theoretical issue of the book: the adoption of Pauline subversion outside of the ecclesiastical or theological context cannot be a mere repetition. Taken out of the realm of religious practice, the reenactment of Pauline discourse focuses mostly on its formal features and often modifies them according to new discursive needs.

The process of the adaptation of Pauline religious performativity to different cultural and historical circumstances deserves special consideration. About the appropriations of performative utterances outside their proper context, Austin writes:

> A performative utterance will . . . be in a peculiar way hollow or void if said by an actor on the stage, or if introduced in a poem, or spoken in soliloquy. This applies in a similar manner to any and every utterance—a sea-change in special circumstances. Language in such circumstances is in special ways—intelligibly—used not seriously, but in ways *parasitic* upon its normal use—ways which fall under the doctrine of the *etiolations* of language.[12]

Since performative power is weakened or erased in a fictional context or with a fictional, unauthorized agent, Austin deliberately excludes such cases from consideration and concentrates only on utterances "issued in ordinary circumstances."

The subversive "discourse apart," however, deliberately reappropriates the foundational performativity of Pauline discourse for extraordinary circumstances and even for directly fictional ones, which could be equated with a reenactment on the stage. A disregard for the distinction between "ordinary" and "hollow," or "parasitic" usage is the most prominent feature of its subversive practice. And it is precisely in this respect that it emancipates itself from the Pauline prototype. This type of subversive discourse takes place on the very threshold between sacred and secular, real and fictitious, old and new. It stretches its idiom across religion, politics, and aesthetics, making a deliberate use of Austin's "etiolation of language."

But the hollowness of such language also accounts for its excessively strong bodily anchorage, in which the performative modality turns upon itself and makes radical use of its latent materiality. The weakening of performative utterance, of quotational idiom, is compensated and counteracted through its bodily invigoration. The speaker often sets out to anchor lax signifiers in his own bodily performance, to deliberately fashion meaning as a procedure. As a result, familiar topoi and iconographic signs and widely circulating religious idioms, often banal in themselves, become indices pointing beyond the text to the objects, images, concepts, and happenings which nourish this discursive practice directly from the context of actuality.

Seeing Austin as excluding fictional performatives from the realm of properly performative statements, Jacques Derrida famously criticizes him for implicitly maintaining the subordination of speech to "a philosophical *ideal*" of Platonic truth.[13] Derrida contests what he sees as Austin's metaphysical anchoring of the performative utterance in consciousness and context, which make it into a unique event. Derrida interprets this as a symptom of Austin's repression of the graphematic nature of performatives.[14] In Derrida's view, the very possibility of iteration in a different context constitutes a sufficient *différance* to detach a reproduced performative utterance from the real presence of both binding intention and binding circumstances, and thus testifies to its nature as writing, that is, to its common share in dissemination.

J. Hillis Miller, in his analysis of Derrida's response to Austin's dismissal of "fictional," "parasitic," or "non-serious" performatives, pointed out the philosopher's full awareness of "the immense accretion of force" that would and could result from embracing the necessity of "being non-serious" and its potentiality in the strategic decisions of discursive and political intervention later theorized by Badiou. Miller quotes Derrida's polemical exclamation against the theoreticians of the speech-act theory (Austin and Searle): "What force they would gain by doing this!! But will they take the risk?"[15] Practitioners of "discourse apart" since Paul have been well aware of this forceful potentiality and have been taking the risk.

Derrida's critique of Austin also helps understand *a contrario* the direction which the subversive discourse that is the subject of this book has taken after leaving behind its historical foundation in the letters of Paul. The performative operation of subversion heads here in the exactly opposite direction—mounting a fierce resistance to the danger of dissemination, of becoming (mere) writing, since its structure foregrounds exactly those nondiscursive forces which are supposed to disappear when a performative utterance is quoted in a fictional context: the agency of intention and the specificity of circumstances, their real presence. And yet, in order to have its full effect, the performativity of the "discourse apart" must be repeatable. But its iterability (askew to both Derrida and Austin) occurs in the mode of positionality.

The performative features of Pauline discourse expand here sometimes to the point of almost total abandonment of language in favor of action, whereas its underlying corporeality is recuperated and intensified by a strong emphasis on the materiality of communication. The subversive "discourse apart" differs from its Pauline predecessor by a drastic degree, in which illocution comes to prevail over perlocution. The verbal subversion is often supposed to be effective at the very moment of its performance. Therefore it often loses its accessibility, or drastically changes its meaning, when approached as a written transmission.

The resulting lack of originality is the major reason for its neglect among the historians of culture. However, its illocutionary performativity explains its elusiveness in this respect. According to Austin, illocution is bound up with effects in three ways: "securing uptake, taking effect, and inviting response" (*How to Do Things with Words*, 118). Therefore "there cannot be an illocutionary act unless the means employed are conventional, and so the means for achieving it non-verbally must be conventional" (ibid., 119).

This discourse wants to be experienced, rather than read. Its originality and actual "content" consist exclusively in what it "does with words," to quote Austin's famous title—in its self-understanding as a means of restructuring a larger social discourse through an unconventional recombination of conventional truths. In the instances of this discourse, the body often takes over the medial vehicle as its actual driver, seeking to imbue the inflated idiom with its vital power. If Paul's presence in his discourse is still a verbally mediated trace of his enunciation, the presence of the author in the "discourse apart" is often consubstantial with its self-reflexive procedure of mediation.

The truth of Pauline discourse, automatically implied from a Christian point of view in his enunciation of belief and in the very procedure of his divinely premised subversion, easily translates into the poetics and materiality of a divinely connoted medium. Due to their ritual and ceremonial nature, emphasized by Austin, "acts of Ethics" (*How to Do Things with Words*, 20) can be engendered in the mediating procedure itself. The performative assertion of belief, which conflates the Christian truth with the ethical and thus makes itself invulnerable to rational scrutiny, allows for the exculpatory self-righteousness driving this type of subversion.

Let us summarize at this point our basic thesis: Paul's foundational discourse on a new law, subversively conceived and performatively implemented, in the name of Christ and from the position of an author who steps into his role as a mediator between the divine and the human and is, to use the modern jargon, wired into his own discourse as its driving force and a medium, delivers a modality and a set of discursive strategies for a specifically Western tradition of subversion.

In the following chapters we will see that this modality, whether in regard to ideas, social or religious customs, representational techniques, or political power, is adjustable to different historical conditions and capable of ever new medial and discursive embodiment and transformation, and that it has produced a "discourse apart" which due to its idiosyncratically camouflaged nature was destined to slip unnoticed through the sieve of cultural history.

This discourse emerges when the performative religious modality crosses into the world of culture and politics, where it constitutes an *a-topia* or *u-topia*. It happens, for good reason, in situations where the strong presence of an authorial intention, of a subject of enunciation, is desired as a way out of a maze of inflated symbolism, as an attempt at the focalization of disseminated signs and at ethical differentiation.

Practiced in a context which is no longer strictly religious, this discourse inevitably embraces a series of misinvocations, misapplications, and misexecutions of the performative formulas (Austin, *How to Do Things with Words*, 17). However, the sacred dimension of its bodily and rhetorical anchorage in the kingdom of God is expected to secure its overall efficacy.

Points of Departure, Diachronic Comparison, Interdisciplinarity:
Toward a Three-Dimensional Reading

This book has been written with the methodology of comparative literature in mind, as we strive to understand it today: "the job of the comparatist is to invent new relations among literary works (and relations with things that have not been previously classed among literary works)."[16] The book proceeds from a series of examples and constructs its own subject matter, Christ's subversive body, instead of merely interpreting an array of canonical texts at hand.

The topics of the six chapters are "points of departure" (*Ansatzpunkte*) in the sense once elaborated by Erich Auerbach in his theoretical essay "Philology and *Weltliteratur*." Each topic offers "a firmly circumscribed, easily comprehensible set of phenomena whose interpretation is a radiation out from them and which orders and interprets a greater region than they themselves occupy." Each of these subjects "is as circumscribed and concrete as possible, and therefore describable in technical, philological terms" (14–15).

Given the historically and culturally diverse set of contexts in which Pauline discourse has been invoked, we are confronted with the situation par excellence where "a single point of departure will not be sufficient—several will be necessary." But "if the first one is present, however," writes Auerbach, "others are more easily available, particularly as they must be of the kind that not only links itself to others, but also converges on a central intention."[17] In fact, all examples of the "discourse apart" in this book, despite a variety of the points of departure, converge on a common pattern.

The book demonstrates how each of these discourses starts as what Michael Warner has described as a "counterpublic discourse" on the ideological margins of society but actively seeks, albeit with different degrees of success, to work its way through the existing public norms by verbally infiltrating and changing the terms of the established discourse.

Each of the discourses is concerned with issues of collective relevance and seeks to address diverse, often conflicted audiences across ideological boundaries and social hierarchies. They do so by taking recourse to the body of Christ as a token of opposition to the perceived forces of societal disintegration, but also as a vehicle through which they hope to achieve centrality and influence for themselves.

All these cases covertly use a conventional public forum for their subversive alternative constructions. Emerging from the interstices of larger systematic discourses, they often make their way into the public sphere by elusive reliance on a heterogeneous media and material culture. "Friction against the dominant public forces the poetic-expressive character of counterpublic discourse to become salient to consciousness."[18]

And in fact, it is through subversive dynamics that all instances of the discourses discussed in this book acquire a "poetic-expressive character" as their authors' idiosyncratically invented, rhetorical artifacts. Even in cases when we are dealing with visual rhetoric, as in Pasolini's films, the concept of the author as indispensable subject of enunciation is valid, having its counterpart in the cinematic concept of the auteur.

The ultimate goal of this book is not to exhibit a collection of cultural curiosities. The archeological unearthing of forgotten or misinterpreted projects is only a side effect of my search for a more fluid understanding of culture, which is approached here not as a dead weight of completed works but as a maze of traces pointing to discursive practices and conflicting intentions, often driven by deception and self-deception. My major methodological assumption is that transmitted texts are always a part of a larger scheme and always respond to their historical circumstance.

The diachronic model of comparison developed in this book through the "points of departure" tries to account for historical contingencies and specificity in the operation of common discursive modalities. In this way the book addresses at least one desideratum of comparative literature today among those eloquently pointed out by Sheldon Pollock in his ACLA keynote address "Cosmopolitan Comparison" in 2010—the inclusion of premodern periods in comparative research.

Without a diachronic comparative approach, Pollock reminds us, "you do not know the contingencies that have made that thing what it is; you do not understand that all products are outcomes of processes that could have been otherwise; . . . that the processes themselves are multiple, that there is in culture no mechanical development from initial conditions, no 'path dependency.' "[19]

The interdisciplinary methodology of this book, on the other hand, raises some further questions which might be of general relevance to comparatists and historians of literature, culture, and religion today: How can we discern, read, and interpret such three-dimensional phenomena as the subversive projects gathered in this book, the very goal of which was to take effect in an inconspicuous and deviant manner? And why should we do it at all, if these projects have quite literally nothing substantial to tell us on their own, their messages having been idiosyncratically fabricated for the needs of the day out of highly heterogeneous stuff, where images, gestures, and objects were meant to work in concert with words or even to communicate in a nonverbal, physical, quasi-magical fashion from within other meaningfully articulated discourses?

In regard to my particular topic, here are some answers. Since a subversive, counterpublic discourse is always of a secondary nature in regard to the notions and conceptions with which it operates, situates itself in interstices of larger and already firmly established patterns of values and ideas, and produces a meaning by way of their rearrangement, it requires a methodology of reading which will account for "a total speech-act" (Austin, *How to Do Things with Words*, 52).

Consequently, one must take into consideration the "operational" aspect of a discourse's inflated semiolinguistic idiom by linking it to both the intentionality of its author (which is in this particular discourse always enunciated, that being an integral part of its performative modality) and to the "circumstantial aspect" of its production (that is, the historical situation in which this discourse was supposed to become effective and in which it was embedded indexically through its verbal references).

This methodology requires archeological and detective work. The body of Christ, unearthed as a device of Pauline discourse, is a relatively easy case because of its rich and well-known connotations. It suggests by itself questions such as: What values are to be overturned? What kind of double-text is constructed here? What social split is resisted and in pursuit of whose interests? What developments in the political and media system force the author into such an archaic, alternative detour? Thus the type of discourse studied in this book is, in effect, a discursive symptom, and as such it can always yield an insight into larger historical and cultural tensions.

The particular structure of "discourse apart" has coincided again and again with historical periods of latent but pervasive tension in constellations of social power and medial systems. For example, the late fourth century's tension between the church and the Roman state went along with tensions over the systems of visual representation of power. The early fifteenth century's clash between Reformation and anti-Reformation movements unfolded during a transition from the culture of handwritten manuscripts to the first technologies of printing (incunabula). The tension between the Enlightenment and anti-Enlightenment movements was accompanied by a transition to a more inclusive society with broader communication (assured mainly by the newspaper). The conflict between the Orthodox Slavophiles and nihilistic Westernizers in nineteenth-century Russia was contemporaneous with the structural transformation of the Russian novel. Or the tensions between the political left and the right-leaning establishment in postwar Italy coexisted with the development of new forms of mass communication and avant-garde performance art.

An insight into an apparent connection between the specific structure of subversive discourse and the social-political turbulences and medial changes of which these discourses took advantage crystallized only in the process of my work on this book. It seemed hardly a coincidence that the medial potential of Christ's body had been called upon again and again at critical junctions in Western cultural history, during periods of preparation for major shifts in the system of human values, in ways of thinking about human beings and society, in the structure of the public sphere, in the constellations of social and political power and in the prevailing media system—in short, during periods when nothing but the authority of a most basic kind of truth still seems to hold the ground.

The sixth chapter, written as a test of this observation, shows that from the last two decades of the twentieth century, the concept of the body of

Christ became instrumental in the formation and promotion of an eclectic Christian ideology in the United States.[20] Initially developed by a relatively small and marginal group of religiously oriented, mostly Catholic, adventurers, this ideology has since the late 1970s progressively claimed the country's political system, economics, law, and government. Its gradual ascent to political prominence under the George W. Bush administration and its further triumph in the election of Donald Trump was to a great extent due to the systematic nature of its underlying corporeal model, its assiduously crafted subversive rhetorical construct, and its strategic reliance on the performative force of its divinely backed claim to truth—the very features that once had made Pauline discourse into a law-giving form of practice. The theoconservative body of Christ seems, moreover, to fulfill the same function of identitarian resistance to the tendency of discursive dissemination enhanced by digital networks, while fully exploiting the advantages of the new media system.

This finding allows me to propose a hypothesis (which this book goes to some length to substantiate) that the discursive function of Christ's body tends to reactivate in historical circumstances when the possibilities of conventional communication appear, justifiably or not, as either politically thwarted or culturally inflated and discredited. Taking advantage of the medial nature of Christianity, which is, in the words of Régis Debray, "*mediation made religion*,"[21] the subversive actors resort to Christ's body in order to forge their message into a medium and convey it in a quasi-ritual fashion, that is, through the reliance on certain performative formulas or forms of enunciation outside the ritual context.

The entanglement of Christ's subversive body with right-wing politics in the contemporary United States is not a necessary phenomenon. The "discourse apart" is a populist discourse, but its political affiliations are blurred and the estimation of its agenda as progressive or regressive is rather difficult. Many of the authors of right-wing theoconservative discourse came from the left and operate within the liberal idiom, while deliberately bending it in favor of a quite opposite agenda.

Similarly, artists like Pasolini or Dostoevsky were quite notorious for eschewing any clearly defined ideological camps. Even more difficult is judgment on the "progressive" or "regressive" quality of attitudes in earlier periods of history. The "ideological operation" of the body of Christ derives its subversive advantage specifically from its discursive aptitude to reconcile and make effective the most paradoxical points of view and sets of ideas.

The examples of discourse collected in this book break out of the canonical frame of ideas usually associated with their epochs in Western cultural history. Their verbal testimonies might strike us today as outdated, nonsensical, or trivial after the invigorating presence of their authors and their performative context had vanished from the historical arena. But we will follow them here as indices marking the path to their once meaningful existence. Their avant-garde sensitivity to some new tendencies in society and their conservative way of approaching them via an archaic and safely righteous detour, their goal of capturing and remaking a totality in the most basic matrix, and the ambiguity of their effectiveness or ethical claims will have our full attention in the six chapters of this book.

Chapter 1

✦

Christ's Body versus Christ's Image
The Iconoclasm of Epiphanius of Salamis

Images are nowhere; images are guilty of nothing.
—Marie-José Mondzain, *L'Image naturelle*

In his "Letter to John, Bishop of Jerusalem," dating to 394, Epiphanius, bishop of Salamis, provides a detailed account of his attack on an image of Christ (or a saint) in a little church in Bethel in John's diocese. The destroyed image was embroidered on a door curtain, such as were common around the time.[1] This ostentatious act of iconoclasm struck the witnesses as so scandalous that the incident soon acquired notoriety, and Epiphanius felt pressed to account for his actions at length:

> Moreover, I have heard that certain persons have this grievance against me: When I accompanied you to the holy place called Bethel, there to join you in celebrating the Collect, after the use of the Church, I came to a villa called Anablatha and, as I was passing, saw a lamp burning there. Asking what place it was, and learning it to be a church, I went in to pray, and found there a curtain hanging on the doors of the said church, dyed and embroidered. It bore an image either of Christ or of one of the saints; I do not rightly remember whose the image was.
>
> Seeing this, and being loath that an image of a man should be hung up in Christ's church contrary to the teaching of the Scripture, I tore it asunder and advised the custodians of the place to use it as a winding sheet for some poor person. They, however, murmured, and said that if I made up my mind to tear it, it was only fair that I should give them another curtain in its place. As soon as I heard this, I promised that I would give one, and said that I would send it at once.
>
> Since then there has been some little delay, due to the fact that I have been seeking a curtain of the best quality to give to them instead of the former one, and thought it right to send to Cyprus for one. I have now sent the best that I could find, and I beg that you will order

the presbyter of the place to take the curtain which I have sent from
the hands of the Reader, and that you will afterwards give directions
that curtains of the other sort—opposed as they are to our religion—
shall not be hung up in any church of Christ.

A man of your uprightness should be careful to remove an occasion of offence unworthy alike of the Church of Christ and of those
Christians who are committed to your charge. (Epiphanius, "Letter
from Epiphanius to John," 9)[2]

A strange episode, with the "murmur" of the custodians and the need of
explaining to John in detail the incident with a torn curtain. Epiphanius's
loathing of "an image of a man" in the church was indeed not at all a self-
evident affair, but strikingly at odds with the sensibility of the time. His
uncertainty whether the image was that of Christ or a saint suggests that the
image in the villa Anablatha could be similar to the popular Coptic hangings,
featuring a big colorful halo around a human face, and thus rather abstract
and decorative in nature.[3] (See fig. 1.1.)

Figurative images of an ornamental kind were common in Christian
everyday life by the end of the fourth century A.D.[4] They often appeared
on embroidered textiles, in mosaics on the floors, in carvings on vases or
sarcophagi, or as illuminations in books. Their usage did not amount to an
image cult. In fact, there is no recorded testimony of Christian image worship
in this period. The veneration of icons, as we know it from Byzantium, was
based on the theological doctrine of the Holy Image. Not in existence yet at
Epiphanius's time, this concept would take centuries to develop.[5] The cult of
the Christian image, and especially the cult of the Christ image, is recorded
not earlier than the second half of the sixth century.[6]

Besides the "Letter to John" describing his iconoclastic outburst, Epiphanius composed other epistles against image worship, which have been
transmitted to us only in scarce and fragmented quotations dispersed through
the conciliar *acta* of the Byzantine image controversy, particularly through
the anti-iconoclastic writings of Patriarch Nicephorus (818–820).[7] Epiphanius vocally appealed to Emperor Theodosius I, to the Christian communities
in Cyprus and Palestine, and to higher clergy. The geographical expanse of
his communications and the hierarchical range of his addressees suggest a
goal no less ambitious than introducing iconoclasm as official state policy in
the whole of the Roman Empire.

Since their first discovery and publication in 1916, the iconoclastic fragments of Epiphanius have been difficult to reconcile with the known religious
practices of the fourth century.[8] Therefore after an initial controversy about
their authenticity, they were shelved as a mere cultural curiosity.[9] Thus
Epiphanius's iconoclasm with its theological untimeliness is a typical instance
of "iconoclash," the term proposed by Bruno Latour for those historical cases
of image controversy which lack a clearly motivated project of destruction,

Figure 1.1. Human face with a halo, Coptic wool tapestry, fourth century A.D. Copyright © The Detroit Institute of Arts.

cases "when one does not know, one hesitates, one is troubled by an action for which there is no way to know, without further inquiry, whether it is destructive or constructive."[10]

Epiphanius carried out his iconoclastic argument in polemical letters, fiery appeals, and concrete actions—that is, politically and rhetorically, not philosophically. The particulars of his rhetoric and performance indicate that his alleged fight against Christian image worship was not a matter of doctrinaire polemics but a strategy of discursive practice invented for the need of the day. The iconoclash of Epiphanius's writings calls for a nontheological approach asking: "What, in all this, was the torn curtain of Anablatha?"

Epiphanius's narration of the iconoclastic incident is remarkably unapologetic. Rather, he turns the tables and presents himself as the offended party. His account of events is dramatic: after celebrating a Collect, the big official mass, together with his fellow bishop of Jerusalem, Epiphanius entered a little, hidden-away church for a private prayer, but—to his shock, as the intensity of his reaction conveys—he found himself face to face with an offensive object—a pictured door curtain—which thwarted his prayer.

Epiphanius's description of his act of loathing of the curtain with an "image of a man" gives a hint at how and why an image in a church could jeopardize the Christian faith: its presence in a house of God turns a prayer into a form of pagan image-worship. Through a complicated maze of meaningful allusions Epiphanius carefully links his proclaimed aversion to a Christian image with the anti-pagan legislation of 392 of Emperor Theodosius.

The pagan theme of the episode is insinuated right away: light lured Epiphanius into the house. The burning of candles was indeed around this time prohibited in Christian churches for its association with pagan worship.[11] Thus Epiphanius intimates that the little church in the villa Anablatha was a compromised space. Its pagan connotation is further strengthened by Epiphanius's exposure of the pictured curtain as a funeral object: after tearing it apart, he says, he advised the church custodians to use the destroyed curtain as a shroud for the burial of a poor person.

The advice is meaningful in its range of allusions. Placing portraits of the dead on winding sheets and coffins was a pagan Egyptian practice. The Roman sarcophagi also were usually adorned with human figures portraying the buried dead. Epiphanius's association of an embroidered image on a door hanging in a little Palestinian church with the funeral portrait in its Egyptian or Roman versions strikes one as deliberate and strategic. His "charitable provision for the poor" metonymically overlaps two types of artifact in the locus: the textile image of Christ should be placed over a corpse and buried because—so the unstated assumption—it is like a funeral portrait, and like a funeral portrait it should be moved to the realm of death. But his advice to turn the pictured curtain into a shroud also puns on Paul's metaphor for the sacrament of baptism: "For as many of you as were baptized into Christ have put on Christ" (Gal. 3:27, Revised Standard Version).

Epiphanius's relegation of the curtain to the dead, his insistence on "taking off Christ" from the body of the church and putting it on a cadaver, hints that this object interferes with the sacrament through which one is incorporated into the living body of Christ, as death interferes with life. The first Christian images emerged indeed from the funerary realm of catacombs and sarcophagi, but at the time they symbolized a prospect of future resurrection. They resisted death.

Epiphanius's portrayal of the church in Anablatha as a space compromised by the pagan veneration of the dead and his treatment of the presumed image of Christ as a dead man who turns the church, the body of Christ, into a tomb instantiate semantic polyvalence in action. The Christians interpreted the Hellenistic Egyptian hybrid god Serapis as a deified dead man. His temple would be destroyed later in the decade.[12]

But the rejection of a "dead man" had also another long and precarious tradition, for the expression "dead man" used to designate among the Christians the images of the emperor. As an example of Christian rebellion against Roman state power at the very beginning of the fourth century, the historian Karl Baus brings up "Fabius, an official in the civil administration and *vexillifer* of the governor of Mauretania, [who] refused to carry 'pictures of dead men,' that is to say, the standard with the device of the divinized emperors." [13]

This context suggests that the pictured curtain of Anablatha took a blow by proxy. Theodosius I, the emperor who endorsed the Nicene faith as the religious foundation of the empire and launched anti-heretical and anti-pagan campaigns in the name of orthodoxy, was notorious for his self-aggrandizement in images.[14] But from a position on the eastern periphery, a precarious iconoclastic attack on the imperial image could be justified as a matter of ancient piety: "an image of a man" in Christ's church contradicts the teaching of the scriptures, and is "opposed to our religion."

This rhetorical gesture of rejection, however, had by this time little foundation in historical reality. The biblical prohibition of images Epiphanius refers to had been disregarded already for at least a century even in the Jewish synagogues. Consider the famous frescoes in the third-century synagogue of Dura-Europos. But even if outdated, the adherence to ancient piety still possessed enough ideological currency to excuse eccentric behavior.[15]

Maybe therefore, Epiphanius prefers to inaugurate his iconoclast policy not by way of an argument but by staging a divinely inspired explosion of rage, that is, from the positionality of a righteous speaker. Through a radically subjective acting-out of the ancient biblical truth Epiphanius could intervene into the order of discourse "not in plausible words of wisdom" (1 Cor. 2:4, RSV) and call on John to follow Epiphanius's example and forbid such images in the churches under his supervision.

In the conclusion, Epiphanius seems to duly redress the local grievance by sending a blank curtain as a replacement for the destroyed textile. But the real conflict created here is not between a pictured and a blank curtain, that is, not between representation and non-representation, but between the image of Christ and the body of Christ. Epiphanius presented them as irreconcilable and even mutually exclusive when he expunged the quasi-pagan textile image from the body of the church, as if in an act of exorcism. The torn curtain of Anablatha comes to signal here an iconoclash between two representational systems and their figurations of power.

Who Was Epiphanius?

The life of Epiphanius (ca. 315–402) falls into the century of the church's formation as a powerful institution. In the course of this formation, its administrative structures had been progressively fusing and competing with

those of the Roman state. According to his *Vita*, Epiphanius was a converted
Jew and the son of a tenant farmer in Palestine.[16] He started his ecclesiastical career as a monk in the Egyptian desert and Gaza. The fourth-century
revival of the monastic movement in the eastern provinces of the empire
(Syria, Egypt, and Palestine, the traditional centers of biblical history and
ancient Christianity) is regarded today as the first expression of ecclesiastical
criticism aimed at the church's officialdom in Rome.[17]

The early phase of fourth-century monasticism was epitomized in the
activities of the movement's founding fathers Anthony (died 356) and
Pachomius (died 345) in Egypt and Hilarion (died 371) in Gaza. Epiphanius
entertained close relations with Hilarion and was, most likely, acquainted
with the others. By the middle of the fourth century the concentration of a
"true," uncompromising faith represented by monasticism on the periphery
of the empire began to prevail over mainstream Christianity in the imperial
centers.[18] Remarkably, already in the monastic period Epiphanius adhered
to the Athanasian theology of the consubstantiality of Father and Son, when
the majority of eastern bishops still supported Arian views subordinating the
Son to the Father.

Epiphanius's stringent adherence to Athanasian orthodoxy made his reputation in religious history. But the church historian John Gager helps throw
into relief its important political aspect. Gager called for social interpretation of Christian dogmas in terms of the body symbolism developed by the
anthropologist Mary Douglas in *Purity and Danger* (1966) and *Natural
Symbols* (1970). In her studies of the anthropological tendency to use the
human body as an image of society, Douglas observed that the body–spirit
dichotomy usually comes to deliver statements about the relation of society
to the individual, where the body represents society and the spirit stands for
the individual.

In applying Douglas's framework to the Christological controversies of the
third and fourth centuries, Gager showed that doctrinal positions that valued
the spirit over the body did indeed signal a tendency of critical revolt and a
desire to separate from the prevalent social-political norms and institutions,
whereas any symbolism declaring the unity of body and spirit conveyed a
tendency to integration.[19]

Consequently, the "spiritual" body-concept of the Arian theology favored
by the monks in the desert can be seen as a reflection of the politically separatist aspiration of monasticism. It sought religious purity and, hence, a distance
from the corrupting influences of the imperial centers. By contrast, the Athanasian theology of consubstantiality, which mingled spirit and matter and
saw spirit as working through matter, implies a politically integrationalist
stance on the tension between church and state.

Epiphanius, who started his career as a monk but then swiftly rose in
the official hierarchy to the status of the bishop of Salamis in Cyprus, displayed the same ambiguity of status as Athanasius, the "urbane bishop and

theological controversialist, on the one hand, and fervent admirer of Anthony and frequent visitor to the desert, on the other."[20] Epiphanius's position might seem paradoxical in its embrace of both the monastic critical differentiation from the "secular church" in Rome and the implicit Athanasian tendency toward an affirmative integration with the state through orthodoxy.

But Gager's approach helps reconcile Epiphanius's theology with his ecclesiastical transformation from monk into bishop. The fact that Epiphanius never belonged to any radical, ascetic wing of monasticism suggests that his early separatist tendency was rather moderate. Moreover, the monastic period of his career testifies to his early preference for the Athanasian version of Christian teaching that had the greatest potential of most effectively advancing the political interests of the church. By the end of the century, Epiphanius was one of the first monk-bishops to have risen to a position of considerable influence by imbuing his ecclesiastical leadership with monastic authority.

The monasticism and orthodoxy of Epiphanius, taken together in their tension, betray his ecclesiastical attitude throughout his life as one of competition with the state. He welcomed integration of the church with the empire as a temporary compromise and a vehicle toward the ecclesiastical takeover. On achieving a high clerical position, Epiphanius finally got a chance to put into practice the critical legacy of monasticism.

In his capacity as a bishop he was entitled to make the most of orthodoxy's increasing influence on the Roman state and to endorse the prophecies of the scriptures regarding the providential history of the church in an official ecclesiastical forum. Moreover, he could do so by advantageously relying on his authority as a former monk, that is, a representative of "authentic," uncompromising faith.[21] This authority aided Epiphanius's rise to ecclesiastical prominence in the reign of Emperor Theodosius I (379–395), who integrated the Nicene Creed into state legislation at the Council of Constantinople in 381.

On becoming an affair of state, the articulation of dogmas turned into a lever of political influence. Epiphanius's pronouncement of the triunity and oneness of the three Holy Persons in the Trinity is considered today the major theological contribution of the council:

> The creedal pronouncements about the Holy Spirit in the three-fold belief of the Church in the Father, the Son and the Holy Spirit . . . , had the effect of establishing the doctrine of the Holy Spirit as perfectly coequal with the Father and the Son in the Holy Trinity, but also had the effect of bringing the doctrine of the Trinity to its full fruition in the mind of the Church. Thus at the Council of Constantinople the doctrine of the *Triunity* of God, "One Being, three Persons," was given full conciliar authority, and was made an ecumenical dogma accepted by the Eastern and Western Church alike.[22]

This creedal pronouncement ultimately endorsed the Nicene faith as the religious foundation of the empire.[23] Epiphanius postulated the Athanasian orthodox dogma in terms that secured it from possible heretical equivocations. It became the basis of the church's institutional identity. Most importantly, by the emperor's legislative move the Christian doctrine of the triunity of God, "One Being, three Persons," was honored as a higher authority than Roman law.

Epiphanius's success at the Council of Constantinople was prepared for by his treatise *Ancoratus* (374), composed seven years earlier at the request of the Christian community in Syedra as an explanation of the major doctrines. This work gives a good insight into the rhetorical mode of Epiphanius's discourse and its significance for ecclesiastical politics. *Ancoratus* demonstrates that he was mostly concerned with the inscription of faith into the network of power while preserving its mystery and event-character through ritual worship.[24]

This goal, shared by Epiphanius's writings in general, is reflected in the nature of his rhetorical performance, which aims at sealing the dogma formally rather than elaborating its content analytically. For example, in Epiphanius's major anti-heretical work *Panarion* (the title means "the medical drawer"), orthodox refutations of heretical teachings are collected and matched with heresies in order to provide their "antidotes."

The performative affirmation of orthodox dogmas and filtering out of the unclean or poisonous unorthodox elements is effectuated here in the very composition of the book. Frank Williams pointed out the formalism of Epiphanius's procedure, which consisted of four parts: introduction, description, refutation, and a closing section comparing the sect to a noxious animal.[25] This textual ritualism conditions the effectiveness of the cleansing performed by Epiphanius's anti-heretical discourse.

Similarly, his explanation of dogmas and refutation of heresies in *Ancoratus* consists simply in a forceful enunciation of the orthodox doctrines: "We call the Father God, the Son God, and the Holy Spirit God . . . When you *pronounce* the *homoousion*, you *declare* that the Son is God of God and that the Holy Spirit is God of the same Godhead."[26] Thus, as to the questions of doctrine, Epiphanius casts himself in the role of a "pedagogue," understood in late antiquity as an overseer of children's proper conduct rather than an educator. Likewise, Epiphanius oversees the correct articulation of the dogma rather than teaching its theological justification.

Ancoratus also provides an insight into another important feature of Epiphanius's discourse—his biblical literalism. In the book he insists that every Christian dogma was exactly prefigured in the scriptures and searches for structural analogies and parallels in the Bible to vouch for each dogma's divine truth.[27] The truth in Epiphanius's discourse is anchored in biblical revelation, and so is his position as a speaker who enunciates this truth.

This logic is most apparent in the late fourth-century Christian testimony book ascribed to Epiphanius. The book "testifies" to the sacrament of

Christian baptism in 102 anaphoric sentences, each of which refers to a structurally similar event in the Bible. Each statement is a concise performative
utterance supported exclusively by the witness of the speaker's enunciative
authority. Each sentence "proves" the truth of the dogma of baptism by sealing it rhetorically. Though the authenticity of Epiphanius's authorship is
disputed, the association of this type of Christian text with his name shows
that his contemporaries were keenly aware of his discursive style.[28]

The structural economy and affirmative intensity of such doubt-proof
dogmatic articulation guaranteed its political success. The council, indeed,
took over the succinct creedal statement crowning Epiphanius's *Ancoratus*:
"We know the Father to be Father, the Son to be Son, the Holy Spirit to be
Holy Spirit, Trinity in Oneness. For One is the Oneness of the Father and
of the Son and of the Holy Spirit, One Being, One Lordship, One Will."[29]
Epiphanius's articulation of the creed paved the way for the church's entrance
into state legislation and thus, in a sense, marked the historical point of balance between ecclesiastical and secular power. With "One Lordship" and
"One Will," the full integration of church and state seemed to be practically
accomplished.

By the time of Epiphanius's death in about 403, the power of the church
was well enough established to become a serious competitor to the administrative mechanisms of the state. The first symptoms of a crisis in the balance
of ecclesiastical and imperial power found their expression in the politics
of Ambrose, the bishop of Milan (died 397), who came to exercise a considerable influence over the emperor. The first concept of Augustine's book
on the interrelation between worldly and divine power, *The City of God*
(traditionally perceived as a response to the sack of Rome in 410), had germi-
nated already in the 390s, in the years of Augustine's acquaintance with and
admiration for Ambrose, the bishop whose ecclesiastical goal was to secure
a leading position for the church in imperial affairs.[30] This is also the time
when Epiphanius had suddenly conceived his hatred for Christian images
while launching a construction of a grand basilica in Cyprus.

Epiphanius was one of those "new protagonists"[31] in the politics of the
late Roman Empire whose rise to a position of influence and control over the
imperial power was discussed in Peter Brown's *Power and Persuasion* (1988).
Brown has shown that with the gradual Christianization of the state and the
legalization of the church, the emperor started favoring as his counselors in
political affairs not men of *paideia*, the wise men of the Greek aristocratic
learning, but members of the clergy who took a position of *parrhēsia* (free
speech) to fashion their authoritative voice according to the role of a plain-
speaking, humble, divinely inspired anti-philosopher in the tradition of Paul
(Brown, *Power and Persuasion*, 65–73).

These new counselors to the emperor acted in the interest of the church as
a competing system of power and thus constituted a subversive force within
the imperial setting. And it was none other than Emperor Theodosius I, the

major addressee of Epiphanius's iconoclastic program, who was the first to
turn to the bishops and monks instead of the profane philosophers and rhetoricians "as the authorized appeasers of his rage" (ibid., 105).

Brown describes how in the famous incident of the Riot of the Statues in
Antioch in 387, when issues of taxation led to an uprising and the demolition
of the statues of the emperor and empress, the holy man Macedonius played
the major part in appeasing the emperor and preventing a punitive massacre
of the population. His forceful, almost fanatically courageous rhetorical performance convinced the emperor to pardon the rebels.

Theodosius I also made concessions to Bishop Ambrose of Milan who
insisted on the impunity of the Christian rioters in Callinicum for their
destruction of a synagogue in 388 (ibid., 105–7). Two years later, Theodosius
accepted public penance imposed on him by Ambrose for his punitive massacre of the residents of Thessalonica. Thus by the early 390s, when Epiphanius
launched his iconoclastic agitation, the emperor had created a series of prec-
edents in which the imperial power yielded to the demands of the church.[32]

Epiphanius, the bishop of Salamis and former monk in Egypt and Palestine,
combines the features of both the learned Ambrose of Milan and the "God-
taught" hermit Macedonius who "acted as effectively as they did because they
found roles into which they could step with confidence. . . . They played the
ancient part of the courageous and free-spoken man of wisdom, but in playing this ancient role they invested it with a heavy charge of novel meaning."[33]
It is this role that Epiphanius fully embraced in his iconoclastic enterprise.

Christ's Body as Christ's Image

The political theology of representation which supported Epiphanius's iconoclastic activism is laid out in the "Letter to John." The letter, which ends
with the iconoclastic episode, opens with Epiphanius's description of another
scandalous incident—his forced ordination of a man named Paulinian to
serve against his will as a priest in a monastery in John's diocese. The incident
with Paulinian bears directly on the problem of ecclesiastical representation
and, therefore, meaningfully relates to the climactic destruction of the curtain
in Anablatha. Within this framework, the letter offers a full scenario of the
iconoclash between Christ's body and Christ's image.

On the surface, the letter had been written as an apology to John for
Epiphanius's administrative trespassing, in defiance of the canons, on the ter-
ritory of John's pastoral care. But on closer inspection, the letter appears to
be a document of ecclesiastical politics bargaining for influence in the Palestinian provinces. Its strategic character is evident already in Epiphanius's very
excuses for the unlawful ordination he had performed.

First, Epiphanius asserts that he ordained Paulinian on behalf of a monastery where most brothers were foreigners and therefore not really subject to

John's jurisdiction. Then, he tries to mitigate the offense by portraying such practice as common in Cyprus where he usually accepts priests ordained by other high clerics in his absence. And finally, he assumes full personal responsibility for the event, depicting the ordination as a violent act committed against the modest will of Paulinian who had to submit not only to Epiphanius's oratory but also to physical force.

But Epiphanius claims to have acted in response to the brothers' complaints about the lack of an officially ordained priest to perform services in their monastery. Notably, he does not try very hard to cover up his subversion of the rules but rather signals this to John as a conscious strategy. Moreover, he not only seeks to persuade the bishop of Jerusalem, in the name of all the brotherly Christian love between them, not to "take it personally," but urges John to imitate him.

> For, although each individual bishop of the Church has under him churches which are placed in his charge, and although no man may stretch himself beyond his measure, yet the love of Christ, which is without dissimulation, is set up as an example to us all; *and we must consider not so much the thing done as the time and place, the mode and motive, of doing it.* (Epiphanius, "Letter to John," 1; emphasis added)

Epiphanius seems to be concerned here with the divine authorization of his actions and, consequently, of his overall discourse. He insinuates that the larger interests of the church, for the wants of which he "simply made provision," are the real cause of his unlawful behavior. And even if he "stretched himself beyond his measure," the love of Christ was his example. If this ordination had not taken place, he further explains, the monastery in Palestine might have been alienated from "the church with its ancient faith." In other words, his concern is that the church could lose the support of eastern monasticism, which was around this time increasingly influenced by the extreme asceticism and spirituality of Evagrius Ponticus.

Evagrian monasticism posed a danger of relegating the church to the position of a purely spiritual appendix of the empire, as it used to be before the edicts of tolerance. Indeed, the actual problem in the monastery for which Epiphanius had ordained a priest was the monks' reluctance to assume the office of priesthood and the presbyters' ascetic refusal to conduct worship with the due ceremonial of the official church, whose administrative structure and regulations were borrowed from the Roman state. Paulinian, whom Epiphanius allegedly ordained against his will, is presented as one of the monastic rebels who defied the representation intrinsic to ecclesiastical ritual performance:[34]

> I saw that the monastery contained a large number of reverend brothers, and that the reverend presbyters, Jerome and Vincent, through

modesty and humility, were unwilling to offer the sacrifices permitted
to their rank, and to labor in that part of their calling which ministers
more than any other to the salvation of Christians. I knew, moreover,
that you could not find and lay hands on this servant of God [that
is, Paulinian] who had several times fled from you simply because
he was reluctant to undertake the onerous duties of priesthood, and
that no other bishop could easily find him. (Epiphanius, "Letter to
John," 1)

Epiphanius's letter thus indicates that the moderate brotherhood of the
monastery in Bethlehem felt endangered by the emergent tendency of extreme
asceticism. On one hand, there were the monks who complained to Epiphanius
about the neglect of liturgical worship in their monastery and hence about the
community's drifting away from the official church. On the other, there were
Jerome, Vincent, and other "reverend presbyters" who seem to have adopted a
proto-Evagrian preference for individual worship in the form of "pure prayer."
Such spiritualized worship shunned all tangible representation in accordance
with the requirement of "passionlessness," modesty, and humility.[35]

The radical splinter group of monks favored private piety over collective
rituals, thus forsaking the representative body of Christ with its institutional
organization. Even more worldly and churchly forms of monasticism could
be considered dangerous by the proponents of the official church, if they
defied ecclesiastical hierarchies and rituals or interfered with them. For
example, Eustathian monasticism, whose members sought their ascetic vocation (in contrast to the Evagrians) within the world and the official church,
were for exactly this reason regarded by some authorities as "dangerously
competitive, rather than in harmony with the church and in submission to
its hierarchy."[36]

The historian of early monasticism Claudia Rapp writes that Evagrius's
ideas, and especially his association of the quest for gnosis with the monastic environment, laid the foundation for "a potential competition between
monks and clergy over the possession and administration of the Spirit": "If,
as Evagrius intends, the monk strives to be a *gnōstikos*, and if, as Clement
and Origen have argued, the *gnōstikos* is also a true priest, this opens the
door for the monastic rejection of the institutional clergy and the services it
has to offer, especially the Eucharistic liturgy."[37]

Thus Epiphanius's forced ordination of Paulinian demonstratively integrates and binds a dissenting monk back into the tangible ecclesiastical
hierarchy. Epiphanius reports in detail about his cunning subjugation of Paulinian: "While, therefore, the Collect was being celebrated in the church of
the villa which adjoins our monastery—he [Paulinian] being quite ignorant
and wholly unsuspicious of my purpose—I gave orders to a number of dea-
cons to seize him and to stop his mouth, lest in his eagerness to free himself
he might adjure me in the name of Christ" (Epiphanius, "Letter to John," 1).

This happens during the High Mass celebrated next door to the monastery, while Paulinian suspects nothing. Interestingly, his violent ordination is followed by an immediate promotion from deacon to presbyter which coincides with the Mass itself, a rite into which he is integrated, first as a passive and then as an active participant.

> First of all, then, I ordained him deacon, setting before him the fear of God, and forcing him to minister; for he made a hard struggle against it, crying out that he was unworthy, and protesting that this heavy burden was beyond his strength. It was with difficulty, then, that I overcame his reluctance, persuading him as well as I could with passages from Scripture, and setting before him the commandments of God. (Epiphanius, "Letter to John," 1)

The unwilling Paulinian ends up administering the sacraments and thus becomes a part of the tangible representation of the ecclesiastical hierarchy: "And when he had ministered in the offering of the holy sacrifices, once more with great difficulty I closed his mouth and ordained him presbyter. Then, using the same arguments as before, I induced him to sit in the place set apart for the presbyters" (Epiphanius, "Letter to John," 1). In other words, Paulinian is kidnapped from the amorphous realm of monastic individualistic spirituality to be installed in the structured, collective space of the church where he assumes a clearly designated place.

Afterwards Paulinian is delegated to the monastery where the presbyters had defied their priestly obligations to conduct collective worship: he is now in charge of organizing monastic religious service in the likeness of the official church. The whole incident is presented as if it had been performed on behalf of the moderate majority of the monastery, though Epiphanius does not conceal that he informed the monks about his intervention and insertion of Paulinian only *post factum*:

> After this I wrote to the reverend presbyters and other brothers of the monastery, chiding them for not having written to me about him [Paulinian]. For a year before I had heard many of them complain that they had no one to celebrate for them the sacraments of the Lord. (Epiphanius, "Letter to John," 1)

Since these "reverend presbyters" were actually the ones who rejected the official collective worship, his delegation of Paulinian "to celebrate for them the sacraments of the Lord" comes across as an unambiguous order to comply with the demands of the church, an order only scantily disguised by rhetorical courtesy and prevarication. The fact that Paulinian was the brother of Jerome, Epiphanius's best friend and political ally in ecclesiastical affairs, suggests that his forced ordination had been most likely just a topos of humility—a strategic homage paid by Epiphanius to radical asceticism in order to endear his envoy Paulinian to the monastic community in question.[38]

But the episode also sends a warning to John: if he fails to force the presbyters to do their duty, there will be others to correct his omission. Thus by not taking measures against a "separatist" monastic tendency, John endangers the unity of the church but also jeopardizes his own ecclesiastical authority. The detailed description of the resistance of Paulinian who allegedly once fled from John and other bishops in order not to be ordained and his subsequent violent subjugation to the demands of the church signal to John that the recourse to the scriptures can be complemented, if necessary, by physical force which can always be justified in the name of God.

Epiphanius as a monk-bishop pits his own "integrationist" position anchored in the authority of the monastic "ancient faith" against Evagrius and his followers. Since Evagrius's Olivet monastery was around this time the major mediator between the desert and Constantinople,[39] Epiphanius's insertion of political allies into a Palestinian monastery betrays his desire to promote his type of monasticism, which could compete for influence in the imperial centers.

To gain leverage for his position, Epiphanius frames his strife with John within a longer and broader history of dogmatic debates. He explains that their disagreement about the breaking of canonical regulations grew out of their different relation to the third-century Platonist theologian Origen, whose spiritual and allegorical exegesis strongly influenced Evagrius. Epiphanius calls Origen "the spiritual father of Arius, and the root and parent of all heresies." Origen's name is, however, used broadly to condemn the whole tradition of spiritual exegesis that at Constantine's time was represented by Arius and had been ever since favored by ascetic monasticism.

Epiphanius's association of Origen with the Arian heresy allows him to lead an attack on the "spiritual" church from the position of orthodoxy. In his letter, Epiphanius seeks primarily to secure John's support as a representative of ecclesiastical administration in Jerusalem. John must prevent a spread of "the heresy of Origen" adopted by Evagrian "separatist" monasticism because it promotes the notion of a purely spiritual and therefore politically impotent church.

Erich Auerbach showed that the tension between the Origenist allegorical exegesis and Epiphanius's type of literalism was indeed a political tension between "philosophical" and "historical" interpretations of the Bible:

> The difference between Tertullian's more historical and realistic interpretation and Origen's ethical, allegorical approach reflect a current conflict, known to us from other early Christian sources: one party strove to transform the events of the New and still more of the Old Testament into purely spiritual happenings, to "spirit away" their historical character—the other wished to preserve the full historicity of the Scriptures along with the deeper meaning.[40]

Epiphanius's attack on Origen's "philosophical" exegesis is launched from an anti-philosophical position once reflected in Paul's words: "See to it that no one makes a prey of you by philosophy and empty deceit, according to human tradition, according to the elemental spirits of the universe, and not according to Christ" (Col. 2:8, RSV). Epiphanius contends that Origen "tampers with the true meaning of the narrative by a false use of allegory, multiplying words without limit, and undermines the faith of the simple by the most varied arguments" (Epiphanius, "Letter to John," 4).

In the steps of Tertullian, the aim of Epiphanius's figural, typological, or literalist exegesis was simply to show "that the persons and events of the Old Testament were prefigurations of the New and its history of salvation."[41] The "attitude embodied in the figural interpretation became one of the essential elements of the Christian picture of reality, history, and the concrete world in general."[42] Therefore it had also provided a perfect discursive tool for the needs of ecclesiastical politics.

At the time of Epiphanius's iconoclastic initiative, these needs consisted above all in securing the sovereignty of the church by endorsing its providential history in all concreteness of state legislation. Epiphanius remembered perfectly well that the church had won access to this legislation only by way of dogmatic articulation. Logically, biblical literalists like him understood any variant of Origen's complex exegesis as a "dehistoricization"[43] of the scriptures, which could only enfeeble the hard-won political standing and influence of the church. Therefore Epiphanius laments: "I grieve, and grieve bitterly, to see numbers of my brothers, and of those in particular who show the most promise, and have reached the highest rank in the sacred ministry, deceived by his persuasive arguments and made by his most perverse teaching the food of the devil" (Epiphanius, "Letter to John," 6).

Besides being confusing and inaccessible to the "simple" ones, on whose popular support the church mainly relies, Epiphanius is especially worried that Origen's teaching might permeate the church's higher echelons. There, the intellectual attraction of Origen could have especially dire consequences for the church as a political institution. It would weaken the "theological" justification of its tangible presence on earth and thus allow for concessions to the worldly might.

Remarkably, at this point the devil makes his entrance in Epiphanius's discourse. The devil had been a traditional accomplice of pagan spectacle and representation.[44] Origen could be responsible for the clergy's succumbing to the devil only because under the spiritual guidance of allegorists the church would have no tangible representation to oppose to the panoply of the state. In fact, the letter's anti-Origenist polemics ultimately amounts to a sophisticated argument against the marginalization of the church and the danger of its institutional invisibility.

Epiphanius makes plain his desire to bring the church down to earth from Origen's heavenly realm. Such a relocation would validate the ecclesiastical claim to overseeing the historical fulfillment of scriptural prophecy, the task that secures its status as an institution. He is especially concerned with the physical reality of paradise.

> Or who can tolerate him [Origen] when he gives us a paradise in the third heaven, and transfers that which the Scripture mentions from earth to the heavenly places, and when he explains allegorically all the trees which are mentioned in Genesis . . .
>
> I have drunk also from the great river Euphrates, not spiritual but actual water, such as you can touch with your hand and imbibe with your mouth. But where are rivers which admit of being seen and of being drunk, it follows that there also will be fig-trees and other trees; and it is of these that the Lord says, "Of every tree of the garden thou mayest freely eat." They are like other trees and timber, just as the rivers are like other rivers and waters.
>
> But if the water is visible and real, then the fig-tree and the rest of the timber must be real also, and Adam and Eve must have been originally formed with real and not phantasmal bodies, and not, as Origen would have us believe, have afterwards received them on account of their sin. (Epiphanius, "Letter to John," 5)

The geographical and physical reality of paradise, which Epiphanius infers from the real existence of the Euphrates and extends to all biblical events, is supposed to guarantee the reality of the kingdom of God to come. There is even a concrete location prepared for this kingdom in the eastern provinces of the empire. And Epiphanius's literal understanding of resurrection as the resurrection of "this flesh" assures that these grounds would be populated with real bodies.[45] Thus the major issue with Origen, as Epiphanius presents it, is that his philosophy undermines the church's historical claim to power and participation in earthly affairs, and hence to a tangible system of representation.

Epiphanius starts his argument against Origen with a defense of the visibility of the Trinity: "What Catholic, what Christian who adorns his faith with good works, can hear with calm Origen's teaching and counsel, or believe in his extraordinary preaching? 'The Son,' he tells us, 'cannot see the Father, and the Holy Spirit cannot see the Son' " (Epiphanius, "Letter to John," 4).

But this visibility is differentiated from a superficial mimetic image-likeness, the sort of "false image" which Plato had banned from the ideal republic. Instead this visibility is understood as a structural relation among the three persons of the Trinity, or in the manner of Plato's "true image," the image understood in terms of mathematical relations as developed in the natural cosmogony of Plato's *Timaeus*. Epiphanius pits this "true image" against what he perceives as Origen's radical denial of visibility as such.

Epiphanius's next objection to Origen is his depreciation of human bodies:

Can anyone, moreover, brook Origen's assertion that men's souls were once angels in heaven, and that having sinned in the upper world, they have been cast down into this, and have been confined in bodies as in barrows or tombs, to pay the penalty for their sins; and that the bodies of believers are not temples of Christ but prisons of the condemned? (Epiphanius, "Letter to John," 4)

Epiphanius alludes to Origen's notion of the body (*sōma*) as a tomb or a dead body, which some call, he says further, a "funeral monument" (*sēma*). Thus he suggests that Origen's spiritualism robs the believers of a real living body, which is a pillar of their collective identity as the living body of Christ. But Epiphanius also excoriates Origen's notion of the loss of "God's image in man," bringing many scriptural references to confirm the opposite: man was without doubt made in God's image, though one should put in abeyance its exact definition. Dechow summarizes Epiphanius's argument as follows:

Some think the image is the human appearance (*plasma*) . . . others the soul (*psychē*), still other the mind (*nous*), virtue (*aretē*), the body (*sōma*), or even baptism (*baptisma*). He refutes all these distinctions and concludes that only God knows the nature of the divine image in the human, but it does exist by grace and faith, as in the action of the Eucharist. It is roundly formed (*stroggyloeides*) and imperceptible (*anaisthēton*) and indicated by the Lord's words, "This is my body." Epiphanius continues: "We believe that it is his [body], and we know our Lord is [the] whole perception, [the] whole aesthetic, [the] whole God, [the] whole of that which activates, [the] whole of that which energizes, [the] whole light, [the] whole Logos, incomprehensibility— yet this which is granted to us by grace."[46]

Thus, Epiphanius's own postulation of the body as a temple of Christ is linked directly with his notion of the image in *Ancoratus*: God's image is the host of the Eucharist and, therefore, a nonrepresentational image, which can be accessed only in liturgical practice.

Epiphanius's understanding of the "image of Christ" as the host stands in the tradition of Tertullian's understanding of the host as a *figura* of Christ, that is, a form understood as a part of the substance: "He [Christ] makes it his own body, saying, 'This is my body, that is, the figure of my body.' For there could not have been a figure unless there were a true body. An empty thing, that is, a phantom, could not take on a figure."[47]

But, as Auerbach has shown, prior to its appropriation through the church fathers the word *figura* meant also an outward likeness. This double meaning allows Epiphanius to extend this dogmatic image-concept to the ritual worship of the Eucharist. The "image of Christ" comes to designate in Epiphanius's understanding the concrete substance and volume of both the host and the congregation united in communion. Most importantly, it provides a model of representation specific to the church, the body of Christ.

The synchronic unity of the body of Christ thus accomplished in worship is additionally cemented on a historical, diachronic axis in Epiphanius's radically anti-ascetic stance on procreation, which secured the continuity of life and therefore the nonmimetic reproduction of God's image in man. Epiphanius insisted that, though Adam was made out of clay in the image and likeness of God, all his offspring maintained this image by generation, including Christ himself who received his body through Mary. This lays a foundation for Epiphanius's argument for a substitution of a mimetic image through a nonmimetic representation: as the creation of Adam was superseded by the incarnation, so handmade images should be surpassed by a generated image of God in Christ, and by implication in the Eucharist, in the communal celebration of the body of Christ.

Epiphanius's naming of the pictured textile as a funeral object emphatically fuses an anti-pagan and anti-Origenist stance. The image on the curtain, he suggests, is a dead body not just like the pagan funeral portraits but also like Origen's bodies, which are merely the tombs of fallen souls, funeral objects and not temples of Christ. Implicitly, Epiphanius links a "false" representation of the textile image of Anablatha with Origen's interpretation of the "garments of skins" (Gen. 3:21, RSV) in which God dressed Adam and Eve after the Fall. Epiphanius alleges that Origen misunderstood "garments of skins" as a mere surface appearance of the body, an ephemeral likeness and not the real flesh.

This quasi-theological disagreement, like everything else in Epiphanius's letter, contained a reference to concrete cultural actuality: tunics covered with embroidered pictures (often bearing Christian content) were indeed fashionable at the imperial court around this time. Adèle Coulin Weibel, for example, references "the 'pictured tunic' that the Emperor Gratian sent, in 379, to his former tutor, the poet Ausonius, on his accession to the consulship,"[48] and thus sheds further light on Epiphanius's linkage of Origenist exegesis with paganism. Origen's concept of the postlapsarian body, Epiphanius hints, fosters two-dimensional superficial representations of the biblical figures in images and leads to a false identification of the pagan realm of death, suggestively linked to imperial fashion, with the Christian realm of life.

Epiphanius's rhetorical camouflage in the letter shows that he was fully aware of the precariousness of his enterprise, which brings to the forefront another aspect of *figura*—the *figura* as a verbal technique of subversion. Roman orators used it to insinuate "something which for political or tactical reasons, or simply for the sake of effect, had best remain secret or at least unspoken."[49] So Epiphanius introduces the iconoclastic episode with a list of current image-concepts (as previously in *Ancoratus*) while ostensibly refusing to commit to one particular understanding.

This "indefinable" image, which in *Ancoratus* constituted the mystery of Eucharistic worship, becomes now a rhetorical device of obfuscating Epiphanius's own definition of "God's image in man." Epiphanius enumerates a variety of image-concepts from contemporary debates and controversies which allows him to engage several meanings at once so that later one could be replaced with another.

Strategically, Epiphanius does not differentiate among the positions of his theological adversaries and allies. For example, the understanding of the image as "sensation" stems from Evagrian asceticism, whereas the interpretation of the image as "virtue" could be from Gregory of Nyssa's *On the Making of Man*. But Epiphanius also smuggles in among them a strange definition from *Panarion*—the image of God "in virtue of which man exercises universal sway," which prompted scholars to speculate: "Epiphanius' view that human dominance over the earth is the central characteristic of 'the image of God' suggests that he may have thought the human copying of God's rulership was the central issue at stake."[50]

In the context of his time, Epiphanius's iconoclasm is legible as an initiative to correct this issue. The "human copying of God's rulership," or "man's exercise of universal sway" hints at the emperor, in whose realm Christianized imperial handmade images were tokens of the divinity of his power. The close association of Christ's image with the image of the emperor pervaded, in Gager's words, "the crypto-political idiom present among the Christian theologians of the fourth century."[51]

The dramatic episodes framing the letter compensate for Epiphanius's rhetorical obscurantism by putting into practice his theology of representation. It is only logical that his ordination of Paulinian, which inscribes Eucharistic worship onto the monastic space as a form of ecclesiastical representation, is accompanied by his removal from the body of the church of a handmade image of Christ, or a saint. This performance obviates the necessity of differentiating between right and wrong understandings of "God's image in man," which is a philosophically complicated and politically precarious task. Instead, Epiphanius differentiates among the image-concepts in an actual act of subversion, that is, by establishing a "true" image of Christ at the beginning and destroying a "false" one at the end of the letter.

Thus, the "Letter to John" has been clearly written to validate an independent system of ecclesiastical representation on the premises of biblical literalism and to win John as an ally in a struggle against imperial image-making. As a "programmatic" text, the letter suggests the strategies of justification for iconoclastic politics for all parties involved: it uses an anti-Origenist stance to address the clergy, but also gives a practical example for emulation to the emperor and the laity, by striking the more accessible tone of ancient piety and anti-paganism.

The immediate reception of Epiphanius's iconoclastic episode is telling: soon after the letter's composition, Jerome excerpted and translated the iconoclastic episode from its original Greek into Latin—as he says, "privately and hastily"—for a guest of his monastery, a certain Eusebius of Cremona. Then the Latin text was allegedly stolen and put into broader circulation.[52] This story suggests that the letter's call for Christian iconoclasm and Epiphanius's performance thereof were directed to the populations in the western provinces of the empire as well.

Epiphanius deploys his strategies of argumentation, proposed and focalized in the letter, separately when he targets the diverse addressees across the empire in his other iconoclastic writings.

Persuading the Emperor

Epiphanius's "Letter to the Emperor Theodosius" was composed around the same time as his "Letter to John." The surviving fragment shows that Epiphanius audaciously challenged even the sovereign himself when urging the introduction of imperial iconoclastic legislation. Seizing on Theodosius's commitment to anti-paganism, Epiphanius launched his attempt at persuasion here by striking the theme of idolatry:

> The devil made idolatry in this world through his wickedness and spread it about in the world and confirmed it and through it turned men away from God. And now once more, after heresies and idols, he has drawn and deceived the believers back to old idolatry. May your reverence consider, and may your God-given wisdom plunge into the depths of thought, whether it is right for us to have a drawn and painted God. Who ever heard of such a thing?[53] (Epiphanius, "Letter to the Emperor Theodosius," 184)

Epiphanius's question is rhetorical. For "such a thing" as a painted image of God was not only heard of but also broadly practiced, especially in Theodosius's imperial sphere. In the grand churches of the imperial centers at this time in history, one could also see compromising representations of biblical figures. Such Christianized images as the magnificent mosaics *Christ in Majesty* in Santa Pudenziana and *Christ the Lawgiver* in the Basilica of Cosmas and Damian in Rome, or *Christ as the Universal Sovereign* in San Vitale in Ravenna, indeed, relied on the iconography of the imperial cult that used to celebrate the emperor as a god.[54] (See fig. 1.2.)

In those churches, Christ, saints, or prophets, represented in the tradition of Roman monarchical art, fell into a liminal zone of power. On the one hand, such images provided Christianity with the official glory of the Roman state; but on the other hand they divinized, now in terms of the new religion, the sacred might of the emperor and the imperial hierarchy.[55] Epiphanius is careful enough to present his objection as a merely theological concern that

Figure 1.2. *Christ in Majesty*, mosaic, Santa Pudenziana, Rome, fourth century A.D.

the making of images of God interferes with the canonical legislation as a form of heresy. Therefore he brings up the Nicene orthodoxy traditionally favored by the imperial family:

> †††(praising the king among the children)††† (that faith) which exists forever and was preserved among a few even during the bad teaching of Arius, was affirmed by our saintly fathers and bishops in the city of Nicaea, and is the same faith which 318 bishops affirmed and countersigned, not putting forth a newly announced faith but agreeing in the one that has always been, (those bishops) whom we too follow like sons ever since our young age, those bishops who have become like parents to us in the faith, we agree in and maintain their faith, just as you do, most reverend king. And this is that faith: We believe in one God, creator of all things (and the rest of the creed). (Epiphanius, "Letter to the Emperor Theodosius," 184)

A fragmented sentence at the beginning of this paragraph praises the orthodox faith of the emperor "among the children." With the reference to the progenitors of the orthodox faith, this praise suggests that the Christian emperor is here given a place as one of the children of the church and is expected to uphold the legacy of the Nicene fathers along with contemporary bishops.[56]

Epiphanius is careful to limit his admonition to the issue of the Nicene legislation, as if he were exclusively concerned with correct religious behavior and is reluctant to interfere with imperial affairs. However, the passage unambiguously tells the emperor to subject himself to the law of the church—a breathtakingly daring step, if one considers that in the political philosophy of the time the emperor's position was still not subject to the law. The church would gain a considerable advantage if it succeeded in postulating its law as a direct manifestation of divine power, binding even on the emperor.[57]

Epiphanius's evocation of the major dogmatic controversy of Constantine's time—Athanasius versus Arius—reminds the emperor of Epiphanius's early monastic loyalty to the Athanasian version of Christianity favored by Constantine. His iconoclastic position should be trusted, he thus suggests, because of his long alliance with the interests of the empire. He continues with a series of rhetorical questions:

> Who ever heard of such things? Who among the ancient fathers painted a picture of Christ and set it in a church, or even in his own house? Who among the old bishops would have done Christ the indignity of painting him on door curtains? Who would have painted on cloths or walls Abraham and Isaac and Jacob and Moses and all the prophets and patriarchs, or Peter, or Andrew, or Jacob, or John, or Paul, or the rest of the apostles, making them a show and a laughingstock? (Epiphanius, "Letter to the Emperor Theodosius," 185)

Epiphanius is right that none of the early fathers made images of Christ, but he also cannot possibly be unaware of the imperial images of Christ in the grand churches of Rome, Milan, and Ravenna.[58] Nor can he be ignorant of the fact that the Jewish patriarchs were important figures in Hellenistic political thought on the nature of kingship and, therefore, were often depicted in the imperial realm. But he chooses to elaborate on the falsity of representation from the position of biblical literalism:

> Moreover, they lie, as they take various imaginary shapes for the saints from their own minds, sometimes painting the same people as young men or old men, although they never saw them. They paint the Savior with long hair, proceeding from the suggestion that he is called the Nazarene, since Nazarenes have long hair. But they err in their attempt to put the pieces of information together, for he drank wine, and the Nazarenes drink no wine. And whenever they form ideas through their own imaginings, they lie: for the rogues paint the holy apostle Peter as an old man, with shaved head and chin; others paint Saint Paul with receding hairline, others paint him bald and bearded, and the other apostles clean-shaven. (Epiphanius, "Letter to the Emperor Theodosius," 185)

Epiphanius seems to object here to the randomness of representation for the same reason as in the "Letter to John" he objects to the randomness of Origen's allegorical exegesis: like Origen's "multiplication of words," biblically unsupported depictions of holy figures dilute the legacy of the scriptures through imaginary and distorted projections. Thus, Epiphanius denounces the multiplicity and hybridity of the images of Christ: for example, the painters who represent Christ with long hair confuse the Nazarene with the Jewish Nazirites.

What Epiphanius omits is that Christ had been usually depicted with long hair in the realm of imperial iconography. Early images of Christ in the catacombs, on the contrary, show him with short hair. Thus, he seems to target the Roman-Christian adulterations of this potent image as if they represented a Jewish-Christian heresy. In *Panarion*, indeed, Epiphanius had chastised the Jewish-Christian hybrid sects as heretical, but the doctrinal and representational hybridity of the powerful Christianized Roman state is a more dangerous terrain where biblical literalism offers the most secure tool for navigation.

So Epiphanius further deduces the nonrepresentational nature of Christ from his social invisibility in the gospel narrative:

> Now if the Savior had long hair, and the other disciples were clean-shaven, and he alone was not shaven and similar to the others, why did the Pharisees and scribes give thirty pieces of silver to Judas as a wage, so that by kissing him he might show them that "this is the man ye seek," since they could have told on their own and with the help of others which was the one they sought, through the sign of his hair, and avoided giving the wage? (Epiphanius, "Letter to the Emperor Theodosius," 185)

Epiphanius's insistence that Christ looked just like everyone else is a variation on his reasoning that man was made in God's image by the generation of an overall human shape and not by a mimetic representation of some overt likeness. In the "Letter to John" this argument buttressed the iconoclastic rejection of pictured surfaces, which in application to Theodosius and the imperial realm acquires more concrete political meaning: the depiction of Christ as the emperor, or the depiction of the emperor as Christ in glory, is a false likeness and an apotheosis of the wrong power.

Epiphanius proposes to the emperor new legislation that would prohibit handmade images of all sorts and even elaborates on the details of removal for each type of representation. His meticulous proposal indicates a carefully prepared program:

> Do you not see, king most beloved of God, that this is a work unbecoming in the sight of God? Wherefore I beg you, God-beloved and

evil-hating king, with the zeal of God in you to suppress every deception with firm legislation and punishment, insofar as this is possible—I
believe that it is possible for you to accomplish this, if you wish it,
in God, so that those textiles on which have been falsely depicted
the prophets and apostles and even our Lord Christ, wherever you
may find them, will be gathered out of churches, baptisteries, houses
and shrines and used for the burial of the poor, and the paintings
made on walls will be covered over with whitewash; representations
in mosaic, because they are difficult to make, you will dispose of as
it will please you, with the wisdom given you by God. If these can be
removed, so much the better, but if they cannot, let people be satisfied
with the images made in the past and let them make no more. For our
fathers made no other images than the sign of Christ, the cross, on
their doors and everywhere else. (Epiphanius, "Letter to the Emperor
Theodosius," 185)

This passage makes clear that in his iconoclastic outburst against a textile
image in Palestine, Epiphanius proleptically performed on the small scale of
a provincial church what he wanted to see accomplished by imperial legislation. Epiphanius gives the emperor an example to follow: Theodosius should
remove the images of Christ, patriarchs, and saints, as Epiphanius removed a
textile image in Anablatha.

The example is tricky because the curtain image in Palestine was a rather
harmless, inconspicuous decoration, not unlike an image of Christ in the vault
of a burial chamber in the catacomb of Commodilla, or a mosaic discovered
on the floor of a Roman building in Hinton St. Mary in Dorset, whereas
the Christian images surrounding Theodosius were gorgeous displays visibly
staged and politically charged with the symbolism of imperial power.

Epiphanius's advice about expensive mosaic images is noticeably cautious.
He leaves the exact decision how to erase them over to the emperor, for, after
all, this concerns his immediate environment. But the emperor's freedom is
even here limited by the options proposed: even if the mosaics are not to be
destroyed, their images should be disavowed and kept out of sight. As an
instance of alternative representation of purely Christian nature, Epiphanius
suggests the sign of the cross. The suggestion harks back meaningfully to the
time of Constantine's conversion. The first Christian emperor, who understood Christianity through the person of Christ, still did not dare to picture
himself in God's likeness. Instead, Constantine introduced a monogram of
Christ (*Chi-Rho*), which looked like a cross and was put on the shields of his
soldiers and the imperial standard.

From the perspective of art history, André Grabar considered Constantine's initiative "a throwback to the first Christian attempt to create religious
figurations, when a small group of new symbolic signs, the image-signs, was
devised."[59] However, this seems to be exactly what Epiphanius wants from

Theodosius when he offers him the example of his great predecessor. Theodosius should give up the rich imperial iconography of divine power and hand over the control of Christian representation to the church, thus effectively sealing the church's victory in its competition with the empire. But Epiphanius presents the issue so as if the abolition of Christianized monarchical art would be merely upholding the venerable tradition of minimalist representation that stemmed from the great Constantine himself.

The same theme of ancient piety is struck in Epiphanius's shortest surviving fragment addressed to his Christian community in Cyprus, "Testament of the Citizens of Salamis," but in the popular context his iconoclastic stance acquires a radically different meaning:

> Take heed and hold fast to the traditions that you have received: lean
> neither to the right nor to the left. And be mindful of this, beloved
> children, not to put up images in churches nor in the resting-places
> of the saints, but keep God in your hearts through memory; nor shall
> you bring (images) to the dwelling house. For it is not permitted that
> a Christian gaze with his eyes and in wandering of his soul, but rather
> let the matters of God be inscribed and impressed (on the soul of)
> each. (Epiphanius, "Testament of the Citizens of Salamis," 187)

This position was introduced in the "Letter to John": the call not to stray from the scriptures is a call to fulfill the providential prophecy of God's kingdom on earth in all concreteness of religious life. And the image posits here a danger of distraction from the collective worship through private, solitary forms of piety, which weaken the unity and dissipate the body of Christ instead of celebrating, consolidating, and empowering it.

The double function of Epiphanius's example for imitation in Anablatha is thrown into relief by these communications to the emperor and the citizens of Salamis: in application to the imperial realm, iconoclasm would mean a subjugation of the imperial power to the church and a weakening of the imperial position. But in the case of the Christian community, the same action calls for strengthening its collective body as the living body of Christ.

The eruption of holy anger, in the populist, anti-philosophical style of Macedonius, at a violation of the scriptures and of the church's living body which Epiphanius staged in Anablatha can be also interpreted as a strategy of self-protection in the context of a highly risky intervention into state affairs. Remarkably, Epiphanius's performance anticipated the logic of "divine intervention" which the Byzantine iconoclasts would seize upon several centuries later. A volcanic eruption in the Aegean Sea, strategically interpreted by the iconoclasts as a sign of God's indignation at Christian images, would prompt Emperor Leo III to take down the imperial image of Christ from the entrance to his palace—the first step in his official inauguration of iconoclasm as a state policy.

Persuading the Clergy

Next to the emperor, Epiphanius seeks to have his iconoclastic initiative endorsed in the forum of ecclesiastical councils and synods having a hand in state legislation. Here he relies on his position as a bishop and dogmatic theologian to whom is entrusted the *cathedra Christi*. The verbal specificity, choice of scriptural quotations, and allusions to the history of ecclesiastical legislation in his longest iconoclastic fragment, "The Speech of Saint Epiphanius Against Those Who Think It Right to Make Images of an Idolatrous Kind of Christ, the Virgin and the Martyrs, as well as of Angels and Prophets," is another example of rhetorical adjustment for a target audience, this time in a legislative forum.

In this fragment Epiphanius apparently tries to accomplish an official transition from the imperial to the ecclesiastical system of representation. Therefore he structures his speech and engages the performatives so as to prompt the listeners to endorse the new law he proposes. Biblical literalism is foregrounded here as Epiphanius's strategy for its legitimization. The layout of the argument recuperates the logic of Justin Martyr, the first prominent Christian apologist of the second century, in his *Dialogue with Trypho*. The choice of the early apologetic style in support of iconoclasm is telling in itself. It implies that the defenders of Christian images are like pagans foreign to Christianity and still need to be converted.

Justin was particularly concerned with the problem of continuity between Judaism and Christianity, which differ in their notion of law. He based his dialogue on the two-part structure of the *figura* showing that Christianity renews and supersedes Judaism. The *figura* of supersession also structures Epiphanius's support of the iconoclastic law. If one keeps in mind that the notion of the Mosaic Law still informed imperial political and legal discourse at the time, Epiphanius's recourse to the apologetic topos acquires a novel political meaning. Now it pertains to legislative competition between church and state. The law forbidding images is supposed to be the ecclesiastical law that will overcome pagan, imperial iconophilia as the New Law of Christ had once overcome the Jewish Law.

Epiphanius's rhetorical performance aims at eliciting from his audience a negation of the image and, thereby, an affirmation of the body of Christ: "Let us observe the patriarchs and prophets who dwelt according to the will of God and imitate them so that we may be genuinely called sons of the catholic and apostolic church. I speak the law to those who know. Those who walked in darkness were deceived" (Epiphanius, "The Speech of Saint Epiphanius," 181).

The fragment starts with an appeal to "imitate in ourselves" the biblical patriarchs from the scriptures instead of "imitating" them in painting. This appeal subverts the notion of *mimesis* as likeness by turning it into a nonrepresentational *figura*: "Being like them" means now to fulfill their prophecy.

The word *mimesis* is strategically preserved but acquires a different meaning. Now it comes to designate the "genuine sons" of the church.

By speaking "the law to those who know," Epiphanius himself imitates a biblical example: he assumes the role of Isaiah, who proclaimed the coming of the Messiah as the New Law. Whereas "those who know," that is the wise, as Paul wrote to the Romans, are "a law to themselves" (Rom. 2:14, RSV), while "those who walk in darkness" need further biblical examples to be set right.

In the context of its time and forum, Epiphanius's differentiation between "those who know" and "those who walk in darkness" could also suggest a division between the right and wrong interpreters of the scriptures, the literalists and spiritualists among the clerics. The spiritualists walk in darkness not only because their misinterpretation of the scriptures obscures its "true meaning" through "multiplication of words," but also because they reject the visibility of dogma altogether and, hence, leave the realm of representation to the state alone, where mimetic likenesses and Christian idolatry blossom as a result.

Consequently, Epiphanius seems to suggest that the right form of imitation should be taught to both groups of Christians, those who accept Christian imagery and those who reject the institutional visibility of the church. Therefore, under pretense of welcoming the notion of imitation, Epiphanius poses a series of questions which allow only one predetermined answer—a binding answer-commitment, which would legally confirm the audience's partaking in the body of Christ and inaugurate the rejection of the wrong imitation.

> Who among the holy fathers ever bowed down to a thing made by hands? Or who commanded that these be revered? Who, among the saints, ever left the boundless wealth that is hope in God through knowledge by painting God and ordered others to bow down to the image? Did not Abraham, the leader of the faithful, become the beloved of the living God when he fled from corpses [Babylonian idols]? And did not Moses, fleeing from the same error, reject pleasures ready to hand [in Egypt]? (Epiphanius, "The Speech of Saint Epiphanius," 181)

The first three questions in the passage above can indeed be answered only negatively. No father, no saint, no one commanded or committed himself to image worship. There is no biblical example to imitate in this respect. But at the same time, the phrase "bowing down to a thing made by hands" skillfully redirects this "no" toward a negation of a different image cult. The sculpted effigies of the emperor and empress were things made by hands, to which one was expected to bow—the only image cult actually celebrated in this period. Dvorník writes:

Some features of the old cult, such as the honors paid to imperial statues and images, were even improved upon in the Christian Empire,
and with Constantine's encouragement, they became very popular.
The text of the law promulgated in 394 by Theodosius, Arcadius, and
Honorius mentions the places where the imperial images used to be
consecrated, just as had been done under pagan Rome.[60]

To address the defenders of the Christian image, Epiphanius points to the
biblical authority of Moses and Abraham. Moses was the famous lawgiver,
whereas Abraham was already according to Philo of Alexandria the Jewish
example of a wise man, embodying the living law all by himself. The fact
that Epiphanius puts Abraham and Moses side by side is meaningful in the
context of then-contemporary debates about ecclesiastical law. The name of
Moses evokes Pauline identification of the Mosaic Law, the killing letter cut
on stone (2 Cor. 3:6–7), with idolatry as a worship of the "elements of the
world" (Gal. 4:3, King James Version). But Moses was also a symbolic figure
in Hellenistic political philosophy justifying the law of kingship.[61] It is in this
second function, most likely, that Epiphanius pairs Moses with Abraham's
living God. Epiphanius wants the Mosaic Law not just to be superseded by
the living law of Christ, foreshadowed by Abraham, but absorbed in the body
of Christ, as it was once absorbed in the imperial law of kingship. Epiphanius
understands that in order to survive and have a historical impact, the church
needs a rigid institutional structure and a tangible system of representation.

Epiphanius now makes figural exegesis into a means of political persuasion. He invites the clergy to imitate Abraham and Moses here and now,
that is to say, to accept the iconoclastic law and throw out the corpses of
those handmade images that divinize the imperial power and weaken the
church. Iconoclastic legislation should historically endorse biblical prophecy.
However, Epiphanius also anticipates objections that the Christian image is
different from the idolatry rejected in the Bible:

> But you will say: The patriarchs despised the idols of the Gentiles, but
> we make images of the saints as a memorial of those same patriarchs,
> and we bow before them as a sign of honor. And indeed, on this rea-
> soning some of you have dared to sully the walls of the holy house
> with variegated colors to figure forth images of Peter, John and Paul,
> as I see from the inscriptions beneath each of those falsely-named
> images, devised by the folly of the painter and according to his think-
> ing. And first, let those who think they are thereby doing honor to
> the apostles learn that rather than honoring, they far rather dishonor
> them. For Paul, angered with the falsely named priest, denounced
> the wall as sullied. Shall we not establish, as images of them, their
> commands, by our good deeds? (Epiphanius, "The Speech of Saint
> Epiphanius," 181)

Epiphanius takes up the images of the apostles as he did the representations of Christ in the letter to the emperor. They constitute a false likeness, for they spring from the imagination of a painter and not from biblical evidence. However, the imagination of the Christian painters around this time relied on monarchical iconography, representing the military, governmental, and judicial powers of the Roman state.[62]

Epiphanius points to the dignitaries of providential history, whose ecclesiastical offices are now occupied by the leaders of the official church. The self-celebration of high clergy in the imperial images is, however, a deceptive triumph because it implies the celebration of imperial patronage over the church, against which Epiphanius now tries to fight. But he also anticipates the objections that the images are made for merely religious, meditative purposes:

> But you may say: We gaze on their shapes as a reminder of them. And where is this command? We have just pointed out that those who do this in ignorance labor in vain. "We know," says John, "that when he appears, we will be like unto him." And Paul announces that the saints are of one shape with the Son of God. How then can you wish to see the saints, who will one day blaze in glory, as an inglorious and speechless corpse, although the Lord says about them that "they will be as the angels of God." How can you bow down while depicting animate and ever-living angels in the corpse form, while the prophet says: "He who made his angels to be spirits and his servants to be a flame of fire"? (Epiphanius, "The Speech of Saint Epiphanius," 182)

Epiphanius seems to polemicize here against the monastic practice of sketching figures on the walls of cells as an auxiliary to prayer. Epiphanius might interpret such sketches as a production of false likenesses as a pretext for the attack on the imperial representations but he also disapproves of the practice as such. He adheres to the idea of Christian collective identity, which should not be disrupted by such individual forms of worship.

Epiphanius sends to the clergy a message that "not even the apostles wanted to be worshipped":

> For when he sent them out to evangelize, they did not ask to be worshipped, but only him who sent them, Christ. For he who received from him the power to bind and to release on earth and in heaven said to Cornelius that "I am a man like you, having the same weaknesses," and he taught them not to bow down before him but before Christ the savior. (Epiphanius, "The Speech of Saint Epiphanius," 182)

The image-making of apostles can amount to their worship only by analogy with imperial effigies. The idiom of "bowing down" before men, not God, alludes to worship in the manner of the imperial cult. But now, to all his

previous points against mimetic representation, Epiphanius adds the weighti-
est one, which directly pertains to the church's competition with the state.
Namely, the idea of portraying the figures of sacred history did not originate
within the institution of the church:

> When the fathers met in Laodicea concerning angels, having come
> together entirely for the sake of this question, they said: "If anyone
> deserts the church of God and calls on angels, let him be anathema."
> The reason was that such a person would be abandoning our Lord
> Jesus Christ and following idolatry. (Epiphanius, "The Speech of
> Saint Epiphanius," 182)

The Synod of Laodicea of 363, which Epiphanius quotes, prohibited the
cult of angels. This allusion shows how desperately he needs, in order to back
up his own legislative effort, to find a precedent within ecclesiastical legislation proper which would connect a cult of a quasi-human shape to idolatry.
In the realm of ecclesiastical law, Epiphanius insinuates, the image had been
always prohibited. The church traditionally tolerated it only in the sphere of
its legal compromise with the state. Now he wants to remind the clergy that
the worship of a human shape, even if in the form of an angel, distracts from
Eucharistic worship and therefore weakens Christ's body. With this preparation, he can finally take up the image of Christ:

> I have heard that some advise drawing even the ungraspable Son of
> God: which is fearsome to hear and blasphemous to believe. How
> can anyone speak of drawing the ungraspable and unpursuable and
> incomprehensible, nay uncircumscribable one, whom even Moses
> could not look in the face? Some say that because he was born a per-
> fect man through the ever-virgin Mary, we can make him as a man.
> And this is why he was made man, so that you, with your hands,
> might draw the ungraspable one who made all things? (Epiphanius,
> "The Speech of Saint Epiphanius," 182)

This passage conveys Epiphanius's anti-imperial stance in the most pronounced way. Not only is the rejection of the image of Christ (around which
the cult of the emperor was centered) articulated here with the most radical
vehemence; Epiphanius also recuperates the very objections to the depiction
of Christ which at the beginning of the century Eusebius of Caesarea had
presented to the sister of the emperor Constantine: the handmade image
diminishes the incarnate nature of God, for it reflects only its earthly hypostasis and is not commensurable with the divine.[63]
Epiphanius's ironic gibe—whether God troubled himself with embodiment so that he could be painted—takes on its full meaning in regard to the
dogmas of incarnation and resurrection. Earlier in the fragment, Epiphanius

reminded his audience that Christ came to embody the new law of human coexistence and human relation to the divine. Hence, his likeness to the Father is not mimetic but functional: like the Father, he brings the dead to life. His restoring Lazarus to life prefigured his own later resurrection as well as the resurrection of all Christians:

> Can it be that he is not like unto the Father, that he did not make the dead come to life? Where did he allow you, as he walked on this earth, to make an image of him and bow down to it or gaze on it? Clearly this is the allowance of the Evil One, so that you might think lightly of God. For it is proper, so it is said, that man should worship the living God in spirit and truth. Nay, will the gangrene continue to spread? (Epiphanius, "The Speech of Saint Epiphanius," 182)

The representation and practice of these doctrines are best accomplished in ritual worship, by partaking in the Eucharist, which prepares Christians for their future life, and not by the veneration of Christ's image. The image-artifact, the homage to Christ's earthly appearance, only interferes with a flow of life and death, with the structure of incarnation and resurrection, the complexity of which is expressed in the many-layered temporal and logical structure of religious service.

Gazing at images leaves Christians outside of the body of Christ, whereas they are supposed to be in it. And it is at this point that the "Evil One" comes into play, for by means of images he makes the Christians think lightly of God. Being outside of the body of Christ is thus directly associated with the devil, or paganism, and thus with the imperial realm, in which the image of Christ does not stand for the new law but glamorizes the emperor's power as divine. The image is in this realm just a surface, a painted wall like Paul's false priest, instead of being the three-dimensional living body of a congregation gathered in worship.

Epiphanius's metaphor of the image-artifact interfering with the church's life-giving force like a gangrene can be best elucidated by a reference to the aforementioned mosaic of *Christ in Majesty* on the concave surface in the apse in Santa Pudenziana (fig. 1.2). Discerning the artists' intent to erase the distance between the onlooker and the protagonist, to turn the congregation into "part of the philosophical assembly, part of this celestial setting,"[64] Epiphanius could well condemn such overwhelming two-dimensional representations, indebted to the imperial style and possibly rising over an altar, as encroaching, quite literally, onto the three-dimensional body of the church. Such gangrenous image-artifacts should be cut away from the body which they threaten with death, this body being unequivocally the living body of Christ.

> For God does away with this in the Old and New [Law], saying precisely: "Thou shalt bow down to the Lord thy God and serve him

alone," saying: "I live, saith the Lord, and to me every knee shall bend." We cannot serve two masters, one living and one dead. "Most accursed," it is said, "is he who honors the creation more than the creator." For the creator contains all things and is not contained by anything. (Epiphanius, "The Speech of Saint Epiphanius," 182)

The persuasion is built here upon a double meaning of the expression "to bow down to": instead of bowing to Christ as represented in a handmade image (by implication associated with imperial power), one should rather bow to his body in the celebration of the Eucharist. Epiphanius's declaration drawn from the Gospels that "no one can serve two masters,"[65] one living and one dead, amounts to an almost straightforward insistence on ecclesiastical emancipation from the imperial domain.

Epiphanius appropriates Eusebius's early warning against Christian images but fills it with a novel meaning. Eusebius's strictures against the representation of Christ were indebted to the tradition of the early fathers, when Christianity was still on guard against conflation and confusion with paganism. The Synod of Elvira (306–312) prohibited the exhibition of images in churches on the same terms as the participation of Christians in pagan games—obviously understanding both phenomena as kindred. This early attempt at differentiation from paganism became topical again at the end of the century when the church sought a way of differentiating its power-symbolism from that of the now Christianized empire.

This legislative fragment culminates in a curse, veiled in a biblical quotation, aimed at anyone who honors the creation more than the creator, "for the creator contains everything and is not contained by anything." The Christian congregation, the church, is contained in the body of Christ as its microcosm. It partakes of this body through liturgical performance.

Christian images are, on the contrary, integrated into a microcosm of the empire. Through its Christian representation, the pagan state claims to contain the Christian universe, whereas, according to providential history, it is the Christian universe that is supposed to contain the state. The very question of which contains which evokes the tension between the empire and the church in their competitive claims to universal power.

Christ's Body versus Christ's Image

The strategic significance of Epiphanius's iconoclastic endeavor becomes fully understandable if one accounts for its historical moment: the juncture when the imperial system seemed to be yielding to the church and a pronounced differentiation in the symbolism of power could become the final touch sealing the church's triumph over the worldly rulership. There was every expectation that the power balance could be tilted in favor of the church through the divinely inspired art of persuasion.[66] But this task required, first of all, some work on language.

Athanasius often elucidated Christian dogmas through analogies with the imperial realm. For example, he famously explained the consubstantiality of the Father and Son through a comparison with the emperor and his image on a coin. Or he clarified the incarnation of the logos in the body of Christ, embracing the whole of the Christian world, through a parable about the monarch who by occupying one house in the city protects and honors the whole community.[67] But in Athanasius's time this reliance of Christian dogmatic rhetoric on monarchical simile and idiom had opened a path through which the church could enter the imperial sphere. By the end of the fourth century, the church felt secure enough to claim its own vocabulary and system of representation instead of relying on borrowed imagery.

In his iconoclastic discourse, Epiphanius sets out to cleanse the religious idiom of its imperial connotations in order to create the basis for an alternative system of representation. It is at this point that the body of Christ enters the political scene as a subversive device. Epiphanius takes over Athanasius's concept of Christ's body, conceived as cosmos, mirrored in the opening of the sacred space and in the organization of the liturgy, but leaves behind Athanasius's imperial similes. Instead, Epiphanius radically opposes Christ's body to the monarchical sphere as the body of a Christian congregation bound by liturgical practice and thus represented in an alternative, three-dimensional "image" of the sacrament of the Eucharist.[68]

This spatial concept of Christ's body becomes Epiphanius's model for the uncompromised representation of the church in architecture.[69] Church buildings, indeed, reflected in their spatiality the collective proceedings of the liturgy. The structure of a cathedral enveloped the body of the congregation with a tangible visual crust, representing the worship as if it were carved and shaped in stone. The church building as an embodiment of communal gathering had signified the triumph of the church since Christianity's very first steps toward an official status.

Eusebius's *The History of the Church* (completed ca. 323–326) famously culminated in the oration on the building of the churches under Constantine. The tenth chapter of the book conveyed a portentous vision of the Christian universe to come and included a symbolic description of its microcosm represented by the newly built cathedral at Tyre in Phoenicia. Its description ends with a meaningful metaphor of the cathedral as a "spiritual image" of the body of Christ, the logos incarnated:

> Such is the great cathedral which throughout the whole world under the sun the great Creator of the universe, the Word, has built, Himself again fashioning this spiritual image on earth of the vaults beyond the skies, so that by the whole creation and by rational beings on earth his Father might be honored and worshipped.[70]

The end of the fourth century was perceived by the clergy as the time of this vision's ultimate fulfillment, resulting in the boom of ecclesiastical architecture in the eastern periphery of the empire, the very cradle of opposition to sanctification of the profane power.

Architecture, indeed, was a traditional realm where the church could make visible its transformative power and influence over the state. Consider Saint John Lateran, the former imperial palace, donated by Constantine to the church and refurbished as a cathedral and residence for the bishop of Rome. While the Christian painters relied on Roman iconography for their visual articulation of dogmas, the imperial palace was, on the contrary, transformed in order to accommodate the needs of the church.

Epiphanius's iconoclasm, in fact, went hand in hand with his foundation of a gigantic basilica in Cyprus. The elements of its construction reveal that the building was meant to endorse Christian expectations from the time of Eusebius (ca. 264–ca. 340). The lavish structure with triple aisles flanking the nave on each side, mosaic decorations, and Corinthian columns represent "a survival of Constantinian planning."[71] Historians of architecture usually link this building with Constantine's basilica on Golgotha. This famous architectural prototype in the very place of Christ's crucifixion marked the first triumph of the church celebrated in Eusebius's expressive allegory of the church's resurrection under the emperor's life-giving power.

In Eusebius's oration, Constantine could be identified with both God the Father who brought Christ back to life and with Christ who raised Lazarus. Ironically, Eusebius's praise of Constantine's patronage of Christianity anticipated the future celebration of imperial power through images of Christ in glory. Perhaps sensitive to this predicament, Epiphanius updated the Constantinian basilica by introducing a striking architectural innovation. The walls separating the apses show unusual passages, which allowed for a greater mobility of the liturgy in the building.[72] (See fig. 1.3.)

As in his rhetoric, Epiphanius's architectural idiom reaffirms but also intensifies Eusebius's vision of the church as a living body. The opening of the structure for a more dynamic ritual is legible as an homage and contribution to the new institutional invigoration of the church, which had overcome its Constantinian condition of a mere survival and reached the point when it no longer needed imperial resuscitation.

This architectural *figura* betrays Epiphanius's iconoclasm as an attempt at recuperation and supersession of Eusebius's celebration of the church on changed historical premises. If Eusebius warned against images of Christ, designating them a wrong form of incarnation,[73] Epiphanius readjusts Eusebius's theological position to the novel political situation and the new forum, with some necessary rhetorical and theological circumlocution.

Describing the control of the Roman state over Christian representation after the official acceptance of Christianity, Grabar speculated about the possibility of a different scenario, such as was proposed by Epiphanius:

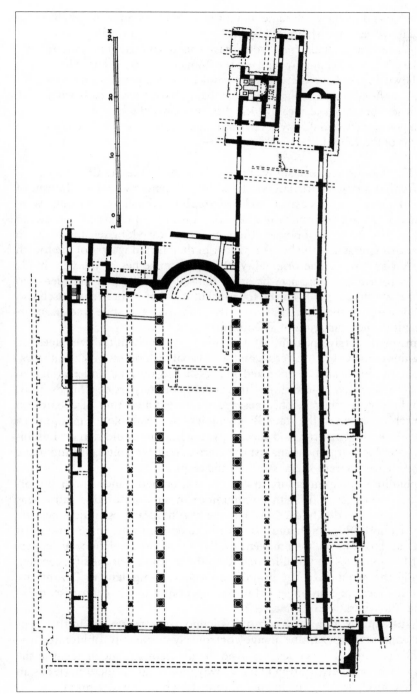

Figure 1.3. Restored plan of the Basilica of Saint Epiphanius in Salamis-Constantia, fourth century A.D. Copyright © 1974, Dumbarton Oaks Research Library and Collection, Trustees for Harvard University. Drawing by A. H. S. Megaw, originally published in Dumbarton Oaks Papers, vol. 28.

One could imagine the same initiative [for a Christian iconography of universal import] directed by the Church, and the probable consequences that such direction would have had in iconographic matters: the Christian community (and not the Roman state) would have been shown to designate the Christian whole; and the essential ideas to be captured in the image would probably have been chosen from those Christological ideas which then animated the best Christian minds—or else would have been taken, more generally, from the dogmas of the Church.[74]

For Epiphanius, iconoclasm was an initiative to make the Christian community designate the Christian whole in the alternative visual symbolism of the ritual space of ecclesiastical architecture. His iconoclastic writings were fashioned so as to constitute a moment of a quasi-legal transaction between two competing systems of power, resolving the century-long tension between the image of Christ and the body of Christ in the blurred waters of the fourth century's visual turn. The originality of his discourse lies in the very mode of his rhetorical performance: he steps himself into the gap between two parts of the political *figura* of the fourth century, that is, between Eusebius's foreshadowing of the church's future triumph over the state and its near-fulfillment in the legislation of Theodosius.

From the discursive position of a righteous, divinely authorized speaker, Epiphanius conveys in both verbal and nonverbal fashion his precarious message that the imperial Christianized image should now be under attack in order to be replaced by the three-dimensional counterpart of Christ's body, the building of the church. This message concluded a century of debates on the church's relation to the state. By giving his own example for imitation to the populace, the emperor, and the clergy, Epiphanius could deploy Eusebius's philosophical argument against the Christian image politically and make it accessible to different social strata of the empire.

Epiphanius's apparent failure to win over the emperor and church authorities and to energize Christian communities in support of this cause was partially due to his death (ca. 403). Having begun his aggressive iconoclastic politics around 390, Epiphanius did not have enough time to gain political leverage and to consolidate a movement. Even though such iconoclastic sects as the Monophysites had proliferated from the beginning of the fifth century, preparing the ground for the grand iconoclastic campaigns in Byzantium, Epiphanius's iconoclasm appeared in retrospect as a lonely enterprise, quixotic and idiosyncratic in its nature.[75]

The subsequent retransmission of his iconoclastic fragments in the theological context of Byzantine image-controversy ultimately obliterated the political character of his endeavors. And the first iconoclastic incident in the history of Christian civilization made its way into religious dictionaries as an anecdote entirely lacking the historical force to which it had aspired.

In more recent scholarship, Byzantine and northern European iconoclasm have been linked with a crisis of iconicity's alliance with power in both the symbolic representation and the philosophical justification of power. Iconoclasm enters the scene when the representation of power ceases to be adequate, and the images fail to protect the Byzantine Empire against the sieges of the Muslims, or when instead of glorifying the Catholic Church in northern Europe they come to stand for its corruption.

The real issues at stake were then rooted not in images themselves but in their participation in a crisis of a more profound nature, the crisis of state, church, and society.[76] This perspective equally applies to Epiphanius's adventure, which did not make history but by taking full advantage of the political tensions of the epoch resulted in the invention of iconoclasm as a strategic form of subversive discourse.

Chapter 2

✦

Corpus Libri as *Corpus Christi*

Subversion, Alchemy, and the
Poetics of Transubstantiation in the
Book of the Holy Trinity

> As you know, all elements contain flesh and blood, so the Holy
> Work goes through this book, when, short or long, the oil out
> of flesh and blood therein is created . . .
> —*Book of the Holy Trinity*

The earliest version of the *Book of the Holy Trinity* (1415–19) is kept in
the Museum of Prints and Drawings in Berlin.[1] This alchemical manuscript
is a rather bleak document, poorly written and amateurishly illuminated. It
would rank very low, if compared to the treasures of medieval book culture.
To be sure, alchemical manuscripts, which contained recipes for early scientific experiments to be conducted in the monastic cells, usually did not aspire
to overt splendor. The modesty of this manuscript is surprising only because
of its close association with feudal rulers of the highest rank.

The manuscript is dedicated to Friedrich VI, Earl of Brandenburg. He
must have commissioned a copy during the Council of Constance (1414–
18), where he received the tenure of Brandenburg from Emperor Sigismund.
Maybe as a sign of gratitude to his benefactor, Friedrich made sure that an
excerpt from his alchemical manual would be presented as a gift to Sigismund as well. The likely reason for these rulers' interest in an alchemical
manuscript was typical for the times: alchemy was perceived as a way of
producing precious metals. Already in 1317, in the bull "Spondent, quas non
exhibent, divitias pauperes alchimistae," Pope John XXII had condemned the
alchemists along with gold-forgers.[2]

The families of both Sigismund and Friedrich of Brandenburg were later
known for their involvement with alchemical experimentations. Friedrich's son John was nicknamed "the alchemist," and the second wife of
Emperor Sigismund, Barbara of Cilli, became notorious for her alchemical

counterfeiting of silver and gold after her spouse's death.[3] The rewards that these rulers must have expected from the possession of this manuscript most likely excused in their eyes the *Book*'s dull and unseemly body.

The first scholar of the *Book*, Wilhelm Ganzenmüller, noticed that the manuscript contained several names of secular and ecclesiastical participants in the Council of Constance, whose coats of arms were placed in the illuminations in a way that reflected their feudal relations. Since these allusions were intriguingly intertwined with descriptions of alchemical processes and alchemical imagery, Ganzenmüller suspected that the role of alchemy here was to support a political message.[4] Considering alchemy's common association with forgery, he assumed that the *Book* was supposed to provide financial backing for Friedrich, Earl of Brandenburg, in his political schemes. (See fig. 2.1.)

Ganzenmüller took his clue from a legend about Raymond Lull. As the story goes, Lull used his alchemical skills to supply King Edward III of England with funding for a promised crusade. However, the king used the money instead for a war against the king of France.[5] The historian of science Hans-Werner Schütt bluntly described the *Book of the Holy Trinity* as a means of ecclesiastical propaganda in a disguise of alchemy. He assumed that the *Book* was supposed to win over the emperor for a crusade against the Turks. Even though his assumption of this political goal was most likely based on a confusion of the Council of Constance, where the *Book* was composed, with the Fifth Lateran Council of Pisa (1512–17), where a crusade against the Turks indeed was considered, Schütt's observation draws attention to the subversive character of the *Book*.[6]

The scholars' suspicion of the *Book*'s dealings with power partially arose from a similarity of its opening gesture with that of the alchemical script *Lapidarium*, once falsely ascribed to Lull. *Lapidarium* opens with a dedication to the virtuous king: "O God, in thy truth I here begin my treatise on the generation of stones by human craft, dedicated to the virtuous king who has given himself to thy service for love of thee."[7] The writer's declaration that his book partakes of God's truth, which justifies the practice of alchemy on behalf of a well-intentioned king, binds the alchemist and the king through their shared religious goal.

The *Book of the Holy Trinity* retains the general matrix of this formula, but it undertakes a significant shift within it, which is reflected already in the incipit:

> This book is not a new belief, but a great revelation of God and his blessed Mother. I have said this for my master's sake who asked me. My master has this *Book of the Holy Trinity* neither as an extract from any other book nor is it studied, or learnt, or copied. The God, the Son and the Holy Spirit gave it to him from the course of the heaven's stars.[8]

Figure 2.1. Symbiosis of alchemical, religious, and political symbolism: Mary's crowning, *Buch der heyligen Dreyualdekeit*, Konstanz, Germany, ca. 1410–19. Illuminated manuscript page, 29.0 × 20.5 cm. 78 A 11, fol. 31 verso, Kupferstichkabinett, Staatliche Museen, Berlin, Germany.

Like *Lapidarium*, the *Book* is written on a master's behalf and customarily asserts that its message is the truth of divine revelation. But this truth is now polemically oriented against "new belief" and inseparable from the *Book*'s claim to authenticity. The writer is careful to stress that the content of this book has not been transmitted from other writings but received directly from heaven through the astrological mediation of the Father, the Son, and the Holy Spirit. Whatever Friedrich's motivation for acquiring an alchemical manuscript, the scribes who compiled or wrote the book on his request seem to have been guided by an ulterior motive behind their overt advertisement of the art of alchemy.

The dedication to Friedrich specifies that the book offered to him contains God's sacraments as medications that should enable him to act as a mediator in the major crisis of ecclesiastical politics which came to be known as the Great Western Schism (1378–1417):

> Burgrave Friedrich, margrave of Brandenburg, God himself sent you all these medications, which he made himself through his holy sufferings. They all are revealed and given to you in this book by the Holy Trinity so that you shall become the loyal healer of poor, sick Christianity, since a number of worldly princes, many ecclesiastical leaders and lords, and all too many common folk have secretly dissented from the holy Christian faith. Truly I write this after God's mouth.[9]

Remarkably, the *Book* does not claim to provide recipes or guidance on how to make those medications but asserts that the medications have already been revealed in the body of the book. Now they are expected to work on Friedrich in a transformative way that would make him into an ally in the efforts to restore the unity of the divided Christian Church. The portrayal of the schismatic troubles as illness and the call for Friedrich's therapeutic help in overcoming the fragmentation of the Christian faith betray a common metaphor of the time.[10] In this context, the medical trope suggests that the *Book*'s goal of influencing the ruler was of a religious nature and that the writer was well attuned to the unification agenda of the Council of Constance, during which the book was composed.

This famous pre-Reformation council was one of the last attempts at achieving religious unity and reforming the church *tam in capite quam in membris* (both "in head and members") before the Protestant movement in northern Europe forever split the Western church internally.[11] The council's immediate agenda was to overcome the schism among three rival popes, to improve the strained relations between the church and the imperial power, to find means and ways for fighting heresies, and to prepare the reform of the church, the necessity of which was acutely felt in the proliferation of religious groups and movements of reformatory and quasi-heretical character as well as in the work of the reform theologians John Wycliffe in England and Jan Hus in

Bohemia.[12] Religious and secular rulers from all over the Holy Roman Empire convened for four years in the town of Constance to achieve these goals.[13]

The historian Jürgen Miethke reconstructed the function of the fifteenth-century council as a public forum in a way that helps illuminate the feedback between the properties of the *Book* and its social context.[14] The council as a legal and cultural institution was already in its own way a subversive forum because it represented the whole church as opposed to its hierarchical top. The council competed with the pope for legislative power and hence for the right to be the institutional anchorage of the church.

The theologians of the fifteenth century understood conciliarism as the only solution to the seventeen-year-long ecclesiastical crisis of the papal schism. When the Council of Constance indeed brought the schism to an end by eventually forcing three schismatic popes to resign and electing Martin V as their sole successor, the council as institution came close to winning the competition with the papal office. Or at least it offered a viable ground from which the power of the head of the church could be challenged by its whole body.

The success of this challenge, according to Miethke, rested on effective communication and collective engagement. Theological deliberations and rhetorical practice were meant to produce new legislation and, therefore, a new constellation of power. In short, the Council of Constance was a political and legal forum where one could "do things with words," a forum where intellectual schemes promised to have concrete and tangible consequences.

Councils of this period were also gatherings of scholars and intellectuals. The medieval universities sent official emissaries to the councils, and the majority of participating clerics held university degrees. The work of the councils was informed by university practices of transmission of knowledge. Scholarly exchange and reflection that took place under the councils' auspices went far beyond immediate ecclesiastical concerns. But most importantly, the councils were self-reflexive institutions, which questioned and negotiated their own status and rights because by the time of the Council of Constance conciliarism was not a unitary theory but rather a highly heterogeneous network of debates and positions that were both theorized and practiced at the council itself.

Besides providing a forum for public opinion, a council was a book fair, where manuscripts from all over pre-Gutenberg Europe were discussed, bought, exchanged, and reproduced. Books were usually publicly dictated (in *reportatio* or *pronuntiatio*) so that anyone could write down and take along a personal copy, or commission a scribe for this task. The rediscovery of important classical manuscripts is usually associated with the scholarly exchange and circulation of books at the fifteenth-century councils of Constance and Basel. Therefore some scholars see them as the incubators of European humanism.

The commotion of an abundant book market must have also offered an environment conducive to the circulation of the most obscure manuscripts of Gnostic, heretical, or alchemical types, not officially endorsed by the church.[15] This opportunity for cross-fertilization of ideas, a strange coexistence of Christian and pagan writings as well as of scholarly and poetic production, had an electric effect on European intellectuals. But the councils were also highly diverse in their social makeup. Feudal rulers, university professors, and ecclesiastics from all over Europe brought along to the convention an army of scribes, courtiers, and servants which raised the number of the participants to about 2,290.

Thus, in late medieval sensibility the church council was a "democratic" forum, where the strictness of social hierarchies was loosened or temporarily lifted. The right to vote extended to so many members as to make Emperor Sigismund uncomfortable. Miethke invokes the much-cited complaint of Enea Silvio Piccolomini, the future Pope Pius II, that "cooks, grooms and domestics in Basel take off in the evening the respectable habit that they wear in daytime at the council in order to serve their masters in their actual functions" (Miethke, "Die Konzilien als Forum," 750).

But the Council of Constance, the legendary "council of unity," was also a forum of utter ambiguity. The dissemination of texts and proliferation of ideas entailed their inflation. The innovatory aspirations were ultimately frustrated. The agenda of reforms faltered, resulting merely in a list of eighteen problems, which the council drew up in conclusion but without any prospect for their concrete solution. In the course of three years, the debates got worn out: "The council's tiredness won over the argument" (Miethke, "Die Konzilien als Forum," 769).

Even if the church seemed to regain its unity due to the resignation of the schismatic popes and the execution of the reform theologians Jan Hus and Hieronymus of Prague, these solutions were superficial and provisionary. Major reform of the church was still outstanding. In the following years, the call for a council faded into a mere "slogan" (Miethke, "Die Konzilien als Forum," 771). Not the councils but local reform movements were historically destined to bring about the changes in the church. Even though they would do so only "in members" and not "in the head," the unity of Western Christianity would be upset forever. The *Book of the Holy Trinity* nestled its subversive scheme at this threshold of the Reformation, in a forum of promise, ambiguity, and frustrated possibility.

Given the growing discursive exhaustion and dissatisfaction with the council's solutions, the non-argumentative magic of verbal action, whether divine or alchemical in nature, must have seemed the most efficient way to proceed.[16] If the *Book* was supposed to have an impact on the ruler to whom it was dedicated, then it was not through the transmission of an alchemical recipe but rather by transforming the ruler himself by means of the holy sacraments singularly embodied in the book.

The goal of winning Friedrich over to the right side of the religious politics, whatever this side might have been, is clearly linked with the *Book*'s claim to truth. The *Book*'s God-given nature, announced in its dedication, presents its composition as a unique event resulting in a unique artifact capable of resisting the dilution of knowledge in the copied transmissions, which was the prevailing mode of intellectual exchange at the Council of Constance.

As in *Lapidarium*, both the religious and alchemical content of the *Book* target the ruler but they don't anymore intersect in the voice of the writer, but rather subordinate the writer as a mere receiver of God's message in a book form to the *Book*'s medial self-consciousness. The material poetics of the *Book* drawn from alchemical and religious discourse and its politically subversive role in the context of the Council of Constance deserve our attention as another instance of discourse apart that takes its idiosyncratic shape at the crossroads of history.

The Book as Medium: Who Speaks?

The relation of the *Book of the Holy Trinity* to its alchemical transmission at this moment in history is best understood through Marshall McLuhan's theory that each new medium incorporates a preceding one as its content. McLuhan observed that any new technological and social environment has a tendency to integrate an old medium as a form of "anti-environment" for the sake of cultural self-reflection. Society becomes aware of its basis in technological innovation through difference and contrast between a new and an obsolete medium brought out by their interrelation. Hence, McLuhan's fundamental formula—"the medium is the message."[17]

The author, or rather the scribe, derives his medial conception of the *Book* from the tradition of alchemy in a way which already in itself constitutes a message. Alchemy had developed in the course of centuries a rich apparatus of concepts, symbols, and tools pertaining to both philosophical speculation and chemical praxis. Together they constituted a medium by means of which human beings sought to decipher the laws of nature in order to communicate with nature in its own language—in the vocabulary of matter and in the grammar of chemical processes.[18] This mythical aspect of alchemy as an ancient form of communion with nature, however, receded in the fourteenth and fifteenth centuries, yielding to the increasing interest in the practice of gold-making, which brought to the fore a social aspect of alchemy as a new means of cultural communication.

The papal bull of 1317 prohibited the practice of alchemy for its association with the forgery of gold and accused the deceptive alchemists of "empty verbosity":

> Those miserable alchemists promise what they can't provide! Though they imagine themselves wise, they still fall into the hole which they dug for others. Ridiculously they pretend to be the teachers of

alchemy but they betray their ignorance by relying always only on the older scribes. And when they don't find what others too have not found, they still consider it possible to find it in the future. When they make false metal pass for true gold or silver, it is a matter of empty verbosity.[19]

The very fact of this indignant prohibition testifies that the alchemical discourse came to be perceived as threatening enough to merit papal attention. The bull reacts to alchemy's exodus from the dark corners of esotericism and legends and signals the fact of its official entry into public life. Once an occupation of inquiring minds in the reclusive corners of the cloisters, alchemy becomes the favorite leisure activity of the powerful. Once based on a strict ethical code of behavior, which stressed selflessness of intention and distance from power, alchemy is now attended to in a hope of profit.

The legal sanction of the papal ban honors alchemy by taking it seriously as a menace to the economic order. From this moment on, alchemy acquires the status of a socially subversive activity. But therefore, paradoxically, it also turns into a means of political intrigue. The cautious reticence of the ancient alchemists is now drowned out by the ostentatious rhetoric of the gold-makers who boastfully advertise their services while seeking employment at the courts. But the new alliance between alchemists and power is precarious and short. Whereas the rulers zero in on speedy enrichment and often punish the absence of the promised gold with the gallows, the adepts try in their turn to defer the expected results as long as possible in order to extend the monarchs' financial support of their experiments.[20]

The *Book*'s incorporation of the old alchemical apparatus in the service of religious politics reflects this social shift in the status of alchemy—the utilization of alchemy for purposes of subversive mediation among social, political, and financial interests. The maker of the *Book* takes advantage of the changed cultural status of alchemy in a way that brings across another radical change in the medial landscape of the fourteenth and fifteenth centuries—the new conceptualization and social role of the book.

The literary historian Jacqueline Cerquiglini-Toulet has observed that in the course of the fourteenth century the ancient understanding of the book as a container of revealed truth gradually yields to a new notion of a book as an individual author's brainchild. Then, in the fifteenth century, the book breaks free from its author as well: instead of merely mediating between a writer and a patron who commissioned it, the book enters the sphere of public circulation.[21]

Dovetailing the two notions of authorship, the author of the *Book* makes this medial change into a pivotal point of his conception and composition of the *Book*'s textual body. First, he announces that he received the *Book* "through God's holy force" (*durch den heiligen Zwang Gottes*) "in the same way as the Virgin" (*von jungfrauen art*). Thus, the author implies that, like the Virgin, he is just a passive receptacle of the book's revealed truth. But he immediately adds that, in the end, it was by his own free will that he recognized his elect status and accepted the God-inspired mission to write the *Book* for the instruction and transformation of the rulers.

The declaration of the authority of God's truth behind the *Book*'s message is a topos, but this topos is charged here with the unconditioned subjective upsurge that is necessary for upholding a radical scheme. Interestingly, during the times of the Schism, the authority of Paul became once again popular among the clerical writers for precisely this quality of his rhetorical positionality. The most often quoted passage of Paul, according to Thomas M. Izbicki, was from the second chapter in Galatians where Paul rebukes Peter, his superior, for refusing to eat with gentile converts.

This "wavering in dealing with uncircumcised converts," Izbicki writes, "could be taken as endorsing Jewish rites that the Church had abandoned as obsolete under the new dispensation. In later medieval thought, this wavering could be understood as not just wrong but bordering on heresy."[22] At the time of the Schism, when ecclesiastics and laymen alike felt that the church had to take into its own hands the matter of ending the Schism and called for a council, Paul's unwavering stance in Galatians was perceived as having "potential to limit papal power, a subversive potential particularly important in an age when the papacy's very power was in question."[23]

But the writer's divinely inspired and self-elected authority in his address to the rulers is transposed here into the body of the manuscript itself. The old understanding of a book as an embodied revelation, "the word made flesh," coexists here with the new identity of the book as a symbolic, manmade cultural artifact. Together they reveal its body as the Eucharist.

The transference of the Eucharistic sacrament onto a manuscript is enabled by the late medieval understanding that "eucharistic beauty . . . cannot be identified exclusively with Christ's divinity, nor with the properties of Christ's glorified, human body. It must extend to the outward signs of the sacrament; to the plain letter of the scriptures; to the simple forms of bread and wine; to the ritual actions of eating and drinking; to the remembrance of Christ's torture, deformity and death."[24] The manuscript usurps those "outward signs of the sacrament" to foreground its medial identity. The Eucharistic concept of the *Book* stresses the ritual character of its composition and reception. The author-priest initiates a congregation of the readers into a mystery of Christian belief by consecrating and administering to them the *corpus libri*.

The transmission of manuscripts through dictation at the council, which most likely informed the composition of this book, is reinterpreted as the incarnation of the word in a written body. The original of the *Book* includes some self-reflexive pointers to the manuscript's sacred materiality. Its paper has watermarks depicting grapes, and its ink is identified with the blood of Christ. On one of the illuminations, the crucified Christ rises in a lily symbolizing the alchemical vapor over Mary surrounded by golden beams of light and positioned on a half-moon. But in a poetically self-reflexive gesture, this Christian figuration of an alchemical process in the *bain-marie* is further transformed into a visual comment on the book's body: A red line drawn from the wound of the crucified Christ conspicuously turns into writing of the names of the virtues. (See fig. 2.2.)

Since the *Book* is meant to work its magic as a physical object, its corporeality becomes paramount. The traditional apparatus of alchemy provides for its material poetics: alchemical cosmogony helps theorize the nature of a medium in a series of images which illustrate the principles of circulation, transformation, and mediation. The alchemical procedures are also evoked in the verbal texture of the book. The alchemical symbolism of *Corpus Christi* is projected onto *corpus libri*. The visible and tangible body of the book becomes a message.[25]

The *Book* enters the public forum of the Council of Constance with an overt promise of silver and gold. However, this new worldly allure of alchemy—a prospect of swift enrichment—is immediately linked with the old alchemical ethic of pure heart and just intentions:

> Who pays careful attention to this book of God and works correctly thereafter will be rewarded through the teaching of this book with both silver and noble red gold. Whoever will try to obtain gold by means of this book, must first set himself right in God, for otherwise one is in danger of obtaining herewith something inhuman. There are hearts hidden in it. (*Das "Buch der Heiligen Dreifaltigkeit,"* 91)

Ganzenmüller, who studied one of the manuscript's later versions, concluded on the basis of its religious content, biographical references, and usage of German that its author was a Franciscan monk.[26] The original, discovered after his article had been published, confirms this conclusion: one illumination, indeed, represents Saint Francis receiving his stigmata and thus provides the *Book* with its most prominent Franciscan signature. But the religious author takes on the persona of an alchemical adventurer with his precarious relation to power: what he ostentatiously advertises as a manual for gold-making turns out to secretly embody "God's new gift from heaven" (*ein newe gabe gotes von himelreich*) (*Das "Buch der Heiligen Dreifaltigkeit,"* 91).

A religious actor practices his inventiveness and political adroitness just like a deceitful alchemist. His religious message seeks social influence under cover of alchemy, and his religious activism, not unlike alchemy, becomes a subversive activity. He turns the alchemy's catering to the *cupiditas* of the powerful into its opposite—a test of Franciscan piety, a guarantee that only those with the right intentions and of the right persuasion would receive the new teaching. The goal of this teaching is nothing less than the deliverance of mankind from original sin: "This is the analogy: This book of God overturns what Eve brought about" (*Das ist die comparatura diß buch gotes vmslag das eua brach*) (*Das "Buch der Heiligen Dreifaltigkeit,"* 91).

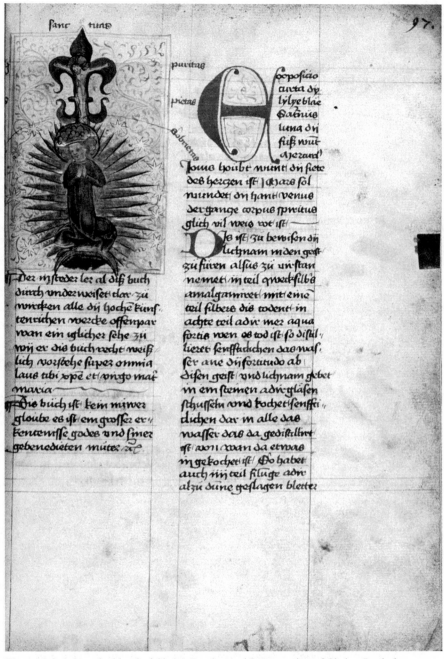

Figure 2.2. Ink as the blood of Christ: Passion and Resurrection of Christ, *Buch der heyligen Dreyualdekeit*, Konstanz, Germany, ca. 1410–19. Illuminated manuscript page, 29.0 × 20.5 cm. 78 A 11, fol. 121 recto, Kupferstichkabinett, Staatliche Museen, Berlin, Germany.

This goal implies a return to *status innocentiae*, a renewal of the paradise-like condition of human beings before the Fall through the pursuit of chastity and poverty. This teaching was widely spread, though in a variety of forms, among many heretical and quasi-heretical groups of the time, including the Hussite Adamites—a sect within the radical wing of the Hussite movement. They believed that the ideal of highest perfection should be sought not through the imitation of Christ and the apostles alone but also through the example of *status primi parentis*, the innocent state of Adam before the fall.[27]

The Franciscans who cultivated poverty and chastity, and especially the more radical representatives of their mendicant order, to which the author of the manuscript most likely belonged,[28] not only sympathized with the views of the Adamites but also patronized and protected semi-religious groups such as Beguines, Beghards, and Tertiaries. These groups rejected the official church and the holy sacraments in a way that was often perceived as bordering on the heresy of Free Spirit.

In the first decades of the fifteenth century, these groups struggled tenaciously and with variable success against accusations of heresy and for acceptance by the pope,[29] and the Franciscans, who supported them, occasionally faced the danger of excommunication.[30] Therefore it is no surprise that an adherent of Franciscan piety would prefer to promote his agenda by way of the *Book*'s material poetics.

In its opening pages, the *Book* specifies its readership as "great rulers and great masters and teachers of the holy Christian writings" (*die grossen herren / und grossen meister und lerer der heiligen schriffte jn der cristenheit*) (*Das "Buch der Heiligen Dreifaltigkeit,"* 91). But it aims also at a different social group, namely, at "all the common, poor, insignificant, secluded" (*alle der gemeynen armen vnbekanten sondern*) and "the Jews, heathens, Christian heretics" (*juden heiden cristen keczern*) (ibid., 95). The *Book* relates differently to these two groups. Whereas the grand and powerful ones are called to justice, mercy, and righteousness, the "secluded ones," that is the heretics, are to be enlightened, cleansed from their erroneous views, and protected.

Concern about heretics is a leitmotif of the *Book*. In one passage, for example, the author refers to them not as a danger to others but as themselves endangered and recommends caution. The *Book*, written at God's own prompting, should ward off this danger from the marginal religious groups and therefore needs to be broadly distributed:

> This whole manuscript should be thus revealed. God knows the vulnerability of all the common, poor, insignificant, and secluded. Therefore, this book should reveal the true Christian belief to the Jews, heathens, and Christian heretics, to all recipients, that Mary stands high in the divine mirror of the Holy Trinity. (*Das "Buch der Heiligen Dreifaltigkeit,"* 95)

The *Book* is indeed remarkable for its strong emphasis on the veneration of Mary. In the Mariology of the book, the Virgin is aligned with Christ and placed as the third person of the Trinity instead of the Holy Spirit. The recourse to Mary for protection of reformist Christian groups and their vindication from the suspicion of heresy is plausible for two reasons. In fourth-century Christianity, Mariology was an integral part of Christological debates. Mary's human person and her virgin parturition of Christ served as a support of the orthodox position against Arianism: it proved Christ's double nature as human and divine at once.[31]

In the pre-Reformation period, this dogmatic dimension of Mary's person became secondary in importance to the problem of her sharing in the burden of original sin. This theological shift brings to the fore Mary's role as a protector and benefactor of sinners.[32] The *Book*'s emphatic appeal to the charity of Mary, the influential intercessor on behalf of wrongdoers, logically follows from its intention of warding off the sin of heresy and standing up for those who were rightly or wrongly accused and persecuted at a time when the definition of heresy was extremely vague.

However, the *Book* engages both aspects of Mariology: Mary's person as a doctrinal touchstone as well as her role as a dispenser of charity. An ancient and theologically outdated function of Mary as a physical mediator between human and divine is brought here in tune with the alchemical theme of mediation, but it is used to support the new social office of Mary as a charitable mediator between divine authority and those who suffer: "Oh, hail Mary— the comforter of us all, the redeemer God Jesus. Maria's human corpus was in itself beginning—middle—end. He must have been through her and still is Jesus-Maria" (*Das "Buch der Heiligen Dreifaltigkeit,"* 102).

Both understandings of Mary as a medium inform the construal of the charitable agency of the book's body. The book that was conceived "in the Virgin's way" should bring about understanding and charity on behalf of those accused of heresies. Through Mary's physical mediation, divinity had once acquired its human hypostasis crucial to the history of salvation. Now the textual body of this book is a product of Mary's benevolence, as was the sacrificial body of Christ.

Truth that cannot be unambiguously articulated or grasped verbally in an inflated discourse is ritually inscribed into the consecrated body of the book. Its appearance at the public forum as a gift to the powerful constitutes in itself a nonverbal equivalent to the enunciation of this truth, which is the truth of Franciscan piety. Franciscans were the most socially engaged religious group of the time. The following passage is remarkable in its self-reflexive attempt to engage alchemy for the book's discursive goal and social cause:

> This book of truth teaches one single meaning that *all things are included in one.* Who understands this could also overcome *all errors of heretics, Jews, and heathens* and convert all of them to the true

Christian belief, to make them accept the one true Christian belief by means of all of God's teaching and by God's force. Time should pass only in God. All devils will be cruelly captured. By God's force they will abandon then their unfaithful will. *God wants to fill in his choirs now all by himself.* (*Das "Buch der Heiligen Dreifaltigkeit,"* 124; emphasis added)

Two moments are especially meaningful in this passage: first, heretics are aligned with Jews and heathens. This implies an old definition of heresy as the rejection of Christian dogma, of the "true Christian belief" (*waren cristenglauben*). The same logic underlies the equation of heretics with devils. However, the late medieval religious debates, unlike those of the High Middle Ages, were no longer focused on Christian dogma but on the institution of the church.[33] The author's archaic understanding of heresy thus appears as a conscious and deliberate differentiation between Christian reformers and heretics.

Here, exactly as in the case of gold-making and anti-heretical Mariology, an obsolete notion is strategically used in application to a modern situation. The end of the passage about God's wish to "fill in his choirs now all by himself" sounds like a stance in the contemporaneous discussion about the definition of the church: the author of the manuscript subordinates the church directly to the might of God. A confession of belief alone, he suggests, should be sufficient as a proof of loyalty to the institution of the church.

By means of this "reversal" (*vmslag*) (*Das "Buch der Heiligen Dreifaltigkeit,"* 91), the author seems to differentiate between the heretics and all those reformist groups who accept Christian dogma. They span a diverse range, beginning with the most radical heresy of the Free Spirit (*geisteskirchliche Häresie*) via quasi-heretical movements of Beghards, Beguines, and Adamites, and ending with the reformist Hussites. The urgency of such differentiation is evident from the fact that even the most orthodox reformers such as John Wycliffe and Jan Hus were condemned at the council as heretics.[34] The alchemical-magical invocation of the unity of all things opening the passage can be interpreted as aiming at an inclusion of all Christians under *one* notion of the church.

In regard to this goal, the visual layout of the book acquires central importance. The medieval understanding of the physicality of vision anchors the process of mediation, which assimilates sensory perception to the taking of a medicament. The medievalist Suzannah Biernoff helps us understand how the logic of embodied vision, of visual participation in the divine, informs the *Book*'s attempt to reach out beyond itself into public space. For it is such nonliterary visual practices as "the transformed host raised for all to see, the character in the mystery play, and the sacred image or exhibited relic"[35] that offer to the maker of the *Book* the models of public exhibition that constitute the collective reception which he seeks for his textual production. It is through the physicality of reading that the *Book* seeks to create its universal audience.

Biernoff observes that in the Middle Ages "vision was a way of relating to oneself, to the sensible world including other animate beings, and to God. As such, it exceeded both viewing subjects and visible objects, as well as determining their mode of interaction" (Biernoff, *Sight and Embodiment in the Middle Ages*, 3). The *Book* engages this medieval excess of vision, its reciprocal, dynamic, and transcendent nature in a variety of ways that contribute to the construal of its circulation as an "ocular communion" (ibid., 134).

In fact, Biernoff shows that medieval perception was defined as assimilation. Therefore the imitation of Christ was performed through contemplation of Christ's wounds and of his crucifixion. "By visualizing Christ's death and resurrection, the meditator could expect to be led to a new state of grace. . . . The emphatic display of Christ's wounds in pictorial representation of the Passion, the elevation of the host, and the exhibition of relics in transparent ostensories performed a similar function" (Biernoff, *Sight and Embodiment in the Middle Ages*, 138).

All these elements also inform the *Book*'s textual body so as to affect the reader through visual perception. According to Biernoff, "Bacon used the term *passio* to denote the 'transmutation' produced in the body of the recipient (viewer) by the agent (object or species)" (*Sight and Embodiment in the Middle Ages*, 139). On this notion of physical transformation of the reader through his or her interaction with the book is based also the material design of the *Book*'s agency. The visual layout of the *Book* reinforces the physical metaphor of reading as drinking of the sacramental wine. In the communion practice of the thirteenth and fourteenth centuries "seeing the miraculously transformed bread and wine became a substitute for 'tasting' Christ" (Biernoff, *Sight and Embodiment in the Middle Ages*, 142).

> Like the display of Christ's wounds in image of the Passion, and their invocation in sermons and devotional literature, the presentation of the host—whether during communion, or in the monstrance outside of the mass—invited participation on the part of the viewer. Extra-liturgical showings of the host began in the early fourteenth century, by which time the *corpus Domini* had acquired the associations and trappings of a holy relic. (Biernoff, *Sight and Embodiment in the Middle Ages*, 143)

The medieval conceptualization of the *Book of the Holy Trinity* as embodied vision might be old-fashioned for its time, but it strategically takes advantage of the novel cultural condition of the public circulation of books, where it could bind its readership in a quasi-devotional way, informed by optical principles but not "in [the] sense of a perspective of a stable, unitary point of view [but rather as] a way of seeing that exploits the ambiguities of thirteenth-century *perspectiva*, including the mutual 'gaze' of subject and object" (Biernoff, *Sight and Embodiment in the Middle Ages*, 149).

The *Book*'s sacramental conception seems to be in tune with the late medieval spirituality which, according to Biernoff, was rooted in the sensuality of carnal vision, overflowing the limits of individual bodies because "the body of the incarnate Christ was *fleshly* rather then passive, bounded and stable" (*Sight and Embodiment in the Middle Ages*, 150). In the *Book*, the author's identification with the expecting Virgin indeed evokes medieval eroticized mysticism of a communion with Christ. As Biernoff pointed out, Christ's body "signifies excessively. And it is literally fluid in its outpouring of redemptive blood" (ibid., 150). The *Book*'s mixture of alchemical scribbling makes its body into such fluid, unstable textual flesh. And its author capitalizes precisely on this semantic instability, which allows for semantic polyvalence of its message. For the *Book* strives to attain a liminal position from which it could mediate among a variety of marginal communities.

Some of the *Book*'s illuminations represent the tortures of Christ, where Christ stands for the sufferings of "all those decapitated, hanged, and broken on the wheel." The contemplation of his passion invites the readers to partake in the sufferings of those punished under the Inquisition, or of those who belong to the Reformation movements and are in danger of prosecution: "The gallows, the beheading, and the wheel, the seven signs earlier in the book show that God also suffered on the gallows of the cross all seven deaths in order to bring us to his eternal peace. Amen" (*Das "Buch der Heiligen Dreifaltigkeit,"* 210).

The *Book*'s Body: Sacraments or Alchemy

Thus the alchemical *corpus libri* is cued to the context of ecclesiastical politics. The figure of a semantic "reversal" performed in the microcosm of the *Book* anticipates the "reversal" which the writer wants to bring about in the world. The inversions that first turned the selfish art of gold-making into a form of Franciscan piety and then redefined a Christian heretic as a heathen in order to exclude from this definition a reformer demonstrate that the *Book* was created as an active agent. Once put into circulation, it is expected to exert its magic on its readers (or rather, users) and through them on the course of historical events.

Consequently, the *Book* is meant to communicate not by way of argumentation or reasoning but by way of magical sympathy, that is, through a system of operations performed in effigy in the process of its composition in order to generate the desired effects in the external world. Corruption, error, and injustice that the author sees as a plague of his times are being corrected and purified through the filter of his book, as if it were the philosopher's stone.[36] The *Book*'s relation to its historical and political context is based on the parallelism between microcosm and macrocosm inherent in the tradition of alchemical-magical visions of nature. But this parallelism is mimicked now in the realm of culture as a relation between society and the book.

The *Book* attempts to reinterpret the notion of heresy by identifying as "heretics" merely those who reject the Christian sacraments, that is, non-Christians. In this way, the diverse reformist Christian groups whose views bordered on heresy could be included under the church's wing. The *Book* also attempts to mediate in a reconciliatory fashion between power (secular and ecclesiastical) and the endangered sects so as to promote the unity of belief and of the church. Both these goals reflect the common aspiration of the epoch. In the area of theology, this drive to inclusion found an expression in the doctrine of concomitant presence (*per concomitantiam*) of the blood and flesh of Christ after consecration.

The doctrine of concomitance was first introduced to the official teaching of the church at the Council of Constance. It was supposed to secure theologically the unity of belief by postulating that each host on each single altar represents the same *Corpus Christi*. This symbolic unity of *Corpus Christi* stood for the unity of the Christian universe.[37]

The message of the *Book*, as reconstructed above, appears in this light as inseparable from the conception of the *corpus libri* as *Corpus Christi*.

The mastermind behind the conception of the *Book* seems to share the sensibility of the quasi-heretical groups: His book claims to contain the blood and flesh of Christ, as if it were in a liturgical chalice. Linguistic "matter" (the written letter) is consecrated here as the sacrament of the Eucharist. In this procedure one could even discern an allusion to the rumored view of the Hussite Adamites that the flesh and blood of Christ can be consumed in a sacramental way in any food. On the basis of this allegation they were accused of a total disregard for the sacrament of the Eucharist.[38]

The *Book* is introduced as a magical object which, like the Eucharist, is capable of working its transformative powers upon the body and soul of those who come in its immediate possession:

> This is a book of wonder-working. One can find here the fair truth. Whoever comes in possession of this book should not conceal it, for *it would be harmful to his body and soul*. But one should present this book, since it comes from God, to the great rulers and to the great masters and teachers of the Holy Scriptures in the Christian world. (*Das "Buch der Heiligen Dreifaltigkeit,"* 91; emphasis added)

The reading of this *Book* thus becomes a form of physical consumption. This construal of the book is reinforced by the syntactic structure of the sentence *wem diss buch wirdet der berg es nit / das were ym an leip und sele verderplich* ("Whoever comes in possession of this book should not conceal it, for it would be harmful to his body and soul"). The pertinence dative *wem diss buch wirdet* is here more than a sign of subjective relation; it is rather a sign of possession, and nearly consubstantiality.

In German language of the later Middle Ages, grammatical constructions with the pertinence dative implied much closer and much more immediate relations, such as the relations of body parts, blood relations, or clothing when put on the body, or dwellings when occupied.[39] Thus the grammar signals that the book's body is designed for incorporation.

The book also contains guidance for its usage and describes the intended effects: "No one should hate this book. One should read and pay attention to it in its entirety. In this way one will really appreciate it" (*keyn menssch sej dissem buch gehass / Er lise es vnd verneme es gancz zu ende alles aus / So wirt er dissem buch von rechte wol gut*) (*Das "Buch der Heiligen Dreifaltig-keit,"* 91). Thus the author instructs the reader not to discard the *Book* at first glance but to peruse it for the teaching it embodies. If one reads through the whole book carefully, the suggestion implies, one will uncover its hidden meaning and value its message as a result. And moreover, one will participate in its magical procedures performing the rites of cleansing, and hence be converted, cured, or protected.

The perusal of the *Book* is characteristically equated with drinking. There is an important nuance in the meaning which is lost in modern translation: *er lise es gancz zu ende alles aus* ("read everything entirely up to the end") sounds indeed almost like *trinke zu ende alles aus* ("drink everything up"). The German *aus* implies a spatial relation between the book and its content which is to be "read up," emptied out by the reader. And in fact, the content of the book deals with the preparation of a medicine which is supposed to be held in its body as if the book were a receptacle. Reading this book is like taking medicine and undergoing its therapeutic effects.

Eating a book as an act of initiation into its transcendent mystery is an ancient topos. Consider the book of Ezekiel (sixth century B.C.), where the prophet swallows a roll of parchment covered with writing on both sides, or a Byzantine ritual, which recommends drinking the letters as a means of learning the alphabet. The letters were to be written in ink on a board, then washed off with wine and given to a child to drink. The art of writing is supposed to be acquired by means of drinking up the written, material substance of the text.[40]

The *Book* seems to share with these ancient examples an understanding of the corporeal transmission of meaning, which can be seen as a subversive expression of the increasing self-reflexivity of the book culture of the later Middle Ages. In *Engaging Words*, Laurel Amtower discussed the explicit intentionality, the construction of readership, and the forms of authorial presence in the writings of this period. "Reading was imagined as a process of interiorization, through which texts are translated into the mental threads that affect ethical action and learned response,"[41] she writes. And "an *auctor* is one who is closer in temporal and spiritual time to the word of Christ as Logos."[42]

The *auctor* of *The Book of the Holy Trinity* creates a subversive medium for a subversive message by rendering the interiorization archaically literal as physical assimilation and Logos as the *corpus libri*. The magical powers of this *corpus* are expected to derive directly from the letter of the alchemical and religious discourse, from the very performance of the book's textual assemblage and visual layout.

The book is a textual mosaic of pieces excerpted from both religious and alchemical sources. They are combined so as to mix and cross-fertilize these discursive types in a way relevant for the transformative impact of the book's body. The genres of religious literature seem to provide a source for what could be called the active type of discourse, or "the word-agent," since they actively aim at rhetorical persuasion and, like sermons, prayers, and mystery plays, address a congregation in a church, a crowd in a market, or God himself. These utterances are geared toward recipients in order to solicit a response.

However, the book owes its actual volume to the passive type of discourse, or the "word-matter," which consists of writing as the undifferentiated letter. Some of this material seems to mimic alchemical procedures, whereas some simply inventories the substances. The pseudo-alchemical recipes constitute the verbal stuff on which the writer labors, enclosed in the receptacle of the book's body. In this respect, the *Book* shares the compositional logic of the ancient magical papyri, studied by William Brashear. Such papyri often contained "the most incongruous material imaginable," literary works compiled along with "mathematical exercises and name lists," and "represented only fantasy, nonsensical scribblings."[43]

Brashear's conclusion about the nature of the papyri's writing is relevant to the *Book*: "Apparently, the content of the written material played a secondary role. Obviously of paramount importance was the presence of writing itself—any writing."[44] The energetic "word-agent" is apparently supposed to charge this matter of the quasi-alchemical writing with the force inherent in the religious rhetoric. The function of the religious passages seems to consist in tincturing the alchemical textuality so as to make it carry the transcendent religious content.

The book's peculiar mixture of German and Latin reinforces this divided function of its textual hybridity. The active "word-agent" largely coincides with the German idiom. It echoes the tradition of German mysticism and sermons, which the representatives of the mendicant orders by this time already pronounced in the national language.[45] The book's alchemical recipes are still mostly in Latin. They are often accompanied by German translations but, remarkably, only those alchemical passages are translated which imitate liturgical procedures and use the religious symbolism of *Corpus Christi*, as if alchemy were to be religiously surpassed and superseded in the process of its filtering through translation.

Alchemy's traditional reliance on religious idiom now becomes a channel for a religious appropriation of alchemical language. For example, in one passage the production of the philosopher's stone, which ennobles the metals, is first codified in a typically alchemical fashion—*prima materia* as virtue, philosopher's stone as *Corpus Christi*, and gold as love. But then, instead of providing a recipe for the procedure, the immediately following religious passages mystically "distill" the religious symbolism of alchemy into a celebration of piety: "Oh, how strong is the body. The *corpus* of pure love is the only desire of our heart. Let us stay in pure love! Chastity is purity, if one proceeds therein right" (*Das "Buch der Heiligen Dreifaltigkeit,"* 99).

The German translation fulfills the function of "tincture" and "sublimation" which separate the religious semantic layer from the alchemical in the Latin text. The former constitutes the book's content, whereas the latter is responsible for the book's physicality. The alchemical verbal mass fills the receptacle of the book like dough. (See fig. 2.5.) The language of matter that alchemy had traditionally developed in the course of its preoccupation with the ennobling transmutations of substance becomes in the *Book* verbal matter, the letter. The legendary inventor of alchemy, Hermes Trismegistos, was indeed regarded as identical with the Egyptian god Thoth, the inventor of writing.

To a large extent, the book consists of an amalgam of alchemical recipes for the production of medicine. Fragments of authentic recipes are mixed up with hardly legible imitative scribblings. The excerpts from religious genres and some authentic recipes as well as the political statements about the fate of the heretics generally follow the rules of grammar. However, most of the book's volume consists of fake alchemical procedures. The language here abandons any semblance of grammatical organization and mimics the formlessness of matter. The text often consists exclusively of repetitive alignments of nouns, the meaning of which is usually defined at the beginning of each procedure.

The names of evangelists and their symbols, planets, virtues, stones, and the basic elements which make up the universe are introduced at the very beginning as verbal substances, which are further rhythmically mixed, stirred, shaken, condensed, pressed thin, stretched long, or ground small. For example, the following passage magically equates word and matter in an act of naming:

> "Chastity," the human substance [*der menschliche leichnam*], castitas leo pater per tot/ Primus est aqua 2° aer 3° thea C "Sanctity," the divine substance, sanctitas columba pater per tot/ "Continence," the human substance, sobrietas aquila pater per tot . . . "Purity," the divine substance, Puritas per deus pater homo per tot/ primus est aqua aer thea. (*Das "Buch der Heiligen Dreifaltigkeit,"* 93)

The German word *leichnam* (corpse) translates here the Latin alchemical term *caput mortuum*, which designates a homogeneous mass that stays behind after the process of distillation has been finished. It is an impure substance. The translation of this particular term into German is meaningful. The usage of the German word *leichnam* allows for a pun on the customary designation of the Host as *unseres herren leichnamen*, whereas the Latin *caput mortuum* (literally, "dead head") does not lend itself to such semantic ambiguity.

In the passage above the names of virtues, which in the alchemical tradition usually define the fortitude of metals, are brought together with the divine and human substance. This magical naming refers to the first stage of the alchemical process of purification, but it also foregrounds the principle of mediation between the human and the divine and their combination into one single substance. The names of virtues as the signifiers become the verbal matter on which the author performs further magical operations, as the following passage shows:

> *Omnia sunt unum esse* Keuschheit Sanctity Continence Caritas Castitas Holiness Sobrietas Love Mildness Mercurius Humility Puritas Pietas Silver, the living Gold, Humilitas Purity, Sun, the eternal Father gives birth to himself, to the Son of God. The son is eternal without a halt, filled with the Spirit. He is himself the Holy Spirit and the Son. *Omnia sunt unum esse* (*Das "Buch der Heiligen Dreifaltigkeit,"* 116; emphasis added)

The virtues, first introduced as powerful substances, are in fact bracketed in this passage between two *omnia sunt unum esse* and mixed together, as if in a receptacle. Both passages quoted above verbally imitate typical alchemical processes of separating and combining. The idea of stirring, or circular motion that results in this portentous mixture of signifiers, is suggested in one of the book's illuminations—a wheel to which are attached the notes with the written names of virtues.

This identity of name and substance is self-reflexively elucidated later in the text: "This brightest stone is the white luna, the crystal substance of earth that has hidden in itself the colors of all virtues and [hidden] itself in their names" (*diß aller clarsten stein ist weiss luna cristallin ein erde leichnam der aller tugende farbe verborgen in ym hat / doch in ym name sich selber*) (*Das "Buch der Heiligen Dreifaltigkeit,"* 140).

Thus the substance is also secretly present in the physicality of the words, hidden in their letter. If the writer is concerned with the purification of morals through the magical body of the book, the names of virtues seem to provide the most plausible verbal material for starting a purifying medicine. This substance is further transformed into the oil of mercy, and finally into the medicine with no less power than that of the blood and flesh of Christ.

The entire process of text construction is thus revealed as a quasi-liturgical act, in the course of which the verbal substance undergoes transubstantiation so that the book, if passed on and consumed, would constitute a communion: "Oh, how greatly we receive into our sinful bodies the bread of the holy sacrament so that we do our best and give up sinful thoughts early and become less proud, greedy, incontinent, unchaste, angry, hating, envious" (*Das "Buch der Heiligen Dreifaltigkeit,"* 134).

The confusingly dense and almost illegible verbal substance of the book prompted some researchers to suspect its scribe of insanity.[46] However, it is better explained through its material conception as a salient feature of its magical production. The leveling of grammatical organization increases the material weight of language, which is consecrated here in place of wine and bread. In fact, many alchemical recipes of the book evoke the preparation of bread and wine and thus can be seen as poetologically self-reflexive.

The philosopher's stone, traditionally associated with *Corpus Christi*, ferments the verbal substance, preparing it for transubstantiation. The stone is pulverized, mixed with the elixir or binding water until it turns into white dough, put into an oven, and so forth. To prepare the elixir, one uses drops of blood from the veins of the stone. The following example should elucidate the whole process of kneading and consecrating of the verbal mass:

> The three most noble stones are [made] out of five wounds: the *wound of the crown of thorns*: the head is a clear white crystal; the *wounds of the feet* are sapphire blue. All together [mixed] with the stone luna they are Emerald. The *wounds of the left side* are dawn-red. The *hand-wound* is red ruby. All together they are one stone. The whole substance is green penetrated with red. The *wound of the side* is identical to the heart, for the water dissolves the blood. Mercurius. This all is the stone of love. Carbunculus is purity. Carbunculus is the whole fiery Corpus Sol. This is the oil of the philosopher, which the philosophers call oleum inconbustibile. And the oleum is like this fermentum auri and elixir and aurum philosophorum. Then it is the fermentum solis, as the fermentum panis is panis. (*Das "Buch der Heiligen Dreifaltigkeit,"* 144; emphasis added)

In this passage the ancient alchemical trope of the fragmentation of a corpse is applied to the body of Christ, and the fragmented limbs are reinterpreted in terms of the Christian allegory of passion and crucifixion. This reinterpretation takes strategic advantage of the northern European iconographic patterns of the time. For example, consider an allegorical image of alchemical fragmentation from the manuscript *Splendor Solis* compiled in the sixteenth century: a black knight with a sword is dissecting a white, salt-like corpse, whose golden head he has already severed and holds up in the air.[47] (See fig. 2.3.)

This alchemical topos of "Die and become!" might ultimately derive from the Egyptian Osiris myth, as some scholars have suggested,[48] but the

Figure 2.3. Fragmentation as dismemberment. Breu, Joerg the Elder, *Splendor Solis oder Sonnenglanz*, 1531–32, Southern Germany. Illuminated manuscript page, gouache on parchment, 33.1 × 22.8 cm. 78 D 3, fol. 18 verso. Kupferstichkabinett, Staatliche Museen, Berlin, Germany.

Figure 2.4. *Caritas*, allegorical fragmentation of Christ's body, Dirck Volckertsz. Coornhert after Maarten van Heemskerck, 1550. Copperplate etching. Rijksmuseum, Amsterdam.

notion of resurrection implied in this image, as well as the iconography of the fragmentation of the body, reappear in the popular religious allegories of *Caritas*. For example, the *Caritas* of Maarten van Heemskerck holds in both hands chalices with the wounded hands and feet of Christ.[49] (See fig 2.4.)

In the *Book of the Holy Trinity*, the alchemical meaning of fragmentation is similarly subsumed and surpassed by the religious symbolism of Christ's wounds layered over the alchemical body. The wounds of Christ are first aligned with the precious stones and then undergo fermentation so as to produce the philosopher's oil. Verbal entanglement reflects the whole procedure of mixing and breaking down of substances.

The fermentation of oil is compared to the fermentation of dough. Somewhat later follows a clear formula of consecration: "All these works are one and the same, as the blood is one, and as the flesh is one. It is not flesh; then be it flesh and also blood again" (*alle diesse werck sind also gleich als eyn blut ist ein fleissch ist / es ist kein fleissch so wirt es fleissch / vnd auch blut wider*) (*Das "Buch der Heiligen Dreifaltigkeit*," 149).

The construal of the *Book* as the bread to be consecrated carries a traditional religious connotation of bread as a unifying medium. For example, according to an old custom, the Eucharistic bread, and later the eulogy bread, or *panis trifidus* (bread divided into three parts by means of three cuts) was to be passed from one church community to another as a sign of unity.[50] However, it is the book's emphasis on Christ's wounds that is especially meaningful. Wounds were paramount to the veneration of Christ's relics because of the blood flowing out of them.[51]

The wounds of Christ surface in the text in an isolated and unmediated fashion: at one point there is the wound of the right foot, at another, the wound of the left foot, or the bleeding head. They seem to be present in order to saturate with blood the verbal mass in which they are hidden, to gradually fill in the receptacle of the book with the blood of Christ. For example, a passage which mentions precious stones in relation to the bleeding wound of the head, whatever this relation might be in alchemical terms, also evokes a vision of a richly decorated receptacle containing the relics, or a liturgical chalice containing the holy substance of Christ's blood: "All elements—earth, water, fire, air—are good, all the precious stones are good, the head becomes the white and red flesh that bleeds" (*Alle elementa gut erde wasser feuer lufft Alle edel gestein gut das haubt ist ein weiss rot fleissch blut wirt*) (*Das "Buch der Heiligen Dreifaltigkeit*," 139).

In the context of the initial command that the book should not remain with one owner but should be passed further, the analogy with a chalice filled with the blood of Christ becomes especially prominent. The right of laymen to take the cup was the major demand of the Hussite reformation. The Hussites' request that the sacrament of the blood of Christ would no longer be a prerogative of an initiated priest alone but would be shared by the whole congregation became the symbol of the whole movement.

Thus the production and insertion in the public forum of a book whose eclectic verbal substance is gradually blended into the medium of the Eucharist endorses in effigy the Hussite demand for both sacraments which was officially rejected at the Council of Constance.

The Book as Communication and Communion

The book, the traditional medium of verbal transmission, becomes in the political context of the Council of Constance an exemplary medium of non-content-oriented, ritual communication in a likeness of a sacral object. The *Book*'s self-consciousness as artifact discernible in its physical makeup is inseparable from its intended functionality. The book's body should match exactly the goals it seeks to reach in accordance with the logic of magical analogy.

Corpus Christi thus charges the *corpus libri* not only with a purifying and reconciliatory potency but also with a healing one. The book makes use of physical health as a metaphor of the social balance, and alchemy helps the book to its self-consciousness as a medium of public communication. Confirming the reservations of Pope John XXII, its "empty verbosity" gives both a strategic cover and practical advice on how to "fake" the Eucharist in the medium of the book, which is offered to a divided public with a promise of gold and silver for the sake of symbolic unity.

According to the magical practice of "healing like with like," the "empty verbosity" of alchemy aims here to match the "empty verbosity" of the inflated ecclesiastical discourse of the schismatic period in order to invigorate the fading power of words and to counteract the council's indecision and legal impotence to accomplish de facto reforms.

The widespread dissatisfaction with the results of the Council of Constance (and soon thereafter, the Council of Basel) concerning the reform of the church is characteristically expressed in the words of the Spanish theologian John of Segovia:

> Those who were concerned about the reform of the church felt by experience then and later how infinite is the distance between saying and doing, between "let there be reform" and "reform is accomplished." And indeed it is pleasant to meditate on the reformation of other estates; advising them is noble, preaching on it is hollow; one is reputed for saintliness as long as no rebuttal is made. But when it comes to the work of reformation in any state, one understands what the proverb says about common justice, namely that it's what we hope will happen to others, but never to ourselves.[52]

It is this "hollow preaching" and the failure of the councils to pronounce "reform is accomplished" that the *Book* attempts to compensate for in the definitive materiality of its *corpus libri*. The book takes recourse to the performative modality of the alchemical and religious ritual and becomes an embodied "speech-act" so that it can fulfill an operative function of tightening up and focalizing the dissemination of pre-Reformation writings into the oneness of its divine body, as its often-repeated formula conveys: "This book is many books and is still one book" (*Dicz buch ist vil bücher vnd ist doch ein buch*) (*Das "Buch der Heiligen Dreifaltigkeit,"* 179).

As a word-deed, the *Book of the Holy Trinity* is posed centrally and singularly against the proliferation of the copied libraries at Constance, as well as against the culture of flyers and the inchoate print culture of incunabula. Moreover, the book seeks to constitute its readership on an imperial scale at a time when handwritten books circulated exclusively in closed communities of friends, religious orders, or universities, established prior to the practice of regular book exchange.[53] In the pursuit of this goal, the *Book* challenges the major limitation of pre-Gutenberg book culture—its inability to constitute a broad, "national" public:

> Manuscript technology did not have the intensity or power of extension necessary to create publics on a national scale. What we have called "nations" in recent centuries did not, and could not, precede the advent of Gutenberg technology . . . The unique character of the "public" created by the printed word was an intense and visually oriented self-consciousness, both of the individual and the group.[54]

The construal of the *Book of the Holy Trinity* as the Eucharist was just another attempt to engage the notion of Christian universalism in order to bring together audiences separated by social hierarchies and to overcome religious sectarianism for the sake of a far larger public (in this case, the western European public) represented in the public forum of the council. The religious notion of communion offered the most plausible, and perhaps the only model of public communication at the time.

Despite its treatment of the most common discursive and visual patterns, the *Book* has a cultural place apart, best demonstrated by its subversion of the phenomenon that Michel Camille described as the "image on the edge."[55] The images drawn on the edges of medieval manuscripts, Camille argues, were an expression of the social unconscious, a testimony to the marginalized culture clandestinely sneaking into the "mainstream." The book is all about the very process of making the hidden, marginalized, unknown, and invisible not only visible but tangibly present and of social consequence. It gives central place to the images of marginalized cultures, whether those of alchemy, or persecuted heresy, or reformation. Symptomatically, it does not have any images on the edge. Its illuminations rather intrude from the margins into the text proper. (See fig. 2.5.)

The *Book*'s illuminations seek to compensate for the illegibility of the text. They take over the actual communicative function by making perceptible and tangible the meaning hidden in the text by conveying it visually. For example, the image of Mary's crowning harmonizes the *Book*'s matching of substances with the names of the evangelists, the coats of arms, and the animals as well as the author's identification with the Virgin. It organizes all these disparate elements into a meaningful whole on one plane of vision. Directional and spatial relations in the image, such as "above," "below," "left," and "right" compensate for the syntactic relations, which are lacking in the text. (See fig. 2.1.)

Ekphrasis contributes to the Eucharistic conception of the *Book* as the embodied vision. For example, the description of an illumination with the Virgin Mary—"Sancta Maria":

Figure 2.5. Text mass and intrusion of the image into the text. *Buch der heyligen Dreyualdekeit,* Konstanz, Germany, ca. 1410-19. Illuminated manuscript page, 29.0 × 20.5 cm. 78 A11, fol. 190 recto, Kupferstichkabinett, Staatliche Museen, Berlin.

Sancta Maria / In the sun with twelve stars around her, Maria means Sol, stands on the moon that speaks: <u>luna sol</u>—Caritas est castitas Jovis. A blue lily with a long blue stem stands behind her. In the lily is the torture of our Lord, and above the lily is written "sanctitas": the lily—$, the right hand—"humilitas," the left hand—"puritas," the wounds in the site—"pietas," the body—"castitas," the right foot— "caritas," the left foot—"sobrietas." The book's continuous teaching shows clearly how to produce them, reveals all the high, artful works. Everyone should see for himself how to understand this wise writing. Super omnia laus tibi criste et virgo mater maria. Amen. (*Das "Buch der Heiligen Dreifaltigkeit,"* 210)

The beginning of the passage is like a mystery play, which ascribes to each character its part. The subsequent description implies the notion of space: Mary appears as if standing on the stage and relates to Christ's torture in spatial terms, as he is in the lily behind and above her. This image visualizes both the alchemical process of distillation in the *bain-marie* vessel and the poetology of the book itself, since it is through Mary's body (with whom the author identifies) that his creation had to go before taking its shape as a book. (See fig. 2.2.)

Elsewhere in the *Book*, both alchemy and poetics coincide in the figure of a lily, which is drawn into the description of an alchemical process of coagulation: "the lily of all seven virtues is purified in three degrees proven as white-yellow-red" (*Die lilie aller siben tugent die wirt beweiset weiß geel rot/ jn drej graden aller metalle purgiret* . . .) (Das "Buch der Heiliger Dreitaltigkert," 273). The "flower" is the term for purified matter that stays behind after the distillation is finished. Therefore the text congeals into the figure of a lily but it also can be seen as spreading out of it. This visual figure draws attention to the book's process of mediation as moving from the image to the text and back.

Similarly, the image of Mary organizes the text mass. It combines the visual iconographies of a mystery play and a devotional image, which since the thirteenth century had conveyed doctrinal lessons in a way that invited participation. And indeed, in the passage *ad medicinem*, the mixture of three virtues and of the human and divine substances is now colored—golden, red, white, green—and linked to Good Friday and Easter Sunday. These dates stand, evidently, for Christ's death and resurrection, but they also indicate the book's liturgical inscription into the temporality of the Christian calendar.

The fragments from the liturgies of the hours and of the Mass are again dovetailed with the astrological calendar so as to relate to profane human activities of everyday life. For example, in one passage, the visual constellations of stars are read as the signs which indicate when to make clothes and weapons, when to marry or undertake a trade, when to start building houses, castles, and churches, and when to go to Mass.

The mundane and religious worlds are linked in an evocation of a liturgical worship of the raised host: "Rest in the hour of Saturn. In the Moon *pater cor corpus*. In the hour of Saturn raise *filius cor corpus*. In the hour of Jove, tinge *spiritus sanctus cor corpus* into one as is taught here and later" (*Das "Buch der Heiligen Dreifaltigkeit*," 118). Thus, the book appropriates the spatial logic of the liturgy centered on the host, on the one hand, and of the temporal logic of the liturgy of the hours and astrology, on the other, to construe its desired reception and circulation—around the clock, around the year.

The appropriation of the liturgical and alchemical rituality for the medial construal of *corpus libri* and its reception becomes possible in the later Middle Ages not in the least because of the changing understanding of the sacramental symbolism. Jürgen Bärsch observed that "in both theology and religious practice the function of the liturgy separated from its form. External ceremonial actions were regarded as playfully imitative depictions of the history of salvation from which the grace intrinsic to the sacrament was largely independent. The visible staging of the liturgy and its symbolism could be explained intellectually."[56] It is in this intellectual realm, now open to invention and experimentation, that the maker of the *Book of the Holy Trinity* rematches the alchemical and liturgical ritual symbolism for the sake of an embodied message.

In its circular flux of symbols, numbers, and names of virtues, the book's organization of signifiers seems to mimic the sensibility of Raymond Lull, who is considered an inventor of *encyclos sophia*, or a "circular discipline." Scholars distinguish between two types of medieval encyclopedia, the "static" ones, which consisted of an inventory of notions, and the "dynamic" ones, which taught how to deduce these notions from certain starting points. Lola Badia observed that the authors of dynamic encyclopedias such as Raymond Lull or Roger Bacon were usually the promoters of social reforms with an underlying ethical purpose.[57] The creator of the *Book* clearly strove to produce such a medium that would codify the expression of his social concern.

The usage of coats of arms to designate alchemical processes unambiguously links the book to the social sphere of politics. At a certain point the book evokes the popular legend about the return of the emperor Friedrich Barbarossa and integrates a description of his coat of arms into the text. The legend had great currency in the political sensibility of the time. It testifies to the *Book*'s longing for the centralized power that Germany lacked in this "diffuse period"[58] of history and that it compensated for with its claim to embody the powers of God.

One could speculate that the presentation of the alchemical book as a holy sacrament at the council was supposed to persuade the ecclesiastical and secular rulers to accept a religious group which stood close to the reform movement and was in danger of being accused of heresy (for example, such a radical sect within the Hussite movement as the Adamites). The celebration of the holy sacraments in the book would demonstrate the group's Christian orthodoxy and thus ward off prosecutions. To achieve this goal through an alliance with the powerful rulers, the supporters of reformation, one would however need first to cleanse the dubious recipients of corruption and injustice and thus make them capable of alliance.

Reformation movements such as the Hussites in Prague and the Cabochiens in Paris were closely bound up with the monarchy. The extension of the purifying and unifying powers of the book to the German rulers could symbolize a restoration of the alliance between reform and the monarchy on German soil, after it had been jeopardized through the execution of Jan Hus. The emperor Sigismund famously failed to protect the leader of the reformation movement in Constance after promising him safe-conduct. By accepting an excerpt from an alchemical book, however, he had, in that book's own terms, unwittingly accepted the major symbol of the reform movement and partaken in effigy of the reformed ritual of communion.[59]

In the last lines of its first part, the book openly casts aside the effectiveness of alchemically produced medicine in favor of the salutary effect of the blood and flesh of Christ: "All medicine can be impaired by the highest nature. I write in God who made all of us whole by means of his own flesh and blood" (*alle medicinen sie eyn eyntracht haben von der hochsten naturen / ich schreibe ingot selber sein fleissch vnd blut vns alle gesunt gemacht hat*).[60]

In addition to its purifying and reconciliatory functions, the *Corpus Christi* also lends the *corpus libri* a healing one. Jointly, the three functions engage the common bodily metaphor of health as a balancing-out of social forces, wherein the book's effectiveness was meant to lie. The alchemy brings the book to a new self-awareness as a medium of public communication. Its hollow-sounding verbal proceedings provided a strategic alibi and practical guidelines for the "counterfeiting" of the Eucharist in the medium of the book. Under cover of the promise of precious metals, the *Book of the Holy Trinity* was inserted in the divided public sphere to achieve its symbolic unification. The question whether from the theological point of view this political aim justifies the means can be put aside.

Chapter 3

The World as Christ and Representation, or Johann Caspar Lavater's Practice of Redemptive Aesthetics

> The rise and fall of Christianity entails the rise and fall in the physiognomic sensibility; the rise and fall of Christianity entails the rise and fall in the beauty of the paintings of Christ.
> —J. C. Lavater, "About the Paintings of Christ"

The epithet of "poet-thinker of the event"[1]—of the event of Christ's resurrection—that Alain Badiou once bestowed on Paul applies quite literally to Johann Caspar Lavater (1741–1801), the pastor-poet from Zurich. Lavater survives in present-day cultural memory almost exclusively because of his association with the doomed science of physiognomy.[2] But Lavater applied himself with equal fervor to a great variety of fields—theology and philosophy, psychology and pedagogy, art and poetry, politics and social thought. His broad range of interests resulted in a plethora of idiosyncratic writings and bizarre activities, which stood out and apart in the second half of the eighteenth century for their obsessive focus on Christ.

The theologian Horst Weigelt suggested a reason for this obsession. Weigelt noticed that in all his preoccupations the pastor-poet was driven by the single desire to find a concrete manifestation of the world of transcendence in the world of immanence: "Though the themes of the particular works are very different, all of them, directly or indirectly, are informed by Lavater's religiosity with its urge for manifest experience of transcendence. This desire was in the end what drove him again and again to reach for the pen."[3] Lavater's search for "manifest religious experiences" (*manifeste religiöse Erfahrungen*)[4] was supposed to prove to his contemporaries that the physical and metaphysical worlds can communicate. Christ's body, the medium of the divinity's access to the human senses, offered, in Lavater's eyes, a historical medium of such communication.[5]

The single-mindedness of Lavater's pursuit of Christ made his views on religion sound "trans-confessional": "In all Christian sects known to me . . . is only one part of the whole Christian teaching, of the meaning of Christ," he wrote. "And their error . . . consists exclusively in that they believe they have him as the whole. They all seem to be caricatures of one original image, in each of which one can see something of Christ, though half truthful, raw, and overdrawn."[6]

Later in life, this trans-confessionalism grew into a trans-religious position. Lavater came to the conclusion that God can be experienced in all faiths: "There are thousands of authentic, though very different, arts of love," he insisted. "How differently the same beam of light breaks through the different pieces of glass! God wants to be known and enjoyed in a million different ways, and Christ to be believed and loved in a million different ways. All believers and lovers will be one, no matter how differently they believe and love."[7]

Weigelt showed that in the end Lavater expected any realm of human knowledge and occupation to have the potential to yield an experience of transcendence. This expectation sustained his lifelong interest in occult phenomena and made him forge contacts with many charlatans of the epoch, including Cagliostro. The pastor became notorious for his experiments with electric magnetism, hypnosis, and mediums who claimed to communicate with ghosts of the apostles and to resurrect the dead. Ultimately, these endeavors only exposed him to ridicule among his educated contemporaries. His fellow Protestant clerics were no less scandalized than the enlightened thinkers. The former accused him of leanings toward Catholicism, or of heresy, and the latter, of irrationalism.[8]

And yet, Lavater's intellectual agenda was a product of the Enlightenment. His goal was nothing less than to put Christianity on a new, empirical foundation, which would confirm the truth of the scriptures on the basis of the observation of nature. When his inquiries into the occult failed to provide the desired proof of a metaphysical world, Lavater did not abandon his project but fell back on his own rhetorical powers. He drafted a philosophical poem on immortality in several volumes, entitled *Aussichten in die Ewigkeit* (*Prospects into Eternity*). This was a systematic outline of the "metaphysical" world which, he professed, awaits Christians in the afterlife and which he construed as the transfigured body of Christ.

The poem's purpose was not just to sing and imaginatively portray the afterlife but above all to logically validate the religious realm of metaphysics on the rational premises of the Enlightenment.

The afterlife as a topic for a poem seems at first to be entirely in line with the literary sensibility of the epoch. Literature on immortality was so popular and common in Lavater's time that he compares his work to Noah's dove, which he "sends off to see if there is a dry spot still left in the inundation of writings."[9] In the fourth letter of the *Prospects* he asks a rather rhetorical question: "Is decay the goal of our existence, the destruction of our whole nature? Or do we continue living on, when our body lies stiff?" (*Aussichten in die Ewigkeit*, 41). Eighteenth-century religious poets answered this question unambiguously with visions of the immortality of the soul.[10]

The "dry spot" whereupon Lavater disembarked in contemporary discourse was, however, the immortality of the body. His vision of transfiguration emphasized the corporeal nature of postmortem existence and provocatively conflated metaphysics with physics. But most importantly, Lavater grounded his poetic vision of the afterlife "scientifically" through the scholarship of the naturalist Charles Bonnet, whose research in what was to become modern embryology combined empirical observations of nature with a religious sensibility. Stephen Jay Gould's *Ontogeny and Phylogeny* provides a comprehensive outline of Bonnet's position and sums up his theory in a way that brings across its special attraction for Lavater:

> Bonnet's philosophical writings encompass nearly everything from the properties of infusorians to the nature of the Godhead. As a dominant theme in all these works, Bonnet extended to the entire universe the basic philosophical tenet of his preformationistic beliefs about ontogeny—development is only apparent; it represents the unfolding of structures performed at the creation itself. God, the clockwinder, has not only ordained the laws of the universe; he had created all its structures as well: one creation followed by the complete evolution of all preordained structure to the appointed end of time.[11]

In his books *Contemplation de la nature* (*Contemplation of Nature*, 1764) and in his subsequent two-volume work *La Palingénésie Philosophique, ou, Idées sur l'état passé et l'état futur des êtres vivants* (*Philosophical Reincarnation, or Ideas on the Past and Future State of Living Things*, 1769), Bonnet defined the world as a living organism which contains a preexistent germ of divine providence. The providential law inherent in nature, according to his views, determines the world's evolution. The providential germ, by analogy with a fertilized egg, starts its tangible, physical development with the beginning of life in each species. This development gravitates toward postmortem perfection, which consists above all in the heightening of human physical potential. Since the human being, as Bonnet insists, is a "mixed being" (*être mixte*) consisting of body and soul, death only interrupts the unfolding of his earthly shell. Bonnet draws an analogy to the changing states in the formation of insects. Souls live on in a condition similar to a butterfly's cocoon until they resurrect in physiologically perfect bodies.[12]

In Lavater's eyes Bonnet's speculations proved the physical reality of the afterlife. Therefore he borrowed the scientist's understanding of the world as a living organism and understood Bonnet's preexistent structure of a divine germ as Christ. For him, Bonnet's germ theory scientifically backed up Paul's metaphor about a seed of the earthly body transforming into a plant of the heavenly body (1 Cor. 15:37–38). On this basis Lavater concluded that "the seed contained in its inner design both the ground of a tree's growth and form" (*das Korn enthielt in seiner inneren Einrichtung den Grund von dem*

Wachsthum und der Gestalt des Baumes) (Lavater, *Aussichten in die Ewig-keit,* 124–25). Thus the seed stands in Lavater's mediation between religion and biology not only for a prototypical form realized in a multiplicity of phenomenal bodies but also for the divine energy (comparable to Schopen-hauerian *Wille* or Bergsonian élan vital) which drives their growth and shapes and diversifies them.

All human beings, Lavater observed, are as different among themselves as are plants coming out of seeds, even if those seeds are of the same kind. The notion of the body of Christ allows for an inclusive relation between the physicality of an individual and the physical whole of the natural world, since the divine will of the invisible God-creator transverses both. The fifth and sixth letters of the *Prospects* convey that "Christ" designates in Lavater's mind the divine energy present specifically in human nature, but through which human physicality partakes of the organic, nonhuman world as well. Thanks to this specific difference, or rather *différance* between human and nonhuman, man can experience nature through observation of his own body.

Thus Lavater's reinterpretation of Bonnet's providential germ as "Christ in man" acquires an epistemological dimension: the notion of Christ becomes an anthropological prop that helps to understand the divine revelation in nature, as it manifests itself in human physicality. Through Christ in man, nature communicates with man's consciousness and acquires a human hypostasis. But Christ also commands a system of perception that translates the divine energy working blindly and invisibly in the human body into a form of vision.

Lavater develops this idea from Bonnet's observation that there must be a part of the brain, the so-called corpus callosum, which is responsible for sense perception and its inscription into memory. Lavater understands this organ of perception as an organ of immortality because it translates the physiological stimuli received through the nerves into spiritual life. Therein he sees the foundation of feeling and memory, and therefore the origin of personality and individuality. Lavater declares the corpus callosum an organ of redemption. By dressing in flesh the "ethereal machine" of the soul, it mediates between the metaphysical and physical dimensions of the human being and thus constitutes a link between his present and future conditions.

Lavater never completed the poem in verse. But its detailed version in prose appeared in three volumes in 1768, 1769, and 1773 respectively, with the fourth volume of revisions following in 1778. This unfinished poem constitutes a theoretical blueprint of Lavater's discursive practice. Lavater's purely rhetorical "proof" of communication between physics and metaphys-ics was carried by that "subjective upsurge"[13] that Badiou recognized in Paul. Weigelt showed that Lavater's charismatic personality, passionate language, and abundant energy were the actual factors that effectively held together both his highly heterogeneous discourse and his public.

The fact that Lavater, who considered himself a poet, ultimately refrained from putting his ideas about immortality into rhyme is usually explained by his lack of poetic talent. However, the poor aesthetic quality of his work did not keep him from writing and publishing religious poetry throughout his life. Even on his deathbed, dwindling physical strength did not prevent him from dictating a last poem commemorating New Year's Day of 1801 for the congregation of his church.[14] His forsaking of the poetic form for the *Prospects into Eternity* rather suggests that the publication of the prose outline of the intended poem was the goal in itself and that his claim to poetry had an ulterior motive.

What this motive really was can be surmised from Lavater's usage of Bonnet in his notorious attempt at converting the Enlightenment philosopher Moses Mendelssohn. Fascinated with the discovery of Bonnet's science, Lavater immediately set out to translate the latter's *La Palingénésie Philosophique* of 1769 from French, limiting his translation to the apologetic part and dedicating the translation to Mendelssohn. Lavater was so convinced that Bonnet provided irrefutable proofs of the Christian truth that he publicly challenged Mendelssohn in an addendum to react to them as "Socrates would have done."[15] According to Weigelt, Bonnet himself openly disproved of Lavater's purpose in using his writings. The ensuing controversy with Mendelssohn, once it had been brought out in print by the publishing house of Friedrich Nicolai in Berlin, created something of a scandal and resulted in many Enlightenment intellectuals taking their distances from Lavater.[16]

Perhaps as a result of this experience, Lavater changed his strategy from overt conversion to insidious subversion and offered his own "philosophical" elaboration of Bonnet as a literary exercise. On the pretext of drafting a poem Lavater could smuggle a religious topic such as resurrection into the forum of his not all too willing target audience—the enlightened public. It is no coincidence that he organized his *Prospects* as a series of letters addressed to his older friend Johann Georg Zimmermann, the medical doctor and writer from Brugg who stood in for Lavater's educated audience.

Interestingly, in 1781 Lavater published an abridged, popular version of his treatise on the afterlife, entitled *Prospects into Eternity: An Excerpt from the Larger Work of This Name for Common Use.*[17] In this version, meant for the "common use" of the broader populace, he neither used an epistolary form nor mentioned the poetic dimension of the project. The larger work used aesthetics and philosophy as a disguise in which a religious theme could be offered to the *raisonnement* of "private persons gathered as a public"[18] (*zum Publikum versammelten Privatleute*). Lavater sought to address his learned contemporaries on their own terms.[19]

But the claim to poetry also possessed another discursive dimension: it provided a rhetorical positionality. The divine presence in nature, according to Lavater, is accessible only in rare instances of the mystical seeing of Christ or through the poetic imagination. The role of a religious poet, supposed to carry a Pauline kind of "proof" in his discourse, is therefore conceived by Lavater as apostolic. "What exactly does 'apostle' (apostolos) mean?"— Badiou writes. "Nothing empirical or historical in any case. In order to be an apostle, it is not necessary to have been a companion of Christ, a witness to the event. . . . There invariably comes a moment when what matters is to declare in one's own name that what took place took place, and to do so because what one envisages with regard to the *actual* possibilites of a situation requires it."[20]

But what were the actual possibilities of the situation that required the invention of Lavater's discourse apart? Frederick Beiser offers a comprehensive answer to this question in *The Fate of Reason*: "If the Enlightenment was 'the age of criticism,' then the last decades of the eighteenth century marked the beginning of a new age, 'the age of meta-criticism.' Intellectuals began to suffer a crisis of conscience and question their own faith in the powers of criticism."[21] Even if the pastor-poet participated in the philosophical self-criticism of the Enlightenment in a rather intuitive, dilettantish, and populist fashion, Beiser's map of the labyrinth of German critical philosophy at the end of the eighteenth century with all its pathways, impasses, dilemmas, and detours helps us understand Lavater's intellectual place in the context of his time.

Lavater had been developing his discourse apart, represented by the poem on the afterlife and the concomitant physiognomic fragments, in the period between David Hume's first prediction of a rift between the claims of reason and faith, philosophy and life in the first book of his *Treatise of Human Nature* (1738) and the full-blown crisis of the Enlightenment, with its animated questioning of the authority of reason, as represented by the philosophies of Kant and Spinoza, in the debates of the 1780s.

Beiser articulates the trends of Enlightenment thinking to which Lavater was responding:

> Kant's philosophy represented an uncompromising philosophical criticism; and Spinoza's philosophy stood for a radical scientific naturalism. But their philosophies also illustrated the dangerous consequences of rational inquiry and criticism. The consequence of Kant's philosophy, if it were to drop its inconsistent postulate of the thing-in-itself, was solipsism; and the consequence of Spinoza's philosophy, if it were to delete its superfluous religious language, was atheism and fatalism. Thus the two philosophies foremost in the public mind seemed to be destructive of morality, religion, and the state. (Beiser, *The Fate of Reason*, 2)

In the intellectual context of the time, Lavater stands in for that "public mind" on behalf of which he had launched his ambitious endeavor of solving this "very painful dilemma"—the necessity of a philosophical choice between a rational skepticism toward all moral, religious, and political beliefs, or an irrational fideism at the cost of reason (Beiser, *The Fate of Reason*, 3). Taken against this philosophical backdrop of the epoch, Lavater's reliance on the body of Christ appears as an attempt to compensate for the fading away of metaphysics. Beiser points specifically to "the decline of the rationalist metaphysics of the Leibnizian-Wolffian school" which had once "seemed to provide a safe middle path between the extremes of Hume's dilemma: an a priori knowledge of the existence of God, providence, and immortality" (ibid., 4).

Lavater's discovery of Bonnet falls within the context of the emergence of vitalistic materialism. Bonnet, who still stood in the tradition of Leibniz, was already pointing to the reemergence of teleological models of explanation by the end of the eighteenth century. Beiser points to the scientific experiments and theories of Haller, Needham, Maupertuis, Wolf, and Blumenbach which showed "that there were organic forces within matter. The essence of matter was not exhausted by dead extension. Rather, it consisted in self-organizing and self-activating forces. Matter appeared to be alive, since, like all living things, it moved and organized itself when no apparent cause pushed it into action" (Beiser, *The Fate of Reason*, 13). Vitalistic materialism "could now explain the mind as the highest degree of organization and development of the forces inherent in the body" (ibid., 14).

The notion of the body of Christ helped Lavater shift, in his own way, the accent within his contemporary cultural paradigm from the Enlightenment of the mind (*Auf-Klärung*) to the transfiguration of the body (*Ver-Klärung*). By placing metaphysics not beyond the physical world but right inside it, he strove to make it into an object of science. So relocated, metaphysics could solicit a quasi-empirical proof via the subject's self-observation in the medium of his own body. But most importantly, the interconnection between physics and metaphysics which seemed to be implicit in the embodied mind could become a matter of discursive practice.

In the epigraph to the *Prospects*, Lavater quotes Paul: ". . . because we look not to the things that are seen but to the things that are unseen; for the things that are seen are transient, but the things that are unseen are eternal" (2 Cor. 4:18, RSV). The "transfigured body" is to become fully visible in the afterlife due to the intensified sensory perception of postmortem bodies: "Jesus Christ will transfigure our mean body so that it will be con-formed [*gleichförmig*] with the body of his clarity; as we have carried the image of the earthly Adam, so we will carry the image of the heavenly one, too!" (Lavater, *Aussichten in die Ewigkeit*, 317).[22] This is a conclusion derived from logical analogy, but carried by a declaration of conviction.

All in all, Lavater's "corporeal metaphysics" was designed to provide a sneak preview of the afterlife. Lavater expected that such a preview would confirm the afterlife's reality and thus open a path to collective happiness. His evocation of Christ's resurrection as a foundation of the afterlife restages precisely this "pure event, opening of an epoch, transformation of the relations between the possible and the impossible."[23]

The refinement of the corpus callosum, Lavater suggested, can bring us closer to redemption already in this world. Sharper eyesight and a more refined sense of hearing would, logically, permit us some glimpses into our future conformity with Christ. Preparation for it should, however, already start in the social community here and now. Therefore the notion of aesthetic education, which Lavater transferred from the contemplation of art to the contemplation of people, becomes central to his concomitant studies of physiognomy.

The goal of training in the visual perception and semiotics of faces is social. Even if divinity is present in man, it is not fully graspable in an isolated living individual. The pure visibility of God, Lavater claimed, is possible only in the quasi-congregational unity of mankind in the afterlife. His determination to teach his contemporaries to see Christ in each other and thus to foresee eternity was a public act of pastoral care. His dictionary of physiognomic signs, ultimately pointing to Christ's body, was mending another painful rift of the Enlightenment—the skepticism about the representational reliability of signs.

In his book on the semiotics of the Enlightenment, David Wellbery observed:

> The sign proves to be at once that which allows man to elevate himself beyond immediate experience, to conceptualize and to perfect his knowledge, as well as that which points out his essential limitation, the finiteness of his soul, his propensity for delusion and error. In this sense, the Enlightenment exhibits a deep suspicion of its own conditions of possibility (signs and language). It resolves this conflict with itself by projecting an ideal future state free of the deceptive opacity of sign use.[24]

Lavater shared this suspicion and a version of this hope. Therefore his declared belief in Christ's transfigured body aimed at mediating between this imperfect world of physiognomic signs and the perfect world of transparency in the afterlife. Relying on his "physiognomic genius," he undertook a task of relating these worlds meaningfully in his own discourse apart. But his phenomenological anchorage of the rationalist semiotics of the Enlightenment could be performed only from a position of extreme subjectivity, in which Pauline enunciation met with the concept of genius as found in the expressive aesthetic theory of Johann Gottfried Herder and the literary movement of Sturm und Drang.

In his practice of discursive bricolage, Lavater successfully conjoined an "aesthetics" with a "corporeal metaphysics," recombining and drawing on the most diverse ideas whenever they could serve his purpose. Like Paul in

Badiou's description, Lavater presents us "with a schema of discourses. And this schema is designed to position a third discourse, his own, in such a way as to render its complete originality apparent."[25]

Lavater "diagonalized" (again Badiou) the thought of the Enlightenment with the revelations of the scriptures to produce the truth that was his own. If belief could be squared with reason, he reckoned, one could win back to faith the Enlightenment intellectuals who were increasingly straying from God. Johann Wolfgang von Goethe was among the many targets who saw through this subversive scheme, but he pinned down best the features of Lavater's discourse when, after seven years of friendship, the poet finally turned away, contemptuously calling the pastor a "sophist" and a "prophet."[26]

Lavater's enterprise is of primary interest to us as a religious phenomenon carried out in the secular public sphere with a social and cultural goal in mind. By aiming at integrating intellectuals into a virtual spiritual community (that is, the body of Christ), Lavater inadvertently joined in carrying out another important social task of the epoch which was perceived by many as especially urgent in the feudally fragmented German-speaking world—a unification of the "German republic of letters" characterized by its parochialism and lack of economic and cultural ties. In his double role as pastor and poet, Lavater actively mediated between the intellectual world, in which he participated through publications, traveling, talks at societal gatherings, and correspondence, and the much more diverse Christian domain represented by his church, in which he had occupied clerical functions throughout his life. Indeed, Weigelt, who approached the eclectic phenomenon of "Lavater" through the pastor's intentionality, saw his historical significance above all in his role as an avatar of communication: "Lavater energetically participated in almost all theological and intellectual movements of his time; maintained contacts with almost all significant persons of the century, and engaged in the most diverse fields with his restless pen; to which one must add his immense epistolary exchange with partners over half of Europe."[27]

The body of Christ, conceived trans-confessionally, was not in the least one of those unifying medial concepts that Lavater invested with a similar potential of "cultural transfer and collective identity" that in the cultural consciousness of the late eighteenth century was associated mostly with the book trade and publishing.[28] In fact, for decades before the establishment of a German nation, publication projects had been compensating culturally for the politically and religiously divided German lands. When in 1774 Klopstock organized a subscription of his self-published *German Republic of Scholars*, Goethe famously praised the "right-thinking" subscribers to this publication as patriots fullfilling a "sacred duty."[29]

In this sense Lavater's relentless mediation among the intellectuals of his time who represented different fields of knowledge and different persuasions can be regarded as an attempt to create a unified cultural space. This attempt might be best understood if compared in its overall agenda with that of Lavater's more pragmatic enlightened contemporary and intellectual adversary, the German publisher Friedrich Nicolai, whose publishing efforts, especially the establishment of the prominent periodical *Allgemeine Deutsche Bibliothek*, strove to mediate among scholarly disciplines and the European educated public.[30]

Yet Lavater wanted not only to create but also to redeem the German republic of letters. Against all the odds, in his discourse that he developed within yet laid athwart to the tenets of the Enlightenment, Lavater set out to teach his contemporaries the art of seeing, paving their path to redemption methodically and systematically with the body of Christ as a map and the topos of *imitatio Christi* as a vehicle.

The Pastor as Poet of the Transfigured Body

In his poetic imagination of the transfigured body, Lavater relied on the scriptural descriptions (Matt. 17:2; Luke 9:28–29) according to which the transfigured Christ on Mount Tabor gave off light:

> After his resurrection, Jesus had an immortal, very healthy body, which was beautiful and resistant to disease. One could, of course, see it with earthly eyes and touch it with one's hands but it also possessed the propensity to fine down to the condition of total invisibility. That an earthly body can be transfigured, which means that it can absorb and emanate light, is clear from the example of Moses and from the transfiguration of Christ. (Lavater, *Aussichten in die Ewigkeit*, 118)

Inspired by the witness of Matthew and Luke, Lavater envisioned the transfigured body as a purely energetic intensity, a luminous human shape that continues living after the earthly flesh has died and decayed. He insisted that all Christians would turn into the ethereal substance of pure light upon their resurrection in agreement with Paul's words about their future "conformity" (*Gleichförmigkeit*) with Christ (Lavater, *Aussichten in die Ewigkeit*, 29). The frontispiece of the *Prospects'* first edition features an image of such postmortal transformation of an earthly body into a heavenly one. It portrays a corpse left behind on the shadowy earth, whereas the new body of the same shape flies up in a beam of light. (See fig. 3.1.)

The transfigured body, as Lavater imagined it, would be of a happy physicality, not only imperishable and invulnerable to all earthly torments of hunger, disease, exhaustion, and desire, but also perfectly mobile and sociable in that it becomes an enhanced medium of transportation, communication, and perception. It could move in all directions at the speed of light, transmit information energetically without language, and have sharpened sight and hearing.

Figure 3.1. Postmortal transfiguration. Lavater's *Prospects into Eternity*, frontispiece of the third volume of the first edition, 1773.

Through its energy, it would always be drawn to the kindred spirits and therefore never feel lonely or alienated from others, even if those others are thousands of light-years away. And moreover, this body would be in happy harmony with the will that drives it, diluting, diffusing, or focusing into a point as it pleases without abandoning its overall shape. In its lack of physical limitations, it is a form of absolute empowerment. These capacities, already there in the human potential, would be fully realized only in the afterlife.

Lavater's wishful projection of the happiness (*Glückseligkeit*) of living in eternity strikes us as a statement on earthly existence as pure suffering, as it is experienced from the point of view of a lonely, sickly, powerless individual. Lavater's vision of the afterlife had indeed a highly personal, subjective dimension. It partially grew out of the religious quest of his youth when he attempted to aesthetically counteract the first inklings of existential discontent.

Max Wehrli's account of the complicated fusion of artistic and religious quest that informed the young Lavater's most intimate reflections makes evident an extraordinary place, a place apart, that Lavater already as a young man occupied in the context of the "enlightened reasonability" (*aufgeklärte Vernünftigkeit*) and "pietistic feeling" (*pietistische Empfindung*) of his contemporaries:

The recently published letters of Lavater at the age of eighteen to twenty testify to an almost horrifyingly intensive, passionate religious life. His consciousness of sin, his thoughts about death and punishment could border on orthodox in terms of dogma. But what is entirely new is the appearance, at the same time, of his desperate eagerness for personal engagement and his attempt to find a way of liberation between prayer and rhetoric.

In the nightly meditations, inspired by Young's *Night Thoughts*, the letter-writer seeks to bring his friends over into a kind of a prayer-community, which would work on bringing about happiness by crying and praying together. Friendship, shared humanity, is revealed herein as the innermost, religious motive of his contemporary joy of communication.[31]

This way of liberation that leads between prayer and rhetoric and implies a strong personal engagement was Lavater's invention of Christ's postmortem body as a model of happy collectivity. His diaries indicate that already in 1763–64 he had started thinking about a poetic work on the afterlife, which would combine philosophical and Christian viewpoints so as to be relevant to his "contemporary way of thinking."[32] At that time, his adopted version of the mild Enlightenment theology was focused primarily on the ethics of religious belief. Only in 1768, with the publication of the first volume of the *Prospects* and with the sudden loss of his bosom friend (*Herzens-Freund*) Felix Hess, did his views undergo a "theological turn" (*theologische Umorientierung*), transforming into a Christ-centered obsession.[33]

When Hess died rapidly from pulmonary tuberculosis, Lavater tried in vain to bring him back to life by means of prayer. To compensate for this failure, Lavater started cultivating the performative aspect of the religious idiom, the language that could "do things with words" and even perform miracles. Several scholars observed that Lavater's expectation of "magic-poetical effectiveness" from his project on the afterlife made his theology border on sorcery.[34] The personal trauma of failing to forestall his friend's death became the event of his conversion to a different type of discourse, which he perceived as his apostolic mission. Lavater came to think of himself as a founder of a new, absolutely original form of "intellectualized Christianity." Therefore he dissociated himself emphatically from all authorities of the Christian tradition, even though he absorbed indiscriminately all of them: "Such names as Zwingli, Calvin, Luther, the Pope, the Council, reformed, Lutheran, Catholic are just nullities for me, and for my inner man, for my religion, for my enjoyment of God."[35] He claims that his position is incomparable to anything else, though he admits to being very well acquainted with the thought of his contemporaries: "For centuries there has been no Christian writer who saw the things as I do, that means, absolutely, no Luther, no Calvin, no one before that, no Augustine, no Origen, even if they said something about the force of prayer."[36]

In the *Prospects*, he claims the same originality for his poem as he does in regard to his theological position. He shrugs off with a quasi-enlightened gesture all traditional metaphysical and moral proofs of immortality as "mere assumptions" (*bloß Vermuthungsgründe*) (Lavater, *Aussichten in die Ewigkeit*, 41). Instead, Bonnet's demand that science take "the liberty of conjecturing entirely from physics" guided his "methodology." Bonnet insisted on the liberty of building theoretical systems on the basis of empirically amassed material in order to resist the reduction of science to a purely descriptive function, that is, to "mere observations."[37]

Following the hint, Lavater projected his "scientific" system of the afterlife entirely from this life, relating the former to the latter as a macrocosm to a microcosm: "There are organic bodies that are related to ours in terms of their size as one to a billion; hence there can equally be a now yet invisible world of organic bodies, to which our bodies are related as one to a billion" (Lavater, *Aussichten in die Ewigkeit*, 27). The idea of an explicitly physical continuity between this life and the afterlife allows him to make the afterlife graspable to the readers through its analogy to this life. In this way, he can present it as a concrete and reachable goal. Moreover, he can construe it as a different but analogous text. Therefore he writes: "My poem should be governed by the idea of a natural connection between all our future and present thoughts and abilities" (Lavater, *Aussichten in die Ewigkeit*, 77).

The systematic discursive mini-model of the world created in his philosophical poem owes a debt to the pioneer of European scientific discourse, Francis Bacon, who argued in *De Augmentis Scientiarum*: "That philosophy only is the true one which reproduces most faithfully the statements of nature, and is written down, as it were, from nature's dictation so that it is nothing but a copy and a reflection [*simulacrum et reflectio*] of nature, and adds nothing of its own, but is merely a repetition and echo."[38] Lavater responded to the idea that besides reflecting the world in abstract concepts and judgments, philosophy is supposed to constitute its simulated model. He construes the perfectibility of the world in Bacon's early modern philosophical manner, that is, by making it intelligible in the very process of its simulation. His philosophical simulacrum performs the transfiguration of the physical world, first, by accounting for reality's imperfections and, then, by filtering them out and postulating an improved and purified version of it in a utopia of the afterlife.

Bacon's philosophy was still closely allied with hermeticism and alchemy. This sensibility carries over into Lavater's poem, as testified by his frequent use of an alchemical idiom. For example, the refined body which the soul would acquire in the afterlife is related to the earthly body in Lavater's parlance as the quintessence to *caput mortuum*, the sediment that is left behind after distillation in an alchemical process (Lavater, *Aussichten in die Ewigkeit*, 89).

In his vision of the transfigured body, Lavater imitates the Baconian scientific method of induction: empirical observations of nature are to be matched with scriptural "hypotheses" about the afterlife and resurrection. Lavater's goal is to show that God's physical revelation in nature is identical with his revelation in the scriptures. The divine certainty of religious propositions allows for conclusions about the natural qualities of the transfigured body: "If it is, for example, certain that our body will be con-form (*gleichförmig*) to the body of Christ (Rom. 6:5), then it is equally certain that it will be free from all disease; because it is obvious that this particular idea is contained in the general premise of the con-formity of both bodies" (Lavater, *Aussichten in die Ewigkeit*, 29).

Despite his claim to scientific methodology, the relation of nature to the scriptures as well as the correlation of this life and the afterlife in Lavater's outline for a poem *Prospects into Eternity* looks much like a poetic metaphor. Its double structure is held together solely by the lyrical subject who in Lavater's discourse acquires apostolic features. To change the contemporary way of thinking through the so-conceived "proof" of the afterlife, Lavater had to enter his discourse in person. It is meaningful that he offered his own body as an object of study and a medium of communication between the physical and metaphysical worlds:

> I start now with observations about my existence, my conception, my growth, my physical and moral force, about the things I perceive outside me, about the reason and origin of this all; and in this way I come to surmise that there is one invisible, omnipotent, reasonable, good creator of the nature. I put myself ahead under the perspective of the well-chosen grounds for this surmise, by means of which it grows into a conviction. (Lavater, *Aussichten in die Ewigkeit*, 33)

Lavater's self-observation imitates Paul, who referred to his own afflicted body and his apostolic sufferings to explain the notion of immortality. Lavater's epigraph to the poem, inviting the reader to "look not to the things that are seen but to the things that are unseen," is extracted from Paul's Second Letter to the Corinthians where the apostle opposes the outer and inner body: "So we do not lose heart. Though our outer nature is wasting away, our inner nature is being renewed every day. For this slight momentary affliction is preparing for us an eternal weight of glory beyond all comparison because we look not to the things that are seen but to the things that are unseen; for the things that are seen are transient, but the things that are unseen are eternal" (2 Cor. 4:16–18, RSV).

Affliction does not discourage Paul because he knows that it does not affect his inner body which is about to resurrect with the Lord. But the certainty of this knowledge is assured merely through his enunciation of belief advanced from the positionality of a poetic subject. In fact, Paul grounds his proclamation of faith with a quotation from a psalm: "Since we have the same spirit of faith as he had who wrote, 'I believed, and so I spoke,' we too believe, and so we speak, knowing that he who raised the Lord Jesus will raise us also with Jesus and bring us with you into his presence" (2 Cor. 4:13–14, RSV).

Poetic subjectivity provides here for the positionality of the speaker. The "subjective materiality"[39] which Badiou discerned in Pauline enunciation and which Lavater sensitively borrowed from the scriptural source informs the poetic self-consciousness of his project on immortality as well as of his discourse at large. Lavater's later work *Worte Jesu* (*Words of Jesus*, 1792) shows that he indeed conceived of a poet of religious lyrics as a medium of divinity. The poet working in the genre is for him identical with Christ himself who "lives and weaves in him. He puts him such words in the mouth that only Him and none other could say, or have said. The poet loses himself entirely in Him. He, the poet, is not noticeable—One sees and hears only the Lord, whose Words he was honored to grasp."[40]

Thus Lavater's claim to the poetic form for his vision of immortality was meant to back up his claim to mediation between the human and the divine: "I am compelled to insist: The creator of my nature must *will* that I am immortal; and to make me calmly convinced that he wills it, he must let me know in some clear, determinate way, that he wills."[41] The pastor-poet aspired to the role of an oracle of Christ, which would empower his discourse as the expression of the divine truth.

The literary historian Hans Wylsing aptly described the apostolic features of Lavater's notorious narcissism:

> The tender confusion between apostolic force and a narcissistic sense of omnipotence characterizes Lavater's historical situation. Today one recognizes narcissism as a form of secularized imitation of God, as self-deification. However, in Lavater this secularization has not yet been accomplished: his self-indulgence is always an experience of the "holy gifts," and this obliges him, despite all bliss, to humility. In his "Mixed Non-Physiognomic Rules to the Knowledge of the Self and Mankind" (1787/88), Lavater described his situation with winning pointedness: "Who does not believe in himself, as he puts it, does not believe in others, nor in God."[42]

This type of deified narcissism with an admixture of humility recalls the Pauline topos of *imitatio Christi*. In the *Prospects*, Lavater, indeed, calls his contemporaries to imitate him as he imitates Christ in doing good and suffering evil "so that Christ can live in me, and I'll become con-form to his death" (*so dass Christus in mir lebe, und ich seinem Tode gleichförmig werde*) (Lavater, *Aussichten in die Ewigkeit*, 117). His call for the imitation of Christ attempts to give a practical recipe for achieving immortality: if one learns how to be "con-form" (*gleichförmig*) with his body in this life, one will be able to also become "con-form" with him in the afterlife.

To the highest moral perfection, of which [Christ] gave the most noble example in the eyes of heaven and earth, should be added intellectual, physical, and political perfections. Human nature rises in him to the highest conceivable perfection. He shines through the unfathomable expanses of the creation as the most perfect example of the wisest belief and obedience to God, and at the same time of the largest, noblest, and most sublime happiness.—*Through him and because of him, numberless new undertakings to make mankind happy are launched and accomplished.* (Lavater, *Aussichten in die Ewigkeit*, 58; emphasis added)

The "scientific" aspect of the *Prospects* is related to the poetic one as the content to its uptake, that is, as are the perlocutionary and illocutionary dimensions of a performative utterance. After all, Lavater was inventing a discourse which would inaugurate the new law and thus promote "the happiness of mankind." Regarding his audacious, if not fanatic, self-appointment as the founder of a "new religion," his presentation of the project as a draft for a poem might have also served as a defense against clerical censorship. Upon the publication of the first volume of the *Prospects*, Lavater was effectively exposed to harsh denunciations by religious authorities who accused him of heresy with regard to the doctrine of resurrection. The accusation resulted in an official investigation by the church. Lavater's insistence on the freedom of poetic imagination, in fact, helped him out of his predicament.

Polemics with Kant

Lavater's quasi-scholarly and aesthetic project was subversively aimed at the educated upper classes, the "philosophical Christians" (Lavater, *Aussichten in die Ewigkeit*, 19). In the introduction to the first volume of the *Prospects*, Lavater announces that there is an appropriate medium of communication with each group in society. His book is meant for a few elect intellectuals, since whatever goes beyond the daily paper in style and content can only be for a limited audience. To the broader populace, however, he prefers not to write but to speak as a pastor in the church (ibid., 21).

The major target of Lavater's polemics against "philosophical Christians" was Immanuel Kant. The *Prospects* was directly aimed at Kant's *Träume eines Geistersehers* (*Dreams of a Spirit-Seer*, 1766).[43] In this early piece Kant bid farewell to metaphysical spiritism, taking the Swedish theologian and visionary Emanuel Swedenborg for its unfortunate, caricatural stand-in. The *Prospects* contain two direct polemical references to Kant's treatise against Swedenborg. The one appears characteristically in the eleventh letter, where Lavater portrays the heavenly, transfigured body:

> I wish that Kant of Königsberg had written something about it. But
> I am afraid that the man would not be concerned with this mat-
> ter, since, despite such rare and considerable philosophical genius,
> he reasons in such an unphilosophical way about the influence of
> the illumination of teaching about the immortality of the soul and
> the nature of our future condition on our moral life. It might be that
> his lack of disposition to philosophize about the future comes from
> moral considerations; he might have seen a lot of people who lived
> in an ever more undignified way the more they philosophized about
> the future; and this might be the reason why he prefers to go culti-
> vate the garden with Voltaire's *Candide*. (Lavater, *Aussichten in die
> Ewigkeit*, 319)

This passage refers to the conclusion of Kant's treatise, where the philosopher denies that a belief in the afterlife is necessary as a guarantor for moral
behavior and jokes that to assure his salvation he had better go cultivate his
garden, like Voltaire's Candide.[44] Lavater voices his regrets about losing in
Kant an enlightened philosophical ally.

The pastor provocatively presents himself as an advocate of the Enlightenment, even if he deals with the traditional problems of the soul. His choice
of the word "illumination" (*Beleuchtung*) in regard to his creative appropriation of Swedenborg for his project on immortality is obviously polemically
opposed to the Enlightenment (*Aufklärung*) of Kant's critical philosophy.
Lavater seems to be committed to the idea of correcting Kant, especially if
one considers that elsewhere in the *Prospects* he emphatically pronounces
that "it is not reason but God's revelation that teaches us" (*Nicht die Ver-
nunft, sondern die Offenbarung Gottes belehret uns, mein Lieber!*) (Lavater,
Aussichten in die Ewigkeit, 97).

The second open reference to Kant appears in the thirteenth letter, where
Lavater enumerates instances of communication between this and that
world. Lavater tells an anecdote about Swedenborg's alleged clairvoyance,
which Kant rejected in his treatise as a distortion of rumors and gossip. But
Lavater subversively presents the issue as if Kant, who considered Swedenborg insane, took it seriously: "Another example is the anecdote that Mr.
Kant of Königsberg—no weak head—recounts about Emanuel Swedenborg,
who saw, from Gothenburg, a fire in Stockholm and described it to a group
of people" (Lavater, *Aussichten in die Ewigkeit*, 429).

Swedenborg, who claimed to be able to see spirits and to communicate
with the world beyond, was, with Bonnet, another great inspiration behind
Lavater's vision of the afterlife. Lavater took Swedenborg seriously. He wrote
to him twice after the death of Felix Hess to inquire about the postmortem
condition of his deceased friend. The fact that in the *Prospects* he counts Kant
among the intellectual addressees of his intended poem signals an attempt to
mediate between Kant's and Swedenborg's seemingly irreconcilable positions.

He sent a published copy of the *Prospects* to both, asking them for feedback. In both cases, his request went without a response.

In his *Prospects*, a Swedenborgian project in spirit, Lavater attempted to silently correct Swedenborg in light of Kant's criticism in order to confront Kant on improved premises. The major point of Kant's objections to Swedenborg and to metaphysics in general is the materiality of spirits. Swedenborg understood them as corporeal beings. In response to Swedenborg's claim that he could see spirits, Kant dedicated a whole chapter to the corporeality of spirits, illustrating that it cannot be experienced and therefore proved but can only be speculated about.

Kant exposed the logical difficulties in thinking "spirit" or "soul" as material, that is, as "spiritual substance." Such a substance would by definition share physical qualities of "matter" and hence immediately comply with the notion of "matter," rendering the word "spirit" meaningless. Even if "spirits" were defined otherwise as "immaterial beings,"[45] their immaterial nature would mean that they do not fill the space in which they are present. But if they can't be experienced through the senses, they are unthinkable: "I cannot think in the concrete of their activity, because it has no analogy with my conceptions from experience" (Kant, *Dreams of a Spirit-Seer*, 46). And further, Kant presents the problem in a way that anticipates his future antinomies: "The possibility of the existence of immaterial beings can, therefore, be supposed without fear of its being disproved, but also without hope of proving it by reason" (ibid., 47).

When Lavater sets out to prove by reason the existence of the afterlife, using analogies between the empirical experience of nature and the text of the scriptures, his enterprise appears as a direct response to Kant's sarcastic provocation: "He who is in possession of means which can lead more easily to this intelligence, should not deny instruction to one eager to learn, before whose eyes, in the progress of research, Alps often rise where others see before them a level and comfortable footpath on which they walk forward, or think they do so" (Kant, *Dreams of a Spirit-Seer*, 48).

Lavater, indeed, sets out in his *Prospects* to instruct Kant on the issue, especially since Kant himself had conceded that organic matter must possess some spiritual essence:

> It seems that a spiritual essence is inmostly present in matter, and that it does not act upon those forces which determine the mutual relations of elements, but upon the inner principle of their state. For every substance, even a simple element of matter, must have an inner activity as the reason for its external efficiency, although I cannot specify in what it consists. (*Dreams of a Spirit-Seer*, 54)

Lavater perceives this spiritual essence, which Kant also admits in matter, as a metaphysical world of divine energy. This inner essence is one and the same in all organic matter, but it presses bodies into different shapes and thus allows for multiplicity in the world of phenomena. In Lavater's theory, in the afterlife this spiritual essence will be experienced physically as pure intensity, light, energy in a way unmediated by the senses, even though it does not fill space as does matter. But Lavater argues that it can be experienced already in this life, though only mediately—as representation.

Kant leaves open the question of how matter and its inner spiritual essence might be combined. This issue, he says, defies reason. He agrees that the spiritual world is conceivable and even explains the operation of thought behind its conception. In his chapter entitled "A Fragment of Secret Philosophy Aiming to Establish Communion with the Spirit-World," he argues that the human mind abstracts through the bodily senses the material qualities of the world and projects them into the realm of metaphysics. The spiritual world is created fully through analogy to the physical one, and consequently is nothing but its representation. In response to this, Lavater's *Prospects* focused on explaining the mechanism of the connection between the physical world and its spiritual essence through the interjection of Bonnet's teaching. But in his polemical fervor, he conceived of this connection not as purely mental but as physical and sensory.

Despite his concession to the "inner essence," Kant absolutely denies any possibility that the physical and metaphysical worlds could communicate. Hence, Lavater's interest in proving such communication—first, through his studies of the occult which he hoped could deliver examples to the contrary and, then, through his own discourse on the afterlife and physiognomy. The message of divine energy, according to him, is incarnated in physical flesh and therefore can be deciphered on the basis of internal self-observation as well as the external reading of faces. He sees the human body itself as a mediator between the earthly and divine realms.

Thus, ironically, it was none other than Kant himself who suggested to Lavater *a contrario* the scenario of his subversive discourse. In the preface to *Dreams of a Spirit-Seer*, the philosopher openly states that metaphysics is purely a matter of verbal manipulation. In the chapter entitled "A Complicated Metaphysical Knot Which Can Be Untied or Cut According to Choice," he debates the deceptiveness of language, insisting that the words "spirit" or "spiritual nature" describe merely the illusions of the senses. "But if you ask, how could this conception arise at all, if not from experience?" Kant continues, "I answer: many conceptions arise in secret and obscure conclusions incidental to experiences, and afterwards are transmitted to other minds without even the consciousness of that experience or conclusion which has first established the conception. Such conceptions may be called 'surreptitious'" (Kant, *Dreams of a Spirit-Seer*, 42).

To counteract this accusation of "secret and obscure conclusions," Lavater makes his choice "to untie the metaphysical knot" in his discourse apart by turning to his advantage the "surreptitious" work of language. Despite Kant's contempt for the rhetorical subterfuge in establishing the alternative realities, when elaborating on his concession to metaphysics, that is, on the spiritual essence of matter, Kant himself went off on a tangent and sketched a discourse, which he placed apart within his own philosophy and marked by a series of asterisks:

* * * * * *

It would be beautiful if such a systematic constitution of the spirit-world, as we conceive it, could be determined, or only with some probability supposed, not merely from the conception of spiritual being in general, which is altogether too hypothetical, but from an actual and universally conceded observation. Therefore I venture upon the indulgence of the reader and insert here an attempt at something of this kind which, although somewhat out of my way, and far enough removed from evidence, still seems to give occasion for not unpleasant surmises. (Kant, *Dreams of a Spirit-Seer*, 62)

The discourse apart that Kant speculatively put forth is about ethics. He recast spirituality as morality modeled on Newton's laws of gravitation, say, attraction:

Should it not be possible to conceive the phenomenon of moral impulses in the mutual relation of thinking creatures as the consequence of an actual force, consisting in the fact that spiritual natures flow into each other? The sense of morality then would be the sensation of this dependence of the individual will upon the will of all, and would be a consequence of the natural and universal interaction whereby the immaterial world attains its unity, namely, by conforming itself to a system of spiritual perfection, according to the laws of this sense of morality, which would constitute its mode of cohesion. (Kant, *Dreams of a Spirit-Seer*, 65)

Lavater built upon this Kantian concession. His body of Christ operates through the Newtonian law of attraction. God's love is the strong magnetic point to which all is drawn. Christ's body functions as an energetic criterion for identifying and integrating the righteous into a moral community while rejecting the unjust. The moral quality of the members, reflected in their energy, determines this body's hierarchy. This answers a problem raised by Kant, who had observed that morality can always be dissimulated among people of finite perception and judgment and is therefore of no consequence in this world. Hence, its consequences are usually projected into the world beyond.

Lavater did precisely that: he transposed into the other world the scenario of the morally transparent, transfigured body. To resist Kant's argument that "he [man] is not entitled to imagine new and arbitrary arrangements in the present or future world, according to some scheme of his own wisdom which he prescribes to the divine will" (Kant, *Deams of a Spirit-Seer*, 67), the pastor-poet boldly assumed the positionality of the imitation of Christ and provocatively asserted the divine will behind his imagining such "new and arbitrary arrangements," and went on to claim its empirical "proof."

The *Physiognomic Fragments*, or an "Education for Eternity"

Lavater's *Physiognomic Fragments, Designed to Promote the Knowledge and Love of Mankind* (1775) were inspired around the same time and by the same circle of friends (Felix Hess and Georg Johann Zimmermann) as the projected poem on immortality.[46] Lavater came upon physiognomy, as he tells in the introduction, when he tried to draw the face of his bosom friend Felix Hess and so discovered the meaningful similarity of his nose with the nose of another friend, Lambert. Zimmermann, the addressee of the *Prospects*, also encouraged Lavater to pursue his investigation about the possible connections between human features and character traits and even published his first experimentations, allegedly without Lavater's knowledge.

The *Fragments* are a practical counterpart to the theoretical speculations of the *Prospects*, and as such they play the major role in Lavater's rebuttal of Kant. With them, Lavater attempted to demonstrate that morality can be visible already in this world and to prove that the connection between physics and metaphysics is not an arbitrary but a necessary one. For Lavater, the art of physiognomic seeing anticipates on earth the transparency and moral readability of human beings which the *Prospects* portrayed as the "natural" result of postmortem transfiguration:

> There is nothing arbitrary here. The separation of the righteous from the unrighteous, the determination of fate, the revelation of the inner-most disposition of everyone, the measure of corporeal perfection and imperfection, all these are the natural consequences which follow immediately from the essence of all things and from the interdependence of all physical, pneumatic and moral forces in accordance with the simplest laws. (Lavater, *Aussichten in die Ewigkeit*, 132)

To Bonnet's biological perfectibility of species, Lavater adds their moral perfectibility. Lavater maintains the biological and providential determinism of Bonnet but differentiates it ethically. In this way it is the necessary natural law that draws the good ones to Christ and repulses the evil ones from him in the afterlife. But the "good" or "evil" energy intrinsic in physical bodies also shapes them into "good" or "bad" appearances: "Bodies drew, absorbed and reflected more or less light in accordance with their souls' will, which formed through their intentions their appearances" (Lavater, *Aussichten in die Ewigkeit*, 119).

Lavater revises Bonnet's understanding that human beings can interfere neither with preexistent conditions nor with the physical development of species toward perfection. Lavater accepts that one cannot influence at will the physical perfectibility of species, but he allows human beings to better their position in the future heavenly orders by improving their moral disposition in this life and thus charging their bodies with positive energy. In the end, it is up to the souls, or rather to the human intentionality, how much energy to absorb and to reflect, and hence what to look like.

This ethical differentiation in Lavater's "scientific" discourse betrays the influence of Swedenborg's teaching about correspondences. In Swedenborg's version of Platonism the world beyond is related to this world as an "idea" (*Urbild*) is related to an "image" (*Abbild*). This relation applies not only to the forms of things but also to all kinds of forces, motions, and actions. The physical world thus corresponds absolutely to the invisible metaphysical one. But most importantly, Swedenborg situates the metaphysical world within the subject so that the correlation of this and that world becomes one of outer and inner man:

> One can also know that such forms don't exist in spirit, as they appear in mimicry, but are just the tendencies, which are so represented; further that such actions don't take place in spirit, as they appear in the actions of the body, but are the thoughts, which are so formed; what belongs to the spirit is spiritual, but what belongs to the body is natural. Hence, it is clear that there are correspondences between the spiritual and natural, and that spiritual things are preformed in the natural ones, or (what is the same), when what belongs to the inner man, is represented in the outer one, then it is that what appears in the outer one performs the inner one, and what coincides is a correspondence.[47]

Since the inner man is supposed to be in the likeness of God, the outer man should also physically correspond to God's image. The body, which in its imperfection is still far from divinity, is not just a mirror of the soul. It can also be used as a tool to achieve inner perfection by conscious effort. Therefore Lavater asks in the sixth letter of the *Prospects*: "The question is thus: in what kind of connection the present and future lives are standing?" and suggests that this life is "an education for eternity" (*Lehrzeit für die Ewigkeit*) (Lavater, *Aussichten in die Ewigkeit*, 63).

The Physiognomic Fragments are conceived as a textbook for this education. The epigraph to the *Fragments* significantly reads: "God created the human being in his likeness" (*Gott schuff den Menschen zu seinem Bilde*), whereas in the concomitant project of *Prospects* Lavater played with the topos of the loss of God's image in man. There he compared God's presence in the human body with a painting covered with dust (Lavater, *Aussichten in die Ewigkeit*, 247–48). Swedenborg explained the loss of God's image in man as a result of hubris, which set the person in place of God and thus resulted in the distortion of human features and the loss of physiognomic transparency. At the origin of mankind, according to Swedenborg, people were innocent and therefore absolutely transparent as to their emotions and intentions. The inner and outer man coincided so perfectly that dissimulation was by definition impossible.

The egotism of the fallen human being destroys the original harmony between inner and outer man. His face becomes a mask that dissimulates egotistical intentions instead of mirroring the soul. The place between human soul (*anima*) and face comes to be occupied by the *animus* of desires and passions. Even though each person carries his or her own mask, which still yields the character traits, its crust-like inflexibility obstructs access to the soul's immediate expression. To reach out to the human soul through the crust of a dissimulating face, one needs the gift of the Holy Spirit.[48] This idea encourages Lavater's belief in his own "physiognomic genius"[49] and inspires his self-appointment as the physiognomic educator of mankind.

The Physiognomic Fragments contain a chapter on images of Christ. This chapter connects the ideas of the *Prospects* with the practice of physiognomy. Its goal is to correlate the metaphysical body of the poem and the earthly human body, the empirical realm of physiognomics. Lavater wants to train human beings to observe each other and themselves so that they can estimate and influence their future position as members of Christ's transfigured body. The difference between future perfection and temporary imperfection is supposed to serve an educational purpose by alerting his contemporaries to the necessity of ethical precautions.

The invisibility of Christ on earth is central to the physiognomic enterprise, the goal of which is to visualize the original divinity hidden in the human body. Lavater comes up with a heuristic device of the "physiognomic body," which is meant to mediate between the transfigured and the earthly body. It is represented by the silhouettes to which in *The Physiognomic Fragments* Lavater reduces human beings in order to decipher their characters because the profiles anticipate their future resurrected shapes. In his discussion of the prophets, who will govern with Christ on earth at the first stage of resurrection, Lavater holds that their bodies will be like a shadow-contour (*Schattenbild*), or a "type" of the luminous one they are going to acquire in heaven.

The physiognomic analysis of profiles had been inspired by Lavater's belief in bone structure, the actual subject matter of his type of physiognomy. The part of the body that he expected to resurrect is the eternal part of the human being. In the eleventh letter about the heavenly bodies of the righteous, Lavater calls this part the "stem." The stem is the skeleton which is left behind after death. After the flesh has decayed, it will be dressed in the glorious raiment of the resurrected body. It is this bone structure that the shadow-profile is expected to pin down, providing a preview of the human "con-formity" with Christ.

In the chapter of the *Fragments* on the images of Christ, he conceives of "seeing Christ" (*Christus Sehen*), traditionally the matter of mystical revelation, as a matter of "aesthetic education." In the *Prospects*, Lavater declares that his intention is "to confirm the invisible in the middle of a storm of visible irritations; to hold the great, enough confirmed truth: Jesus is alive, even if we don't see him any more!" (Lavater, *Aussichten in die Ewigkeit,* 162). The *Fragment* is designed so as to fully embrace this dilemma. It opens with the words: "Maybe no mortal should dare to draw an image of Christ. Certainly, nobody could draw a dignified one. It is strange that the evangelists, even the favorite one of the Lord, tell us nothing about his appearance and features."[50]

The word "dignified" (*würdig*) is the central aesthetic category which anchors Lavater's reflections on the image of Christ in the intellectual context of his time. In fact, he defines "dignified" later as "correct" (*richtig*). The lack of this kind of images was already noted, he says elsewhere, in Herder's reflections on the lack of authentic iconology in German religious art. The impossibility of a "dignified" mimetic likeness of Christ reflects the impossibility of representing the divine energy living in human bodies. The evangelists' silence in this regard, says Lavater, implies that words might be powerless to provide an adequate description of Christ, who defies any representation in paint or language. And yet, it is only through the representations of our mind that one can have an access to Christ: "I don't think that we should not make an image of him for ourselves. It is partly unavoidable because of the nature and condition of things and partly impossible because of the nature of our imagination that we would not think him in some imprecise or precise human form" (Lavater, *Physiognomische Fragmente,* 104).

Lavater uses the lack of objective testimonies to Christ's appearance to situate his image in the subjective realm of imagination. It is in the nature of our cognition to picture Christ in a more or less definite human form, and this mental image defies both the ecclesiastical prohibition of images as well as the aesthetic requirement of imitation of nature. But whether it be as a mind-image or as a painting, the representation of Christ is always at odds with our innate sense of a "dignified," that is, "correct" image of Christ: "But as much as it is impossible that we make a dignified, that is, a correct image of him, it is very easy for us to sense the lack of dignity and falsity of many of his images. Without being able to sketch his ideal, we can say with certainty: Of all existent heads of Christ is none worthy of the great character" (Lavater, *Physiognomische Fragmente,* 104–5).

The notion of dignity (*Würde*) that Lavater engages here can be traced back to Henry Home's sensualist aesthetics (*Wirkungsästhetik*). In the *Elements of Criticism*, Home defined dignity as a natural principle of human self-understanding: "Man is endowed with a sense of the worth and excellence of his nature: he deems it more perfect than that of the other beings around him; and he perceives that the perfection of his nature consists in virtues, particularly in virtues of the highest rank. To express that sense, the term *dignity* is appropriated."[51]

On the basis of this innate sense of dignity, Home develops the category of aesthetic judgment. An artistic performance is judged in terms of its impact on the human being and his sense of dignity. The category of dignity is anthropological in nature and is applied, first of all, to human actions as they are depicted in art. In this sense the "dignified" image of Christ is supposed to match his actions, narrated by the evangelists, and make the same impression on the viewer as the reading of the Gospels. Since, according to Home, "virtuous actions justly possess the highest of all the ranks," it is easy to conclude that the depiction of Christ would be the highest of arts.

The sympathetic relation between the artistic subject matter and the recipient, postulated by Home, understands dignified art as an edifying experience for the human being, which heightens and ennobles his spirits. Lavater, however, employs the concept of dignity negatively. For him, it is a measure of how faulty the rich tradition of Christ iconography has been. He seeks to disengage himself from this tradition and free the grounds for his transfigured, visible Christ, the Christ of the afterlife.

As examples of such undignified, inappropriate images of Christ, he offers Winckelmann's descriptions of the Christ images by the Italian painters Carracci and Guercino.[52] Winckelmann himself praised these images as lively and heroic and opposed them to the lowbrow Christ figures of Michelangelo. He valued the youthfully beardless Christ figures modeled upon antique statues over Michelangelo's plebeian naturalism. Lavater, however, rejects both styles of representation: "At least, all those that I have seen are, if not simply offensive, then weakly expressed, either too much human, or too little, without being divine for that reason" (Lavater, *Physiognomische Fragmente*, 105).

Michelangelo's images are thus "too human," whereas the standard of Winckelmann's taste is to Lavater's judgment "too little human without possessing godlike divinity." The features borrowed from mythological antiquity do not match the character of Christ as transmitted through the Gospels. Lavater adds in a footnote:

> Why is there no one among the antique heads, of which a painter or a connoisseur of men would ever say: "This one could look like Christ!" Among many other reasons, because of the lack of humility and love. Apollo has no sparkle of spirit of Christ's physiognomy, and

he is still the most human one among the old gods. And any face of Jupiter has much less of it.—There is no face among gods, of which one could say: In una sede morantur majestas et amor. (Lavater, *Physiognomische Fragmente*, 105–6)

But as for Michelangelo, his Christ images are "too human" because they are modeled upon real human beings. Thus Lavater feels free to dissociate himself from the tradition of the Christ portraits in both their Italian and—with a reference to Herder—their German versions. Neither one suits his sense of dignity because "there is always at least one major integral part, without which Christ is no longer Christ, that is forgotten or ignored. Either the *human*, or the *divine*, or the *israelish*, or the *messianic*" (Lavater, *Physiognomische Fragmente*, 105).

His Christ is conceived as a whole embracing elements which are human and divine, past and future (called "israelish" and "messianic") at once. They can never be represented in full because any representation would be a reduction. As Lavater puts it: "it is possible to find such lines, but impossible to find all of them, and to bind all of them together." And nevertheless Lavater insists on the importance of ever-new attempts at visualizing Christ: "Meanwhile it is still important to make attempts 'non ut dicatur quid,' as Augustine says at a certain point, 'sed ne taceatur'" (Lavater, *Physiognomische Fragmente*, 107). The *Prospects* explains why:

> Christ is in every sense the original image of the perfectibility of human nature; the goal of the highest virtue and bliss accessible to the human nature. . . . In the future we should become similar to him in glory; — and this glory should consist in something moral, or rather, in the possession of intellectual, physical, political power directed to moral goals. (Lavater, *Aussichten in die Ewigkeit,* 160)

Christ's mediation (*Mittlertätigkeit*) between the force of God and the physical and historical world of phenomena is a crux of Lavater's theory of perception. Even if Christ can't be represented, he still can be experienced as a drive to perfection, which is reflected in the multiplicity of images and in the history of Christian iconography.

"The better images of Christ repress the worse ones, erase their fatal impression, and make it unbearable. The better the images of Christ are, the stronger is the faith in Christ. A beautiful sight of Christ produces the belief in Christ" (Lavater, *Physiognomische Fragmente*, 107). The better images of Christ are thus closer to the divine essence of his transfigured body expected in the afterlife. Therefore they also serve as a testimony to immortality. But the image of Christ, Lavater finally admits, is actually nothing but a projection of an artist's own image. Consequently, Christ's image reflects the ethical condition of humanity, which the artist embodies and represents:

Not every Christian can draw a face of Christ; but certainly even the most skilled painter would not create anything bearable without love for Christ. Each painter paints more or less himself. (In a rendition of Christ by Rubens, which is in possession of Mr. Mechel in Basel, the face of Christ is the bodily Rubens himself.) As one is, so one paints, too. (Lavater, *Physiognomische Fragmente*, 108)

The realms of ethics and aesthetics merge in Lavater's thought. In the first letter of the *Prospects*, Lavater characterizes the thinking Christians among his readers as having an "incorruptible moral, Christian, philosophical sense." He compares it to "the musical ear of a musician, and to a "painterly eye of a painter" (Lavater, *Aussichten in die Ewigkeit*, 23). In the *Fragments*, he equally relates the true Christian sensibility to the sense of perception:

The Father can draw to the Son through everything. Everything bears a testimony to Christ. To hear and see the thousand voices of the omniscient testimony to Christ: this is what I call having faith and spirit. Whoever has recognized the living fact of Christ, and therein the likeness of the Father, has faith and a sense of all truth and divinity. (Lavater, *Physiognomische Fragmente*, 107)

Christ's crucifixion, he explains, was due to the lack of physiognomic savvy: people failed to recognize the son of God in Christ and therefore in themselves. It is in order to prevent a similar mistake that one should learn to recognize the first features of Christ's transfigured image already here and now, that is, in the human potential for perfection. The better the moral condition of mankind, the finer its physiognomic sensibility, reflected in the quality of the images of Christ: "The rise and fall of Christianity entails the rise and fall in physiognomic sensibility; the rise and fall of Christianity entails the rise and fall in the beauty of the paintings of Christ" (Lavater, *Physiognomische Fragmente*, 108).

But this relation seems to be as reversible here as the one in Swedenborg's physiognomy because the beautiful images of Christ, in their turn, inspire faith. Their aesthetic perfection entails ethical perfection and vice versa. Lavater's complaint about the lack of "dignified" Christ images is thus a complaint about the ethical condition of his contemporaries. The images of Christ, the self-portraits of painters, in the end, reflect the features of Christ to the extent that any human face does. These are just individual, unaccomplished refractions of the single shining essence of Christ.

Lavater concludes the chapter by resuming the Pauline topos of the *Prospects* about the invisibility of Christ in this life: "But maybe, whoever truly believes and loves, knows Christ not after the flesh, and won't know him (this way), or shudders to dare a sketch. No one dares to paint the full sun!" (Lavater, *Physiognomische Fragmente*, 109).

Christ's "Common Image," or Physiognomic Truth

In the *Physiognomic Fragments*, Lavater comes to practice the ethics that was the goal of the outlined poem on immortality:

> With publication of his *Prospects into Eternity*, Lavater ultimately pursued an ethical goal. The future glory of the Christians could and should be adumbrated to some extent already here and now. He was thus concerned neither with a systematic development of an eschatology nor with the conception of a utopia in a narrow sense of a word, but with a proof that postmortem existence implies a requirement of a morally qualified life. With this he worked another variation on the favorite theme of his life, namely the manifestation of the transcendent in the immanent.[53]

In the chapter of the *Fragments* about images of Christ, Lavater staged a moment of such manifestation. Among eleven images that Lavater reproduced in his book, including the famous Van Dyck painting and his lesser known contemporary Chodowiecki, he smuggled one "authentic" image of Christ.[54] (See fig. 3.2.) This image is a copy of the Christ profile from an emerald which the Turkish sultan Bajazet II gave as a present to the pope in 1492. Both the legendary letter of the Roman official Lentulus testifying to the authenticity of the profile and the carved emerald itself turned out to have been faked in the fourteenth century. The image became well known from a series of medals, created around this time in imitation of the emerald. (See fig. 3.3.) Ironically, they portrayed Christ in the likeness of a fifteenth-century Flemish painting in Berlin and bore no relation to first-century iconography.[55]

Lavater reinterpreted the legend in his own terms. He separated Christ's profile from its background on the medal and from its holy nimbus, which signified its kingly and saintly status. One socially subversive aspect of Lavater's discourse that emerges in this procedure is worth mentioning. Lavater's major concern with the materiality and form of the body after death and the body's physical resurrection recuperates the dogmatic discourse of the first centuries of Christianity. In terms of its political symbolism, Lavater's construal of the afterlife as an ideal community of physically resurrected Christians is typical of the integrational social attitude.[56]

Coming from the political margins of Europe, with the Swiss Confederacy circa 1800 wedged between revolutionary France and feudally fragmented Germany, Lavater envisions a middle path as an ideal social community of the righteous gathered around Christ.[57] This vision of the community of citizens turns the monarchical political model of "the king's two bodies" into a duality of the collective earthly body of Adam and the collective heavenly body of Christ, with a prospect of empowering and elevating the righteous commoners to kingly status.

Das gewöhnliche Christusbild.

Figure 3.3. Prototype of Lavater's "common image" of Christ: medal, circa 1500. Florence, Bargello.

Figure 3.2. Lavater's "common image" of Christ. Johann Caspar Lavater, *Physiognomische Fragmente: Zur Beförderung der Menschenkenntniss und Menschenliebe: Erster [-vierter] Versuch. Mit Vielen Kupfern.* Leipzig: Weidmanns Erben und Reich, 1775. Special Collections Research Center, University of Chicago Library.

The socially subversive aspect of this project is stressed in the ninth letter of the *Prospects* through his reference to Paul's words about God's might "which he accomplished in Christ when he raised him from the dead and made him sit at his right hand in the heavenly places, far above all rule and authority and power and dominion, and above every name that is named, not only in this age but also in that which is to come" (Eph. 1:20–21, RSV) (Lavater, *Aussichten in die Ewigkeit*, 140).

This aspect of Lavater's vision acquires a strong rhetorical force in the context of his polemics with Kant, who in *Dreams of a Spirit-Seer* had accused metaphysics of an alliance with this-worldly political power. Lavater attempts to counter, but de facto confirms this accusation on his own terms by celebrating a "common image" of Christ which anticipates the shining glory of the future partaking of his kingly body by the righteous. Paradoxically and eclectically, in his project the progressive notion of the unification of mankind is still realized within the matrix of the ancien régime, though conventionally inverted in moral terms.

Lavater also omits the legendary origin of the "common image" of Christ with its claim to authenticity. Instead, he relies on his own physiognomic genius in interpreting the profile. This image, he concludes, reflects the perfect piety of the artist. Thus the truthfulness of this image becomes solely the matter of Lavater's enunciated belief. His veneration of the image becomes a veneration of the virtuous artist, who was already in this life capable of discerning Christ's transfigured body.

Lavater insisted that the "common image" of Christ is present in almost every household. His contemporaries needed only to be taught to recognize its beauty. Lavater's exalted *ekphrasis* seems to fulfill this task:

> This harmless peace of innocence pours over the whole face. It is in the form, in the harmony of the parts, it is totally gorgeous in the eye, even more gorgeous in the nose, and the most gorgeous in the mouth. If I saw such a man endowed with such calm, I believe that I could embrace his knees. . . . Calm and humility which characterize so inimitably everything divine and the most divine of all divinity. . . . What a dream, what inalienable purity, what loyalty! When the brow alone, the eye alone, the nose alone, the mouth alone, each separate part is a standing expression of pure kindness. I bow to the shadow of a man who invented this image, created it, and refreshed himself in its shadow. (Lavater, *Physiognomische Fragmente*, 111)

This image, for Lavater, also exemplifies the ideal "physiognomic language" of Swedenborg's theology: in it the inner and outer man absolutely coincide because, in Lavater's eyes, it matches exactly Christ's words in the Gospel: "Blessed are the meek, the compassionate, the pure of heart, the peace loving!" Lavater comments: "This all is spoken from the soul, there cannot be found any betrayal in this mouth. The more I see it, the more I love, the more my innermost spine trembles for a breath of this divine calm and simplicity" (Lavater, *Physiognomische Fragmente*, 112).

The ideal physiognomic language cannot dissimulate, being rooted in the phenomenal body as a form of being. Physiognomic language is hieroglyphic, that is, verbal and pictorial at once and, therefore, both successive and instantaneous. In the *Prospects*, Lavater wrote:

> Even the most perfect verbal language of the earth has a very essential imperfection in that it is only successive; whereas the language of images and signs is instantaneous to the eye. The language of heaven, if it is supposed to be perfect, should be successive and instantaneous at once; that is, it should represent the whole simultaneous heap of images, thoughts, sensations, like a painting at the one and the same time, and yet also represent successive images, thoughts, sensations,

with the greatest and truest speed. It must be a painting and language
at once. (Lavater, *Aussichten in die Ewigkeit*, 451)

The realization of such paradoxical divine language is expected only postmortem. But Lavater embarked on his physiognomic project in order to cheat
time by cultivating his readers' capacities for wordless physiognomic communication already in this life: "As Christ is the most telling, living, perfect
likeness of the invisible God, so is each human being totally an expression, a
simultaneous, true, all-encompassing, non-exhaustive, inimitable expression:
he is entirely the language of nature" (Lavater, *Aussichten in die Ewigkeit*,
452). The "common image" of Christ is the sacred threshold between phenomenal reality and transcendental ideality. If the religious poet in Lavater's
vision is the mouthpiece for Christ and his poetry is art in touch with the
divine transcendence, the painter paints in the likeness of Christ nothing but
himself and thus is fatally steeped in the world of immanence. The "common image" of Christ constitutes the point in Lavater's discourse where these
separate worlds finally communicate. The power of the physiognomic message of this image is of the same nature as that of a performative utterance,
which is successive and instantaneous at once and sets in motion a new order
of things in immediate and irrevocable fashion.

However, without Lavater's personal enactment of this physiognomic
truth this connection, which Kant rigorously denied, would not be possible.
With his insistence that Christ's words in the Gospel match absolutely this
image, Lavater stages the moment of the triumph of physiognomic truth:
this "common image" of Christ is that ancient image of God in man which
humanity lost and which Lavater works so hard to restore in the modern
world. This image is an index of the divine, but this divinity is assertively
located inside a pious artist's body. In fact, in the most emphatic moment of
religious enunciation, Lavater subverts the veneration of the divine in favor
of the veneration of the human: his claim that he would desire to embrace the
knees of the man who created this image turns the ritual genuflection to the
sacred image in the Byzantine tradition into a genuflection to a virtuous man.

Thus Lavater's rhetorical performance connects the world of transcendence with the world of immanence in the medium of the human body and
makes it accessible to the human senses by means of aesthetic representation
of "an intrinsic moral instinct in man," the only point on which Lavater and
Kant would agree. He makes this image of Christ visualize "the seal of the
double and equally noble thought" (*das Siegel von dem gedoppelten gleich
erhabenen Gedanken*) that "in the future we should become similar to him
in glory; and this glory should consist in something moral, or rather, in the
possession of intellectual, physical, political power directed to moral goals"
(Lavater, *Aussichten in die Ewigkeit*, 160).

In the *Prospects*, Lavater is highly aware of the power of belief as the
power of veridiction when he reminds his readers that

the apostles and first Christians could perform, in accordance with the strength of their belief and love, works which very far surpassed all human insights and forces. Their insights and power to do the good were equal to the power of their intention. To such moral intention I also count above all the *belief*; the upholding of the great truth that has been confirmed to you: Jesus is alive, even if we do not see him any more! (Lavater, *Aussichten in die Ewigkeit*, 161–62)

The "common image" of Christ might well be as fake as Lavater's intellectual construct, but on the purely discursive level it emerges as true through his personal fanatical commitment to "the upholding of the great truth."

Changing the Paradigm

As to Lavater's subversive agenda of winning the German republic of letters to the side of religion, his discourse can be considered a failure. When as an echo of Lavater's debate with Mendelssohn, two young Jews showed up in Zurich in November 1770 seeking conversion, Lavater proudly gave a speech at their baptism which he did not fail to publish. But this small triumph was undermined soon thereafter by Lavater's prominent enlightened opponent Georg Christoph Lichtenberg, who penned a biting satire published anonymously two years later under the title *Timorus, the Defense of Two Israelites Who Motivated by the Force of Lavater's Proofs and the Sausages from Göttingen Accepted the True Faith* (1773).[58]

And yet, in his heavy religious idiom and on the crutches of Pauline performativity, Lavater was already pointing to a radical shift in the intellectual paradigm of his epoch. To understand this shift, one should look to the philosophy of Lavater's much more sophisticated follower Arthur Schopenhauer. While sharing Lavater's obsession with the manifestation of the world of transcendence in the world of immanence, the philosopher far surpassed the pastor in his skillful synthesis of religion and science. Lavater's criticism of early Kant indeed anticipates the major features of Schopenhauer's philosophy by placing the realm of metaphysics within the human body and understanding the human being as an embodied mind which is subject and object at once. Lavater's "Christ-germ," or divine drive working through physical phenomena, adumbrates Schopenhauer's notion of "will," which the philosopher would advance on the basis of his interpretation of Kantian transcendental ideality. For Schopenhauer, the will, like the "Christ-germ," would manifest itself in the phenomenal world, objectified in human bodies. And consequently, like Lavater, he would embrace physiognomy.

In fact, Schopenhauer's "will," accessible to the human being in mental representations through sensory perception, is not unlike Lavater's notion of the innermost divinity hidden in this world and visualized in our mental or painted images of Christ. Lavater's preoccupation with the corpus callo-sum betrays his intuition that sensory perception might be intellectual—the major concern of Schopenhauer's "Criticism of the Kantian Philosophy." To establish a connection between the world of phenomenal reality and tran-scendental ideality, Schopenhauer would provocatively equate the Kantian paradigm with Platonism and interject the world of Platonic ideas in place of "things-in-themselves," thus implicitly reiterating the logical move of Christian theology in the model of incarnation. Maybe, therefore, Lavater's explicitly naive reliance on this model anticipates Schopenhauer's solution of the embodied subject and his sensory perception. Through the perception of the senses, both grant the artistic genius an immediate access to the world of transcendence and endow art with the capability of transmitting transcen-dent knowledge to the rest of mankind through representations. And finally, both enunciate their theories emphatically as truth.

Thus it is hardly surprising that Schopenhauer gives the best description of Lavater's discourse apart when he writes that

> the solution to the riddle of the world must come from an under-standing of the world itself; and hence that the task of metaphysics is not to pass over experience in which the world exists, but to under-stand it thoroughly, since inner and outer experience are certainly the principal source of knowledge. I say, therefore, that the solution to the riddle of the world is possible only through the proper connexion of outer with inner experience, carried out at the right point, and by the combination, thus effected, of these two very heterogeneous sources of knowledge.
>
> Yet this is so only within certain limits inseparable from our finite nature, consequently so that we arrive at a correct understanding of the world itself without reaching an explanation of its existence which is conclusive and does away with all further problems. Consequently, *est quadam prodire tenus* ("It is right to go up to the boundary" [if there is no path beyond]), and my path lies midway between the doc-trine of omniscience of the earlier dogmatism and the despair of the Kantian Critique.[59]

Christ's body was for Lavater the exact point of the "proper connec-tion" of outer and inner experience, and a discursive operator that allowed one to combine into one logical construct "very heterogeneous sources of knowledge." As awkward as Lavater's enterprise might sound today with its paradoxical coexistence of enlightened worship of reason and a provocative demand for blind acceptance of the scriptures, Lavater was revolutionizing a thought that had not yet developed its own vocabulary.

In the period, often described as witnessing the decline of Christianity, he set out in his pastoral way and with the discursive means at hand to help mankind to overcome the trauma of existential solitude, the inevitable byproduct of religious emancipation and self-determination. Without rejecting reason, he wanted to keep the soul but to keep it as a body. The relation of Lavater's discourse to that of Schopenhauer can be described in Schopenhauer's own words as the relation of Plato or the sages of India to Kant:

> Plato and the Indians . . . had based their contentions merely on a universal perception of the world; they produced them as the direct utterance of their consciousness, and presented them mythically and poetically rather than philosophically and distinctly. In this respect they are related to Kant as are the Pythagoreans Hicetas, Philolaus, and Aristarchus, who asserted the motion of the earth round the stationary sun, to Copernicus.[60]

In *The World as Will and Representation*, Schopenhauer refers directly to Lavater's "beautiful allegorical vignette . . . , which must have so heartening an effect on every champion of truth: a hand holding a light is stung by a wasp, while in the flame above, gnats are being burnt."[61] And he quotes its motto as follows:

> And though it singes the wing of the gnat,
> Destroys its skull and scatters all its little brains;
>   Light remains light!
> And although I am stung by the angriest of wasps,
> I will not let it go.[62]

This truth to which both clung fanatically was the truth of a shift they both strove to enact within the Kantian paradigm. Even if far superseded by Schopenhauer's achievement, Lavater's idiosyncratic, cumbersome discourse nevertheless yields a valuable insight into the heuristic function that Christ's body came to fulfill in the early formation of the new philosophical episteme. In Schopenhauer's masterfully succinct articulation, Lavater's redemptive aesthetics came to inform the culture of European modernism, leaving its clumsy pioneer in oblivion.

Chapter 4

✦

Christ's Vanishing Body in Dostoevsky's Genealogy of Ethical Consciousness

> Yes, believe me, you naive person . . . believe me that your
> Christ, if he were born in our day, would be the most ordinary
> and insignificant person; he would simply vanish in the face
> of contemporary science and of the contemporary movers of
> mankind.
>
> —Belinsky to Dostoevsky, *A Writer's Diary*

In Dostoevsky's eyes, Hans Holbein's *Dead Christ in the Tomb* (1521–22) posed a challenge to the belief in Christ's resurrection. "A painting like that can make you lose your faith,"[1] the writer told his wife after seeing it on display in the art museum in Basel in August 1867. (See fig. 4.1.)

Dostoevsky was reacting to the painting's merciless design: the famed naturalism of a life-size dead body shown in close-up. Holbein's representation of the dead Christ, according to art historians, indeed has remained unique for its unsettling treatment of the subject.[2] The long narrow panel completely coincides with the space of a tightly sealed stone tomb that encapsulates the savior's decaying corpse. Stretched out horizontally, his body lacks any pictorial dramatics of graphic suffering or romantic slumber. The bluish-green face is tipped up, indifferently, with the eyes and mouth open. The limbs are already gangrenous. The wounds have paled and sunk in, with their blood long curdled. Muscles still strained from the suspension on the cross bulge under the decomposing skin. They make the waxen arms and legs, already streaked with grey, look furrowed.

The painting derives its unique power from showing what nobody has seen—Christ's body as it would have really appeared three days after he had been laid to rest, that is, on the verge of resurrection. Holbein, allegedly, portrayed the real cadaver of a drowned Jew, foregrounding matter and space so as to convey viscerally the deadliness of the scene. The tight space, the heaviness of stone, the decay of flesh slice through the viewer's mind. Sensations of claustrophobia, silence, and morbid fumes make clear that only an object could possibly endure this compression. No vestiges of life could be imagined

Figure 4.1. Hans Holbein the Younger, *The Dead Christ in the Tomb*, 1521–22. Painting, oil on limewood. Kunstmuseum, Basel.

here stirring and recapturing this body. Holbein's illicit voyeurism seems to divulge a dark secret hiding inside the tomb.

Forsaking the iconographic solace of grieving bystanders as in paintings of the "Descent from the Cross" genre, Holbein withdrew a narrative of human or divine transcendence, laying bare belief as a conundrum glossed over by the pictorial tradition. Lonely, quiet, and cold, his picture can impress us as a mere testimony to the fact of death. Dostoevsky sensed the challenge. His wife left a prodigious record of the encounter:

> The painting had a crushing impact on Fyodor Mikhailovich. He stood before it as if stunned. . . . I went into other rooms. When I came back after fifteen or twenty minutes, I found him still riveted to the same spot in front of the painting. His agitated face had a kind of dread in it, something I had noticed more than once during the first moments of an epileptic seizure. . . . Luckily this did not happen. He calmed down little by little and left the museum, but insisted on returning once again to view this painting which had struck him so powerfully.[3]

Whether Dostoevsky indeed returned to the museum is unknown, but the painting haunted his thinking ever after. In his novel *The Idiot*, which was germinating in the writer's mind around the time of his museum visit, the painting is discussed twice precisely in the terms of its challenge to faith. One of Dostoevsky's characters, the nihilist Ippolit, wonders about Holbein's Christ: "if all those who believed in him and worshipped him had seen a corpse like that (and it was bound to be exactly like that), how could they believe, looking at such a corpse, that this sufferer would resurrect?"[4]

And yet there is another dimension to Holbein's painting. It hinges on the dead body's allegorical framework. Light emanates inside the tomb with no possible source other than the cadaver. The stone plate beneath the body is draped with a white sheet, riffled as if a breeze ran through it. The folds under the wrist are denser. They repeat the loincloth's curves which spread like shining beams from the savior's bulging crotch. In Renaissance art the loins of Christ, according to Leo Steinberg's famous study, allegorized the resurrection.[5] In fact, the tomb's right solid wall is cracked through at the bottom.

The chipped triangle inevitably draws the eye. In the grave's putrid odium, this tiny detail becomes only more potent as a desired hint at near liberation.

With the source of light placed in the body itself, the painting evokes the words of John: "In him was life, and the life was the light of men. The light shines in the darkness, and the darkness has not overcome it" (John 1:4–5, RSV). Holbein's illusionism only enhances the salvational scheme: the body, flattened if looked at straight on, acquires a third dimension if seen from the low left angle. The shifting of perspective implies a motion, almost an anamorphosis, within the image. Change and transformation are thus implicit in the composition itself but are to be discovered only through the viewer's interaction with the image.

In baroque fashion, the painting opens eerily onto the viewer's world. The corpse's hair, right wrist and foot, as well as its white winding sheet, spill out of the tomb into the space where the fourth wall would naturally be. This marked artifice creates a tension with the realism whereby Holbein seems to take the "ecce homo" to its ultimate degree. The savior's light shines forth toward the viewer. But maybe, after all, it is merely a candle in an inquisitive viewer's hand, or a lamp, or the sun, or the mind that throws light onto the mystery of Christ's dead body.

Holbein's paintings abound in puzzling details and are well known for their tendency toward allegory. Ambiguity and paradox are their *modus communicandi*. This feature has been long recognized as the rhetorical dimension of his art.[6] Holbein's paintings "speak differently" (allegorize) in that they reach beyond the literal toward a figural expression. In the case of the dead Christ, duality becomes especially eloquent. Thanks to the allegorical framework, transcendence, which the painting of Christ in the tomb might seem utterly to lack, is transposed into the beholder's mind. The painting stages the very process of flesh turning back into the Word which it had once embodied.

That Holbein's rendition of Christ's body was fully in line with Reformed theology is today a matter of consensus.[7] Having given so much attention to the intensive scrutiny of this tableau, the Russian writer could not have missed the painting's paradoxical light. Ippolit's musings about the feelings that Christ's followers must have had with regard to his corpse stem from the tension between body and word that animates the painting. "They must have gone off—Ippolit imagines—in terrible fear, though each carried within himself a tremendous thought that could never be torn out of him."[8] The "tremendous thought" of a teacher, not a savior, is the logos, or bluntly put, the consciousness and language which perpetuate a religious mystery, even when the mystical body with its sacrificial scheme had lost its persuasive powers.

Through his writings, Dostoevsky too searched for an adequate expression for the "tremendous thought" of a Christianity which could reinvigorate belief as a conundrum and paradox and effectively take the place of the sacred rituals and institution of the church, the body of Christ. The author of *Crime and Punishment* (1866) interrupted his trip from Baden-Baden to Geneva to see for himself what he had already heard or maybe read about in the Russian historian Nikolai Karamzin's *Letters of a Russian Traveler* (1801)—this painting of the dead Christ in which "one doesn't see anything of God."[9]

Holbein helped the writer situate himself in more pronounced fashion within his time's conflicting paradigms of reason and belief. Karamzin's simple description of the painting pinned down the intellectual tendency of the dawning nineteenth century "to regard God and Jesus as purely human attributes and to regard religion either as a natural, predictable human phenomenon or as something having a primarily practical function for human life."[10] In Dostoevsky's eyes, the *Dead Christ* condensed the epochal developments of the nineteenth century that the writer was preparing to overturn.

Anna Dostoevskaya's stenographic diary adds a telling detail to her memory of the writer's encounter with the painting: "But F. admired this painting. Wishing to have a closer look at it, he stood on a chair, and I was very afraid he'd be asked to pay a fine."[11] This somewhat comical scene of Dostoevsky perched on a chair, however, literalizes a metaphor of the authorial position. His physical positioning toward the painting captures graphically the writer's search for a viewpoint from which he could respond to the nineteenth century.

This viewpoint was soon thereafter self-reflexively articulated in *The Idiot* as that of someone who like Christ has faced up to death and come back: "Maybe there's a man who has had the sentence read to him, has been allowed to suffer, and has then been told, 'Go, you're forgiven.' That man might be able to tell us something."[12] It is from this existential experience of the imitation of Christ that Dostoevsky felt entitled to respond to Holbein's *Dead Christ* and to everything that in his eyes the painting came to stand for, with the motif of the "Russian Christ," first in the novel *The Idiot*, then in *The Brothers Karamazov*.

The protagonist of *The Idiot*, Prince Myshkin, narrates how he was brought in a condition of mental stupor from Russia to Switzerland for a cure. But he was "roused" from "that darkness" on entering Basel, the hometown of Holbein's *Dead Christ*, when his mind abruptly cleared in response to "the braying of an ass in the town market" (Dostoevsky, *The Idiot*, 56). Finally, after several years of sojourn in Switzerland, with the support of a German doctor, he returns to Russia, in the words of one character: "As if sent by God!" (ibid., 51). A stranger in his own country, he speaks in parables, proclaims, "It's said: 'Don't kill'" (ibid., 22), tries to mediate conflicts, to calm deadly passions, and to intervene on behalf of the fallen and downtrodden. One of his first interlocutors immediately recognizes his mission: "You're a philosopher and have come to teach us." To which the Prince responds, "Perhaps I really am a philosopher, and, who knows, maybe I actually do have a thought of teaching . . . It may be so; truly it may" (ibid., 59).

Prince Myshkin ultimately fails, returning to the nonverbal darkness of idiocy and to the mental asylum in Switzerland. What stays behind, however, is Dostoevsky's six hundred pages in which the "tremendous thought" of Christianity is squared mercilessly with his contemporary Russia and the reader is led through a maze of the characters' drama of choice. In *The Brothers Karamazov*, the homage to Holbein is even more literal. The decaying corpse of the saintly elder Zosima that against all expectations of believers fails to resist corruption shakes both the monastery and the parishioners. The incident provokes a crisis of belief in the protagonist Alyosha Karamazov, who consequently decides to abandon his monastic life to carry Zosima's "tremendous thought" into the world itself.

Dostoevsky split Holbein's allegory in two—he left the motionless *Dead Christ* to the medium of painting, which he considered "incapable of providing a model for how Jesus's life could be repeated in our day,"[13] but reserved Holbein's drama of belief and resurrection for his experimentation with the novel of consciousness. In the polemical context of the 1870s wrangling about Russia's cultural destiny between Slavophiles and Westernizers, Dostoevsky let the dead body remain in the "West," but reserved the resurrected body for Russia. Needless to say, the line between the West and Russia runs not along the country's borders but cuts right through Russian cultural identity itself. Dostoevsky chose Holbein's early-modern painting to designate a body of a discourse that he was to subvert within his own novels.

But this subversion could be accomplished only from a position of faith, or what Badiou called "conviction."[14] Rowan Williams pinned down the rhetorical interplay of faith and fiction in Dostoevsky's novels: "Faith and fiction are deeply related—not because faith is a variant of fiction in the trivial sense but because both are *gratuitous* linguistic practices standing over against a functional scheme of things."[15] This observation echoes Badiou's understanding of Pauline discursive positionality as "a subjective upsurge" that "cannot be given as the rhetorical construction of a personal adjustment to the laws of the universe or nature."[16] Such a "subjective upsurge" also drove Dostoevsky.

The literary scholar Steven Cassedy has shown that the writer's "religion" was an act of anti-philosophy that offered an idiosyncratic gloss on German Protestant thought with an admixture of messianic Judaism—the author's personal invention, to wit, a discourse apart.[17] In 1883, two years after Dostoevsky's death, the writer's friend, the philosopher Vladimir Soloviev, felt pressed to publish a defense of Dostoevsky against an accusation that the writer had invented his own "New Christianity" consisting in a mixture of "sentimentality" and "abstract humanism."[18]

Soloviev insisted that Dostoevsky's humanism was driven by faith, that "the very creation of true culture was to Dostoevsky first of all a religious 'orthodox concern,' "[19] and the writer merely repeated the Gospels, specifically John's revelation, "with his own words."[20] But the philosopher did not deny here and elsewhere that Dostoevsky's religious vision was to be channeled into another body, the social body of "humanity"[21] per se—"the Church as a social ideal."[22] This vision has been seen variously as a "theocracy"[23] or as a "democracy."[24] But whatever idiosyncratic construct Dostoevsky came up with for his social utopia, it took its point of departure from Christ's dead body that in its very crumbling made room for replacing a religious body with the discursive space for Christ's "tremendous thought."

The *Dead Christ* versus the "Russian Christ"

Steven Cassedy's *Dostoevsky's Religion* has provided Dostoevsky's writings with a detailed context of mostly German thought, from Kant and Hegel via Feuerbach and Stirner to Strauss.[25] With our focus on the rhetorical operation whereby Dostoevsky substituted his "Russian Christ" for what the writer tagged as Holbein's *Dead Christ*, this context needs to be recapitulated only in the broadest of terms.

For Dostoevsky, Western culture stepped toward modernity, rather scrupulously, over Christ's dead body. This perception, though later to be contested by social anthropologists,[26] was in Dostoevsky's time not totally unjustified. The philosophical theology of Friedrich Schleiermacher and the philosophy of G. W. F. Hegel marked a brief period of forethought, lingering, and deliberations before Christ's mythical, supernatural body was dealt its actual, fatal blow.

In *On Religion: Speeches to Its Cultured Despisers* (1799), Schleiermacher defined "true religion" as a "sense and taste for the Infinite."[27] But his critique of the confusion of true religion with its mere trappings still presented itself as a defense of religion. In *The Christian Faith* (1830–31), he still moved safely within the sacred circle of belief in the "perfection and blessedness of Christ,"[28] in his "living influence" as a redeemer who stimulated "God-consciousness" in man.[29] Hegel, who prepared the grounds for sublimating Christ's sacred body into the philosophy of consciousness, still preserved in his published work the incarnational model of "revealed religion": "God is attainable in pure speculative knowledge alone and is only in that knowledge, and is only that knowledge, and is only that knowledge itself, for He is Spirit; and this speculative knowledge is the knowledge of the *revealed* religion."[30]

For the philosopher, the incarnational scheme reflected the stages through which individual self-consciousness emerges in its first sensually immediate perception of God-turned-flesh, then overcomes this immediacy through creating a distance in time and space to the incarnated God's death, and finally arrives at a universal self-consciousness of the Spirit in the community: "He [God] rose up for consciousness as a *sensuous existence*, now He has arisen *in the Spirit*."[31] The incarnation of the Spirit mediates between the individual and collective, sensual and spiritual elements of knowledge: "The dead divine Man or human God is *in himself* the universal self-consciousness; this he has to become explicitly *for this self-consciousness*."[32] The redemptive plan taken as an allegory of the progression of human knowledge from the individual to the universal might read more abstractly, but it still has not abandoned all mystical undertones.

Hegel's early essay "Life of Jesus," where he made Jesus into a representative of the Kantian moral philosophy, remained unpublished until 1907.[33] Not unlike Thomas Jefferson's Bible, this was a private experiment in separating Jesus's social teaching from its mythical and dogmatic accretions. Despite such private or anonymous ventures of the philosophers into the realm of theology, it was not before the first publication of *Das Leben Jesu* (*The Life of Jesus*) by the German theologian David Friedrich Strauss in 1835 that the vanishing of Christ's body as the medium of divine revelation was inaugurated publicly and in an outspoken fashion. In his textual analysis of the Gospels, Strauss sought to filter myth from historical fact. In so doing he demonstrated the contradictions of the scriptural text and dared to conclude that Christ had never predicted his resurrection.[34]

Instead of the mythical incarnation of the divine, or Schleiermacher's "God-consciousness," Strauss proposed to see "in the life of Christ an objectification of the church's consciousness of the human spirit as divine."[35] This proposal resulted in Strauss's demotion from his clerical office to the position of a schoolteacher and his retirement two years later. But his introduction of "critical theology" stirred the minds of the epoch and signaled a radical turn toward secularization in Western thought.

Strauss's French follower Ernest Renan soon thereafter extended the revolution in the realm of dogmatic theology to the realms of history and literature with his *Life of Jesus* (*Vie de Jésus*, 1863). Renan's teaching career also came to an abrupt end as a consequence of this publication. But Renan's book not only cleared the way for a scholarly and historical approach to the figure of Christ and to the study of Christianity, but also made Christ's life into subject matter for literary imagination and fictional narratives.

Renan's contemporary, the French critic Charles Augustin Sainte-Beuve, wrote about his work:

> To be historian and story teller from this new point of view, [Renan] had to begin by being above all a diviner, a poet drawing inspiration from the spirit of times and places, and a painter able to read the lines of the horizon, the least vestiges left on the slopes of the hills, and skilled in evoking the genius of the region and the landscape. He has thus succeeded in producing a work of art even more than a history, and this presupposes on the part of the author a union, till now almost unique, of superior qualities, reflective, delicate, and brilliant.[36]

In Renan's approach the focus on Christ as an individual and on his historical role as a leader of the oppressed and a teacher of social ethics replaced the theological focus on Christ's body. "Since the publication of the *Life*, this whole field, hitherto set apart as a field of magic and miracle, has been reclaimed for history and the normal life of man."[37] "You won for us," wrote Sainte-Beuve, "the right of discussion in this matter, hitherto forbidden."[38]

By the end of the nineteenth century, this discussion most memorably culminated in Friedrich Nietzsche's radical repudiation of David Strauss's groundbreaking achievement as a philistine and cowardly half-measure which never managed to fully abandon metaphysics and did not go beyond "explosive outbursts against parsons, miracles, and the 'world-wide humbug' of the Resurrection."[39] In his own aphorisms about God's creation in the likeness of man and God's death, Nietzsche sought to compensate for what he perceived as Strauss's failure to tell his readers directly: "I have liberated you from a helping and pitiful God: the Cosmos is no more than an inflexible machine; beware of its wheels, that they do not crush you."[40]

Nietzsche was the one in whose thought Christ's "un-resurrected death" entitled human beings to put their faith instead into a religion of their own making, that is, into the experience of art with its unlimited possibilities of transcendence. The fading of Christ's divinity, the profanation of the sacred, which used to anchor the human being firmly within the context of universal meaning, inaugurated European literary modernism.[41] Perception of time was now the matter of subjectivity. Aesthetically intensified, human consciousness became all-encompassing: it usurped the cosmic expanse and it ventured beyond the "old prejudice" of good and evil.[42] On the theological ruins of Christianity Nietzsche inaugurated a big dream of "the higher man": "Well! Take heart! ye higher men! Now only travaileth the mountain of the human future. God hath died: now do *we* desire—the Superman to live."[43]

With some assistance by the Russian philosopher Lev Shestov, Dostoevsky was placed next to Nietzsche in the psychological genealogy of literary modernism with its "apotheosis of cruelty."[44] Shestov saw Nietzsche as a great successor to Dostoevsky in what he called "an attempt to rehabilitate the rights of the underground man,"[45] that is to give voice and justification to the most unsavory traits of human nature and to penetrate into the workings of a mind tormented by self-doubt and contradiction. But it was also Dostoevsky's tendency to condense novelistic time into one instance of the here and now that came to set him in literary history alongside Nietzsche as the father of the literature of consciousness.[46]

Thomas Mann was the first to differentiate between Dostoevsky and Nietzsche along ethical lines in his essay "Dostoevsky—Within Limits" (1946).[47] Mann wrote his essay in American exile during his work on *Doktor Faustus*, the novel dealing with what the writer perceived as the ethical failure of German modernism. In these post–World War II reflections on Dostoevsky, Mann still insists on Shestov's vision of the proximity between the two thinkers in their "diseased genius," or in their "criminal desire for knowledge," and especially emphasizes their congenial conceptions of time—the "aesthetically heightened instant" and the "eternal return."[48] But he does so only in order to distinguish between them more trenchantly in ethical terms.

Mann observes that both thinkers had been concerned with the expansion of consciousness in an ecstatic moment, an experience that in both cases was bodily rooted in illness. The distinct logic of their respective diseases, however, informed the structure of their thought. Mann discerns in Dostoevsky's epilepsy an explicit figure of reversal (Bakhtin would later call it "the carnivalesque"): the subjectively heightened, blissful moment preceding an epileptic fit always loops back into depression and feelings of guilt.[49] Thus, there is a "historical" dimension to the self-analysis and afterthought in the psychological condition of an epileptic. Conversely, Nietzsche's "waves of intoxicating feeling of happiness and strength" (*Wellen rauschhaften Glücks- und Kraftgefühls*),[50] as Mann put it, lead in a linear fashion up to an ecstatic climax that results in the irreversible mental collapse of syphilitic paralysis.

In other words, Mann describes the structure of consciousness in Dostoevsky as one of death and resurrection, fall and ascent. It yields a posthumous reflection, differentiation, critical distance to the self, and hence, responsibility. The time structure of "self-consciousness" in Dostoevsky (Bakhtin) allows for awareness of guilt and thus contains the potential for correction and regeneration. Dostoevsky's model of subjective time, so conceived, is consequently a literary model of an ethically alarmed consciousness, that is, of bad and good conscience. Its moral torment renders it exceptional in the modernist tradition of literature.

Mann emphasizes the national difference between the two writers as a way of delineating Dostoevsky's closeness to as well as his distance from the Western paradigm: Nietzsche could have perceived Dostoevsky as a "great teacher" (Mann, "Dostojevskij—mit Maßen," 174) because the novelist was "not German" and thus lacked some humanist impediment that conditioned Nietzsche's thought and from which the latter wanted to break out (ibid., 169). But at the same time, Mann observes that the religious charge of Dostoevsky's novels still sets him far apart from what Mann saw as Nietzsche's secular humanism.

Precisely for this reason, Mann himself adopted Dostoevsky's style and narrative innovations for his *Doktor Faustus* (1947), a novel struggling to respond to recent history.[51] Through Mann's own reception, Dostoevsky's "non-German" identity made him once again into one of the "great teachers" of Western culture, but this time instead of offering a lesson in uninhibited irrationality, the Russian writer becomes an avatar of the cultural awakening to the necessity of an ethical revision of modernism. In the aftermath of World War II, Mann perceived Dostoevsky's novels as a valid, ethically differentiated alternative to Nietzsche's consciousness-construct.

Mann's position was not unique. The Marxist critic Georg Lukács interpreted the victory of the Soviet Union in the war as a testimony to the ideological superiority of the Russian critical realism of the nineteenth century over what he had dismissed already much earlier as the aesthetic of "Western decadence." In his book, written during wartime in the Soviet Union, *Russian Realism in World Literature*, Lukács called for a postwar revival of the Russian realist tradition, which he invested with the political potential to take on a new edifying function of democratizing and spiritually transforming nations recovering from fascism.[52]

In 1962, in his second, revised book on Dostoevsky, *Problems of Dostoevsky's Poetics*, the Russian critic Mikhail Bakhtin likewise turns to Dostoevsky in a search for a model of ethically differentiated discourse. Inspired by Thomas Mann's reception of Dostoevsky in *Doktor Faustus* as a response to the experience of totalitarianism, Bakhtin sees in Dostoevsky's work a "metaphysical threshold, a watershed in novelistic consciousness": "No heroes of Russian literature prior to Dostoevsky had tasted from the Tree of Knowledge of Good and Evil. Within the bounds of their novels, therefore, one could still find naive and integrated poetry, lyric, poetic landscape."[53] Notably, in his Dostoevsky essay Mann rejected the psychology of Proust's novels in favor of Dostoevsky, justifying his preference in a congenial fashion. He argued that in Dostoevsky's writings one is faced with "psychological lyric in the broadest sense of this word, with confession and shattering admission [of guilt], and therefore with the fearsome moral force, the religious horror of Dostoevsky's inquiry into souls [*Seelenkunde*]."[54]

Dostoevsky's anticipation of a novel of consciousness in his "polyphonic novel" indeed implied a differentiation within the inchoate paradigm of literary modernism, within which the writer has offered an alternative of Christianized consciousness, that is, of conscience. "In writing fiction in which no formula is allowed unchallengeable victory, Dostoevsky has implicitly developed what might be called a theology of writing, specifically of narrative writing."[55] In 1920, the Russian philosopher Pavel Florensky reinforced this differentiation by adding a visual counterpart to Dostoevsky's polyphonic writing in his theoretization of the "reversed perspective" of the Russian medieval icon.[56]

In its conscious embrace of poly-perspectivism, the icon expressed "liberation" from the constraints of naturalism and the drive for "spirituality," Florensky argued.[57] The philosopher's criticism of perspective as an illusionist, bourgeois technique originating in the tradition of theatrical decoration throws light on Dostoevsky's rejection of Holbein's *Dead Christ* as a literal rendition of God's death. Florensky was implicitly offering a theology of avant-garde art, as reflected in the adaptations of icon aesthetics by Natalia Goncharova, Wassily Kandinsky, or Marc Chagall. In doing so he still moved within that Russian Christianized variant of modernism once broached by Dostoevsky.

In his discourse apart, Dostoevsky transformed the notion of Christ's body, the church, into a "big dialogue" on the ethics of social coexistence. He raised Christ's dead body, abandoned as in Lautréamont's *Chants de Maldoror* as a useless remainder by the side of the road taken by "Western" civilization, into consciousness and presented its polyphonic structure as a specifically

"Russian understanding."[58] This national emphasis had above all a structural meaning. It was to demarcate that place apart that Dostoevsky wanted his own utopia to assume within the shared context of what he perceived as the common and inevitable decline of institutionalized Christianity. His own way of participating in the relentless transformation of the sacred into culture was to rhetorically oppose the West while repurposing and subverting the medieval presence of the Russian Orthodox Church.

In his introduction to *The Idiot*, Richard Pevear draws attention to Dostoevsky's hint about the historical origins of Prince Myshkin, the Russian Christ, expressed through a marginal character, the clerk Lebedev, at the very beginning of the novel: "the name's historical, it can and should be found in Karamzin's *History*."[59] Lebedev's suggestion, if followed, reveals that in Karamzin's *History of the Russian State* (1816–26), a monumental work of national history writing, the name is recorded as belonging to one of the architects of an ambitious cathedral, the building of which was miscalculated and collapsed in 1474. While dropping this hint, Dostoevsky was signaling to his readers his poetology of subversion.

The Christianization of Consciousness

In *Problems of Dostoevsky's Poetics*, Bakhtin famously pointed up Dostoevsky's tendency to ground speech in the bodies of his characters. The scholar explained this prominent feature of the novelist's poetics with his literary adaptation of a carnivalesque sense of timelessness, the panhuman sensibility and familiarity of a marketplace. Only recently has Bakhtin's approach to Dostoevsky been recognized as "a usage of semiotics in the advancement of . . . an ontology."[60] Taking a detour through folk culture under Soviet censorship, Bakhtin addressed the problem of Dostoevsky's restructuring of the secular discourse of his times in religious terms.[61] In fact, in the inseparable trio of hero-idea-word that Bakhtin described as an inalienable feature of Dostoevsky's novels is discernible a variant on the incarnation of the word, which the writer sought to adapt to the realm of social communication.

Bakhtin drew attention to the characters' embodied discourse, their quasi-authorial self-consciousness, and thus to their partaking of the same ontological plane as their author. This phenomenon of an authorial voice joining the discourse on an equal footing with the characters, or the "integral authorial position,"[62] can be seen as a literary version of the Nicene Creed's equality among the persons of the Holy Trinity. Bakhtin elaborated on the relation of the character and the author in Dostoevsky's novel as follows:

> It might seem that the independence of a character contradicts the fact that he exists, entirely and solely, as an aspect of a work of art, and consequently is wholly created from beginning to end by the

author. In fact there is no such contradiction. The characters' freedom we speak of here exists within the limits of the artistic design, and in that sense is just as much a created thing as is the un-freedom of the objectivized hero. But to create does not mean to invent.

. . . Thus the freedom of a character is an aspect of the author's design. A character's discourse is created by the author, but created in such a way that it can develop to the full its inner logic and independence as *someone else's discourse*, the word of the character himself. As a result it does not fall out of the author's design, but only out of a monologic authorial field of vision.[63] (Emphasis in original.)

The logic of this reflection reveals the relation of the author to his character as that of God, the Father, to the Son. The Son who is "begotten not made" is the embodiment of the Father's intention but has life and mission on his own. He is no mere instrument (as in Arianism) but addresses the Father as an equal, even if he is ultimately dependent on the latter's will. Bakhtin meaningfully relates this orthodox Christian feature of Dostoevsky's poetics directly to his resistance against "a reification of man, of human relations, of all human values under the conditions of capitalism."[64]

Joseph Frank in his biography of Dostoevsky provided a detailed account of the tendencies in the culture of the writer's time which he felt compelled to resist—the inflation of language and knowledge, the reconfiguration of Christianity through socialist utopias, the advancement of English political economy with its rationalization of social relations, the historicization of religion in speculative, academic Christ narratives, as well as cultural criticism playing with the idea of Christ's return and failure.[65] Dostoevsky absorbed all these tendencies in his discourse apart, engendered in the microcosm of his novelistic world, and subverted them by deliberately building this world as a point of convergence between religious and secular discourse.

This convergence becomes programmatic as a strategy of the Christianization of consciousness in *The Brothers Karamazov*, the most self-reflexive of Dostoevsky's novels in regard to his poetics. Part 1, book 2 of the novel, tellingly called "An Inappropriate Gathering," stages a meeting between the two seemingly mutually exclusive worlds: the secular, mundane, and corrupt world represented by the Karamazov family and the solemn religious world of monastic piety represented by the elder Zosima and his fellow monks. These worlds converge in the figure of Alyosha, a novice in the monastery and the youngest Karamazov brother, who also attends the gathering when his biological father Fyodor Pavlovich Karamazov comes to his monastery to seek help, advice, and mediation from the elder Zosima, Alyosha's spiritual father, in a familial argument over issues of inheritance with his unruly older son Dmitri.

Fyodor Pavlovich arrives in the company of his intellectual son Ivan and their neighbor, the landowner Miusov. Miusov is a liberal gentleman educated in the Western style who sees the gathering as an opportunity to settle his outstanding business about fishing rights with the monastery. To satisfy his idle curiosity about the place, he is ready "to observe all their customs." Ivan is a natural scientist, atheist, and a writer doubting and seeking God. The arrival of this worldly company at the monastery inevitably results in a dissonance of values and ultimately in a profanation of the sacred space. The landowner Maximov's behavior upon entering the courtyard signals the impropriety of the situation right away: Maximov calls the elder "un chevalier parfait!," "the splendid elder," and "the honor and glory of the monastery," projecting into a place of humility clichés pertaining to the realm of aristocratic vanity.

The shallow conversation of the group abounds in meaningless and frivolous puns. Fyodor Pavlovich first remarks that Maximov looks like the murderer von Sohn, whose case has been all over the tabloid papers. Then he addresses Zosima as the "sacred elder." And finally, he cracks some jokes interspersed with plays on words. However, Fyodor Pavlovich's incessant provocations, despite his frivolous topics and language and inappropriate joviality, carry meaningful connotations. The anecdote about the Metropolitan Platon and his conversion of Diderot, or the story about the headless Saint Denis borrowed from Voltaire vividly associate the intrusion of secular sensibility into sacred space with the tradition of Western atheism, where the devil is at home. It is hardly a coincidence that Miusov—"such a Parisian, such a progressive-minded gentleman"—continues cursing in the devil's name throughout Fyodor Pavlovich's buffoonery.

Soon the conversation takes a serious turn as the discussion focuses on the relation between church and state. The episode puts into philosophical perspective the meaning of the "inappropriate gathering" and thus provides the most important poetological reflection on the goals of Dostoevsky's discourse. The participants in the conversation are Ivan Karamazov, the atheist; the monks, including the elder Zosima; and the liberal Miusov. In the course of their debate in the chapter, which bears as its title the performative utterance "So Be It! So Be It!," the transformation of the institution of the church into a structure of conscience and ethically differentiated discourse unfolds before the reader's very eyes.

The conversation starts with Ivan Karamazov claiming that the state should develop into the church. This idea is handled polyphonically through a discussion of some faulty versions of the church's fusion with the state as they can be found in the Western understanding of Catholicism, Lutheranism, and socialism. But in the end, Ivan's initial proposition reappears in the light of the "Russian understanding," which takes it to a different level, the level of ethical consciousness.

The transformation of the church, the body of Christ, into a structure of conscience, as presented in "So Be It! So Be It!," deserves closer attention. It is significant that Ivan Karamazov had articulated his criticism of the separation of church and state in a journal article, "On the Subject of Ecclesiastical Courts and the Scope of Their Rights."[66] Thus the whole question about what place the church should occupy in society emerges within an explicitly juridical framework that poses the problem of judgment about crime and punishment. Ivan's article is a polemic against a liberal churchman's insistence that the church should have a clearly delimited place within the state. The monastery's librarian, Father Iosif, summarizes Ivan's objections to the following propositions of his opponent:

> First, that "no social organization can or should arrogate to itself the power to dispose of the civil and political rights of its members." Second, that "criminal and civil jurisdiction should not belong to the Church and are incompatible with its nature both as divine institution and as an organization of men for religious purposes." And finally, third, that "the Church is a kingdom not of this world." (Dostoevsky, *The Brothers Karamazov*, 60)

In response to these topographies, the atheist Ivan argues that "the Church should contain in itself the whole state and not merely occupy a certain corner of it." His argument seems to be made in a utopian mode, since "the mixing of elements, that is, of the essences of Church and state taken separately, will of course go on eternally, despite the fact that it is impossible." But nevertheless, he puts his proposition in abeyance as a goal for the future: "If for some reason that is impossible now, then in the essence of things it undoubtedly should be posited as the direct and chief aim of the whole further development of Christian society."

On the one hand, Ivan's vision of the state turning into the church critically opposes the failed project of Roman Catholicism, in which the church never managed to transform the pagan state but ended up being included within the state as an entity lacking any transformative power over the state itself. On the other hand, Father Paissy adds a further objection to the scholarly and scientific progress in Europe, which took place under the auspices of Protestantism:

> According to certain theories, which have become only too clear in our nineteenth century, the Church ought to be transforming itself into the state, from a lower to a higher species, as it were, so as to disappear into it eventually, making way for science, the spirit of the age, and civilization. And if it does not want that and offers resistance, then as a result it is allotted only a certain corner, as it were, in the state, and even that under control—as is happening in our time everywhere in modern European lands. (Dostoevsky, *The Brothers Karamazov*, 62–63)

In saying this, Father Paissy joins the position of Ivan Karamazov whose goal is to subvert Western secular tendencies on the Russian soil: "Yet according to the Russian understanding and hope, it is not the Church that needs to be transformed into the state, . . . but, on the contrary, the state should end by being accounted worthy of becoming only the Church alone, and nothing else but that." Most importantly, he seals this proposition with an explicitly performative endorsement of this hope—"So be it! So be it!" (Dostoevsky, *The Brothers Karamazov*, 63).

Ivan's proposition is, however, double-edged. From this point on, the liberal Miusov and the elder Zosima take over the discussion. Miusov interprets Ivan's argument that the church should contain the whole state and administer the criminal law as the establishment of ecclesiastical control over human rights and, quite literally, over the punishment and execution of criminals. In fact, Ivan can be easily understood as demanding such unlimited jurisdiction for the church, since he reasons as follows: "If everything became the Church, then the Church would excommunicate the criminal" as a punishment. The excommunicated man "would then have to go away not only from men, but also from Christ. For by his crime he would have rebelled not only against men but also against Christ's Church" (ibid.).

Ivan elaborates here on a totalitarian system of punishment which, in his view, would strip the criminal not only of civil rights and social identity but also of his humanity as such because "to go away from Christ," to lose God's image in which man was created, boils down to being reduced to what Giorgio Agamben would later call "bare life." This line of argument culminates in Ivan's legend "The Grand Inquisitor," a poignant allegory of ideologically rooted power. Thus it is for a good reason that Miusov sees in Ivan's entire argument a Christianized version of socialism—the most dangerous socialism in the view of the French gendarmes, as he claims. In its own right, Miusov's concern is fully legitimate, since Ivan's further development in the novel leads him to total rejection of any form of forgiveness, reconciliation, and regeneration under the wings of the church for offenders against children, as he confesses to his brother Alyosha in the chapter "Rebellion."

However, the elder Zosima harks back to a different aspect of Ivan's argument, that is, to his thought-experiment about the potential of the church to reform the state on Christian ethical premises. His critique of secularism asserts that in the present day only the church can awaken an ethically differentiated consciousness, the criminal's conscience about his crime before God. Zosima responds to Ivan's utopian vision of the criminal's moral restoration under fear of excommunication from the body of Christ as follows:

> But, you know, in reality it is so even now. . . . If it were not for Christ's Church, indeed there would be no restraint on the criminal in his evildoing, and no punishment for it later, real punishment, that is, not a mechanical one such as has just been mentioned, which only chafes the heart in most cases, but a real punishment, the only real, the only frightening and appeasing punishment, which lies in the acknowledgement of one's own conscience.

> . . . If anything protects society even in our time, and even reforms
> the criminal himself and transforms him into a different person, again
> it is Christ's law alone, which manifests itself in the acknowledge-
> ment of one's own conscience. Only if he acknowledges his guilt as
> a son of Christ's society—that is, of the Church—will he acknowl-
> edge his guilt before society itself—that is, before the Church. Thus,
> the modern criminal is capable of acknowledging his guilt before the
> Church alone, and not before the state. (Dostoevsky, *The Brothers
> Karamazov*, 64)

Consequently, only the church can reform the criminal. But for Zosima, it
is exactly the church's opposition to and difference from the state that assures
its moral superiority and impact: "But the Church, like a mother, tender and
loving, withholds from active punishment, for even without her punishment,
the wrongdoer is already too painfully punished by the state court, and at
least someone should pity him" (Dostoevsky, *The Brothers Karamazov*, 65)
For this very reason, the church is expected to be able to overturn the
state's bureaucratic approach to the human being as a statistical entity and to
become a force capable of regenerating the wrongdoer and reintegrating him
or her into the social community. Russian society could be different from that
of Europe exactly because

> besides the established courts, we have, in addition, the Church as
> well, which never loses communion with the criminal, as a dear and
> still beloved son, and above that there is preserved, even if only in
> thought, the judgment of the Church, not active now but still living
> for the future, if only as a dream, and unquestionably acknowledged
> by the criminal himself, by the instinct of his soul. (Dostoevsky, *The
> Brothers Karamazov*, 65)

The Russian church does not excommunicate the criminal, Zosima explains,
but harbors him after his rejection by society. Thus mercy constitutes the only
force that could bring about the criminal's moral transformation. Zosima
first subtly reverses Ivan's argument and then seemingly accepts Ivan's point
about the totality of punishment as a utopia of moral reformation. He affirms
Ivan's construct in this corrected form and even gives it his blessing:

> "What has just been said here is also true, that if, indeed, the judg-
> ment of the Church came, and in its full force—that is, if the whole of
> society turned into the Church alone—then not only would the judg-
> ment of the Church influence the reformation of the criminal as it can
> never influence it now, but perhaps crimes themselves would indeed
> diminish at an incredible rate. And the Church, too, no doubt, would
> understand the future criminal and the future crime in many cases

quite differently from now, and would be able to bring the excommunicated back, to deter the plotter, to regenerate the fallen."

"It is true," the Elder smiled, "that now Christian society itself is
not yet ready, and stands only on seven righteous men; but as they
are never wanting, it abides firmly all the same, awaiting its complete
transfiguration from society as still an almost pagan organization,
into one universal and sovereign Church. And so be it, so be it, if only
at the end of time, for this alone is destined to be fulfilled! And there
is no need to trouble oneself with times and seasons, for the mystery
of times and seasons is in the wisdom of God, in his foresight, and
in his love. And that which by human reckoning may still be rather
remote, by divine predestination may already be standing on the eve
of its appearance, at the door. And so be that, too! So be it!"—"So be
it! So be it!"—Father Paissy confirmed with reverence and severity.
(Dostoevsky, *The Brothers Karamazov*, 65–66; punctuation altered)

Already the Church

The title of the chapter "So Be It!" reiterates the performative utterance
directly in the authorial voice. In this chapter, Dostoevsky allows his readers an insight into the performative operation of his discourse. The ideas on
the relation of the church and state presented through the five characters'
discussion constitute its perlocutionary dimension with the sentence "So Be
It!" making up its illocutionary seal. This affirmation throws into relief the
conflation between religious and secular discourse throughout the meta-text
of Dostoevsky's novels as a part of his subversive scheme.

Dostoevsky makes fiction into an arena for the performative implementa-
tion of his positive program of the "Christianization of consciousness." This
positive program, polemically aimed against Western and Westernized socialist utopias with their Christian underpinnings, is implicit in his alternative
utopia, the utopia of a gradual reformation of the state, and hence of the secular discourse on the ethical premises of Christ. This reformation, allegedly
expected in the future and advanced in the mode of hope, is however already
proleptically accomplished in Dostoevsky's quasi-realistic novels where the
reality of contemporary Russia appears already as the "Church."

The consciousness of his modern characters is a battlefield between good
and evil as defined by the tenets of Christian ethics. It is not a coincidence that
the discussion about the future of the church and the ethical mission of Orthodoxy blends smoothly into the sphere of Ivan Karamazov's consciousness in
the next chapter. Ivan externalizes and makes public his intimate thoughts
when he confesses his doubts about the ethical consequences of faith in the
immortality of the soul. This ethically tormented conscience, so typical for
Dostoevsky's characters, becomes a theme of Ivan's dialogue with Zosima:

"Yes, it was my contention. There is no virtue if there is no immortality."

"You are blessed if you believe so, or else most unhappy!"

"Why unhappy?" Ivan Fyodorovich smiled.

"Because in all likelihood you yourself do not believe either in the immortality of your soul or even in what you have written about the Church and the Church question."

"Maybe you're right . . . ! But still, I wasn't quite joking either . . . ," Ivan Fyodorovich suddenly and strangely confessed—by the way, with a quick blush.

"You weren't quite joking, that is true. This idea is not yet resolved in your heart and torments it. But a martyr, too, sometimes likes to toy with his despair, also from despair, as it were. For the time being you, too, are toying, out of despair, with your magazine articles and drawing-room discussions, without believing in your own dialectics and smirking at them with your heart aching inside you . . . The question is not resolved in you, and there lies your great grief, for it urgently demands resolution. . . ."

"But can it be resolved in myself? Resolved in a positive way?" Ivan Fyodorovich continued asking strangely, still looking at the elder with a certain inexplicable smile.

"Even if it cannot be resolved in a positive way, it will never be resolved in the negative way either—you yourself know this property of your heart, and therein lies the whole of its torment. But thank the Creator that he has given you a lofty heart, capable of being tormented by such a torment." (Dostoevsky, *The Brothers Kara-mazov*, 70)

Thus the heart of Dostoevsky's heroes is already the church. Not only do they measure every personal step and every choice of everyday life against the moral scale given in the scriptures, but also every social and political problem is approached in Dostoevsky's novelistic universe in a Christian idiom and from the point of view of Christian love for one's neighbor as opposed to the socialist, systemic "love of mankind."

The performative modality of Dostoevsky's discourse, which postulates his utopia as a reality, resorts to the conventional genres of the nineteenth-century novel—detective story, romance, family melodrama, Bildungsroman, political conspiracy, and historical Christ narrative. But he transforms and transfigures their linear *chronotope*, as if in a performance of a ritual, into a hermetic microcosm of mythically condensed time and space. Joseph Frank identified this condensation of time and space as a characteristic of modern literature. Dostoevsky anticipated the "spatial form" of many modernist writers who intended "the reader to apprehend their work spatially, in a moment of time, rather than a sequence."[67] But what sets Dostoevsky apart is that his novels' "spatial form" is modeled upon the spatiality of the church, the body of Christ.

Dostoevsky abandons the focus on the linear chronology of Christ's life, which his contemporaries Strauss or Renan saw as one historical narrative. Instead, he shifts the attention to its polyphonic presentation by the four evangelists, each of whom repeats the story with a slightly different accent. Dostoevsky's tendency to condense novelistic time into one instance of the here and now, which often caused him to be assimilated to Nietzsche, has as its goal a polyphonic leading of voices in a dialogue. In this way he transforms the modernist model of consciousness with its solipsistic experience of intensity into a collective, social form of intensity, carried out not outside but within a collective structure. Dostoevsky wants to transform individual existence into social coexistence, the model of which he borrows from ritual worship.

In fact, the commotion and polyphonic leading of voices in Dostoevsky's novels recall the peripatetic Orthodox liturgy, but transposed into the secular urban spaces of modern St. Petersburg and Russia's provincial towns. The iconographic transfiguration of those secular spaces often adumbrates heavenly orders and apocalyptic visions, familiar from the frescoes on the walls of medieval Orthodox churches. The narthex room and the wall in the West of the nave delineate a zone of transitory earthly life and death, displaying images of the passion and the Last Judgment. The opposite end of the nave and the apses in the East represent a zone of eternal life and heaven. In them arise the images of saints, prophets, and evangelists.[68]

Dostoevsky often crafts his mise-en-scène so as to convey such dramatic confrontations between "good" and "evil." For example, the participants in his "inappropriate gathering" are depicted visually and arranged in the space so as to evoke the spatiality of the church:

> The elder sat down on a very old-fashioned, leather-covered mahogany settee, and placed his guests, except for the two hieromonks, along the opposite wall, all four in a row, on four mahogany chairs with badly worn black leather upholstery. The hieromonks sat at either end of the room, one by the door, the other by the window. The seminarian, Alyosha, and the novice remained standing.[69]

The one side of the room alludes to the Russian iconostasis with its symmetrical alignment of ecclesiastical, saintly characters in their solemn dignity and calm, centered around Zosima, who occupies the place of God the Father. The representatives of hell are recognizably positioned along the opposite wall. The worldly buffoon Fyodor Pavlovich Karamazov quarrels here with Miusov, scatters frivolous anecdotes left and right, pulls grimaces and skits, giggles, and provokes. However, the hieromonks face him like icons who "showed no change at all in their physiognomies . . . watching with grave attention for what the elder would say."[70]

Zosima's little cell where the gathering takes place is after all an integral part of a monastery. Therefore, a religious allegory, conveyed here through the spatial arrangement of characters in the mise-en-scène, might seem to be less striking. But similar spatial configurations of "good" and "evil" appear in the drawing rooms of St. Petersburg apartments as well as in the other secular urban spaces of Dostoevsky's novels. For example, the wake in honor of the poor drunkard Marmeladov in *Crime and Punishment* (1866) transforms the living room of his family into a church. At the one corner of the room there is a display of icons in front of which Katerina Ivanovna, the widow, kneels with her children and prays. On the opposite side, her evil neighbor Luzhin makes his entrance to libel the innocent Sonechka, accusing her of stealing his money.

In the middle, a crowd of guests congregate around the table, witnessing this tableau vivant of an uncanny mythical confrontation between sanctity and hell. It is up to the community to judge, to decide, to make choices. The result is a triumph of justice, that is, a disclosure of Luzhin's intrigue and his ousting.[71] One can speak about verbal predetermination of the spatial mise-en-scène in Dostoevsky's novels in the same way as one speaks today about the "verbal predetermination of the visual" in Cervantes.[72] This predetermination suggests a path of reception: as *Don Quixote* lends itself to pictorial or cinematic adaptation, so the "spatial form" of Dostoevsky's novel lends itself to social emulation.

Dostoevsky's ethically differentiated spaces anticipate the transformation of the secular state with its public ethics and social responsibility into the church. They pull the reader into moral melodrama and inspire similar differentiations to be drawn in life. However, the Orthodox Church as institution is in Dostoevsky's understanding merely a matter of history. In the process of its fusion with the secular world, the "state," the official church with its panoply of rituals and relics, rescinds its sacrality and religious authority. Christian teaching ultimately turns into a governing principle of human ethical self-consciousness, into an internalized moral imperative.

An episode from Dostoevsky's novel *The Adolescent* (1875) provides a remarkable description of the church's transformation from a ritual space into the internal virtual space of human conscience. In this episode, the secondary character Trishatov explains how he would set up the cathedral scene in the opera *Faust*. Because of its poetologically self-reflexive character as to the workings of Dostoevsky's discourse apart, Trishatov's imaginary scene is worth quoting at length:

> If I were to compose an opera, I'd choose a theme from *Faust*. I love Faust. I keep composing music for that scene in the cathedral—oh, just in my head, of course. . . . The interior of that Gothic cathedral, the choir, the hymns. . . . In comes Gretchen . . . the choir is medieval—you can hear the fifteenth century at once. Gretchen is in despair. First, a

recitative, played very softly, but full of suffering and terror, while the choir thunders grimly, sternly, and impersonally, "*Dies irae, dies illa!*" And then, all of a sudden, the devil's voice sings the devil's song. You can't see him, there's only his song mingling with the hymns, almost blending into them, although it's completely different from them—I must manage to convey that somehow. The devil's song is long, persistent. A tenor—it absolutely must be a tenor. It begins softly and tenderly: "Do you remember, Gretchen, when, still an innocent child, you came here with your mother and lisped your prayers from the old prayer book?" But the devil's voice grows louder, more passionate, more intense, it floats on higher notes that contain despair, tears, and infinite, irretrievable hopelessness: "There's no forgiveness, Gretchen, no forgiveness here for you!" Gretchen wants to pray but only cries of pain come from her breast—you know, the breast shaken by sobs and convulsions. . . . And all this time the devil's song continues and pierces her soul deeper and deeper like a spear—the notes get higher and higher and then, suddenly, it all breaks off in a shriek: "Accursed one, this is the end!" . . . Gretchen falls on her knees, her hands clasped in front of her. And then comes her prayer. Something very short, a semi-recitative, but completely simple, without ornamentation, again very medieval, only our lines—Stradella has a passage with a score a bit like that. . . . And then, on the last note, she faints! There's general confusion, they pick her up, and suddenly the choir thunders forth. It must sound like an explosion of voices, an inspirational, triumphant, irresistible outburst, somewhat like "Borne on high by angels . . ." So that everything is shaken to its foundations and it all merges into one single overwhelming, exalted "*Hosanna!*"—like an outcry from the whole universe. . . . And they carry Gretchen off, and just at that moment the curtain must fall . . . ! Ah, I wish I could do it![73]

The polyphony of voices within the ethically differentiated space of a cathedral is internalized and transposed here into the internalized space of Gretchen's consciousness as conscience. The transposition takes the form of an aesthetic fiction, an opera, which is set on the stage of Trishatov's mind. The devil's song and an angelic choir will, according to Trishatov's concept, finally break out of the confines of a single consciousness into a form of universal dialogue. The disagreement of good and evil is not to be transcended in an ethically indifferent ecstasy. To the contrary, it is supposed to extend itself into an endless *mise-en-abîme* of discourses. But that is what already happens in the novelistic world of Dostoevsky.

Alex de Jonge has pointed out Dostoevsky's affinities with French modernism. He observes that "the characters of Baudelaire and Dostoevsky are in the process of losing [the] sense of cosmic and indeed social wholeness."[74]

Figure 4.2. Consciousness as the church: Mary of Burgundy reading, *The Hours of Mary of Burgundy*. Illuminated manuscript page. Cod. Vindobonensis 1857. Vienna, Austrian National Library.

However, this comparison requires a differentiation: Dostoevsky's characters are not just *losing* the sense of cosmic wholeness. Much rather they are partaking in a transformation of that "cosmic wholeness" (represented by the body of Christ or the cathedral) into a social wholeness, which is cemented by the logos of the social discourse and social conscience.

Remarkably, Trishatov takes up precisely this theme in his discussion of a scene from Dickens's *Old Curiosity Shop*. He describes a young girl standing at the threshold of a cathedral and contemplating the sun and concludes sententiously: "There is a double mystery: the sun is God's thought and the cathedral is man's thought."[75] The ethical reformation of the human mind, Dostoevsky suggests, should start with the internalization of the cathedral space, which tangibly allegorized good and evil in the building itself. His own novels aspire to be such virtual cathedrals. They are supposed to draw readers into their ethically dramatized space.

Trishatov's recourse to fifteenth-century sensibility and to a Gothic cathedral as a model of consciousness is also poetologically revealing. The medievalist Laurel Amtower has shown how the consciousness of reading, and especially of religious reading, crystallized in the course of the fifteenth century. Reading was understood as an activity which can pull the person into the virtual world of the book, as if it were a cathedral. Therefore one expected reading to exercise an immediate influence on the reader's inner disposition, to engage the reader with the content of the book practically.

In the illuminations of the time, an open book often symbolized Christ as the logos, whereas the space of a cathedral came (as in the arts of memory) to allegorize the consciousness of the reader. Consider an illumination from the fifteenth-century *Hours of Mary of Burgundy*. (See fig. 4.2.) In the foreground, the image shows Mary absorbed in reading. She sits at a window, which opens not onto the outside world of the street but into the inner space of a Gothic cathedral, the physical projection of her mind. In the cathedral of her mind, the content of the book, presumably the Bible, is represented and allegorized in three-dimensional shape. Reading thus provides an experience on the very borders of subjectivity, myth, and history. The cathedral, "man's thought," as Trishatov puts it, connects the microcosm of the human mind with the macrocosm of the universe. This transitional place links together the internal and external, the individual and collective in the life of the human being.

In the late Middle Ages, according to Amtower, Western culture comes to conceive of reading as a passageway to human "self-awareness" and "self-actuation":

> Books were thus symbols of a new kind of status to which anyone could aspire. They represented potentiality and worldly escape. But more than that, books offered the semblance of egalitarianism. For the gentry, in particular, the act of reading embodied something

of a utopian promise: projecting conversations, places, and identities romanticized by their very distance from reality, the contents of books provided an illusion, however transitory, of class freedom. In books one could converse with the saints, the church fathers, even the Virgin herself. If the Church promised that all were equal before God, books upheld that promise, creating worlds in which anyone "intellectually enlightened" enough to read the words or even meditate upon the images might find an audience with the greatest figures of history and tradition.[76]

Amtower's study on medieval reading helps us understand the archaic dimension of Dostoevsky's restructuring of the modern novel's chronotope in terms of the spatiality of a cathedral. The cathedral offers a model of a collective, public space. Therefore it aptly allegorizes that social dimension of reading and of the human mind which Bakhtin described as carnivalesque. The emergence, democratization, and proliferation of the culture of reading that had progressed in Russia rapidly from the establishment of the first fashionable literary almanacs in 1820s to the serious "thick journals" of the 1840s was the social reality behind this allegory.[77] Dostoevsky's own publications were carried on its wave.

In Dostoevsky's discourse, the spatial allegorization of the mind's work transforms into a virtual model of consciousness, private and collective at once. This consciousness leaves the religious realm of the sacred, which had reached its vanishing point with the inevitable progress of scientific and critical thought, but it does so in order to claim validity in the profane, secular sphere of human coexistence, in the state.

"Russian Understanding"

Surprisingly, Dostoevsky characterizes his model of ethical consciousness, originally inspired by the Gothic cathedral, Goethe, and Gounod, as a specifically Russian model. This differentiation, drawn in emphatically national terms, is usually shrugged off as a trace of Dostoevsky's idiosyncratic pan-Slavism. Nevertheless this national differentiation of Christianity has an important structural function. It sets up an alternative path for the church's destiny in an increasingly secularized society, the path of transformation of the cathedral into a cathedral without walls, the cathedral of an ethically differentiated discourse.

Dostoevsky's younger contemporary Vladimir Soloviev discussed the writer's social project with rare poignancy in his "Three Addresses in Memory of Dostoevsky": "If we want to specify and designate the social idea at which Dostoevsky arrived with a single word, then this word will not be the nation, but the *Church*."[78] But Soloviev also differentiated "the Church as a social ideal" in Dostoevsky's sense from the belief in the church as the mystical body of Christ, or the practice of the church as the collective of believers. He captures the whole outline of Dostoevsky's discourse apart so precisely that it is worth quoting at length:

> Dostoevsky did not have any theological pretensions, and thus we also do not have the right to look within him for any logical definition of the Church in its essence. However, in preaching the Church as a social ideal, he expressed an absolutely clear and definite requirement, just as clear and definite as the requirement declared by European socialism—although in direct contrast to it. (Therefore, in his last diary, Dostoevsky also called people's faith in the Church our Russian socialism.) European socialists require a violent reduction of all to one purely material level of satiated and complacent workers; they require the reduction of the State and society to the level of a simple economic association. "Russian socialism," about which Dostoevsky spoke, on the contrary, elevates all to the moral level of the Church as a spiritual brotherhood, although with the preservation of an outward inequality in social circumstance; it requires the spiritedness of the entire State and social structure through the embodiment of Christian truth and life in it.[79]

As a writer, Dostoevsky practices this elevation of all "to the moral level of the Church" by emulating the logic of the spiritual transformation represented in the visual and spatial outline of the Russian cathedral with its Byzantine origins in the mystical theology of Pseudo-Dionysius the Areopagite.[80] The inner space of the Byzantine cathedral, inherited by the Orthodox churches, was supposed to evoke a sense of the building's dematerialization. Frescoes of the saints covered all the walls of the Byzantine cathedral so densely that the members of the congregation found themselves in the midst of religious figures whose solemn, intense gaze focused on them from all directions. In this way the building fused with the community horizontally, whereas the concentration of light in the dome and the thinning out of the stone into lighter substances conveyed an impression of the building's gradual rising away from the earth.[81]

Orthodox architecture was premised on the understanding that the church building would foster spiritual growth and communal feeling. Dostoevsky translated this understanding into the social internalization of Christ's teaching. He turned the mystery of Christ's resurrection into the structure of human consciousness. Characteristically, Dostoevsky's heroes find themselves constantly inspected, penetrated, judged by the silent gaze of their fellow human beings. This gaze, originating in the frescoes of martyred saints inspecting the Christian congregation, is now embodied in the flesh and blood of the modern residents of St. Petersburg.

The philosopher Pavel Florensky, who provided a rich modern study of the metaphysical, ethical, and psychological meaning of the inner space of an Orthodox church, called the material iconostasis a "crutch of spirituality," the function of which is to highlight the mystery of the altar in compensation for the "feeble spiritual vision" of the believers.[82] Dostoevsky had to preserve such a crutch of spirituality while challenging his contemporaries with the extremes of religious ethics and psychology. The meta-text of Dostoevsky's novels abounds in elements of ecstatic Orthodox worship. They are recognizable in recitations of the scriptures, prostrations and kneeling, emphatic gestures of crossing, kissing of icons, confessions, and the like. But they spread throughout Dostoevsky's novels as allegorical ruins of the church's external shell.

In the historical reality of Dostoevsky's Russia, this eccentric world stretched between good and evil, ironically, represents an ultimate farewell to ritualized performances of belief. Raskolnikov confesses his crime by kneeling and bowing not in the church but at a crossroads in St. Petersburg because the Russian metropolis had already superseded the church. Prince Myshkin kisses the portrait of Nastasya Filippovna in the apartment of General Epanchin as if it were an icon, because the church has already been subsumed in the secular dwellings of the citizens. Such baroque gestures show that Dostoevsky implements the utopian program of the state becoming the church, articulated in *The Brothers Karamazov*, in the performance of his own discourse.

In the West, as Dostoevsky saw it, the blows of progress emptied the church of its sacred content and left behind merely a dead building. The hierarchy of Western Christianity survives as a relic. It is a superfluous atavism within the modern world, void of any real influence on human consciousness. Ivan Karamazov, the theoretician of the dead church, articulates its failure regarding the situation of a criminal in Western society as follows:

> The foreign criminal, they say, rarely repents, for even the modern theories themselves confirm in him the idea that his crime is not a crime but only a rebellion against an unjustly oppressive force. Society cuts him off from itself quite mechanically by the force that triumphs over him, and accompanies that excommunication with hatred (so, at least, they say about themselves in Europe)—with hatred and complete indifference and forgetfulness of his subsequent fate as their brother. Thus, all of this goes on without the least compassion of the Church, for in many cases there already are no more churches at all, and what remains are just churchmen and splendid church buildings, while the churches themselves have long been striving to pass from the lower species, the Church, to a higher species, the state, in order to disappear into it completely. So it seems to be, at least, in Lutheran lands. And in Rome it is already a thousand years since the state

was proclaimed in place of the Church. (Dostoevsky, *The Brothers Karamazov*, 65)

The cell of the dying elder Zosima symptomatically contains numerous representations of this dying ecclesiastical "officialism," as the liberal Miusov puts it contemptuously. The room, seen from Miusov's point of view, is cramped with old, useless objects of religious worship, which stem from all periods and denominations and reflect the religious "tastes" of the Christians of all standings:

> . . . there were many icons in the corner—including a huge one of the Mother of God, painted, probably, long before the schism. An icon lamp flickered before it. Next to it were two more icons in shiny casings, and next to them some little figurines of cherubs, porcelain eggs, an ivory Catholic crucifix with the Mater Dolorosa embracing it, and several imported engravings from great Italian artists of the past centuries. Next to these fine and expensive prints were displayed several sheets of the commonest Russian lithographs of saints, martyrs, hierarchs, and so on, such as are sold for a few kopecks at any fair. There were several lithographic portraits of Russian bishops, past and present, but these were on other walls. (Dostoevsky, *The Brothers Karamazov*, 39)

This jumble allegorizes the dusty past of the church as an institution and its outdated system of representation. Out of this ecclesiastical lumber room the dying Zosima, the novel's equivalent of God the Father, sends his spiritual son and follower Alyosha on a mission into the wide world. He insists that Alyosha leave the monastery because his presence is needed more among people. Zosima's death with its lack of saintliness or miracle becomes an important test of Alyosha's faith. Instead of divine transfiguration, which according to the old legends awaited the monastery's elders, Zosima's corpse starts decaying and smelling like any regular corpse.

Dostoevsky counts the type of miracle that the populace expects from Zosima's death among the devil's temptations of Christ, temptations to which the official church had succumbed. The novel stages instead a "miracle" of moral transformation that the despairing Alyosha all of a sudden witnesses in his encounter with Grushenka. Instead of seducing Alyosha, she opens herself to him in friendship and tells him the "onion story," which allegorizes her moral awakening. The story reveals her ethical self-consciousness. Grushenka's change of character happens not without the help of Alyosha's kindness and respect for her. This is the miracle that happens in the characters' dialogue, in the living word, freed from ecclesiastical constraints.

The two Christlike, saintly characters—Alyosha Karamazov and his novelistic predecessor Prince Myshkin—fulfill an important structural function in Dostoevsky's novels. They trigger a dialogue, provoke the characters to open themselves in conversation, and mediate between disparate narrative lines in a fashion germane to the genre of the novel—by walking and talking. It is through their particular discursivity that the other characters experience their conversions and revelations. It is through them that the characters' ethical consciousness, the differentiation between good and evil within themselves, is triggered.

In their mediating function, these two figures are comparable to the Eucharist that circulates among the congregation and unites its members through the partaking of Christ's body, or in Dostoevsky's case of Christ's word. Bakhtin called this narrative feature quite unambiguously "participatory thinking." Dostoevsky conceived of such sharing of Christ's word as material and literal, but at the same time as deeply psychological. For example, Prince Myshkin spends his conscious life copying a manuscript transmitted from the Russian elders. In his examination for employment as a copyist, he reproduces the signature of the sixteenth-century Russian saint Pafnuty Borovsky so exactly that in the course of copying he comes to completely identify with the saint and his words. This identity is also what in the end assures his narrative function as a trigger of dialogue.

Or consider the counterexample of the scene wherein Rodion Raskolnikov comes to the police to inquire about a bureaucratic bagatelle, after he has already committed a crime. Suddenly, he is incapable of writing down and signing a note that a clerk dictates to him that obliges him to stay in town until he pays an outstanding check. The alienation from the community of people, Christ's body, which he experiences in this scene makes him incapable of talking to others:

> A dark sensation of tormenting, infinite solitude and estrangement suddenly rose to consciousness in his soul. . . . Even if he had been sentenced to be burned at that moment, he would not have stirred, and would probably not have listened very attentively to the sentence. What was taking place in him was totally unfamiliar, new, sudden, never before experienced. . . . Not that he understood it, but he sensed clearly, with all the power of sensation, that it was no longer possible for him to address these people in the police station, not only with heartfelt effusions, as he had just done, but in any way at all, and had they been his own brothers and sisters, and not police lieutenants, there would still have been no point in his addressing them, in whatever circumstances of life.[83]

When transposed into human consciousness, Christ's body becomes the very guarantor of language, conscience, and discursive mobility. Raskolnikov's inability to sign his name on a form which is supposed to bureaucratically bind him with the community is indicative of his fall from

Christ's word: "'You can't even write, you're barely able to hold the pen,' the clerk observed, studying Raskolnikov with curiosity."[84] The state's formal attempt at binding a citizen into community creates a pronounced dissonance with Raskolnikov's condition of inner alienation. Right after signing the form he suddenly overhears the clerks talking about his crime and faints in the middle of the office.

The rest of the novel pursues the gradual reintegration of the alienated criminal into the social structure of human community. This happens dialogically through two unconventional characters and outsiders—the prostitute Sonechka and the non-bureaucratically perceptive detective Porfiry Petrovich, about whose homosexuality some hints are dropped. Both speak in a religious idiom and see faith as a way of overcoming the exclusion that a criminal endures in a secular state. These two marginalized figures share Dostoevsky's vision of a social necessity for Christianization, that is, the humanization of the state.

The Chronotope of Conscience

In his adjustment of the nineteenth-century novel's linear chronotope to its new function as a medium of conscience, Dostoevsky resorts to a religiously rooted, allegorical vision of history. Allegory's vision is backward-oriented and indiscriminately crowds different pasts together in space, as Walter Benjamin has shown in *The Origin of German Tragic Drama*. The history in Dostoevsky's novels is a church history represented in an allegorical mode through its spatial and visual dimension. It is no coincidence that Fyodor Pavlovich calls Zosima's bowing at the feet of Dmitri Karamazov, the novel's martyr, "some sort of emblem."[85] This gesture from the point of view of the secular world appears eccentric and outlandish.

In Dostoevsky's novel, spatially construed religious history opposes the secular, rational understanding of history as a linear progression in time. The constitution of the "self-consciousness" of Dostoevsky's heroes, discussed by Bakhtin, necessitates such a spatial transformation of a linear narrative into the "inner cathedral" of the human being, the walls of which are thinned out into the purely verbal performance of discourse. The echo effects of liturgical singing are translated here into verbal echoes of the voices of others.

The allegorical mode allows Dostoevsky to acknowledge the historical dimension of Christianity without abandoning the tension between transcendence and immanence underlying faith. In his portrayal of the emergence of "Christian consciousness" atop the institutional ruins of the church, Dostoevsky integrates historical Christ narratives with rationalizing social utopias. By transposing Christ's teaching into the inner self of a human being, he creates his own social utopia of a Russian collectivity that is based in an ethically differentiated consciousness.

The Western versions of Christianity did not manage in Dostoevsky's vision to undergo such a reviving fusion with the society and therefore they constitute a counterpart to the dead body of Holbein's Christ, a copy of which Prince Myshkin contemplates in his romantic rival's somber house. The painting is so important for the conception of the novel that it is discussed twice, once by Myshkin and Rogozhin and once by the nihilist teenager Ippolit. Despite their philosophical differences, all heroes agree that this painting allegorizes that "dark, brazen and senseless eternal force, to which everything is subordinate,"[86] that "enormous, implacable, speechless animal,"[87] ugly as a tarantula, the nothingness which annihilates life and poses a test to faith.[88]

Holbein's Christ represents the dead body over which Nietzsche's Zarathustra danced singing his ominous song about the Last Man. Void of the hope for resurrection, all other human aspirations, in Dostoevsky's eyes, lose their sense and élan of faith. European civilizational ideas turn into a drab graveyard over which Dostoevsky's heroes can only weep. That is why Ivan tells Alyosha:

> I want to go to Europe, Alyosha, I'll go straight from here. Of course I know that I will only be going to a graveyard, but to the most, the most precious graveyard, that's the thing! The precious dead lie there, each stone over them speaks of such ardent past life, of such passionate faith in their deeds, their truth, their struggle, and their science, that I—this I know beforehand—will fall to the ground and kiss those stones and weep over them—being wholeheartedly convinced, at the same time, that it has all long been a graveyard and nothing more. (Dostoevsky, *The Brothers Karamazov*, 230)

For centuries Russian culture had been embracing Western thought and looking up to superior Western achievements. But now, as Ivan's words suggest, Russia is ready to recognize the death of its Western idols and to embark on its own independent path. "Russia must reveal to the world her own Russian Christ, whom as yet the peoples know not, and who is rooted in our native Orthodox faith,"[89] Dostoevsky wrote to Strachov on March 18, 1869. Prince Myshkin's confrontation with a copy of Holbein's painting, like that of Dostoevsky himself with the original in Basel, constitutes the pivotal moment when Myshkin as the Russian Christ faces an emblem of the dead Western church which had lost all hope of resurrection.

In his "Russian" version of belief, Dostoevsky replaces this dead body with a vanishing body that yields its place to Christian consciousness. Prince Myshkin facing Holbein's *Dead Christ* reminds us of Makar Devushkin, the poor clerk in Dostoevsky's early novel *Poor Folk* (1846), who suddenly faces himself in a mirror. The mirror augments the self-consciousness of Dostoevsky's "small man," the literary ancestor of Myshkin. Bakhtin observed that when Makar views his reflection, his physical attributes are "transferred from one plane of representation to another" in such a way that "we see not who he is, but how he is conscious of himself."[90] Thus the very moment of Myshkin's encounter with the dead Christ which seems to reproduce the topos of Nietzsche and French aestheticism about Christ's failure becomes the actual point of departure for the subject's self-awareness.

While looking at Holbein's painting, Prince Myshkin becomes conscious of himself as a dying body and of his imitation of Christ as an imitation of Christ's death. In fact, this realization in front of the painting anticipates Myshkin's near-death under Rogozhin's knife soon thereafter. At the very point when Rogozhin raises a knife to kill his romantic rival, the narrator takes over from the fainting Prince Myshkin to provide an omniscient insight into his consciousness:

> Then suddenly it was as if something opened up before him: an extraordinary *inner* light illuminated his soul. This moment lasted perhaps half a second; but he nevertheless remembered clearly and consciously the beginning, the very first sound of his terrible scream, which burst from his breast of itself and which no force would have enabled him to stop. Then his consciousness instantly went out, and there was total darkness.
>
> He had had a fit of epilepsy, which had left him very long ago. It is known that these fits of epilepsy, *falling fits* properly speaking, come instantaneously. In these moments the face, especially the eyes, suddenly become extremely distorted. Convulsions and spasms seize the whole body and all the features of the face. A dreadful, unimaginable scream, unlike anything, bursts from the breast; everything human suddenly disappears, as it were, in this scream, and it is quite impossible, or at least very difficult, for the observer to imagine and allow that this is the man himself screaming. It may even seem as if someone else were screaming from inside the man. At least many people have explained their impression that way, and there are many whom the sight of a man in a falling fit fills with a decided and unbearable terror, which even has something mystical in it.[91]

Dostoevsky, who experienced the same feeling of mystical terror himself in front of Holbein's *Dead Christ* in Basel,[92] chooses to place Holbein's painting in the house of Rogozhin. The future murderer confesses to Myshkin that he often looks at the image. In the novel one habitually calls it "Rogozhin's painting." This painting also appears in the nightmare of the dying Ippolit, the novel's young atheist who offers this poignant *ekphrasis*:

> Depicted in the painting is Christ, who has just been taken down from the cross. I think that painters have usually been in the habit of

depicting Christ, both on the cross and when taken down from it, still with a nuance of extraordinary beauty in the face; this beauty they seek to preserve in him even during his most terrible torments. But in Rogozhin's painting there was no trace of beauty; this really was the corpse of a man who had endured endless torments even before the cross, wounds, tortures, beating from the guards, beating from the mob while he carried the cross and fell beneath it, and, at last, the agony of the cross which lasted six hours (by my calculations, at least). To be sure, it is the face of a man who has *just* been taken down from the cross, that is, retaining very much that is still alive and warm; nothing has yet had time to go stiff, so that on the face of the dead man one can even see suffering, as though he were experiencing it even now (this is very well captured by the artist); but on the other hand, the face is not spared at all; here there is only nature, and this is truly what the corpse of a man, whoever he may be, must look like after such torments. I am aware that the Christian Church established in the first centuries that Christ did not suffer figuratively but actually, and that therefore his body must have been wholly and completely subject to the laws of nature on the cross. In the painting, the face has been horribly lacerated by blows, swollen, with terrible, swollen and bloody bruises, the eyes open, the pupils narrow; the large, open whites of the eyes gleam with a deathly, glassy sheen. But strangely, as one looks at this corpse of a tortured man, a peculiar and interesting question arises: if this is really what the corpse looked like (and it certainly must have looked just like this) when it was seen by all his disciples, his chief future apostles, by the women who followed him and stood by the cross, indeed by all who believed in him and worshipped him, then how could they believe, as they looked at such a corpse, that this martyr would rise from the dead?[93]

Holbein's painting of the dead Christ indeed becomes a test of faith for the characters in the novel. In the young Ippolit, it triggers doubt and introspection. It shatters Rogozhin's faith, but only strengthens that of Prince Myshkin who contemplates in this painting his own epileptic death. His body might be similarly battered and bruised, or his face distorted in a fit that would throw him down the stairs under Rogozhin's knife, but his epileptic death is nevertheless only a temporary one, from which he comes back to life. In a way, *The Idiot* practices an "allegorical fragmentation" (*allegorische Zerstückelung*) of Holbein's dead Christ: each time the painting resurfaces in the novel it provokes a discussion about life and death, and therefore about good and evil. Thus, in Dostoevsky, Christ resurrects discursively in the dialogue of the heroes and Christ's dead body, in fact, becomes that "metaphysical threshold to the novelistic consciousness of good and evil" emphasized in the later Bakhtin.

In Performative Mode: Utopia as Reality

The proleptic feature of Dostoevsky's poetics which he called "realism in a higher sense of the word" describes his discursive strategy of presenting his vision of an ethically differentiated state as a reality already achieved.[94] Therefore he depends on the kind of language that can "do things with words." But Dostoevsky seeks a specific performativity that can bridge fictional diegesis and the author's personal experience. Only through the real presence of the author who establishes himself as a medium of truth can discourse appear to be rooted in phenomenal reality and thus become existentially important to the characters as well as to the readers.

This performative aspect of Dostoevsky's language comes from religious discourse. "So Be It!" is its underlying matrix. Symptomatically, the monks chide the author of a book on an ecclesiastical topic for his unacceptable "worldly pun" on the words "a kingdom not of this world." Though a literal quotation from the Gospel accounts of Jesus's dialogue with Pilate, the expression has a different connotation from the original: "unworldly" as in lacking practical knowledge or applicability. Given the fact that the monastery's elder has been asked to repair the rift in the Karamazov family, the pun directly undermines any possibility of his mediation's successful outcome. Such puns also permeate the irresponsible language of Fyodor Pavlovich Karamazov. Plays on words, the monks hold, convey the sensibility of the secular world. As a vehicle of relativism, they are not permissible in the earnest realm of ultimate questions.

The religious dimension of Dostoevsky's discourse, its ontological anchorage in the phenomenon, was not in the least to resist the general tendency toward the "etiolation of language" that alarmed many European intellectuals of the second half of the nineteenth century. Dostoevsky saw the loss of faith as responsible for the banalization of discourse. The writer's French contemporary Gustave Flaubert exposed the phenomenon of ideas turning into commonplaces in *Bouvard and Pécuchet* and the *Dictionary of Accepted Ideas*. In his own way, Flaubert also connected religious relativism with the inflation of language. In the words of Pécuchet, "What does it matter what people believe in? The main thing is to believe."[95] The emergence of mass society, the blurring of differences among social strata, and universal suffrage brought about the phenomenon of "public opinion" which Alexis de Tocqueville famously discussed in his nineteenth-century bestseller *Democracy in America* (1840). The development of the printing industry enlarged the circulation of newspapers and therefore increased the weight and influence of public opinion, accelerating the hardening of language into clichés.[96]

Inspired by the mass media of newspapers and magazines, Dostoevsky's novels often appeared in installments in serialized periodicals and did not shun cheap tricks of suspense for the sake of public entertainment. They were designed to counter and overturn the predominant public discourse, but to do so within the same medial paradigm. He was transfiguring broadly circulating ideas into existential questions of life and death by rooting them solidly in the "real presence" of his characters and approaching them from multiple perspectives in dialogue.

In *A Writer's Diary*, Dostoevsky lamented the phenomenon of the "cliché-ization" of language and ideas:

> Think carefully about today's common opinions, about today's "rational demands," about today's flat judgments—not only upon Thackeray but upon the whole Russian People: what *simplicity* there is at times! What a straight-line approach; what quick satisfaction with the petty and insignificant as means of expression; what a general rush to set one's mind at rest as quickly as possible, to pronounce judgment so as not to have to trouble oneself any longer.[97]

Dostoevsky's insistence on spoken expression can be seen as another way of addressing this cultural tendency. Bureaucratic cliché is mocked in the writing style of Dostoevsky's most despised character, the social parvenu Luzhin in *Crime and Punishment*. Dostoevsky's learned criminals Rodion Raskolnikov and Ivan Karamazov, who like Judas fell away from Christ, publish in journals and operate with the fashionable *idées reçues* of the time. But their intellectual constructs tragically crumble to pieces when put to the test of reality. Flaubert treats the similar failure of Bouvard and Pécuchet, those lovers of museums, collections, journals, manuals, dictionaries, and university lectures, in the comical mode of parody. After all the ordeals and disappointments that the unfortunate followers of learned discourse had gone through in their attempts at a practical application of knowledge, Flaubert, with cruel irony, turns them into copyists.

To such analysis of reality and pronounced admissions of defeat, Dostoevsky responds by postulating a utopia. He reverses the direction taken by Flaubert and transforms his copyist Makar Devushkin, the protagonist of the early and still secular novel *Poor Folk*, into the great copyist Prince Myshkin, the protagonist of the later and already religiously transfigured novel *The Idiot*. Whereas Devushkin, himself a copy of Pushkin's and Gogol's heroes, is hopelessly entrapped in his identity as a copyist, Prince Myshkin's copying of the Russian elders' transmission nourishes his imitation of Christ in day-to-day life. Dostoevsky moves from iteration, or copying in a sense of writing and literary intertextuality, which leads to the "etiolation" of discourse, to a lived experience of the imitation of Christ as an imitation of his discourse.

Prince Myshkin's copying leads to the internalization of Christian teaching in his own consciousness and his own word. Characteristically, he refers to Christ not as the incarnation of God but as an author of a discourse ("Christ talked about this") or as a thinker ("Christ's thought"). Joseph Frank points out that this understanding goes back to the time of Dostoevsky's early alliance with the "revolutionary" reformers of society:

> All the Utopian Socialists of any importance in the 1840s saw Christ (much as Dostoevsky had done in 1838) as a divine figure come to prescribe the laws governing the organization of earthly life in the modern world, and whose teachings, freed from centuries of perversion, were at last to be put into practice. . . . When Belinsky became converted to French Utopian Socialism in 1841–1842, he accepted a doctrine, it will be recalled, strongly informed by Christian moral-religious values.[98]

But in *The Idiot*, Dostoevsky's vision of Christ acquires a new dimension which sets it apart from socialist utopias. The novel shares the sensibility of the writer's famous credo as expressed in his letter to the historian, sociologist, and the father of Russian liberalism Konstantin Kavelin: "Christ was mistaken—it's been proved! A burning feeling tells me: better to remain with a mistake, with Christ, than with you . . . Living life has flown away from you, and only formulas and categories are left."[99]

Dostoevsky sees the socialist understanding of human being as one of positivist calculation. "Dostoevsky objects," Frank writes, "to what might be described, in a loose sense, as the behaviorist world-view. Behaviorist science is rooted in the empirical method and nineteenth-century positivism."[100] Thus, turning away from the political aspect of Christ's discourse, Dostoevsky dismisses a "behaviorist" approach to the human being in favor of a religious and existential one. He turns to Christ as a theoretician of extended consciousness.

Meaningfully, Christ's authority as a thinker is quoted in the episodes which deal with the human condition on the threshold of death: for example, in the salon of the Epanchins, when Myshkin suggests a decapitation scene as a subject for a painting and reflects on the extension of human perception of time in the last moment before death, or Christ is referred to in the episode of Myshkin's epileptic fit which rescues him from Rogozhin's attack. Dostoevsky's vision of Christ's discourse as truth about the human condition goes back to his religious conversion at his mock execution and the consequent labor camp in Siberia.[101]

The Idiot exposes a direct link between this experience and Dostoevsky's poetics. Therefore this novel can be seen as a point of Dostoevsky's personal entrance into his discourse. Prince Myshkin shares his author's most intimate existential experience, which came to inform the time structure of Dostoevsky's big novels—the extension of consciousness preceding an epileptic fit, or in the face of a near-death. Dostoevsky anchors the truth claim of his discourse in his own body. In a discursive *mise-en-abîme*, his protagonist embodies the authorial position. He triggers the extended dialogue of the novel, but also links the diegetic pattern of ideas with a social discourse of Dostoevsky's time.

The Allegorical Figuration of a New Discourse

Prince Myshkin, a modern allegory of Christ, whose bodily presence is conveyed exclusively in negative terms of sickness, meagerness, and impotence, appears as a vanishing body, the body on the brink of letting loose the word it engenders. This conception of Christ responds to the critic Belinsky's disparaging words that "Christ, if he were born in our day, would be the most ordinary and insignificant person; he would simply vanish in the face of contemporary science and of the contemporary movers of mankind."[102] Dostoevsky makes this process of Christ's vanishing into a means of his allegorical figuration of a new discourse.

Walter Benjamin has shown that the first banalizations of Christ owed much to the spirit of allegory. For Benjamin, allegory as a form of discourse was born out of the seventeenth century's religious crisis, when Christ's dead body became an important vehicle of transcendence precisely because of its negative anchorage in the decay of immanence. Benjamin writes about the allegorical sensibility of the seemingly diminishing Christ images of the baroque and Sturm und Drang:

> The attempt to gather all worldly events into the graphic foreground is not undertaken only in order to heighten the tension between immanence and transcendence, but also in order to secure for the latter the greatest conceivable rigour, exclusiveness and inexorability. It is an unsurpassably spectacular gesture to place even Christ in the realm of the provisional, the everyday, the unreliable. The *Sturm und Drang* provides strong support; Merck writes that it "cannot in any way detract from the great man if it is known that he was born in a stable and lay in swaddling clothes between an ox and an ass."[103]

Benjamin's book on German baroque drama captures the origins of modernism in Christ's dead body. It charts a path between Nietzsche and Dostoevsky. Benjamin emphasizes the transcendence of *physis* into a social, cultural form of discourse. The discursive transfiguration of nature into allegorical meaning is also valid for Dostoevsky's poetics. The Russian writer replaces Nietzschean transcendence through dialogization and intensification of consciousness and situates it within the discursive sphere of immanence so that any moment of transcendence loops back to social reality and the full presence of conscience.

Prince Myshkin's reflections on the epileptic condition illustrate precisely this dialogical and self-conscious variation on Nietzsche's Dionysian theme, as if they were written in a direct response to the philosopher:

> The sense of life, of self-awareness, increased nearly tenfold in these moments, which flashed by like lightning. His mind, his heart were

lit up with an extraordinary light; all his agitation, all his doubts, all his worries were as if placated at once, resolved in a sort of sublime tranquility, filled with serene, harmonious joy, and hope, filled with reason and ultimate cause. . . . Reflecting on that moment afterwards, in a healthy state, he had often said to himself that all those flashes and glimpses of a higher self-sense and self-awareness . . . were nothing but an illness, a violation of the normal state, and if so, then this was not the highest being at all but, on the contrary, should be counted as the very lowest. . . . Was he dreaming some sort of abnormal and nonexistent visions at that moment, as from hashish, opium, or wine, which humiliate the reason and distort the soul? He could reason about it sensibly once his morbid state was over. . . . However, he did not insist on the dialectical part of his reasoning: dullness, darkness of soul, idiocy stood before him as the clear consequence of these "highest moments." Naturally, he was not about to argue in earnest. His reasoning, that is, his evaluation of this moment, undoubtedly contained an error, but all the same he was somewhat perplexed by the actuality of the sensation. What, in fact, was he to do with this actuality? Because it had happened, he had succeeded in saying to himself in that very second, that this second, in its boundless happiness, which he fully experienced, might perhaps be worth his whole life.[104]

In the context of the debates between Slavophiles and Westernizers on the question of "national consciousness,"[105] Dostoevsky polemically claims this model of self-doubting, self-searching, self-evaluating, and thus moralizing consciousness for a Russian subjectivity to be achieved under the auspices of Russian Orthodoxy but in a gospel of his own writings. About a hundred years later the French psychoanalyst Jacques Lacan would rely on the same model of the basic Christian myth of death and resurrection for his articulation of the notion of the subject. Importantly, Lacan put forth his notion of the subject as a revision of Freud in the aftermath of the Second World War.

As in Dostoevsky, there is no energetic drive in Lacan that would not be inscribed into a structure of meaning, climaxing in the notion of the "unconscious structured like a language." Lacanian signification starts, as perhaps it had to, with Christ's death on the cross, which is for him a prototypical instance of symbolic representation, the instance where the Name-of-the-Father is called out to become a trigger of the metaphor, and thus of a cultural signification at large.[106] The notion of resurrection is intrinsic in his concept of *jouissance* describing the subject's potential of sexual desire and its sublimation in an act of cultural creativity.[107] Lacan's biographer Elisabeth Roudinesco testifies to the psychoanalyst's own claim that his teaching possessed a religious dimension.[108]

The socially redemptive relevance of Lacanian discourse is difficult to overestimate. His early treatises on the treatment of psychosis appear in the context of the 1950s as an attempt to bring European civilization out of that very torpor where the Nietzschean ecstasy of transcendence threw it with the collapse of the Second World War. In Lacan, the crucified Christ who calls the Name-of-the-Father comes to stand for postwar consciousness, for the subject overcoming the existential forlornness of corporeal and mental destruction. Postwar culture testifies in a variety of ways to the awakening of the industrialized nations to that form of self-consciousness and dialogic imagination that Dostoevsky broached in the second half of the nineteenth century.

In her famous discussion of Holbein's painting of the dead Christ, which stood in Dostoevsky's thinking for the Western and Westernizing lack of belief, Julia Kristeva, characteristically, recaptured for the modern subject Dostoevsky's dissolving of Christ's body into a structure of polyphonic, ethically differentiated discourse.[109] In the steps of Lacan, Kristeva attempted to reinscribe Christ's dead body into a structure of meaning. On the level of a psychoanalytical reflection, she tried to resurrect that Christ over whose body Western civilization once ruthlessly stepped:

> The break, brief as it might have been, in the bond linking Christ to His Father and to life, introduces into the mythical representation of the Subject a fundamental and psychically necessary discontinuity. . . . Because Christianity set that rupture at the very heart of the absolute Subject—Christ; because it represented it as a Passion, as an interdependent opposite of his Resurrection, his glory and his eternity, it brought to consciousness the essential dramas that are internal to the becoming of each and every subject. It thus endows itself with a tremendous cathartic power.[110]

The "tremendous cathartic power" which Julia Kristeva sees in Holbein's Christ, Dostoevsky invested in Prince Myshkin, whom he conceived as a Russian counterpart to this painting. In his eyes Holbein's picture emblematized atheism and the inability to overcome the laws of nature, and hence stood for a mental state that is incapable of regeneration. Dostoevsky described this mental state as "some enormous machine of the most modern devising, which has senselessly seized, smashed to pieces and devoured, dully and without feeling, a great and priceless being—a being which alone was worth the whole of nature and all its laws, the whole earth, which was, perhaps, created solely for the emergence of that being!"[111] In his polemical fervor, he labeled it "Western."

The necessity to postulate the cathartic power of Christ's death in the wake of state-sanctioned mass murder starts in the postwar discourse with the Dostoevskyan appropriation of the structure of resurrection, first of all, for an individual psyche. But Dostoevsky also understood an individual consciousness as always already collective. The epileptic logic of resurrection, pointed out by Thomas Mann, might have allowed Dostoevsky to construe the cathartic potential of consciousness, but he also endowed consciousness with the social potential for ethical differentiation. He did so by distinguishing between Christ's two bodies, one physically dead and one discursively transfigured.

Theologically incorrect, but rhetorically overpowering, these two bodies stand in his novels next to and against each other as life and death, good and evil, as heaven and hell do in the frescoes of the Orthodox Church, the body of Christ. Dostoevsky accounted for its historical vanishing in a way that allows for a transition from religious corporeality via morally punctuated space to an ethically alarmed discourse.

Figure 5.1. Fabio Mauri, *Intellettuale: "Il Vangelo secondo Matteo" di/su Pier Paolo Pasolini*, 1975 (cropped). Galleria Comunale d'Arte Moderna, Bologna. Photo: Antonio Masotti. Courtesy Studio Fabio Mauri, copyright © Eredi Fabio Mauri and Stefano Masotti.

Chapter 5

✦

The Scene of Christ, or the Cinematic
Body of Pier Paolo Pasolini

God is a scandal in this world. Christ, if he returns, will be
again a scandal.

—Pier Paolo Pasolini

At the inauguration of the Gallery of Modern Art in Bologna on May 31,
1975, the Italian performance artist Fabio Mauri staged a happening entitled
Intellettuale: "Il Vangelo secondo Matteo" di/su Pasolini (*Intellectual: "The
Gospel According to Matthew" by/about Pasolini*). The happening consisted
in a projection of sequences from Pasolini's *Gospel* film (1964) onto the
director's own body.[1] (See fig. 5.1.) Pasolini sat on a chair in the lobby of the
museum with his back to the entrance door. He wore a white shirt so that
his chest and shoulders could serve as a screen. His face and legs remained in
the dark. The film critic Giacomo Manzoli interpreted the patch of light on
Pasolini's torso as an allusion to a television screen, and thereby to Pasolini's
role as a public intellectual, whose major medium of expression was journalism, and especially telejournalism.[2]

The screened segment of the film displayed the story of Christ's passion
on the director's telechest. On his body, shadowy lineaments of characters,
landscapes, and buildings looked like bruises and gaping wounds. The dis-
proportion between the small size of the images projected and the loud
soundtrack, typical of a cinema-hall screening, contributed to the general
sense of disorientation. Pasolini complained later that the volume of sound
prevented him from following his own film. Witnesses recall that his face
bore an expression of suffering throughout the event.[3]

This *ecce homo* scene, reminiscent of religious iconography, tragically
and uncannily anticipated the photographic images of Pasolini's dead body,
which several months later would be discovered on a football field in Ostia.

Intellettuale hinged on two of Pasolini's lifelong obsessions: his Gramsci-
inspired concern with the role of intellectuals in society and his fascination
with the figure of Christ.[4] The performance suggested that these two obsessions, inseparable as they were, amounted to a coherent artistic life-project,

163

of which Pasolini's cinematic theory and practice, as these had developed since the *Gospel* film, were an integral part. Pasolini claimed that in his *Gospel* film he portrayed Christ as an intellectual.[5] In response, Mauri invited Pasolini to endure a crucifixion through his own film, to face up to the role of Christ on which the filmmaker-poet had patterned much of his public action.

The happening foregrounds the phenomenological dimension of Pasolini's art, which tended to originate in real-life experience and which he tested on location: in the public forum, in the street. Pasolini understood the identity of an intellectual as a public mission which, like that of Christ, implied suffering and sacrifice. *Intellettuale*, according to the curator of the 1994 retrospective of Mauri's works, called intellectuals to responsibility for their thought and words.[6] Mauri dared Pasolini, as he dared his fellow communist director from Hungary, Miklós Jancsó, earlier in that same year, to endure the consequences of their ideological commitments on their own skin.[7] This call echoed Pasolini's lifelong challenge to his intellectual contemporaries to give up their sheltered position of privilege and enter history and social reality, not as representatives of a political party or a trend but as independent individuals living up to their own discourse—an existential position for which he himself stood as an example.[8]

Pasolini took up Mauri's challenge. *Intellettuale* has the same function of delineating clearly and unambiguously Pasolini's enunciative position in his discourse—of making it visible as "the statement's protocol." "Can one imagine Rousseau without the *Confessions*, Kierkegaard without our being informed of the detail of his engagement to Regine, or Nietzsche not inviting us to pay witness, through *Ecce Homo*, to the reasons entitling him to ask the question 'Why am I a destiny?'"[9] In fact, one can't understand Pasolini's discourse apart as a whole without *Intellettuale*'s explicit answer to the question upon which this discourse was hinged: "Who speaks?"

Mauri's performance about Pasolini throws into relief the same feature of the director's life in cinema that Teresa de Lauretis pointed out only a few years later in her rereading of Pasolini's film theory of the 1960s: Pasolini's cinema constituted a form of social discourse and practice.[10] Consequently, it has been an integral part of his output at large, including fictional and nonfictional writings, poetry, pedagogy, linguistics, and politics. But the scene of Christ staged in Bologna had yet another revelatory dimension. Mauri exposed Christ's body as an unlikely but potent medium, which organized and focalized Pasolini's heterogeneous discourse by anchoring it in the corporeal presence and intellectual responsibility of its author.

The Scandal of Christ and Structural Reforms

Self-fashioning as Christ was interlocked with Pasolini's intellectual and political agenda. In 1946, as if to prepare his future role as a cultural reformer,

Pasolini described the founding moment of his identification with Christ in his diary, *Quaderni rossi*. In the entry, he recalled an erotically tinged childhood fantasy about Christ's crucifixion that triggered his desire to imitate Christ's sacrifice on the cross.

> There rose up before me, I believe, as I saw or imagined it, an effigy of Christ crucified. That naked body, barely covered by a strange piece of cloth over the thighs (which I took to be a discreet convention) awoke in me thoughts which were not openly illicit and although I very often looked on that silken band as a veil spread over a disquieting abyss (this was the absolute gratuitousness of childhood), yet I quickly turned these feelings of mine into piety and prayer. Then in my fantasies there insistently flowered the desire to imitate Jesus in this sacrifice for others, to be condemned and killed although innocent. I saw myself hanging on the cross, nailed to it. My thighs were scantily draped with that light strip of cloth and an immense crowd was looking at me. This public martyrdom of mine ended up by becoming a voluptuous image and gradually I was nailed there with my body entirely naked. High above the head of those present, who were rapt in veneration, with their eyes fixed upon me, I felt myself [blank] in front of an immense turquoise sky. With my arms open, with my hands and feet nailed, I was perfectly defenseless, lost.[11]

Pasolini's internalization of the topos of the imitation of Christ betrays that "certainty as to being personally chosen" which gives a rhetorical charge to the founders of groundbreaking discourses.[12] Pasolini's elaboration of his discursive positionality is first cast here in pictorial and theatrical terms. His gaze, initially focused on the loins of Christ, is then redirected inwardly to his own imaginary exposure, presented as a *tableau vivant*, a canvas of a painting coming to life. The theological dimension of Christ's sexuality as a code for resurrection—which Pasolini discerned in Renaissance art long before the art historian Leo Steinberg broached this tabooed subject—merges here with the libidinous drive which cues a subject into the realm of the symbolic: religion, society, and art.[13]

Pasolini presents his Christ experience as an instance of "the intrusion of the signifier in man's psyche," which Jacques Lacan would theorize a decade later in his writings on the treatment of psychosis.[14] The French psychoanalyst postulated that the evocation of the phallus is necessary in the psychoanalytic cure of psychotic delusion, the failure of the subject's imaginary functions.[15] The imaginary function of the phallus constitutes in Lacan's psychoanalysis the basis of the symbolic process of cultural signification. Christ's death on the cross is for him a prototypical instance of symbolic representation, the instance where the Name-of-the-Father is called out to become a trigger of the metaphor.[16]

Pasolini's imaginary embracing of death on the cross as the path to signification partakes of the Pauline "antidialectic of death and resurrection," where resurrection is expected to suddenly come forth "out from the power of death, not through its negation." One could say with Badiou that "the Christ-event, the fact of there having been this particular son, out from the power of death, retroactively identifies death as a path, a dimension of the subject, and not a state of affairs. Death is not a destiny but a choice, as is shown by the fact that we can be offered, through the subtraction of death, the choice of life."[17]

Pasolini's Christ fantasy anticipated the Lacanian logic implicit in Badiou's understanding of the Pauline subject. Pasolini integrated phallic symbolism into the dynamic substitution of Christ's dead body through his own living body, the body of *jouissance*, endowed with a potential of desire, and therefore of creativity. Pasolini invoked the imaginary death on the cross as the very moment triggering the process of signification, the emergence of an imaginary painting. Whether a recollection or a retrospective invention, it is significant that Pasolini's thinking of Christ in terms of phallic signification dates back to the immediate aftermath of the Second World War. In the postwar discourse on art and society, his erotic appropriation of this cultural icon acquires scandalous but socially therapeutic potential, the potential of renewal and reform.

The body of Christ provided Pasolini with a model much needed in the attempts to revivify a traumatized collective consciousness, to account for the fiasco of Western civilization discredited and compromised by fascism. In 1954 Pasolini further elaborated on his discursive positionality in his letter to the poet Carlo Betocchi. His letter shows that by this time his identification with Christ's martyrdom had evolved into an identification with Christ's moral imperative about the destiny of culture and society.

This Christian imperative demanded "structural reforms," sublimating love into new social signification, that is, into an economically just, socially humane, and more civilized organization of human coexistence:

> Note that Christ, becoming man, accepted history—not archaeological history but the history which evolves and therefore lives: Christ would not be universal if he were not different for each different historical phase. For me, at this moment, Christ's words "Love thy neighbor as thyself" mean "Carry out structural reforms." And the souls of others are more important than our own. And this is why I am convinced that a drama of choice exists: it is a question of choosing by which road society can become more civilized and economically better organized; and it is the first step, but an essential one. I do not think there is any better way of spending that mite of love we possess.[18]

Like Paul, Pasolini "is in no way a theoretician of oblatory love, through which one would forget oneself in devotion to Other. This false love, which

Figure 5.2. Pasolini as the medieval painter Giotto directing *Decameron*. Production photo, copyright © Mario Tursi/Archivio Storico del Cinema / A F E.

claims that the subject annihilates himself in a direct relation to the transcendence of the Other, is nothing more than narcissistic pretension."[19] By switching his declaration of faith from "I" to "we," and to a view of society and social reform, Pasolini participates in "the theorem of the militant," according to which "no truth is ever solitary, or particular."[20]

Pasolini's declared positionality of the imitation of Christ is a manifestation of what Leo Bersani identified as "the corrective will"[21] at the core of culturally redemptive projects. This "corrective will," indeed, drives Pasolini's structural reforms. One example of such "structural reform" is his short film *La Ricotta* (1963) where the director filled in a hollowed-out cultural signifier—the scene of the crucifixion—with the martyrdom of a hungry subproletarian extra. Stracci, playing the good thief, really dies of exhaustion on the cross next to the studio star's Christ during the production of a luxurious blockbuster film of a passion play. In anticipation of Vatican II (1962–65) with its attempts to modernize and liberalize the Catholic Church, Pasolini showed how social consciousness leads to a restructuring of the Christian iconography of suffering, updates its content, and makes it acutely relevant.

But "structural reforms" are not just about a social cause. They are also about the medium in which this cause is to be carried out. Pasolini's self-fashioning in imitation of Christ anchored his agenda of revivifying the dead load of cultural heritage in his creative mediation as an artist and intellectual. Seven years later, a production photo of *The Decameron* (1971), the film where the director also played the role of a medieval painter, staged his commitment to updating Christian art through cinema in an almost programmatic fashion. In the photograph, Pasolini poses in front of the painting of Christ crucified so as to suggest that he takes up the baton from Christ, as his cinema does from the pictorial art. (See fig. 5.2.)

But as the blasphemy trial provoked by the release of *La Ricotta* demonstrated, "structural reforms," on which cultural and social renewal or reinvention depend, are inevitably scandalous in their breaking of convention. "God is a scandal in this world. Christ, if he returns, will be again a scandal," Pasolini wrote in 1969 about his film *Teorema*.[22] Pasolini's understanding of Christ as a figure of scandal links him up with nineteenth-century cultural criticism: for example, Nietzsche, Lautréamont, Dostoevsky, and Ensor. The idea of Christ's return and failure in modern society was a frequent thought experiment in that epoch of the reevaluation of all values, and was inevitably scandalous for its profanation of sacred history.

The nineteenth century, the time of the emergence of mass society and mass media, was the first to make scandal into a device of communication, a way of broaching public discussion about tabooed contents. Mikhail Bakhtin drew attention to the discursive function of scandal in the poetics of Dostoevsky, whose journalistically inspired novels were microcosmic versions of the larger social debates of his time. In Pasolini's life, as in Dostoevsky's novels, scandal was not an accident but a method of opening up public space for so-called ultimate questions.

One such ultimate question during Pasolini's time was epitomized by Theodor Adorno's famous 1949 essay "Cultural Criticism and Society," which addressed the survival of the notion of culture after it had been manipulated and degraded in the service of the Holocaust and high capitalism. Adorno rejected those representatives of the tradition of cultural criticism whom Pasolini had read voraciously during the war (Nietzsche, Dostoevsky, Lautréamont) as discredited and irrevocably obsolete under post-1945 social conditions. Theirs was a tradition of cultural criticism from within. Its carnivalesque profanation of inflated values aimed at cultural renewal. Adorno, for his part, questioned the possibility of cultural criticism itself, given the threatened disappearance of the very notion of culture.

Adorno postulated the necessity of a new beginning that would start from the dialectical differentiation between culture and barbarism, tragically erased in the era of Auschwitz. If barbarism had come to be regarded as culture, then culture should be created anew, from the ground up, in a dialectical paradox, by the barbaric act of writing poetry. What Adorno expects from the new generation of intellectuals is a radical, primordial act of creation, not a relativist critical reflection upon the tradition's rights and wrongs. The only real criticism is that which weaves its paths along and across culture's dialectical curves.[23]

The young Pasolini consciously situated himself at the crossroads of the old tradition of criticism and the necessity for the new definition of culture. A poet after and even during Auschwitz, Pasolini anticipated Adorno's scenario. Pasolini's first book of verse, *Poesie a Casarsa*, appeared in 1942 and shocked by rejecting the civilized language of literary Italian in favor of a dialect. Pasolini composed this poetry in the period in which, according to his biographer Enzo Siciliano, he cultivated "a personal nonfascism of his own."[24] A review of *Poesie a Casarsa* connected for the first time the word "scandalo" and Pasolini's name (Siciliano, *Pasolini: A Biography*, 61). The scandal lay in Pasolini's invention of his own written version of the Friulian dialect, which resisted both the technocratic, standardized Italian of the fascist establishment and the traditional literary usage of the oral Friulian dialect for the sake of exoticism. The new language informed a new poetry. And in the act of this creation, Pasolini was concerned with no less a goal than the reinvention of humanistic culture (ibid., 73).

What is it if not plotting barbarism, as Adorno uses the term, when Pasolini contemplates a return of the dialect as a vocation to be accomplished from outside, "from one language (Italian) to another (Friulian)"? In Pasolini's own words, the Friulian dialect became "an object of mournful nostalgia, sensual in origin (in all the breadth and depth of the term), but coinciding besides with the nostalgia of one who lives—and knows it—in a civilization that has reached a linguistic crisis, the desolation and violence of a Rimbaldian 'je ne sais plus parler.' "[25]

The reference to Rimbaud connects Pasolini's linguistic project directly back to the nineteenth century's literary lament about the imminent end of Western civilization which took on new urgency in the 1940s. Pasolini's self-definition by recourse to nineteenth-century cultural criticism would have been obsolete if he had not transfigured it in his own redemptive terms by taking recourse to the twentieth century's public forum and media such as cinema and performance. But these media had to be redesigned and adapted in their own turn to the needs of a civilization silenced by the horrors of the war, the civilization whose truths were discredited as lacking any foundation in political reality.

To rehabilitate the notion of culture—despite the fact that it had been used as the pretext for dehumanizing human bodies, turning them into flesh to be ground up in the machinery of war, or subjecting them to other industrial processes—meant, first of all, to assert life through yielding to the body's sensuality and creativity, to reestablish the human body as a culturally meaningful agent.

Pasolini embarked on this project in *Poesie a Casarsa* by giving a unique expression to homoerotic longing. His scandalous creation of a new Friulian language was indeed one of those "structural reforms" based on creative sublimation. A further "structural reform" was the film *Il Vangelo secondo*

Matteo (*The Gospel According to Matthew*, 1964), a barbaric act of poetry which aimed to reinvent the medium of cinema as a body-centered performance and communication.

Cinema's Signing Body: Polemics with Body Art

In his essay "The Cinema of Poetry," written at the time of the release of the *Gospel* film and presented as a paper at a conference in Pesaro in 1965 (where it caused a scandal among the cine-semioticians), Pasolini came to conceive of the cinematic apparatus itself in corporeal, human terms, thus further elaborating his redemptive project for postwar culture. In his call for a cinema of poetry, Pasolini joined the film-theoretical discourse on the language-like character of cinema.[26] But he did so in terms that distinguish him from the theoreticians of cinema, like Christian Metz, whose domain was the syntagmatic analysis of cine-texts.

Pasolini's ideas are much closer to those of the French critic and filmmaker Alexandre Astruc, who had coined his famous metaphor of the camera as pen in order to emphasize the expressive capacities of camera work over its representational ones.[27] But Pasolini goes a step further in rethinking camera work in terms of a three-dimensional signifying body using a language system composed of what he calls—by analogy with gestures—"naturally communicative archetypes": the sign language of the deaf.

> This system of signs by gestures which, in practice, accompanies the system of linguistic signs as its complement, can be isolated as an autonomous system and become the object of a study. One can even suppose, by abstract hypothesis, the existence of a unique system of signs by gestures as a unique instrument of communication for man (in sum: deaf and dumb Neapolitans): it is from such a hypothetical system of visual signs that language derives the foundation of its existence and the possibility of allowing the formation of a series of naturally communicative archetypes.[28]

In fact, when Pasolini speculates about "the existence of a unique system of signs by gestures as unique instrument of communication for man," he is as always ingeniously in tune with contemporary discourse. In 1960 the American linguist William Stokoe published the first linguistic study of sign language, which helps illuminate certain aspects of Pasolini's oeuvre.[29] Stokoe's innovation was to show that sign language, which had been for centuries considered a spontaneous "language of reality," had as systematic a grammatical basis as any other language.

Pasolini's speculations about sign language as equivalent to the "language of reality" are reminiscent of the characterization of sign language as the "language of natural signs" by the French priest l'Abbé de l'Épée who started developing a transcription system for sign language for the sake of the methodical education of the deaf and mute in the middle of the eighteenth century. Gesture was indeed traditionally perceived as a "language of reality."[30]

The fact that sign language operates through the natural medium of the body by means of gestures places it, for Pasolini, on the same ontological level as physical reality (which is in turn always already capable of communication because it similarly constitutes a natural medium for another agency, the "sign language" of God). In an interview, Pasolini explained his understanding of the "language of reality" as follows: "my religion is a form of immanentism: that is to say, reality itself is a hierophany, but since I don't believe in a transcendent God—and furthermore reality is hierophany—which means that reality itself is God."[31] Pasolini's theology is advanced here clearly in service of a three-dimensional semiotics of physical reality.

The idea that things communicate in themselves and not merely as signs scandalized the cine-semioticians of the 1960s. In the 1990s, Giuliana Bruno showed that this aspect of Pasolini's thinking foreshadowed post-structuralism.[32] However, the post-structuralist features of Pasolini's cinema theory seem to stem from the linguistic property of sign language, which is oral and written at once. It is oral as far as it communicates by the very presence of a signing body and resists two-dimensional notations so that filming constitutes the most adequate form of its material recording, and it is written as far as the gestured sign is a material signifier uncoiling in space that again makes it akin to a moving image.[33] The sign language specialist Bauman saw an analogy between manual signing and Derrida's deconstruction:

> If non-phonetic writing interrupts the primacy of the voice, deafness signifies the consummate moment of disruption. Deafness exiles the voice from the body, from meaning, from being; it sabotages its interiority from within, corrupting the system which has produced the "hearing" idea of the world. Deafness, then, occupies a consummate moment in the deconstruction of Western ontology.
>
> Further, deafness does more than disrupt the system of "hearing-oneself-speak"; it creates an embodied linguistic system which, unlike speech, is not fully present to itself. Signers, unless gazing into the mirror, do not fully see themselves signify. While they may see their hands, they cannot see their own face perform much of Sign's grammatical nuances. The eye, unlike the ear in the system of "hearing-oneself-speak," can only partially "see-oneself-sign." There is always a trace of nonpresence in the system of signing.[34]

With this in mind, one can see Pasolini's language of cinema as describing the theoretical implications of sign language with its bridging of natural and cultural signifiers, its performance character, and structurally meaning-ful bodily motions. Pasolini's cinema of poetry, in fact, implies a model of deafness:

> The fact of walking alone in the street, *even with our ears stopped up*, constitutes a continual dialogue between ourselves and an envi-ronment which expresses itself by the mediation of the images which compose it: the physiognomy of the passers-by, their gestures, their signs, their actions, their silences, their expressions, their collective reactions (people waiting at red lights, a crowd around a street-accident or around a monument); besides, traffic signs, indicators, counterclockwise rotaries are in sum objects charged with meanings and which utter a brute "speech" by their very presence.[35]

The objects that Pasolini enumerates signify by movement, as do bodies in the process of gesticulation. Thus, their expressivity appears as simultane-ously natural and codified. Like signing bodies, objects are both media of signification and signifiers. Accordingly, the camera's relation to profilmic reality (the reality in front of the camera) is conceived in participatory terms, as corporeal interaction in a signed dialogue.

The process of filmmaking itself becomes as meaningful as live perfor-mance and as important as the final cinetext. In "The Cinema of Poetry," Pasolini requests that this third dimension of cinema—the presence of the camera, and by implication of the auteur's body—be integrated into cine-text and felt on the screen. This request corresponds to Bauman's emphasis on the partial character of the sign language system, the subject of which can only partially see himself sign. However, Pasolini's emphasis is on the phenomeno-logical dimension of camera work.

The poetic language of cinema consists in those creative deviations which the filmmaker's camera wrings from the profilmic and filters through its lens. Pasolini sees the body of the camera as an extension not only of the body of its operator but also of the director's mind. By means of its movement, it externalizes the "inner cinema" that exists in the mind of the filmmaker and brings it into dialogue with the image-signs of reality.

> There is more: in man, an entire world is expressed by means of significant images—shall we therefore propose, by analogy, the term "im-signs" (image-signs). This is the world of memory and of dreams. . . . And all dreams—are a series of im-signs which have all the characteristics of the cinematic sequence: close-up, long shots etc. (Pasolini, "The Cinema of Poetry," 544; emphasis in original)

The im-signs of memories and dreams appear in Pasolini's description in a cinematic format, delivered to the individual's mind through certain positions and movements of his body, as if it were through the camera and its lens. Sign language helps theorize both the choice of the profilmic (as one might choose a dialogue partner—the most eloquent and responsive one would be the best) and the individual bodywork, that is movement of the camera.

This double articulation of camera movement and profilmic reality yields the cinematic style of "free indirect discourse" (Pasolini, "The Cinema of Poetry," 549). Deleuze, sensitive to the philosophical dimension of Pasolini's cinema, recognized his theory as an attempt at establishing cinema as a medium of the sacred.[36] In fact, Pasolini calls this corporeal visual communication, which in his view underpins cinematic language, "of a virtually pre-human order," something "at the limit of humanity":

> Indeed, gestures, the surrounding reality, as much as dreams and mechanisms of memory, are of a virtually pre-human order, or at least at the limit of humanity—in any case pre-grammatical and even pre-morphological (dreams are unconscious phenomena, as are mnemonic mechanisms; the gesture is an altogether elementary sign etc.).[37]

The idea of the body as a recording device was not new in Pasolini's time. For example, the French anthropologist Marcel Jousse had discovered in the early twentieth century that many preliterate peoples used the body to record verbal content. The rhythmic gestures of ritual dance functioned as a bodily memory. The movements triggered the words in the process of the ritual performance. This anthropological discovery became important for some modern studies in the psychology of memory, which expected bodily movements to become effective in the cure of amnesia and traumatic memory losses.[38]

Against this background, Pasolini's provocative discussion of cinematic apparatus in corporeal human terms appears as a part of his redemptive project for postwar culture. Conceptualized in terms of body language, cinema could remedy the loss of cultural memory in the society of his time. As an alternative kinesic system of communication, sign language helps a child born deaf to overcome his disability.[39] Signing is the paralinguistic means of survival par excellence.

Pasolini's recourse to the modes of expression operating with meaningful movement seems consistent with his therapeutic program for a traumatically silenced civilization. "The theoretical significance of 'deafness' . . . takes on new historical and metaphysical importance that pathologized 'deafness' cannot."[40] In fact, in "The Cinema of Poetry," Pasolini turned deafness from a form of pathology into a form of a normative theory. Sign language, if taken seriously as the linguistic model for Pasolini's cinema, makes him appear less of a theoretical prophet and more of an astute observer of his time. Pasolini's freelancing for the newspapers in Rome in the early 1950s coincided with the First International Congress of the Deaf that convened in Rome on

September 19–23, 1951, and established the World Federation of the Deaf, an organization advancing and supporting the human rights of the deaf. In the spirit of the time, Pasolini borrowed the model of sign language for his own cultural project.

Pasolini's "structural reforms" consist in reevaluating civilization's less important, subordinate, or excluded areas by making them the most important, creative, and culturally valid ones. He finds in the "barbaric" remnant of kinesic communication more linguistic potential than in the normative language compromised by technocracy. Savage rituals become a strategy of lifting from oblivion the iconographic resources of a culture. In their very silence and traumatic exclusion from an inflated and corrupt culture, the speaking bodies of the deaf preserve the dignity of language, consciousness, artistic creativity, and sociopolitical legitimacy. In Pasolini's eyes, they suddenly provide the non-compromised, pristine platform from which to begin.

Pasolini's polemics with the avant-garde of the 1960s throws into relief the centrality of the signing body to his cinematically driven project of the reinvention of culture. His turn to the cinematic medium in this decade and his subsequent body-centered film theory coincided with the appearance of performance and body art in all industrial nations. The genealogy of body art is usually traced back to the experience of technologies of destruction during World War I. The Viennese artist Oskar Schlemmer epitomized the legacy of the battlefield with the conclusion that "the new artistic medium is a much more direct one: the human body."[41]

In the 1960s body art burst on the cultural scene as a belated reaction to the mass slaughter of World War II. It is usually seen as a reenactment of new technological atrocities that mutilated the bodies. The art historian Lea Vergine described the sensibility of performance and body artists such as Beuys, Marioni, Chiari, and Zaza in a way that applies to Pasolini, who shared their desire "to act as a function of 'the other,' . . . to live collective ethos and pathos, . . . to grasp the existent in all of its brutal physicality, to communicate something that has been previously felt but that is lived in the very moment of communication, . . . to return to the origins without leaving the present."[42] But despite the shared ethos and common focus on body and technology, Pasolini's and body artists' understanding of their respective media differed significantly.

One signature of body art is the technological extension of the human body. Body artists are often equipped with cameras and gadgets and interlocked in a variety of ways with machines and apparatuses. For example, in Dan Graham's performance *Body Press* (1970–72), two filmmakers stand within a completely mirrorized cylinder, rotating the running cameras around their bodies and exchanging them at a certain point.[43] The resulting films are then projected simultaneously on two facing walls so that viewers find themselves surrounded by a mass of flesh pressing from all sides. This filmmaking is participatory and bodily oriented, but its goal is exactly opposed

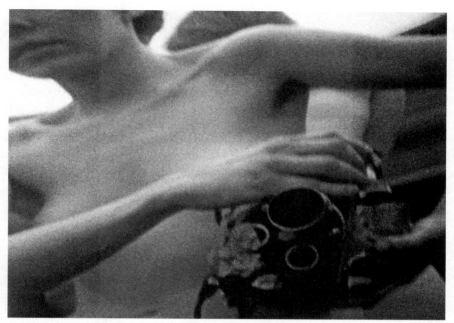

Figure 5.3. Dan Graham, *Body Press*, 1970–72. Film installation: two films, 16 mm, color, silent, synchronous projection on two opposite walls, eight minutes (loop). Edition 2/3 + 1 A.P. Performers: Susan Ensley, Ed Bows. Copyright © Generali Foundation Collection—Permanent Loan to the Museum der Moderne Salzburg.

to Pasolini's: it seeks to defy cultural symbolism by decomposing the body as a form and presenting it as pure matter. (See fig. 5.3.)

Body art stages a body-wound which conveys nothing but its own trauma and even that merely by means of technological props, or through its most basic physiology. For the poet Pasolini, cinema was the medium in which he could polemically explore an alternative relation of body, art, and technology through the body of the auteur. With the camera work understood in terms of communication, the filmmaker is not shooting reality, according to the aggressive metaphor, but interacting with it in language of im-signs. The technological body of the camera is humanized through its alliance with the human operator. Man and machine reconcile in a creative process. So understood, the implications of Pasolini's film theory are momentous.

Recasting filmmaking as communication, Pasolini made cinema into a legitimate participant in a social discourse and even endowed it with the responsibility to revive the humanistic cultural tradition on new technological premises. To the defeat of culture postulated by body art, Pasolini opposed the speaking body of the deaf as a silent and marginalized but nevertheless meaningful body: a body-logos.

An Aesthetic of Deafness

Il Vangelo secondo Matteo (*The Gospel According to Matthew*, 1964) real-
izes this program most completely. Here Pasolini uses the auteur's embodied
camera to produce the language of poetry. The dialogue between the profilmic reality and the camera, which yields a visual counterpart to the gospel,
is best understood in terms of sign language. Every sign-unit of deaf and
mute communication consists of three parts—designator, tabula, and signation. The designator is a configuration of the hand, a hand-shape. The tabula
is the upper part of the body against which the movement of the hand is
positioned. It can be an upper or a lower arm, a left or a right shoulder, the
chest or different parts of the head.

The signation is the performance of the sign, the meaning of which depends
on the particular movement of the designator in relation to the tabula: the hand
can be positioned at a distance to the body, or it can touch it. It can move in
circular movements or go up and down, or to the left or right. The tabula itself
can be totally static, or moving this or that way, especially as a means of syntactic indication, for syntax in sign language is conveyed through turns of the
torso in relation to a certain point in space as well as through facial expression.

The two salient stylistic features of the *Gospel* film, the camera's frontal
take on the profilmic and the profilmic's pushing toward the camera, appear
to be an outcome of such a "signed dialogue."[44] Either the profilmic serves as
the tabula in relation to which the camera "gesticulates" as a designator or,
conversely, the camera assumes the static position of the tabula, in relation
to which the profilmic motion is organized, becoming in its turn a designator. An example of the first constellation is the long tracking shot of Joseph's
gaze striking the static panorama of the mountain dwellings of "Bethlehem"
(Matera), until it arrives through a semicircular movement at a still point and
focuses on a group of playing children.

The shot of children then offers an example of the second constellation,
since, from its static position, the camera comes to contemplate the movement of the profilmic, the commotion of the jumping children. The reciprocal
repositioning of the sources of movement appears indeed as a modulation
between two different types of signation, with the motion originating in turns
either in the camera or in the profilmic, as if two signing agents were taking
turns in a silent dialogue.

The opening sequence of the film is self-reflexive in this respect. Pasolini's
visual transliteration of the gospel starts with the story of Jesus's birth. The
first image of the film is a close-up of the young Mary's face—Mary whose
pregnancy by the Holy Spirit has just been discovered by Joseph. The alternating close-ups of their faces that follow suggest a conscious departure from
the logic of dialogue, which in narrative cinema would have been staged by
the shot-reverse-shot exchange, preceded by an establishing shot situating the
protagonists spatially in relation to each other. (See fig. 5.4.)

Figure 5.4. Opening close-ups of Pasolini's *Il Vangelo secondo Matteo*. From top to bottom: (a) Mary; (b) Joseph; (c) Mary; (d) Joseph.

The close-ups of Pasolini's film are image-signs conveying the predicament: (a) Mary's anxiety about Joseph's reaction to her pregnancy; (b) Joseph's surprise and questioning look; (c) Mary's downcast, confirming eyes; (d) Joseph's subtle movement toward the camera as a sorrowful, silent "exclamation." These mute images translate the following words of the gospel by means of rhythmical alternation and syntactic mimicry.

> The birth of Jesus the anointed took place as follows: While his mother Mary was engaged to Joseph, but before they slept together, she was found to be pregnant by the Holy Spirit. Since Joseph was a decent man and did not wish to expose her publicly, he planned to break off their engagement quietly.[45]

The quiet breakup is rendered in mute signifiers—facial emotions and bodily motions are spatially detached from each other and thus imbued with the abstract austerity of mere signs. The dramatic intensity of the scene is the pure intensity of emotion, with the context already provided by Matthew.

The alternation of close-ups is followed by a rhythmical exchange of long shots of the pregnant Mary and of Joseph, both given, presumably, from their reciprocal points of view. The transition from the trans-spatiality of the close-up to the grounding format of the long shot is too radical to reconcile the viewer with the physical reality of protagonists in their cinematic space, as the protagonists never appear together in one shot. The long shot is deprived here of its space-establishing quality and thus comes to signify third-person narration: he/she sees, she/he goes, and so on.

The next alternation of shots appears in a different format: long shots of Mary and Joseph. First, Joseph turns and leaves through the yard-gate, then Mary who suddenly appears positioned against a different background from the previous shot walks toward the still camera so that the shot's format slowly changes to the medium shot. The following extreme long shot is given from Mary's point of view. This shot shows Joseph moving away from the camera in the arid landscape.

This long shot is intercut with two further close-ups of Mary's sorrowful face. The same expression, the same casting down of the eyes, the same shot-format, create a sense of lyrical continuity slightly varied by a change in lighting and in shot-composition. The first cadence of the mute opening ends with the close-up of her sorrowful face.

The subsequent cadence is even more dramatic with its radical contrast of falling and rising rhythms of camera movement in pursuit of Joseph. His consternation about the predicament is conveyed by means of his wanderings, until finally an angel visits him in a dream and resolves his doubts by telling him what to do:

> While he was thinking about these things, a messenger of the Lord
> surprised him in a dream with these words: "Joseph, descendant of
> David, don't hesitate to take Mary as your wife, since the Holy Spirit
> is responsible for her pregnancy. She will give birth to a son and you
> will name him Jesus—the name means 'he will save his people from
> their sins.' "[46]

Joseph's arrival in the town is conveyed first by a melancholy horizontal
tracking shot brushing along the mountains and then by a shot focused on
a group of children. Here again we are confronted with alternating shots
of Joseph's downward movement, when he falls asleep, and of the children,
in whose place the angel appears to encourage Joseph to take his wife and
to accept the child conceived from the Lord himself. From this moment on,
sorrow turns into joy, and the jubilatory camera swings upward to focus
on Mary's dwelling in an extreme high-angle shot from the perspective of
heaven.

The last cadence of this silent sequence shows Joseph's rapid return in a
symmetrical reversal of the order of the previous shots from the very beginning
of the sequence. To the beat of the glamorous declamation of the prophecy
about Jesus's birth, Joseph strides hurriedly across the same arid landscape in
a number of shots whose format changes rapidly from an extreme long shot
back to a close-up, indicating his approach in an almost digitally abrupt and
interrupted fast-forward fashion.

In response, Mary leaves the house and walks toward the camera; then
a close-up of her anxious face; then Joseph entering the yard through the
same gate followed by another close-up of Mary's face; a close-up of Joseph's
accepting smile and his subtle head-dip, followed by a close-up of Mary's
happy smile of acknowledgment.

This mute exchange between Mary and Joseph recalls Dreyer's *La Passion
de Jeanne d'Arc* (1928) in which the drama of faith, doubt, and suspicion
was carried out almost exclusively through close-ups of the protagonists'
faces. The religious sensibility of this silent classic endorsed the metaphysical,
revelatory potential with which the close-up had been charged in the history
of cinema.[47] But while Dreyer's close-ups are provided with inter-titles that
are supposed to be "heard" in the expressions of the protagonists, Pasolini
makes the characters' microphysiognomics and their position in respect to
the camera into the exclusive medium of communication, as in sign language.

Pasolini's focus on facial mimicry in the close-up and corporeal motion in
the long shot reflects the corporeal aspect of the film's underlying aesthetic.
The eye-lowering, head-dip, subtle paralinguistic smile, and questioning look
indeed fulfill a syntactic function in sign language indicating question and
response. Stokoe speculated that such facial activity most likely inspired earlier students of sign language to call it "the language of natural signs."[48]

The rhythmical organization of the silent opening sequence alternates "feminine" and "masculine" shots of Mary and Joseph, as if they were differently stressed syllables of a poem. Pasolini's embrace of rhythmical repetitions of locations, shot compositions, camera movements, and contrasting shot-formats indeed evokes the techniques of sign-language poetry.

Consider the sign poet Clayton Valli, who has advanced such techniques as "rhymes" in signed poetry. A signed rhyme is produced through a repetition of particular hand shapes, movement paths, sign locations, or non-manual markers such as facial expressions or body postures. For example, in Valli's poem "Snowflake," a visual rhyme consists of five repeating movements of the hand shape: first, the palm opens with all fingers extended to sign "tree," then it draws the outline of the leaves on the tree, and then shows the leaves falling to the ground.[49] The opening sequence of the *Vangelo* shows Pasolini's camera creating similar visual patterns of rhyme.

The camera's signed poetry is most obvious in Pasolini's filming of Christ's preaching, when a long sequence of close-ups zooms rhythmically on Christ's face, showing it from different angles and in different light. The camera's zoom punctuates the spoken text. The stop of the zoom marks the period. Specialists today speak of the cinematic nature of sign language, as Pasolini spoke about the signed nature of the language of cinema. In both cases, the movement is codified in space.

As a visual performance art, sign poetry bears more similarity to painting, dance, drama, film, and video than to poetry and fiction. A "line" in sign poetry, for example, is more accurately modeled after the concept of the "line" in painting or a choreographed "phrase" in dance. Instead of moving from left to right, the sign poet draws lines through space in all directions.[50]

Pasolini's understanding of cinematic language as body language presupposed the camera's presence in the film. In the scene of Christ's baptism, Pasolini staged the camera's divine embodiment and its integration as an actor into the cinetext: (a) first, John the Baptist prophesizes the coming of Christ. (b) Then suddenly the image of Christ materializes on the screen. John recognizes and baptizes him. (c) After the baptism, Christ raises up his head. (d) In response, a high-angle shot focuses upon the scene of baptism accompanied by the words coming from God himself: "This is my beloved son, in whom I am well pleased." (See fig. 5.5.)

The Christ image here points to the camera, which responds with gestures of centering and elevation. The camera mediates between the incarnate son and the father in heaven, alternately taking both positions but connecting them through a single gaze. The director stages the camera's fusion with the body of Christ. Like the Byzantine icon, the cinematic image figures here not as a representation but as an index, a pointer, according to Merleau-Ponty's maxim, that where the gaze is, there is the body. (See fig. 5.6.)

Essential to Pasolini's cinema of poetry is the camera's mediation of divine presence. For example, in the mute exchange between Joseph and Mary,

Figure 5.5. Indexical presence of the body of Christ in *Il Vangelo secondo Matteo*. From top to bottom: (a) John the Baptist; (b) Jesus before the baptism; (c) Jesus after the baptism looking at the Father; (d) God's point of view in the baptism scene.

Figure 5.6. Camera's interpolation of Christ's body into the cine-text. Pasolini directing the baptism scene in *Il Vangelo secondo Matteo*. Production photo, copyright © Angelo Novi / Archivio Storico del Cinema / A F E.

the camera's invisible presence fills in the diegetic gap between two frontal im-signs of the protagonists, who are uprooted from their physical space in the profilmic and are related to each other exclusively through the camera's gaze. Its three-dimensional presence in the real space right between Mary and Joseph is made visible in retrospect: when Joseph finally moves to leave, the camera tangibly pans after him, betraying its earlier presence in between the protagonists. In light of this move, the previous frontal address of the characters inevitably appears as a result of the camera's full rotation in space between them. Thus, the camera's implied presence ensures continuity in the flow of images leading from one image to the next in rhythmical patterns of its bodily movements, which Pasolini prefers over the narrative logic of continuity editing.

Thus, Pasolini's camera fuses with the auteur's body in their shared claim to incarnate the divine vision. Pasolini's cinematic icons—disembodied high-angle and panoramic shots brushing over the surface of the earth as well as the synchronization of the divine words with such images—endow the camera work itself with the status of divine authorship, reminding us of Merleau-Ponty's phenomenological observation that "the body, by withdrawing from the objective world, will carry with it the intentional threads linking it to its surroundings and finally reveal to us the perceiving subject as the perceived world."[51]

Pasolini's cinema, in which Deleuze discerned such phenomenological perception-image, had the ambition of inscribing the hollowed-out iconography into the world of phenomena before the camera, thus filling it with life. The embodied camera makes the viewer physically identify with its movement and gaze and thus partake of the divine itself. Pasolini's perception-image points to the body of the non-diegetic, non-cinematic space. His films are traces of what was happening beyond the film, of the social discourse of his epoch.

The viewing experience consequently acquires a character of cultural communion, of a collective reception of the gospel cinematically figured in the thousand-year tradition of Christian iconography. It is hardly a coincidence that Mauri's performance *Intellettuale* was also the event inaugurating the city of Bologna's new Gallery of Modern Art.[52] Pasolini's cine-gospel, cast onto his body as the redemptive sacrifice, was that barbaric act of poetry which, according to Adorno, was needed to restart the modern culture from scratch.

Cinema's Other Body: Mauri-Sade-*Salò*

In the performance *Intellettuale*, the anthropocentric cinema of Pasolini was mercilessly confronted with the cinema of Mauri, who a decade later reminisced about the self-reflexive nature of the event:

> This event "by/about Pier Paolo Pasolini" was an extra "installment" in our friendship. Undoubtedly in mine. One of those moments in which the agitation of the passions seems to be calmed, the wind drops, to reveal a landscape fraught with meaning, in which everything, past and present, all those risks miraculously overcome, falls back into some sort of intelligent order, and gives us back the people we were in that intellectual enterprise: survivors, friends, serene at heart and worthy of those ideals of poetry or art to which, careless of our personal fortunes, we remained faithful.
>
> I see that evening in Bologna, so decisively clear and final, as a confirmation. Of something steady and beautiful: the steadiness and beauty of poetry, intent on capturing the world and its works because they are there. Or intent on explaining them, and fatally, making them understood.[53]

Since the late 1950s Mauri had been concerned with the materiality of the cinematic medium. His work focused on such aspects of cinematic apparatus

Figure 5.7. Mauri's cinema: Fabio Mauri, *Schermi-Disegno*, 1957. Tempera on paper, 69.5 × 98.8 cm. Courtesy Studio Fabio Mauri, copyright © Eredi Fabio Mauri.

as the screen, the film reel, and the beam of light, usually left out of film theories. In 1957 he came up with his first series of installations, *Schermi* (*Screens*), which conceptually anticipated Pasolini's embodiment of the screen in *Intellettuale*. The first screen, *Schermi-Disegno* (*Screens-Outline*), featured a rectangular white paperboard. Its edge was painted black, as if it were a frame. (See fig. 5.7.) Its similarity to the cinema screen suggested that the screen doesn't just deliver the cinematic image to the viewer, but is an entity with a life of its own, which partakes in the physical reality of things and therefore reinforces the phenomenological dimension of the cinematic image.

Mauri inverted the famous trope about cinematic illusionism seen, for example, in Edwin S. Porter's short *Uncle Josh at the Moving Picture Show* (1902), where the naive uncle confuses the film and reality. In his desperate attempts to enter the world projected onto the screen, he comically upsets the show. But Mauri insisted that those who attempt to grab an airy projection are not totally deceived by their instinct. They sense the material reality of the cinematic embodiment, when a beam of light touches the screen. Mauri worked to show that the traces of an illusion are tangible. They stay behind, even after the projection has evaporated. Mauri's screens expose cinema as a violent enterprise.

Figure 5.8. Mauri's cinema: Fabio Mauri, *Grande cinema a luce solida giallo*, 1968. Plastic and neon, 220 × 100 × 97 cm. Galleria Nazionale d'Arte Moderna e Contemporanea, Rome. Photo: Soprintendenza Galleria Roma. Arte Contemporanea-Galleria Nazionale d'Arte Moderna, Rome. Courtesy Studio Fabio Mauri, copyright © Eredi Fabio Mauri.

Figure 5.9. Mauri's cinema: Mauri posing as a director. *Director*, 1967. Emulsion and paint on canvas, 114 × 120 cm. Courtesy Studio Fabio Mauri, copyright © Eredi Fabio Mauri.

Figure 5.10. Mauri's cinema: a frame from *Che cosa è il fascism?*, 1971. (Giornale LUCE). Centro per l'Arte Contemporanea Luigi Pecci, Prato 1993. Photo: Claudio Abate. Courtesy Studio Fabio Mauri, copyright © Eredi Fabio Mauri and Claudio Abate.

Figure 5.11. Fabio Mauri, *Linguaggio è guerra*, 1975. Photographic images and stamping, 41.8 × 29.9 cm. Courtesy Studio Fabio Mauri, copyright © Eredi Fabio Mauri.

Figure 5.12. Pasolini in *Intellettuale: "Il Vangelo secondo Matteo" di/su Pier Paolo Pasolini*. Galleria Comunale d'Arte Moderna, Bologna. Photo: Antonio Masotti. Courtesy Studio Fabio Mauri, copyright © Eredi Fabio Mauri and Stefano Masotti.

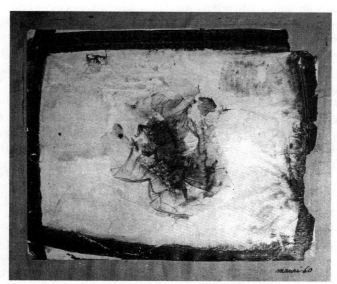

Figure 5.13. Mauri's cinema: Fabio Mauri, *Moviola 3*, 1960. Collage, oil paint, and tempera on canvas (45 × 65 cm). Courtesy Studio Fabio Mauri, copyright © Eredi Fabio Mauri.

In 1968 Mauri added a series of installations about the materiality of the beam of light. *Pile e cinema a luce solida* (*Battery Torch and Cinema with the Solid Beam of Light*) featured a torch with a paperboard light. Looking like a baseball bat, the beam of light seemed to have just hit the ground and bent. Or *Grande cinema a luce solida giallo* (*Big Cinema with the Solid Yellow Beam of Light*) conveyed the idea of the materiality of cinematic projection with its plastic pyramid of light hitting the wall. (See fig. 5.8.) The installation played with two meanings of the Italian word "giallo" as "yellow" and "thriller," as in "film giallo." Later, in his more explicitly political happenings, for example, Mauri often directly analogized cinematic cameras to weapons.

For Mauri, the cinematic apparatus was just another form of military machinery, and the filmmaker was a commander on a battlefield. (See fig. 5.9.) His investigation of cinema as a technology of destruction critically reflected on the glorification of violence in Italian futurism. His screenings of military footage in *What Is Fascism?* evoked the spirit of Marinetti's famous slogan "We extol aggressive motion . . . ," exposing the violence inherent in cinematic projection as such, and by extension in any representation or ideology. (See fig. 5.10.) A series of installations elaborating on this topic were tellingly entitled *Language Is War*. (See fig. 5.11.)

In *Disegno* Mauri outlined a surface of exposure, a crime scene, where the invisible wounds dealt by a cinematic projection could be rendered visible. Many other screens, covered with tangible marks of projections, followed. Some of them were tinted with color and patterned, some were shadowed, some were divided and multiplied, and some were torn open and bruised. Mauri's conceptualism offered a rationale for the aesthetics of body art. Body artists interrupted the symbolic continuity of the space for their enactment of the traumatic dissolution of form. They staged the wound as a gap within the signifying order of the institutions of culture. *Disegno*'s black edge alluded to this sensibility. Like a mourning postcard, it bore an air of grief, waiting for a message of death to be inscribed.

In the projections *Intellettuale*, the white rectangle of Pasolini's chest, taken out of darkness by a beam of light, obeyed the brutal logic of Mauri's understanding of cinema. Pasolini's body faced the cinematic apparatus as a vulnerable screen, as a body to be covered with gaping wounds. "It's a question of facing up to death through life, rummaging around in the under and seamy sides of life, bringing to light the secret and the hidden,"[54] Vergine wrote about the aesthetics of body art in 1974, just a year before Mauri's projection.

The close-ups of faces uncannily merged with the director's torso—behind those faces hid not brains, but guts. The spectacle taking place on the director's chest evoked the words of Katherine Mansfield: "There are certain tremendous moments in life when a creature comes out of his corner and looks around, and it's frightening."[55] Under the shimmer of the *Gospel* film, the creature gazed from Pasolini's body. (See fig. 5.12.)

However, the destructive scenario underlying *Intellettuale* was in line with Pasolini's own later vision of cinema. He articulated this vision in the essay "The Unpopular Cinema" (1970)—a theoretical counterpart to "The Cinema of Poetry" (1965). In this essay, he continued his reflections on filmmaking as a corporeal enterprise but this time focused on editing. The brutal cutting into the celluloid evoked the fantasies of torture at the Moviola editing machine. In the process of filmmaking, one always dies, he argued, but this is always a "spectacular death," the death that becomes visible in the final product. This sensibility harks back to Mauri, whose installation of a wounded screen of 1960 was about such understanding of *Moviola*. (See fig. 5.13.)

In his speculations, Pasolini returned to the sacrificial erotic fantasies of 1946. Now they are explicitly linked to cinema. Christ crucified is discernible in the description of sadomasochistic pleasure, of pain and exposure inherent in any creative process. The condition of balancing between life and death, between creation and mutilation through the cinematic apparatus, culminates in an ultimate delivery to the viewer. The viewers who witness the director's dissolution in the apparatus appear as complicit in his death.

In their collaboration, Mauri and Pasolini have recourse to the notion of the embodied cinema. Pasolini's body-logos and Mauri's wounded screen are logically dovetailed in *Intellettuale*, a spectacle that stages the sacrificial death of the filmmaker through the cinematic apparatus. Pasolini participated in Mauri's performance during the time when he was working on the final cut of his adaptation of Marquis de Sade, entitled *Salò, or 120 Days of Sodom* (1975). In his novel *120 Days of Sodom*, Sade created a prototypical concentration camp, where a group of victims are brought together with the sole aim of sexual exploitation and annihilation. This simple plot made Sade's dusty writings suddenly relevant for the twentieth century. A famous issue of *Tel Quel*, published in 1967, signaled a renewed interest in Sade's writings among postwar intellectuals who wanted to reflect on the political failure of European civilization.

Pasolini joined the discussion by cinematic means. In *Salò* he embarked on investigation of the nature of fascism. *Salò*, dedicated to the body-object, body-wound, and body-victim of a culture gone berserk and to the oppressive potential of the cinematic apparatus, was a nod to body art. However, in his portrayal of sadistic tyranny, the director adapted the problematic of body art to his own redemptive agenda. In *Salò* Pasolini staged his camera's descent into the harrowing of hell, laid out according to Sade's atheistic universe.

Sade linked atheism to a quadrangular mode of representation. His vision of the human being was inspired by the eighteenth century's concept of the body-machine. The boxlike spatiality suggested by his narrative reinforces the sense of geometrical artificiality. The novel has four parts, with four storytellers in charge of each part. The preparation for the debauchery takes place at the four extremities of Paris. This space is then narrowed down to the cubicle of the château of Silling with four apartments, each located at a corner, where four major protagonists withdraw themselves with their four wives for the purpose of libertinage.[56] The number four is the cornerstone of both the novel's quadrangular narrative and its atheism, symbolically expressed in its defiance of the Trinity as well as in its profanation of the four evangelical narratives.

Sade's linkage of atheism to a quadrangular mode of representation allows Pasolini, who famously argued that the rejection of the sacred is bourgeois, to import a political charge to the cubicle spaces of upper-class villas and perspective views. Pasolini's film restages the peephole world of Sade's novel. In a peepshow, the model of a prison cell—a prototypical scene of visual power and surveillance—is fused with the scene of entertainment. Peepshows usually presented exotic faraway countries and landscapes, military and religious scenes, or pornography—all subjects based on an appeal to the viewer's voyeuristic imagination.

Richard Balzer showed that the peepshows, popular in the eighteenth century, were usually accompanied by stories narrated live by showmen who used to pull a string at the side of the box in order to change the views. To attract the audiences on the marketplaces, bells and drums were used to advertise the performances.[57] These features are salient in the novel. Sade's configurations of bodies change in a mechanistic manner and then "fly" back into the initial position, as if they were animated cutout figures. The libertine tableaux are typically separated by the ring of a bell. This simple mechanics of moving cartoonlike figures is present in Sade's innumerable descriptions of intercourse: "she sighed and panted and moaned, her thighs rose mechanically," or "she is adjusted, obliged to yield, she obeys automatically" (Sade, *120 Days of Sodom*, 308).

The visual logic of a peepshow box comes to symbolize for Pasolini the cultural philistinism of fascism; it draws both viewer and filmmaker into complicity with the camera's offensive voyeurism. A self-reflexive shot for this visual sensibility is given at the end of *Salò* where the torture scenes are located in the quadrangular yard and observed by the perpetrators, taking turns with binoculars from a distant window.

In the context of the time, Pasolini's reception of Sade stands out for its sensitivity to the very strategy of Sade's cultural criticism. Sade took on his contemporary culture on its own terms by bringing out the self-destructive potential intrinsic in traditional forms of representation. Sade hinged his novel of destruction on a visual paradox. He interconnected two visual orders at odds with one another—that of the peepshow and that of the camera obscura. Both these apparatuses of art, scholarship, and entertainment, cultural apparatuses par excellence, were broadly popular by the end of the eighteenth century.

The camera obscura projects into a closed box a precise reflection of the outside world. This logic can be discerned in Sade's framework of a war as the basic premise for the scene of libertinage. The fact that the theme of the war has no further development or mention in a novel otherwise based on the innumerable permutations and repetitions of all its themes, ideas, and actions establishes war once and for all as the unquestionable horizon of the novel, within which it is to be read. War as a prototypical setting of cultural demise in all its forms and expressions thus provides an underlying matrix for Sade's "quadrangular" narrative. The visual illusionism of a peepshow clothes this matrix in details.

This schizophrenic interconnection of two discrepant visual regimes—a viewer of a peepshow enclosed within a camera obscura—excludes a priori the omniscient presence of a unified subject in the novel. The narrator's competence consists exclusively in a construction of an intricate clockwork mechanism, which having been wound up once, is supposed to work by itself. Such combinations of a clock-box with a peepshow, decorated as if it were a theatrical stage or a boudoir, had been popular since the seventeenth century.[58] Detailed descriptions of the participants, of the château, and a declaration of the timetable and statutes characteristically precede Sade's narration so that the characters appear to be flawlessly matched within the narrative mechanism through their accurately assigned places and functions (Sade, *120 Days of Sodom*, 253).

Sade's plot, clock-driven and peepshow-inspired, was meant to produce the voyeuristic pleasure of pornographic configurations. But this pleasure inevitably wears out in the course of time. Incessant repetition and acceleration discard one symbolic layer of the show after another, until the reader confronts a purely mechanical set of torture machines and destructive tools, which reduce the bodies of the participants to bloody pulp. The mutilation of the bodies is reflected in the progressing fragmentation of narrative, which eventually bursts into mere chaos of signifiers. The only means of bringing the destroyed diegetic world back into the symbolic order is to draw a posthumous summary of the numbers of victims, as Sade does on his last page.

The Duke's address to the victims, in which he denies them any hope for pity and survival despite their compliance with the prosecutors' wishes, reveals how the de-sublimation of desire is bound up with Sade's project of the destruction of representation: "Roused in fury against the altars that have been able to snatch from us some few grains of incense, our pride and our libertinage shatter them as soon as the illusion has satisfied our senses, and contempt almost always followed by hatred instantly assumes the preeminence hitherto occupied by our imagination" (Sade, *120 Days of Sodom*, 250).

Sade's contemplation of post-coital destruction aims at the eradication of culture's very origin in productively transformed sexual energy. The Duke's metaphors of religious worship ("altars," "incense") warn here against love and happiness as a possible transcendent pitfall of intercourse. The Duke's program consists in turning the mechanism of pleasure into a mechanism of destruction. As soon as desire is gratified, the altars should be broken and the incense should evaporate, preserving contempt and hatred unchallenged.

This contempt and hatred are epitomized in the novel's underlying matrix of war, which Sade carefully specifies as the very condition for the horrors of the debauchery to follow:

> The extensive wars wherewith Louis XIV was burdened during his reign, while draining the State's treasury and exhausting the substance of the people, none the less contained the secret that led to the prosperity of a swarm of those bloodsuckers who are always on the watch for public calamities, which, instead of appeasing, they promote or invent so as, precisely, to be able to profit from them the more advantageously. (Sade, *120 Days of Sodom*, 191)

But war, for the former military officer Sade, is always already implicit in the imaginary world of culture and representation. The destructive force in Sade is not the repressed unconscious but the exuberance of sexual energy in the absence of all those taboos which absolute power claims as its privilege. Sexual expenditure which is not creatively channeled into production of new forms exhausts itself in an inflation of the old ones. The cultural apparatus has an in-built potential to turn into the counter-production and counter-creativity of war.

Thus Sade's novel exposes to the reader a representational machine gone berserk. The participants in the orgy are subordinate to the anonymous and elemental power of nature, as the Duke conveys: "I am in her hand but a machine which she runs as she likes, and not one of my crimes does not serve her: the more she urges me to commit them, the more of them she needs; I should be a fool to disobey her" (Sade, *120 Days of Sodom*, 199). Nature is, for Sade, however, identical with culture because of its symbolic value as god's creation. Sade's alleged atheism is in this respect nothing but an attack on the symbolic nature of creation, represented by the human body in its prototypical likeness of God.

The Eucharist exemplifies the religious symbolism on the level of culture. There is a series of narrative fragments in *Sodom* dedicated to the destruction of the host. In the style of libertinage, it is supposed to be shat upon or inserted into the vagina of a prostitute. However, the supposed desacralization of the Eucharist just refashions the orgy as a "negative" community, held together not by communal consumption of wine and bread but by partaking in the Eucharist through the lower bodies.

The inversion of unity and communication was the central theme in Simone de Beauvoir's famous essay on Sade. She argued that Sade's negation never breaks out of a pre-given cultural matrix, but rather exhausts it from within. And in fact, Sade's originality consists exactly in his lack of originality. Pornography was broadly used in the anticlerical and antiaristocratic satire of the time. Sade situates himself in the tradition of social and cultural criticism by endowing his villains with the highest social and governmental positions.

Sade's imagination by no means transgressed the conventions of the sexual imagery of the time. Aretino's postures, images of harems, of debaucheries, of flagellation were broadly circulated in the age of libertinage. The combination of sex and crime, rape and incest, or dismembering of corpses were popular topics. For example, the coprophagous meal in Sade recalls such French eighteenth-century political caricature as "the Brits cooking a pudding." This lack of originality allows him to lay bare the destructive potential of the repetitive cultural mechanism. Sade anticipated the sensibility of body art in his staging of the wound inflicted upon the collective body by the representational apparatus itself.

In 1951 Simone de Beauvoir highlighted those features of Sade's sexualized worldview, which had become relevant again for postwar civilization. She sees in Sade an attempt at communicating the incommunicable.[59] Body art's silent traumatized body wounds, like those of Sade, "do not constitute a living experience within the framework of the subject's psychophysiological unity." Sexuality in Sade is conceived as a "bodily accident." The cerebral aspect of Sade's sexuality, its "autism," and its nature as "a social fact" and a "spectacle" equally characterize the conceptual nature of body art (Beauvoir, "Must We Burn Sade?" 33–43).

"Sade does not give us the work of a free man. He makes us participate in his efforts of liberation. But it is precisely for this reason that he holds our attention. His endeavor is more genuine than the instruments it employs" (Beauvoir, "Must We Burn Sade?" 55). This attempt at communication and liberation out of traumatic silence makes Sade into a predecessor of Lautréamont, another adept of thwarted communication who greatly inspired Pasolini. "I received life like a wound, and I have forbidden suicide to heal the scar. I want the Creator—every hour of his eternity—to contemplate its gaping crevasse. This is the punishment I inflict upon him,"[60] cries out Maldoror, the hero of Lautréamont's *Chants*.

This declaration is in line with the "negative theology" of body art. Maldoror's violations and mutilations of the speechless bodies of his innocent victims convey his material dialogue with the impotent, discredited Creator, to whom he speaks in the idiom of the wound. Lautréamont's *Chants* were as scandalous in their testimony to the embarrassment of culture in which communication can be conceived only negatively as a way of destruction, as was body art's response to the aesthetics of destruction once celebrated by the European avant-gardes.

With *Salò*, Pasolini joined this tradition. The turn entailed a recasting of the director's embodied, participatory camera in oppressive terms. The film restages the perspectival view of the cubicle rooms in a villa that appears as a strange hybrid of a bordello and a death camp. The camera acquires the rigid body of a lascivious voyeur, or a prison guard whose gaze does not converse with reality but merely controls it. With greedy lust, it fixates on spatial configurations of human bodies in a distant format of long and extreme long shots.

The distance obstructs full visual access to the anonymous human torsos interlocked and caught in the space in order to tantalize the viewers' imagination, to heighten their desire to see. Magritte's painting *The Rape*, in which the contour of a face is filled in with an image of a female torso, provides an insight into the imaginary world of *Salò*. In this universe, the faces, distorted by tears or lust, don't matter.

The embodied camera and its operations are modeled self-reflexively upon a rigid doll used in the film for lessons in masturbation. In the end, the libertine rulers watch the torture scenes while sitting on a throne in a position of such masturbatory prop. In response to the close-up of a torture-scene, the president's hand goes into the pants of a young guard standing next to him.

Pasolini reduces the expressivity of the body language to the monotony of masturbation—a single gesture performed for a single goal. This impoverished communication, nevertheless, stays within the same corporeal paradigm of sign language. The Duke's comments on a masturbation scene in *Salò* are characteristic in this respect:

> Observing as we do with equal passion and apathy Guido and Vaccari masturbating the two bodies belonging to us inspires a series of interesting observations. We, Fascists, are the only true anarchists, naturally, once we are Masters of the State. In fact, the one true anarchy is that of power. Nevertheless look! The obscene gesticulation is like deaf-mutes' language with a code none of us, despite unrestrained caprice, can transgress. There is nothing to be done.[61]

The paradigm of body language sets the limits to the notion of power, and therefore of evil, since for Pasolini any power is evil. Once power has reached its utter limit, it has to bounce back. Pasolini's cinematic universe allows for a reversal, a conversion, or undoing of the wrongs which occurred for no reason but the system's exhaustion. This is a lesson he had learned from Sade, whose "theory of culture" is congenial to Georges Bataille's principle of "general economy," according to which the cultural expenditure of excess energy and resources results in destruction and human sacrifice.

In *The Accursed Share* (1967), a reflection upon the causes of war, Bataille distinguished between productive and nonproductive expenditure. This distinction pins down the nature of Pasolini's polemics with body art. Whereas body artists postulated an ultimate rupture in the system of representation, Pasolini wanted to transfigure the inflicted wound within the system, to reinscribe the rupture into the cultural symbolic framework of "productive expenditure." The prevention of further destruction consists for both Pasolini and Bataille in bringing the phenomenon of destruction to consciousness. Bataille's solution was to raise the "level of life" (*le niveau de vie*). It echoes Pasolini's insistence on "social reforms."

A Scenario of Redemption

Pasolini's discourse apart was without doubt a project of the "aesthetic morality" which Leo Bersani dismissively called "the culture of redemption."[62]
Nothing brings out better Pasolini's belief in "art's beneficently reconstruc-
tive function" than his response to body art in *Salò* (1975). The parade of
suffering bodies that has ruptured the cine-text of Pasolini's films until this
point culminates in Pasolini's last film.

Symptomatically, the scenes from *Salò* are included in a book on body art,
Body Probe: Torture Garden, as a kindred phenomenon.[63] But in *Salò*, the
ghastliness becomes so all-pervasive that it acquires a redemptive dimension
of the Dantean hell. From this nadir of destruction, one can only ascend. Two
guards who have participated in the crime all of a sudden put aside their rifles
in order to dance to a radio tune. Their simple dialogue at the end of *Salò*
constitutes a powerful intrusion of life and normality into a show-box of horror—a "redemptive" move from the side of non-culture. *Salò* was supposed
to be just a stage in the pilgrim's progress of Pasolini's biographical passion as a filmmaker. In the screenplay for his next film, *Porno-Teo-Kolossal*,
which the director had planned to start shooting at the time of his death, the
protagonists continue the Dantean trajectory started in the hell of *Salò* by
ascending to paradise.[64]

The imitation of Christ once again comes to the fore in the negative project of *Salò*. The artist's self-fashioning as Christ is an old topos which goes
back at least as far as Dürer's famous self-portrait, which created a paradigm
for such identifications. Pasolini's Christ betrays the Renaissance sensibility
which generally permeates the modern world of his films. In fact, Pasolini's
aesthetics mirrors Jacob Burckhardt's vision of Renaissance art as a way of
transcending the dark, sinister, muddy grounds of political reality. The director transfigures the slums and low passions of the Roman sub-proletariat in
the semblance of Renaissance iconography. The subtle beauty of images is
supposed to transcend their origin in misery. In the *Gospel* film, this artistic
capacity of Pasolini's embodied camera conveys the divine.

The *Gospel* film, dedicated to the memory of Pope John XXIII, not only
marked Pasolini's turn toward political allegory. In search of locations for
the *Gospel* film, he visited *terra sancta* and entered Jerusalem. The trip to
Palestine possessed all the features of a religious pilgrimage and inaugurated
the director's intellectual passion—his investigation of his own class and his
own culture's involvement with the guilt of fascism.[65] After the *Gospel* film,
the director started his cinematic descent into the harrowing of hell: *Teorema*
(1968), *Porcile* (*Pigsty*, 1969), and ultimately, *Salò* (1975).

The color scheme of the last film evokes medieval illustrations of Dante.
Consider, for example, a late fourteenth-century illumination of "Inferno,"
Canto XXXIV, from the *Divine Comedy* in the Bodleian Library at Oxford,
which shows Dante and Virgil in front of Lucifer. The image displays the

same messy, saturated colors mixed with dark undertones.[66] The bloody mutilated bodies swallowed by Lucifer recall *Salò*'s articulated reminder that the bourgeoisie swallows its own children. The concept of the participatory camera meant a shared responsibility for the horrors Pasolini filmed, especially since members of his own class had perpetrated these horrors in the cultural context of his own time.

Against this background, Pasolini's return to the *Gospel* film in *Intellettuale* and his bodily exposure to the apparatus appears in a new light as an emergence from hell. The body artist Eliseo Mattiacci's performance entitled *Remake Oneself* (1973) gives a clue to the redemptive logic of the happening *Intellettuale*. (See fig. 5.14.) In the process of his remaking himself, Mattiacci covered his face with mud as Pasolini's face was obscured during the projection. *Intellettuale* quoted the dark, enclosed spaces of *Salò*. And Pasolini's rigid posture uncannily repeated those of a body-automaton and a body-oppressor, the victim and perpetrator at once. The visual regimes of *Salò* and the *Gospel* film clashed on Pasolini's body, placing him at the very threshold between death and resurrection.[67]

The stylistic counterpoint between *Salò* and the *Gospel* film evoked in *Intellettuale* was already prepared in *Porcile*. This political allegory stylistically paved the way from the *Gospel* film to *Salò* by establishing a programmatic connection between the bourgeois sensibility and the perspectival view. The film takes place in the halls and parks of a villa in Bonn whose respectable owner, the industrialist, bears Hitler's features and turns out to be a willing collaborator with the National Socialists. His lethargic, blasé son is consumed by a passion for pigs.

At the same time, the quadrangular enclosures allegorizing proto-fascist ideology are intercut in *Porcile* with long panoramic views of the naked earth, the signature of the *Gospel* film. There such panoramic shots were to convey the divine gaze striking over the primordial expanses, empty and unformed before the event of incarnation. In *Porcile*, the panoramic shot shows the sacred work of creation undone by the corruption of the bourgeoisie. Only a preverbal cannibal roams over the desert and swallows anything alive in his desperate search for food.

The sequence where the cannibal detaches the head of a fellow human being and throws it away while keeping the torso for nourishment signals a change in the bodily paradigm of Pasolini's ideology-critical project: *Porcile* transitions from the faciality of the *Gospel* film to the objectified bodies of barbaric consumption. But *Salò*'s condemnation of bourgeois culture is even more radical: the faceless victims of fascist ideology find themselves in the midst of the "cultured" space of a bourgeois villa, the walls of which abound in the masterpieces of European art. The prototype of this space is already adumbrated in the abodes of Herod, the high Roman officials, and the Philistines, which are contrasted to the barren earth trodden by Christ and the apostles in the *Gospel* film.

Figure 5.14. A key to the redemptive logic of *Intellettuale*: Eliseo Mattiacci, *Rifarsi*, 1973. Cast iron table, clay. Action at Alexander Iolas Gallery, Milan. Image courtesy of the artist, Pesaro. Photo: Claudio Abate.

In the corporeal scenario of *Intellettuale*, a torso meets a face. The projection of the faces from the *Gospel* film onto the rigid faceless body of the director in *Intellettuale* undoes the logic of Magritte's *Rape* by providing the torso with a face and thus closes the wound. But the re-humanization is staged as a new human sacrifice. Marcel Mauss argued that in sacrifice the consecration extends beyond the thing consecrated. Among other objectives, it touches the moral person who bears the expenses of the ceremony.[68]

In the case of *Intellettuale*, the sacrificial event touches the cinematic apparatus, that is, the representational technology. Pasolini clears himself and the apparatus of *Salò*. Pasolini, indeed, was engaged in remaking himself. His camera's redemptive as well as oppressive potential are related here in a religious scenario of satanic inversion and Christian conversion. John Freccero discerned this scenario at work in Dante's *Divine Comedy*, which he called a "novel of the self." Freccero argued that the frozen Satan stuck upside down in Dante's hell inverts Christ's crucifixion. Therefore, it constitutes that very zero point where corruption meets generation.[69]

Dante partakes of the medieval tradition in which Christ's descent into the harrowing of hell is "correlative with Christ's death on the cross and his ascent with the Resurrection."[70] As the embodiment of exorcised evil, the crucified Satan participates in the plan of salvation. His body is the very ladder via which the pilgrim undergoes spiritual conversion and passes into purgatory.

The movement to grace in the medieval perception, always dear to Pasolini's artistic sensibility, is *motus ad formam*. It implies the leaving behind of sin, of a corrupted form, and an acquisition of a new form.[71] Conversion was understood in Dante's scheme of salvation in physical terms as a turning of the soul. Sandro Botticelli's illustration to Dante shows the pilgrim and his guide Virgil turning over on a disc located in the area of Satan's genitals. (See fig. 5.15.) This detail is especially meaningful in the context of *Salò*, through which Pasolini returns to the very point of his cinematic departure, to the redemptive potential of the body of Christ. Mauri's performance evokes such logic of circular movement towards form.

If Sade took apart representation and descended to the "real" (Lacan), Pasolini uses him in order to integrate the "real" back into the symbolic, to give matter a form, to render it meaningful. Mauri helped him reinscribe the "iconography" of body art back into the symbolic sacrificial scenario. He thought of *Intellettuale* as a "radiography of spirit." In the event, the performance artist wanted to melt Pasolini and his work into a "sculpture of flesh and light as a compact unity."[72]

Dante's verses about Virgil and the pilgrim climbing out of hell capture the latent message of *Intellettuale*:

> By that hidden way
> My guide and I did enter, to return
> To the fair world: and heedless of repose
> We climbed, he first, I following his steps,
> Till on our view the beautiful lights of heav'n
> Dawn'd through a circular opening in the cave:
> Thus issuing we again beheld the stars. (*Inferno* 34.133–39)[73]

A medieval illumination of this scene is strikingly similar in its mise-en-scène to a photograph from Mauri's projection. (See fig. 5.16.) In a dark, cavern-like lobby of the new museum opening onto the lit space in the background, the artist stands in profile next to Pasolini and touches his shoulder-screen—the endearing gesture of accompaniment that Virgil once offered to Dante's imagination. (See fig. 5.17.)

Figure 5.15. Conversion around the Devil's genitals: Sandro Botticelli, illustration to Dante's *Divine Comedy*, "Inferno," canto XXXIV. Center of Hell, Lucifer in full figure; departure from hell, after 1480. Pen and ink on vellum. Inv. Cim. 33 Inferno XXXIV-2. Kupferstichkabinett, Staatliche Museen, Berlin.

Figure 5.16. Virgil and Dante leaving hell: Dante, *Divine Comedy*. Illuminated manuscript page, detail. MS. Holkham misc. 48, fourteenth century. Copyright © Bodleian Libraries, University of Oxford.

Figure 5.17. Fabio Mauri and Pier Paolo Pasolini in *Intellettuale: "Il Vangelo secondo Matteo" di/su Pier Paolo Pasolini.* Galleria Comunale d'Arte Moderna, Bologna. Photo: Antonio Masotti. Courtesy Studio Fabio Mauri, copyright © Eredi Fabio Mauri and Stefano Masotti.

In this public event, as in Pasolini's numerous adaptations of antique myths and medieval tales, the drama of Western art loops through the medium of the cinematic body. Its destructive potential can be redeemed only through the creative updating of tradition, as Pasolini self-reflexively concluded in "The Unpopular Cinema": "If a Power which is 'less worse' than others is conceivable, this could only be a Power that, in preserving or reconstituting the norm, took into account the appearances or possible reappearances of Reality."[74]

Bersani's criticism of artistically redemptive projects as "dependent on a devaluation of historical experience and of art" corroborates the nature of Pasolini's meta-project as a discourse apart, where historical experience is indeed to be overcome and opened up onto a future, and art is always a device for achieving this goal. The redemptive or corrective function of Pasolini's discourse is, however, carried out not by his individual artworks but by the unfolding of the overall intermedial meta-discursive trajectory, in which Pasolini participates not merely as an artist but as a public intellectual, or as Bersani puts it in Nietzsche's contemptuous terms, as a "theoretical man."[75]

"Circuit Reversal"

The performance *Intellettuale*, when the director self-reflexively steps into his own discourse, inaugurates cinema's entrance into postwar intellectual life as the medium of the self. Hans Magnus Enzensberger's new socially engaged media theory helps understand the social polemics at the bottom of the event. In his influential essay "Constituents of a Theory of the Media" (1970), Enzensberger polemicized with progressive intellectuals who disdained the media as a mere tool of capitalist manipulation of the masses. Enzensberger drew attention to the democratic potential of the new media of telecommunication: media are a necessary platform for the criticism of the establishment. They could and should become the arena of mass creativity and mass control over the flow of information.

> For the first time in history, the media are making possible mass participation in a social and socialized productive process, the practical means of which are in the hands of the masses themselves. Such a use of them would bring the communications media, which up to now have not deserved the name, into their own. In its present form, equipment like television or film does not serve communication but prevents it. It allows no reciprocal action between transmitter and receiver; technically speaking, it reduces feedback to the lowest point compatible with the system.
>
> This state of affairs, however, cannot be justified technically. On the contrary. Electronic techniques recognize no contradiction in

principle between transmitter and receiver. Every transistor radio is, by the nature of its construction, at the same time a potential transmitter; it can interact with other receivers by circuit reversal.[76]

Enzensberger's scenario of "emancipatory" versus "repressive" usages of media corresponds to Pasolini's exploration of ideologies of the camera work in the *Gospel* film and *Salò*. The technological metaphor of "circuit reversal" is at work in the idea of the director as a receiver of the film that he has once produced. The filmmaker's entrance into the circuit of production and transmission reenacts the demise of the individualist bourgeois intellectual that Enzensberger foretold within the public sphere of new mass media:

> More radically than any good intention, more lastingly than existential flight from one's own class, the media, once they have come into their own, destroy the private production methods of bourgeois intellectuals. Only in productive work and learning process can their individualism be broken down in such a way that it is transformed from morally based (that is to say, as individual as ever) self-sacrifice to a new kind of political self-understanding and behavior.[77]

The passion scene of a bourgeois intellectual that Mauri staged inaugurates "a new kind of political self-understanding and behavior." At a time of Pasolini's radical dissociation from Nietzsche and Nietzsche-inspired modernist aesthetics, his autobiographical happening appears to take on the provocative usurpation of the topos of Christ's sufferings in Nietzsche's deliriously self-glorifying intellectual autobiography, *Ecce Homo*. Pasolini's passion scene is supposed to constitute his transition to a new type of intellectual in Gramscian terms. Its path goes through cinematic apparatus.

In Italian postwar culture, the notion of the "intellectual" was closely associated with the communist activist and theoretician Antonio Gramsci. As an editor of the socialist magazine *Ordine Nuovo* (1919–20), Gramsci was already in the 1920s engaged in building a stratum of responsible thinkers as political organizers of their class.

In his notebooks, written during his incarceration under fascist rule and published for the first time in 1949, he continued his reflections upon the necessity of educating "new intellectuals"[78] who would not be mere rhetoricians like "the traditional and vulgarized type of the intellectual . . . given by the man of letters, the philosopher, the artist."[79] He thought that "in the modern world, technical education, closely bound to industrial labor even at the most primitive and unqualified level, must form the basis of the new type of intellectual."[80]

In his theoretization of the self through the cinematic apparatus, and in his ultimate confrontation with the projector, Pasolini aspired to the role of the Gramscian "new intellectual" as a technician of culture. In the climactic sacrifice of *Intellettuale* Pasolini tried to live up to Gramsci's notion of the "organic intellectual" as the consciousness of his class. Unlike in Pasolini's earlier films *Accattone* (1961), *Mamma Roma* (1962), and *La Ricotta* (one episode of *RoGoPaG*, 1963), the sacrificial role fell now not to the Lumpen-proletariat but to a son of the bourgeoisie.

His poem "Oh, My Naked Feet . . . ," dedicated to a bourgeois intel-lectual's attempt to break out of his class, already adumbrated the scenario of this sacrifice. The poem concludes Pasolini's script of *Teorema*, where he depicted an industrialist who consciously endorses the Marxist prediction of the end of the bourgeoisie by renouncing his ownership over the means of production. With an excruciating expression of guilt, the renegade capitalist takes off his clothes and walks out into the desert.

The poem, unlike the film, comments on this "act of salvation" with a pessimistic lament: "Wretched, prosaic conclusion—a lay one because of the imposition of a culture of oppressed people—of a process begun in order to lead to God!"[81] In the script, the poem's existential questions only augment the melancholy utopia of a cinematic allegory: "And what of me? Of me, who am where I was and was where I am, the automaton of a real person, dis-patched into the desert to walk through it? I AM FILLED BY A QUESTION WHICH NO ONE CAN ANSWER . . ."[82]

Pasolini was always aware of those gaping existential dead ends even in the midst of his political passions. In his screenplay *Porno-Teo-Kolossal*, the episodes from which Abel Ferrara integrated into his film *Pasolini* (2014), the protagonist Epifanio and his companion arrive at the doors of paradise only to discover that paradise doesn't exist. They decide to sit down and wait to see what happens.

Intellettuale takes on "a question which no one can answer" but at the cost of a body stripped to its essentials—an action whose meaning has to be accepted as an unknown, a form of communication akin to the existential scream at the end of *Teorema*. The bourgeoisie's demise, even if in a Christ-like willing self-sacrifice, is nothing but a crucifixion through "the imposition of a culture of oppressed people." In the film, this sacrifice was triggered by a mysterious visit of a stranger to the bourgeois family.

In an interview, Pasolini comments upon Terence Stamp's character of a mysterious visitor: "I made Terence Stamp into a generically ultra-terrestrial and metaphysical apparition: he could be the Devil, or a mixture of God and the Devil. The important thing is that he is something authentic and unstoppa-ble."[83] Upon his "authentic" touch the family fell apart into all those elements upon the repression of which it was founded: the father became a homeless vagabond, the mother a whore, the daughter a handicapped autist, the son a body-artist, whereas it is only the peasant maid who acquired sacred powers to work wonders.

The *Gospel* film, imposed over the body of a bourgeois director in the projection, indeed glorified this culture of proletariat and peasantry. But the sacrifice, as expressed in the poem, might lead the bourgeois class down to a wretched existence without bringing about the transcendent experience of grace, or even simply that of social justice. Skepticism in the way of religious or socialist redemptive projects rounds up and transfigures their teleology as circularity. The Gramsci-inspired intention of dissolving a bourgeois intellectual in his confrontation with the cinematic apparatus, ironically, results in a defiant affirmation of individualist hubris: a circuit reversal? If there is a redemptive dimension to *Intellettuale*, it is, as always with Pasolini, social and public. Its "superior patching function"[84] was to be performed from outside art.

The Gospel by/about Pasolini

Mauri's *Intellettuale* may provide the most insightful comment on the conundrum of Pasolini's art and politics. Pasolini famously claimed that Italians do not read the Gospels, therefore the purpose of his adaptation was to disseminate Matthew's gospel cinematically.[85] But this goal implied a much broader social and cultural agenda, which Pasolini chose to organize through the body of Christ. The logic of Mauri's performance drives home, quite literally, the essential moment of Pasolini's discourse, its rootedness in a ritualized, meaningful body. In cinema, this body is that of the camera, which figures as an extension of its human operator, or in a broader sense, of the filmmaker himself.

Mauri's projection returns Pasolini's film back where it originated, in the three-dimensional space once occupied by the camera's bodywork. The German critic Karsten Witte wrote about bodily geography in Pasolini's films—of bodies as locations and locations as bodies. His essay "Körper/Orte" fused in its title the words *Körper*, "body," and *Orte*, "locations," as bodies and locations fuse on Pasolini's screen. *Intellettuale* revealed that their fusion is implicit in the very ritual of filmmaking. The presence of the camera in the film is always the presence of the human body that once was united with it, and therefore cinematic art is always rooted in life and accountable to it.

The evocation of Christ's sacrifice on the threshold of a new museum also implies a procedure of mourning. Eric Santner has argued for the German context that the auteur cinema, and specifically that produced for television, compensated for the inability to mourn verbally.[86] Cinema comes into play where one senses a need for another language. To be socially effective, mourning can't be structurally abstract. As another form of "lived experience," cinema, Santner observed, possesses the capacity to bring back to memory the repressed past and in this way to master the traumatic loss. Moreover, cinematic remembrance is collective, as crimes and histories were collective.

Like a homeopathic procedure, cinema can make the viewer relive trauma on a small scale; it introduces a minimal dose of poison in order to help heal the whole system. The auteur cinema, according to Santner, offers a possibility of such homeopathic ethics. In *Intellettuale*, Pasolini's cinema of poetry in its nexus with Mauri's conceptual art of weapon, wound, and matter was accomplishing precisely this.

The interjection of the director's sacrificial body within the maze of the discourses on art, politics, and technology reconnected them to the phenomenon, endowed them with history, relevance, and personal responsibility. Most importantly, the event drew the visitors attending the performance to participate in collective mourning over the notion of culture struggling to survive—a rite of passage necessary for the intellectual and his public alike, before they can enter the pristine space of a new gallery and see the light.

Chapter 6

A "Sacred Enterprise"

Christ's Body in the Contemporary United States

When it is the Lord's battle you are fighting, politics takes on
an aura of deadly earnestness.
  —R. J. Neuhaus, *The Naked Public Square*

Nobody fucks with the Jesus!
  —Coen Brothers, *The Big Lebowski*

The emergence of *theoconservatism* as an ideological current distinct from
conservative or neoconservative streams in the United States became public
in the course of the 1996 presidential elections. In September of that year a
group of prominent antiabortion lobbyists, among them Paul Weyrich and
Gary Bauer, gathered in the antechambers of the Senate majority leader Trent
Lott to condemn in unusually fiery terms the Senate's failure to overturn
President Clinton's veto of a ban on "partial-birth abortions." The group
loudly questioned the legitimacy of the "American regime" that "sanctions
infanticide" and likened the current Clinton administration to both China
and Nazi Germany.[1] Such extreme rhetoric, openly displayed in the Republican quarters of the U.S. Senate, drew the attention of Jacob Heilbrunn of the
New Republic, who was the first to report on a new political development.

Soon thereafter, the same actors felt bold enough to go to the broad conservative public with a call for a religious coup d'état. In November 1996, *First
Things* (a leading far-right religious journal cofounded by theo- and neoconservatives in 1990) published a symposium entitled "The End of Democracy? The
Judicial Usurpation of Politics." The document revealed a systematic ideology
and a radical political agenda on the part of the theoconservative movement
at the moment of its coming-out as a new avant-garde of the American right.

The symposium built upon the journal's May 1996 editorial "The Ninth
Circuit's Fatal Overreach," dedicated to the case *Compassion in Dying v.
State of Washington* (1996). In *Compassion in Dying*, Judge Stephen Rein-
hardt, regarded as the most liberal among the federal judges, upheld a lower

court's decision to grant a right to physician-assisted suicide for mentally competent, terminally ill adults dying protracted and painful deaths.[2] The case gave the theocons a convenient pretext for a rhetorical exercise in the emotionally charged language of life and death, chastising the liberal courts for "imposing" euthanasia on the old, sick, and disabled.[3]

The theocons' objection to *Compassion in Dying* was, however, motivated not by the protection of life.[4] What outraged them in Reinhardt's decision was its underlying understanding of the courts' function in a liberal democracy, that is, the decision's emphasis on the protection of individual rights rather than on upholding a particular ideological stance:

> Some argue strongly that decisions regarding matters affecting life or death should not be made by the courts. Essentially, we agree with that proposition. In this case, by permitting the *individual* to exercise the right to choose we are following the constitutional mandate to take such decisions out of the hands of the government, both state and federal, and to put them where they rightly belong, in the hands of the people. We are allowing individuals to make the decisions that so profoundly affect their very existence—and precluding the state from intruding excessively into that critical realm.
>
> The Constitution and the courts stand as a bulwark between individual freedom and arbitrary and intrusive governmental power. Under our constitutional system, neither the state nor the majority of the people in a state can impose its will upon the individual in a matter so highly "central to personal dignity and autonomy." . . . Those who believe strongly that death must come without physician assistance are free to follow that creed, be they doctors or patients. They are not free, however, to force their views, their religious convictions, or their philosophies on all the other members of a democratic society, and to compel those whose values differ with theirs to die painful, protracted, and agonizing deaths.[5]

It is instructive to compare Reinhardt's stance with the *theoconservative* rejection of precisely this model of "advanced democratic societies":

> In such societies government is forced to be relatively modest and even self-limiting. The state is seen as the pragmatic broker between countervailing interests; it is not the generator or promulgator of values. On this view, the state does not presume to address ultimate issues nor to claim transcendent authority for its decisions. It is a classically liberal view and is highly unsatisfactory to those who want politics to deal not only with procedural questions but also with the substantive questions of justice, the common good, and even transcendent destiny. (Neuhaus, *The Naked Public Square*, 133)[6]

In response to Reinhardt's affirmation of individual freedom in matters of life and death, the May editorial of *First Things* had insinuated the illegitimacy of the American government in the light of its tolerance of "immoral" jurisprudence and pondered the possibility of withdrawing its popular support. The November *First Things* symposium[7] extended the journal's earlier attack on *Compassion in Dying* to a wider range of Supreme Court decisions, especially *Planned Parenthood v. Casey* (1992), upholding women's right to choose; *Romer v. Evans* (1996), upholding gay rights; and *United States v. Virginia* (1996), granting women the right of admission to the Virginia Military Academy.

Besides the rhetoric of baby-killing in regard to *Casey*, theoconservatives raged that by extending the protection clause of the Fourteenth Amendment to homosexuals in *Romer*, the Supreme Court had shown "approval of homosexual conduct" and overruled *Bowers v. Hardwick* (1986), a decision which allegedly articulated the original meaning of the U.S. Constitution by allowing a state to criminalize homosexuality ("The End of Democracy?" 22). At the same time, according to the contributors to the *First Things* symposium, women's military education interfered with the natural role of women, since in the lone dissenting opinion of Justice Scalia the equality of women was nothing but one of "the smug assurances of [the] age" (ibid., 22).

In an unsigned introduction, the journal's editor in chief, Richard John Neuhaus, declared religion to be "the first political institution" of American democracy. This statement of principle was based on an inversion of Alexis de Tocqueville's observation about the interplay of the political and the religious in America. Tocqueville wrote in 1835: "Religion, which never interferes directly in the government of Americans, should therefore be regarded as the first of their political institutions, for, if it does not give them the taste for liberty, it enables them to take unusual advantage of it."[8] Neuhaus and the participants in the symposium subverted Tocqueville's meaning by insisting on religion's direct interference in government. "What happens to the rule of law," Neuhaus further asked indignantly, "when law is divorced from, indeed pitted against, the first political institution?" ("The End of Democracy?" 20).

The contributors answered this question with an apocalyptic vision of the godless country's collapse. In "Kingdoms in Conflict," Charles Colson, the former Watergate felon turned evangelist and chairman of Prison Fellowship, consequently declared that "given the demonstrated animus of the current judicial regime against believers—a showdown between church and state may be inevitable" ("The End of Democracy?" 37). He transformed Augustine's concept of "just war" into "just revolution" and contemplated a strategy of consolidation of power by the religious right, which would make possible a political takeover: "It seems to me, however, that only the Church in some corporate capacity, not the individual Christian, has the authority to answer the question of our allegiance to the present regime. . . . Only the

Church collectively can decide at what point a government becomes sufficiently corrupt that a believer must resist it" (ibid., 35).

Colson reminded readers of the successful 1994 initiative "Evangelicals and Catholics Together: The Christian Mission in the Third Millennium," which he and Neuhaus had launched in the pages of *First Things* in pursuit of exactly this goal—the consolidation of American right-leaning religious groups and denominations into one Christian coalition that would constitute an effective political force. "But would even active disobedience be effective against our current judicial state?" he wrote. "When peaceable means and limited civil disobedience fail—according to the Protestant theologians Knox and Rutherford—revolution can be justified from a Christian viewpoint" ("The End of Democracy?" 37).[9]

However, it was Russell Hittinger, professor of Catholic studies at the University of Tulsa, who provided the strongest statement of the symposium's militant anti-secularism by revealing the Catholic notion of the "common good" as a foundation of the group's shared political theology. The symposium proudly pointed to the papal 1995 encyclical *Evangelium Vitae*, the document where Pope John Paul II talked about the necessity of moral foundations for democracy, as the ultimate authority behind their endeavors. However, the participants were conspicuously silent about their more radical and immediate ideological source—*The Way of the Lord Jesus*, a voluminous textbook written for students of American Catholic seminaries by Germain Grisez, professor of Christian ethics at Mount St. Mary's University.

Responding to theological attempts to bring Catholic morality more up-to-date with the modern world, Grisez developed a comprehensive defense of Catholic moral principles based on a natural-law theory derived from Saint Paul and Thomas Aquinas. Grisez declared that "the judgment of conscience, which characterizes each possible choice as right or wrong, cannot be deduced from facts or logic. How things are cannot finally determine how one ought to live. Moral principles and judgments neither can be established nor overturned by experience or the sciences."[10] Consistent with this stance, Grisez dedicated his life to fighting abortion and contraception.

In the contemporary landscape of Catholic theology, Grisez's interpretation of the Vatican's missives stands out for his position on Christian civil disobedience. In *Catholic Moral Principles* (1983), the first volume of his textbook, he argued that civil laws should be tested for their Catholic moral truth, which is superior to the laws of the government. In the second volume, *Living a Christian Life* (1993), Grisez radicalized his thinking so as to wage an outright war against the decadent culture of secular humanism, which, he claimed, is irreconcilable with the Catholic way of life, a way of life that implies sacrifice and suffering. He encouraged the Christians to break secular law openly or stealthily if it interferes with the truths of the Catholic Church.[11]

Grisez's encouragement fell on fertile ground and did not stay unheeded. In *Ourselves Unborn*, Sara Dubow offers statistics: "Between 1977 and the end of September 1998 alone, pro-life activists performed more than 3,385 bombings, arsons, blockades, acts of vandalism, stalking, assault and harassment at abortion clinics around the United States. Between 1993 and 1998, four physicians, two clinic employees, a security guard, and a clinic escort were assassinated."[12] But Grisez went even further: "Rarely, force may be used to replace a bad regime."[13]

In "A Crisis of Legitimacy," Hittinger argued in the steps of Grisez that "citizens can have a duty not to obey a law if it seriously injures the common good" ("The End of Democracy?" 26). A law upholding the rights of women and sexual minorities exemplified such injury to the "common good" (ibid., 25). How the liberty of citizens to make their own decisions about their bodies and intimate lives injures the political common good is difficult and even impossible to understand, however, on the basis of a secular concept of state and citizenship. American abortion law, for example, hinges on the right to privacy. Consider its evocation in Judge Reinhardt's reference to *Casey*: "In discussing a woman's liberty interest in securing an abortion, the *Casey* Court stated that pregnancy involves 'suffering [that] is too intimate and personal for the State to insist, without more, upon its own vision of the woman's role, *however dominant that vision has been in the course of our history and culture*'."[14]

The theocons' insistence that the state forbid abortion as an injury to the common good is, in fact, not "without more": their position is based on the assumption of a shared body politic. It betrays an understanding of society not as a diverse group of individuals of varying persuasions and competing interests who want to be left alone, but as one self-identical, undivided, unanimous collectivity. The common good of a society so conceived is not that of liberal democracy but that of Catholicism and is better understood with Grisez's words in mind: "Human life itself belongs to individual organisms, but it also exists in the common functions of sexual intercourse and procreation. Thus, there are no categories of human good inherently private or inherently social."[15]

The common good is for Grisez an intelligible category; as such it transcends the empirical good of individuals. He argues this against Aristotle and Thomas Aquinas, both of whom saw the members relating to society as parts to the whole and hence understood the "common good" as "the only true and complete good of the individuals." Grisez, on the contrary, understands the individual's relation to society as a synecdoche: each member carries full responsibility for the whole. He insists that one member can indirectly damage the health of another member, or of the whole, in which case that member can be amputated. His argument makes clear that individual empirical rights can be trumped in the name of the intelligible good, such as, for example, the concept of life.[16]

Without mentioning Grisez's name, Hittinger defined the "common good" rather narrowly and in Grisez's wording as that of the "citizens of rightly formed conscience," that is, of the church: "Unless the new constitutional order is profoundly reformed, citizens of rightly formed conscience will find themselves in a crisis" ("The End of Democracy?" 28). Hittinger substituted the common good of a group of the faithful for the varying values of all citizens of American liberal democracy by interjecting the Christian eschatological presumption that everyone, believers and nonbelievers alike, knowingly or not, participates in divine history and is bound by Christian law.

Thus Hittinger boldly posited the United States as a Church where all citizens constitute one common body so that an abortion performed on one logically implicates all, the non-procreative homosexuality of some affects the procreation of the whole, and an individual choice to die interferes with the living body of the collectivity.

"In the Lord Jesus, the identity and self-consistency of the Church is assured,"[17] wrote Grisez. The theocons' audacious wager was to take Grisez's parochial views beyond the narrow precincts of the Catholic Church and into the big world of American domestic and international politics. They seized upon Grisez's teaching on Christian civil disobedience, but chose to express it in the parlance of a legal authority, Supreme Court Justice Antonin Scalia: "A Christian should not support a government that suppresses the faith or one that sanctions the taking of an innocent human life."[18] Grisez's Catholic moral principles, scantily dressed as a discourse on the alleged abuse of constitutional law, were posited as a directive for conservative political action.

Many evangelists, for example Colson or Jerry Falwell, subscribed for strategic reasons to the Catholic pro-life and antihomosexual causes, since the Catholic Church possessed a solid and tested institutional body and a systematic political philosophy, necessary for an organized political effort. Already in 1983, writing during the surge of the evangelical movement with its drive for political influence, Grisez had speculated about the failure of Protestantism's "disincarnate Christianity" and its possible accommodation under the wing of Catholicism:

> Today's Catholic Church is confronted with substantial opportunities for ecumenism and evangelization. . . . Christians today can see clearly the result of allowing the world to go its way without the illumination of faith; few are satisfied with a disincarnate Christianity which isolates faith in the individual relationship of the soul before God. Rationalistic philosophy no longer shapes Protestant theology, and most Protestant theologians who believe in divine revelation realize the difficulty of sustaining the claim that it is enshrined in the Bible, to be found there by individuals without a community whose faith somehow transcends and sustains the individual's faith.[19]

To return to the *First Things* symposium, its ideological project of politicized incarnate Christianity culminated in the contribution "The Tyrant

State" by Robert P. George, professor of politics at Princeton and an ardent follower of Grisez.[20] Focusing on the papal understanding of democracy in *Evangelium Vitae*, George articulated the parties' mutual consent that the leading force in the enterprise of Christianizing the United States would be Roman Catholicism. John Paul II had pointed out that "fundamentally democracy is a 'system' and as such is a means and not an end. Its 'moral value' is not automatic, but depends on conformity to the moral law to which it, like every other form of human behavior, must be subject."[21]

For the symposium, this moral law, to which democracy must conform, was unambiguously the Catholic moral law, and the American democracy was nothing but "a means to an end": be it through contempt of court, civil disobedience, armed revolution, or the long-term subversive work of provoking a constitutional crisis and legal and governmental reform that would strip the liberal courts of constitutional review, the ultimate goal of all the forms of sabotage suggested by the theocons was to annul the separation of church and state and replace the value-neutral proceduralism of the American government with an inherently valorized and moralized system. That is, with the body of Christ.

In 1983 Grisez wrote: "Eventually, the inhumanism of secular humanism will become obvious to everyone. At that point, a new phase of history, with new opportunities for evangelization, will begin."[22] The theocons felt that the electoral campaign of 1996 offered such an opportunity for evangelization: To bring in an administration that would agree to bind all citizens, regardless of their personal beliefs and persuasions, by Catholic moral law issuing from the Vatican would not only accomplish a missionary task, but also constitute the first step toward fulfillment of the Christian prophecy and 2,000-year-old hope of harnessing the powers that be as a vehicle to ride toward the kingdom of God.

However, in 1996 the *First Things* symposium's attempt to influence the electorate through the rhetoric of urgency and moral indignation turned out to be a flop. The primary contender most closely allied to their positions, Alan Keyes, made no headway. The Republican nominee, Bob Dole, proved a disappointment: despite his initial flirtation with the Christian Coalition, he did not push their agenda concerning "moral values" in the debates. Finally, the publication of the symposium instantly caused a radical rift and warfare among the ideologues of the religious right and their former neoconservative allies and supporters.[23] The inflammatory tone and Christian political theology, which blurred the distinction between the political system of the United States and the Catholic Church, caused a scandal and alienated the neoconservative members of the journal.

The aggressive rhetoric, accusing the United States of baby-killing and comparing it to Nazi Germany, must have rung the wrong bells. Many of the neocons were Holocaust survivors or came from survivors' families. Moreover, by publishing the symposium without the neocons' knowledge or consent, the theocons hijacked the coedited periodical for their own radically religious agenda and thus bluntly demonstrated their emancipation from their former patrons.[24]

Midge Decter, the de facto editor of the journal, and Norman Podhoretz, the founding father of neoconservatism and editor of *Commentary*, dissociated themselves from the radical and subversive goals of the symposium group in their letters and publications. The neocon political theorists Walter Berns and Peter Berger as well as the historian Gertrude Himmelfarb resigned from the editorial board, and neocon periodicals such as *National Review* and the *Weekly Standard* published their own demurrals.

As Heilbrunn observed, the intellectual genealogy of the neocons' understanding of the United States went back to Leo Strauss's *Natural Right and History* (1953). Strauss saw American democracy as based on the Aristotelian notion of natural rights and insisted on its Athenian model. He did not deny a role of religion in society but believed the state must not explicitly endorse any religious code. However, the participants in the symposium did not share Strauss's restraint.

The Orthodox Jewish theocon Hadley Arkes tried to put the symposium's agenda into a broader perspective of resistance to modernity with an emphasis on its overall anti-civilizatory impetus: "Perhaps Rousseau, with an edge of madness, had it right: that all of this simply came along with the ethic of modernity, as it was spread through the diffusion of the sciences and the arts. 'We have all become doctors, and we have ceased being Christians'" ("The End of Democracy?" 33).

But the theocons' project was not a Rousseauist one: in its underlying Catholic concept of the church as "one Eucharistic fellowship, the communion of those united with one another by being united in Jesus,"[25] there survived a premodern, pre-Lockean notion of polity in which one partakes through blood kinship, and not through a rational notion of citizenship. Obviously, up to this moment, the neocons had misinterpreted the theocons' efforts in Straussian terms as a case of ordering American society according to Judeo-Christian ethics and thus had been ready to accommodate them as a moralizing force bringing support to their neoconservative agenda. However, they were not ready to sacrifice the freedoms of the secular state and their own political influence.

Himmelfarb's reaction to the symposium was characteristic of this misunderstanding. In her open letter of resignation, she pointed out that the contributors' description of the American political system as a "regime" targeted not just a particular institution or branch of government but "the very nature of the American government," an attitude she expressly rejected:

> This is not, it seems to me, a proper mode of political discourse, still less of conservative political discourse. Indeed, it discredits, or at the very least makes suspect, any attempt by conservatives to introduce

moral and religious considerations into "the public square"—as if morality and religion necessarily lead to such apocalyptic conclusions. It can only confirm many Americans in their suspicion that cultural conservatism is outside the "mainstream" of American politics, that it is "extremist," even subversive.[26]

Richard John Neuhaus's Theory of Subversion

Himmelfarb's letter gave away the source of the long-lasting neoconservative misunderstanding of the theocons' actual political goals—Richard John Neuhaus's *The Naked Public Square* (1984). This founding text of theoconservative ideology was written in the immediate wake of the aggressive appearance on the political scene of Christian fundamentalists, or evangelicals, mobilized and organized into the so-called Moral Majority by the evangelist Jerry Falwell in 1979.[27] Their overwhelming electoral support for Ronald Reagan was counted among the factors that brought him into the White House and thus effectuated a serious political and religious reorientation of the country from left to right.[28]

Neuhaus, a Lutheran pastor, who had started his career in the 1960s on the religious left marching with Martin Luther King, astutely estimated that the victory of the new right over liberalism signaled by Reagan's election was far-reaching and promised to be lasting.[29] Disappointed that in the 1960s the mainline Protestant churches entered the public space merely to endorse the civil rights movement on ethical grounds, but did not use the opportunity of popular upheavals to claim moral and political domination over the American state, Neuhaus reckoned that by engaging the potential of a new popular front, now on the right, the established church would have another opportunity—however "uncertain" and "filled with risk"—to revamp its identity as a political actor (Neuhaus, *The Naked Public Square*, 13).

He expected that "Christianity ranged along the conservative evangelical-fundamentalist spectrum may well become the largest and most vital constellation of religious forces in American life" (Neuhaus, *The Naked Public Square*, 17). Therefore he urged the leaders of the predominantly liberal mainline Protestant denominations to do as he had done, that is, to switch under the expediency of the moment to the winning conservative side and to accommodate the fundamentalists as the populist force for the common Christian cause. After all, "God's purpose cannot converge so conveniently with any political agenda" (ibid., 7).

Neuhaus's enthusiasm for the political potential of Christian populism might have been inspired as well by concurrent political events in Iran, where the Islamic revolution of 1979 had just resulted in the foundation of an Islamic state under the guardianship of Islamic jurists. Mentioning this outcome of

militant Islamism in Iran as a potential scenario for the outcome of radicalized Christianity in America, the scenario he allegedly wanted to prevent
(Neuhaus, *The Naked Public Square*, 162–63), Neuhaus set out an astonish-
ingly similar plan for the political transformation of the United States.[30]

Employing the well-worn Cold War strategy of "scar[ing] hell out of the
country,"[31] Neuhaus painted the United States as being in imminent danger of either an armed insurgence of Christian fundamentalists who were
about to install an Iran-like theocracy on their own, rather unsophisticated,
theological terms, or of Soviet or Nazi-like totalitarianism issuing from an
overreaching secular state. The only way of preventing either of these dire
prospects, he insisted, was to replace the fundamentalists' crude biblical literalism with a more sophisticated theology and to allow religion to become a
"mediating structure" between the secular state and American society, which
he claimed was deeply religious.[32]

In this scenario, the religion would "promulgate belief in a transcendent
reality by which the state can be called to judgment" (Neuhaus, *The Naked
Public Square*, 82). Religious institutions would dress the "naked public square" of American liberal democracy with moral meaning and values
binding on both citizens and the state, and the notion of individual freedom
would be redefined as the freedom to be bound by what is "authoritative"
(ibid., 17).

In the last climactic chapter of his book, entitled "Law and the Experiment
Renewed," Neuhaus claimed that law's power to bind (*religare*) is rooted in
religion (Neuhaus, *The Naked Public Square*, 250). The law's "premise, from
which it derives its perceived legitimacy and therefore its authority is that it
strives to anticipate and give expression to what a people believes to be its
collective destiny or ultimate meaning within a moral universe" (ibid., 253).

"In law or any other field, the search for ultimate meanings that provide
morally binding legitimacy for an enterprise is a theological search," Neuhaus continued. In Christian theology, the meaning of any thing is in the end
of that thing. The "meaning of all history is revealed—if the Christian gospel
turns out to be true—in the end time of the consummation of history in the
Messianic Age" (Neuhaus, *The Naked Public Square*, 256). Since the foundation of the United States—the American experiment—was in Neuhaus's
vision a "sacred enterprise" (ibid., 7), not the state-made laws, but religious
law should bind God's chosen country.

It would follow as a matter of logic that this religious project strove for
legal and political realization by targeting civil laws premised on liberal
democracy's notion of individual autonomy. *Roe v. Wade* (1973) was Neuhaus's major example of secular state law lacking a foundation in a higher
law; it is therefore "an instance of law against life, of individualism's assault
upon the individual, of the eradication of the personal and communal bonds
without which it is not possible to be an individual" (Neuhaus, *The Naked
Public Square*, 259).

Neuhaus was correct that a woman's right to seek an abortion was not founded on religious principles, but rather was established in *Roe* as an individual freedom, a private choice that is not accountable to the *civitas'* communal body. The proposition to establish Christian law as the law of the land sought to bring about precisely such accountability and, in consequence, ecclesiastical control over the citizens' collective body.

"Some theological abstractions to the contrary," Neuhaus wrote, "Christianity *as religion* is engaged in the struggle for power, despite its message being centered in the powerlessness of the cross" (Neuhaus, *The Naked Public Square*, 131; emphasis in original). The agenda of dressing the allegedly naked public square of liberal democracy in Christian symbolism was integral to this struggle. Neuhaus understood very well that the one who owns the symbol owns the power: "Rhetoric is almost never *mere* rhetoric. Terminological disputes bear upon substance and power, as witness arguments 'pro-life' and 'pro-choice' in the abortion debate" (ibid., 11; emphasis in original).

Consequently, the Christianization of the state, Neuhaus suggested, should start with a Christian rearticulation of the law. Consider the example of his discussion of New York's prohibition of child pornography. It outraged him that this prohibition had been advanced not on moral grounds but on the basis that the production of child pornography harms the child psychologically. His objection to so secular an articulation of the judicial opinion was not substantive but strategic from the position of the church: he claimed that the testimony of psychological experts could be questioned and appealed, whereas the judicial assertion of the same law from a moral Christian viewpoint would make it impervious to any further challenge (Neuhaus, *The Naked Public Square*, 111).

Revision of the American legal system on unchallengeable religious premises would, without doubt, significantly simplify procedure, obviating the need for appellate courts and judicial review altogether. But what such religious articulation of law would really accomplish is not public morality but the practical fusion of church and state. The language used by the judicial and legislative branches of government is indeed not mere rhetoric. Such language has a performative, law-giving function. Clothing legal language in religious symbolism would give de facto legal status to Christian absolutes.

Neuhaus made clear that his vision of American society as a *civitas Dei* with a transcendent and binding point of reference was to be understood concretely as a society governed by religious law in anticipation of the kingdom of God, where the state is not the source of laws, but a law-enforcing agent of the church. There "the lawyer and public officer have a quasi-priestly role, mediating between human conflicts and what is hoped is a moral universe" (Neuhaus, *The Naked Public Square*, 255).

Neuhaus called such an organization of society not "theocracy" but "theonomy," allegedly quoting the renowned Protestant theologian Paul Tillich.

However, Tillich used the term in an explicitly theological sense as distinct from the political. His use of the word "theonomy" described "the state of culture under the impact of the Spiritual Presence," the kingdom of God: "The *nomos* (law) effective in it is the directedness of the self-creation of life under the dimension of the Spirit toward the ultimate in being and meaning." Tillich unambiguously rejected political projects of the type put forward by Neuhaus: "It is certainly unfortunate," he wrote, "that the term 'theonomy' can indicate the subjection of a culture to divine laws, imposed from outside and mediated by a church."[33]

Neuhaus's proposal for American social reorganization falls, however, exactly under Neuhaus's own definition of theocracy: "Theocracy is in fact a form of heteronomy in which an institution, namely, religion, claims to embody and authoritatively articulate absolute truth" (Neuhaus, *The Naked Public Square*, 188). In his chapter on law, he finally discarded the disguise of Tillich, who after all admitted that "Protestantism is aware that a new theonomy cannot be created intentionally by autonomous reason."[34] The intentional creation of theonomy is, however, exactly what Neuhaus wanted to achieve by turning a new theonomy into the goal of the political process. At a certain point, he conceded that his theonomy was in fact not that of Tillich's liberal Protestantism but that of Catholicism, glossing over Tillich's warning: "Catholicism, too, demands a new theonomy but what it really wants is the re-establishment of ecclesiastical heteronomy."[35]

Not coincidentally, Neuhaus was careful to defer a direct answer to his opponents' alarmed question: considering the great diversity of religious persuasions in the United States, "whose religion" was supposed to play the law-giving role (Neuhaus, *The Naked Public Square*, 21)? First, he went through all potential sources for the spiritualization of the American public square, rejecting them one by one. The European tradition of secular moral philosophy is valid but not appropriate for America, which is a religious country.

Liberal churches and liberation theology are too secular, basically an appendix of good causes defined by others. Mainline Protestantism is too individualist, fragmented, and institutionally weak to be a public force of major influence, whereas all forms of religiously inspired public ethics are politically ineffectual for their lack of powerful religious symbolism. Only at the very end of his book does Neuhaus put his cards on the table: it is Roman Catholicism that now should have a turn at the culture-forming task in America.

> In many ways, this ought to be "the Catholic moment" in American life. By virtue of numbers, of a rich tradition of social and political theory, and of Vatican II's theological internalization of the democratic idea, Catholics are uniquely posed to propose the American proposition anew. Not least among their strengths is that in John

Paul II we have a historic figure who is singularly persuasive about the ominous alternatives to the human freedom that democracy protects. The Catholic moment was not, as some say, in 1960 when John F. Kennedy was elected, in large part because he reassured the electorate that he was not a very serious Catholic. The Catholic moment is now. It may be missed, however. (Neuhaus, *The Naked Public Square*, 262)

Neuhaus observed that in their drive for power, conservative Catholic leaders merge most harmoniously with evangelicals: "Their meeting point is in the passion for authority and, therefore, in the necessity of challenging, or even overthrowing, the authorities that have allegedly undermined legitimate authority in the modern world" (Neuhaus, *The Naked Public Square*, 45). Catholicism would be, in his view, the most appropriate safeguard for religious sensibility in American public life and politics because "in a more far-reaching way, the Catholic spirit is not amenable to the 'strict separationist' program that would elevate to the level of dogma the proposition that America is a secular society" (ibid., 51).[36]

For reasons of rhetorical strategy, Neuhaus equated secularism with the danger of "totalitarianism." The Soviet Union, Nazi Germany, and China—always enumerated as a set without any historical or political differentiation—offered an example of the totalitarian threat that the secular American state poses to its citizens. He chose to represent the system of "totalitarianism" as an all-powerful state promulgating civil values and imposing them violently upon the disempowered citizenry. This system, he insisted, originates in secular liberal democracy, which has purged religion from its public space.

His representation obfuscated the fact that the totalitarian regimes of the Soviet Union, Nazi Germany, and China were not the offspring of secular democracy, which in all those countries was weak and short-lived. Quite to the contrary, their oppressive regimes were virtual surrogates for the divinely established oppressive monarchies that had governed them in previous centuries, whereas it had been precisely the traditional liberal democracies of England and France that were able to avoid the totalitarian experience and were especially resistant to its temptations.[37]

For similar strategic reasons, Neuhaus omitted the fact that in actual totalitarian states, the state is never in direct and exclusive relation to the citizens, but is always controlled and directed by a third entity, the party. Liberal democracy, a value-neutral structure, can accommodate a variety of parties. In the totalitarian systems, however, it was not the state but the party with its parallel hierarchy of power that promulgated the ideological values which were binding on both the state and its population. The totalitarian state, at least in the given historical examples, was merely a neutral, pliable mechanism accountable to this powerful ideological institution.

By misrepresenting liberal democracy as a precursor of totalitarianism, Neuhaus obscured the insight that the totalitarian three-part model "Party-State-Citizenry" was precisely the one that he proposed for the United States, in which the Catholic Church, as a "mediating structure," was supposed to play the ideological role of the Communist or National Socialist Party.

The party, precisely like the Roman Catholic Church in Neuhaus's model, was above the state because it claimed to be in possession of the absolute truth. It had its own institutional structure and functioned as a mediator between the state and citizens who were bound by the precepts of its ideology. Moreover, in the totalitarian systems, the party, regarded as the avant-garde of the people whose citizenship is predicated on a shared ideology, was said to generate these values on behalf of the people as the "free" expression of their will. Neuhaus expected precisely such "free" surrender of American citizens' individual liberties to the ideological authority of the church.

Neuhaus opposed the regimes of the Soviet Union, Nazi Germany, and China so fervently not because of the oppressive idealistic nature of their totalitarian political systems, which annihilate individual liberties in favor of the abstractly defined "common good" and bind all citizens into one monolithic body by one single set of principles, but because the principles they advocated were secular.

Conspicuously absent from his list of totalitarian dictatorships was Spain under Franco (self-styled "leader by the grace of God"), where the Catholic Church indeed promulgated the binding values. While exuberantly condemning Nazi Germany, Neuhaus mentioned its Catholic ally and counterpart only three times as an example of Roman Catholicism's ideal of a "Christian" society. Despite putting "Christian" in quotation marks, he carefully avoided a designation and repudiation of the Spanish Christian regime as "totalitarian" because in his calculation the Catholic promise of American democracy was about to supersede this ideal.

The suggestion that American-style liberal democracy is the best societal organization to carry the message of Roman Catholicism came from the American Jesuit John Courtney Murray, whose work had been rejected by the Curia until Vatican II. In his book *We Hold These Truths: Catholic Reflections on the American Proposition* (1960), Murray insisted that the United States and its political system were founded on the medieval principles of natural law and that Americans have been tacitly bound by Catholic morality throughout their history.

Building upon Murray's masterpiece of historical revisionism, Neuhaus insisted that the United States was, in fact, a better ground than Catholic Spain to restore the church's true monopoly on the *potestas spiritualis* destroyed by Luther's Reformation. He wrote that "in some places, such as Spain under Franco, the monopoly had a degree of believability, but generally the claim to monopoly ran counter both to sociological fact and, increasingly, to ecclesiological doctrine. . . . Only a great ecumenical advance that would once again institutionally 'center' the religious dynamic could change the fragmentation of moral authority in the modern world" (Neuhaus, *The Naked Public Square*, 174).

Catholicism's domination of Franco's Spain was imperfect, Neuhaus made clear, because of its limited missionary possibilities: being in charge of one isolated and none too powerful state, Spanish Catholicism lacked any influence on Protestant, non-Christian, and secular societies. The United States, on the contrary, is a world power that would offer Catholicism a muscular shoulder for universal expansion, especially if American Catholicism could integrate under its leadership all other Christian denominations:

> It is said that the failure of Christianity to be the culture-forming force that it ought to be is attributable to the division of the church. The ecumenical task, then, is to consolidate churchly resources in order to exercise greater clout in society. This regrouping is the prerequisite for another go at establishing the complete Christian commonwealth. (Neuhaus, *The Naked Public Square*, 228)

In light of this proposition for America published already in 1984, Heilbrunn's irony about the sudden scandal within the conservative camp in 1996 was not unjustified:

> When Neuhaus and Dobson and Grisez hear Podhoretz and Kristol and Decter accuse them of not acting like true conservatives—of being radical and subversive—they must be at least a little tempted to laugh. Well, yes. Of course they are radicals and subversives. That is what they intended to be all along; that is what they have always been. (Heilbrunn, "Neocon v. Theocon," 24)

Secular and Jewish neoconservatives had, indeed, been among those who in 1984 cheerfully applauded the publication of *The Naked Public Square*, the book proposing an aggressive, missionary, expansionist religious policy and openly contemplating subversion of the American state and its political organization. Having little interest in Christian-sounding speculations and concerned primarily with the use of religious rhetoric for funneling the Christian vote in imitation of Reagan, the neocons found the smooth-looking and soft-talking Neuhaus, seemingly preaching an ecumenical compromise, better company than the radical evangelical ruffians.[38]

To be sure, Neuhaus's book included here and there a nod toward neoconservative and even liberal readers, claiming that "the alternatives to secularistic views of American society . . . cannot be permitted to violate the imperatives of pluralism or to undo the great constitutional achievement represented by the 'free exercise' and 'no establishment' clauses of the First Amendment" (Neuhaus, *The Naked Public Square*, 52). Or specifying the book's goal as designing forms of interaction between religion and politics "which can revive rather than destroy the liberal democracy that is required by a society that would be pluralistic and free" (Neuhaus, *The Naked Public Square*, 9). And of course, guaranteeing "a thoroughly internalized Christian understanding of the continuing importance and theological status of living Judaism" (ibid., 174).

At first glance, such passages jar with the context of the book, as if they had been cautiously inserted to provide quotable backup in case there should be a need to mend public relations. But the implausibility disappears if one notices that the author had previously redefined the meaning of "pluralism," "freedom," "liberal democracy," and the "First Amendment."[39] The double-coding of these passages allows Neuhaus to maintain their logical integrity within an overall antidemocratic argument while setting a trap for reviewers thumbing through the text for accessible sound bites. In fact, if the redefinitions are overlooked, and the passages are read in a conventional way, as most reviewers certainly did, they offer a string of well-minded democratic clichés by which the book's subversive construct could be safely pulled into the mainstream discussion.

This superficial homage to the received wisdom of secular democracy, picked up by gullible reviewers, indeed helped veil the book's questionable propositions, which otherwise would have sounded the alarm.

Neuhaus was highly aware that propaganda works not by rational engagement but by Pavlovian reflex. And the word "democracy" is to the American ear a magic word in the name of which anything goes. Even erudite intellectuals like Harvey Cox, at the time professor of theology at Harvard, succumb to the reflexive reaction of approval when this bell is rung. In his review of Neuhaus's book in the *New York Times Book Review*, Cox wrote: "Democracy thrives best 'where the political order is held accountable to a transcendent truth,' he [Neuhaus] says, but to know the truth does not mean to 'have the truth,' so persuasion, not coercion, must permeate the public sphere."[40]

The danger of Christian totalitarianism inherent in Neuhaus's project did not escape Cox, who forthwith listed counterexamples to Neuhaus's model of quasi-democratic Christianity—the church's unholy involvement with oppressive regimes in South Africa, Nazi Germany, and especially in Spain under the Falangists, where church, state, and party were ideologically merged. But Cox was not alarmed by the inconsistency between what he took to be Neuhaus's thesis about democratic pluralism and its application, which, he said, was "so questionable as to mar a case that desperately needs to be heard."[41] Cox mistook a handbook of political strategy written for the church for an academic treatise on the sociology of religion and ascribed its inconsistency to the clergyman's methodological difficulties, not to a deliberate strategy of planting a subversive discourse and giving it currency amidst its most likely opponents, such as Cox himself.

Despite all his critical insights, Cox endorsed the thesis that "the political order should be accountable to a transcendent truth," when the Pavlovian bell rang "persuasion, not coercion"—never mind that this "persuasion" would be assured in Neuhaus's plan through the establishment of Christian law.

That a theocratic argument, if skillfully packaged, could have currency even with critical intellectuals is best demonstrated by the example of Michel Foucault, who praised the "political spirituality" of the Islamic revolution in *Le Nouvel Observateur* in 1978.[42] Foucault succumbed to the Iranians' ideal of an Islamic government as an expression of basic formulas for democracy and lauded the politicization of the traditional social structures of Islam as a form of resistance to the shah's secular Westernizing regime. His fascination with the idea of Islamic government "as a form of 'political will' . . . in its attempts to open a spiritual dimension in politics"[43] represents the same secular naïveté about the religious drive for power that Neuhaus exploited in his book.

Neuhaus praised Christian revivalist politics as "a democratic stirring against conventional notions about a secular society" (Neuhaus, *The Naked Public Square*, 106) and emphasized the liberating aspect of religion "as a countervailing force to the ambitions of the state" (ibid., 82). His interpretation of politicized fundamentalism as the spiritual opening of the American political system to the demands of "those who want politics to deal not only with procedural questions but also with the substantive questions of justice, the common good, and even transcendent destiny" (ibid., 133) went along the lines suggested by Foucault's defense of the Islamic state.

Ironically, in 1991 Slavoj Žižek would take up this line of criticism of "formal democracy" as a "heartless abstraction" violating "the fantasy-space" of individuals.[44] Žižek reproduced almost verbatim Neuhaus's arguments against the value-neutral model of "advanced democratic societies" (Neuhaus, *The Naked Public Square*, 133) and Rawlsian distributive justice (ibid., 257–58), which radically contrast with the liberal understanding of democratic proceduralism as a guarantee of the individual freedom of actual human beings as, for example, advanced by Judge Reinhardt in *Compassion in Dying*.[45]

With his background in the liberal left, Neuhaus knew how to handle liberal clichés. The easiest way for the church to enter public discourse and the political process was indeed through the mechanism of liberal democracy itself, which is not to be confused, he warned, with the liberal political agenda: "We can remember that our deeper stake is not in the policy specifics of liberalism or of conservatism but in the larger movement of liberal democracy that makes both possible and necessary the continuing redefinition of partisan positions and postures" (Neuhaus, *The Naked Public Square*, 9).

The liberal notions of "freedom" and "pluralism," redefined so as to support the right and freedom of "religion" to enter the public space—first, as one among many other political actors—prepared for a rather simple subversive move: once admitted to the public debate, religion was the sure winner, since religious postulates a priori constitute the absolute truth, impervious to scientific fact, practical experience, or logic.

Thus in Neuhaus's plan the admittance of religion to the "public square" guaranteed its positioning as the absolute binding authority beyond bipartisan politics, just as totalitarian ideologies, in a religious manner, claimed such authority for themselves.[46] Despite the transparency of this scheme, the American mainstream press conceded to disseminating the idea that the American polity should constitute the body of Christ.[47]

In Search of a Compromise: The Theory of Incarnate Capitalism

In the wake of the scandal caused by the *First Things* symposium in fall 1996, Heilbrunn predicted the weakening of the right through factional struggle, since the neocon and theocon visions of American statehood seemed to be irreconcilable. He expected the neocons to fall victim to their self-destructive strategy of "strengthening the devil's hand," and the theocon agenda, standing on its own, seemed disastrously nonviable. However, after a period of altercations both sides realized the advantages of a mutual compromise. The neocons needed the palliative of Christian ideology to accompany their dismantling of the public sector and the social security network, whereas the theocons needed the neocons' financial backing and political support. Despite the diplomacy that the theocons invested into mending their relations with the neoconservatives, there was no return to their initial plan of achieving Catholicism's ideological domination over the United States. It was clear that the neocons would never allow the Catholic Church to be the institution in charge of the American government and legislature, unless it was done on their own terms favoring free enterprise.

The American Christ needed a new body. It was at this point that another branch of theocon ideology, formerly held in abeyance, all of a sudden came to the rescue of Neuhaus's subversive scheme: Michael Novak's theory of incarnate capitalism.

Novak was another political adventurer of the American experiment who received his training in Catholic theology at the Gregorian University in Rome and, like Neuhaus, changed sides from left to right in the course of the 1970s. He has been scholar-in-residence at the American Enterprise Institute (AEI) since 1980, lending Christian support to the institute's agenda of deregulating the American economy and politically empowering corporations.[48] In the late 1970s and early 1980s, the AEI sought to counter the problem of the growing unpopularity of corporate capitalism in the United States by developing rhetorical strategies for drowning out the criticism of multinational corporations mounted by the Democratic think tanks and public policy institutes.

For example, consider Richard J. Barnet's 1975 report *The Crisis of the Corporation* for the American Management Associations. Barnet drew attention to the extraordinary power of the multinational corporations, resulting from their ability to internationalize and at the same time centralize production, finance, and marketing. This power, he warned, poses the real threat to the nation-state: "While national governments retain the trappings of sovereignty, notably the power to make war, they have lost some of the essential attributes of sovereignty, principally the power to protect their money supply, the power to maintain stable employment, and the power to collect revenues."[49]

Barnet observed that the multinational corporations had become institutions provoking a crisis of values. In light of the widely publicized accounts of corporate bribery and corruption of the political process, the corporation's legitimizing myths of free enterprise, efficiency, equality, and democracy were crumbling. Its unprecedented economic power was accompanied by an ever-growing difficulty to justify that power as a social institution. The response to this crisis, Barnet suggested, would be more stringent structural and legal reforms ensuring the public ethics of corporate behavior (Barnet, *Crisis of the Corporation*, 5–8).

In response, the AEI made a concentrated effort at public justification of corporate capitalism by promoting the status of the big multinational corporation as a culture-forming and value-setting institution. And it did so in a rather surprising way. Encouraged by the Christian fundamentalists' electoral support for Reagan's administration and their proclaimed commitment to free-market enterprise, the AEI went for an attempt at a religious legitimization of corporate capitalism, a step as radical as it was old-fashioned. Novak was hired to integrate biblical literalism with the laissez-faire ideology of the free-market economy. His mission was "to create a language for discussing theology and public policy, with a focus on economic systems" and "to change the paradigms in which the discussion is conducted." To specify his task, Novak wrote: "The new paradigms must take into account the dimensions of meaning, of transcendence, and of moral consideration. Such concerns are not merely private. They are social, communal, public."[50]

As Damon Linker pointed out, Novak's major strategy for creating such new economic paradigms consisted, first of all, in a Christian rearticulation of Irving Kristol's pragmatic neoconservative and explicitly antireligious defense of the free-market economy in *Two Cheers for Capitalism* (1978).[51] Kristol's book was written as a polemic against the socialist utopias of the recent student movement in an attempt to give a more balanced and objective view of the advantages and flaws of American corporate capitalism. Kristol took American capitalism as it existed in the mid-1970s to be a 200-year-old demonstration that capitalism represents a social order under which, although prosperity may be unequally shared, "over the longer term everyone does benefit, visibly and substantially."[52]

As a product of Cold War patterns of thinking, the book was not without the usual logical subterfuge: Kristol (and in his steps Novak) praised the results of the resistance to capital—governmental regulations, public oversight, labor rights, and environmental protections—as capital's very own accomplishments and, therefore, argued for dismantling all governmental agencies in charge of corporate oversight, which, in his view, represented an oppressively overreaching "state capitalism." But above all, Novak seized upon Kristol's major claim that the future of American liberal democracy depends on such undemocratic formations as big business corporations (compared by him to the Catholic Church) as a counterbalance to the authority of government.

In his writings for the AEI, Novak criticized American theologians for their failure "to relate the Word of God *incarnationally* to every fiber of modern civilization," especially economics.[53] For Novak, the system that incarnated the Word of God economically was corporate capitalism. Therefore, he suggested, the role of the corporation in the society should be modeled upon the body of Christ:

> One idea that suggests itself is the Latin phrase corpus Christi, "body of Christ." The human body has been the traditional metaphor for the Christian community—and, as the Second Vatican Council said, this Christian body includes everybody (so that, as the joke went, even Satan is a "separated brother")—but the corporation might be an even more illuminating metaphor. A corporation contains multiple models of human community; it is not an individual, but it is not just a community, either. It doesn't operate the way a sensitivity session operates. It includes unions and other subgroups just as the Christian community does. In any case, theologians have much to learn about the history, legal structure, types, functions, limits, and problems of corporations.[54]

Novak called for a theology of corporations, which would establish the big multinational enterprise as a "redemptive agency of the world," "a moral-cultural institution," a "mediating structure" for American society as a whole, a mediating structure which would be "neither individualistic nor statist, yet efficient and concrete." This theology, he suggested, should consist in a neoliberal interpretation of certain Christian doctrines.[55] For example, the Trinity stood for "pluralism-in-unity," "a political economy differentiated and yet one,"[56] where differentiation meant that "inequality of income is no more a scandal than are inequalities of looks, personality, talent, will, and luck."[57]

Or consider the doctrines of the Incarnation and original sin. These were supposed to assure public acquiescence to the corporate crime. The divine ideal of free enterprise might be incarnated in imperfect form, Novak admitted, but original sin is precisely what makes economic liberty thrive. Hence, his response to the "socialist" request for strengthening regulatory laws: "A political economy for sinners, even Christian sinners (however well intentioned), is consistent with the story of Jesus. A political economy based on love and justice is to be found beyond, never to be wholly incarnated within, human history."[58] In Novak's proposed theology, the political economy of democratic capitalism "imitates the demands of *caritas* by reaching out, creating, inventing, producing, and distributing, raising the material base of the common good" (Novak, *Spirit of Democratic Capitalism*, 357). But at the same time, his notion of *caritas* is practically indistinguishable from social Darwinism: "In the economic sphere, creation is to be fulfilled through human imitation of the Creator. Creation is no morality play. Nor is it a Panglossian perfect harmony. Many species perished in its evolutionary emergence, and within each species countless individuals have been untimely stricken" (ibid., 356).

Novak's use of Christianity, generously rewarded by the one-million-dollar Templeton Prize for Progress in Religion (1994), was modestly subservient to the neoconservative expectation that religion would reconcile the populace to the unequal distribution of wealth and rewards. Novak's incarnate capitalism was supposed to help the working class accept their economic disadvantages as a token of freedom because democratic capitalism "creates a noncoercive society as an arena of liberty, within which individuals and peoples are called to realize, through democratic methods, the vocations to which they believe they are called. Under God, they may expect to meet exact and just judgment" (Novak, *Spirit of Democratic Capitalism*, 360).

Novak did not strive to turn Catholicism into the governing institution of the United States. He even explicitly rejected "the subordination of the political system and the economic system to a single moral-cultural vision" as a feature of "a *command* society" irreconcilable with democratic pluralism (Novak, *Spirit of Democratic Capitalism*, 68; emphasis in original). Despite his modeling of the corporate social function and moral authority on the body of Christ, Novak seemed to value the personal freedoms of pluralistic liberal democracy.

In his system, power and favorable legislation could be easily bought with money and needed no other forms of coercion: "Respect for the transcendence of God and for full freedom of conscience—respect for the common human wandering in darkness, is better served, however, even in Christian and Jewish terms, by the reverential emptiness at the heart of pluralism than by a socially imposed vision of the good" (Novak, *Spirit of Democratic Capitalism*, 67–68). Precisely on this point Novak and Neuhaus disagreed in the mid-1980s. In *The Naked Public Square*, Neuhaus explicitly rejected Novak's vision of "reverential emptiness at the heart of pluralism" as "the naked public square" presaging totalitarianism (Neuhaus, *The Naked Public Square*, 121). However, his rejection in 1984 was of a competitive nature: Novak's "incarnated capitalism" was co-opting Christianity for the ideological pro-motion of a far more powerful institution which harbored a greater and more realistic potential for subverting the American state and its political system than the Catholic Church.

The prospect of transforming American liberal democracy in accordance with the one-party corporate model and the eradication of liberal dissent were also voiced at the AEI conferences organized by Novak.[59] The contribu-tors praised corporations as "the monasteries of a scientific age" (Novak, *The Corporation: A Theological Inquiry*, 17), as organizations expressing the "will to power" (ibid., 169, 176) and fitting the ideal of the medieval total-izing worldview (ibid., 177), which some of them wanted to see reclaimed in the United States. These proposals of a corporate model of government were not groundless fantasies. They were building upon the inherently antidemo-cratic, top-down structure of corporate organization, the medieval features of which were thrown into relief by the business ethicist Marjorie Kelly.

In her book *The Divine Right of Capital* (2001), Kelly has shown that the functioning and hierarchy of the modern business corporation still preserve the ancient feudal logic eliminated from other areas of democratic society. Membership in corporate society, like membership in an aristocracy, is based on property ownership, which today takes varied forms of wealth, or finan-cial assets.[60] Accordingly, in a corporation, the interests of stockholders are on the top, and the interests of the employees are on the bottom. Stockhold-ers alone have a voice in governance, though apart from providing the initial capital they may have been long detached from further involvement with the business (Kelly, *Divine Right of Capital*, 58, 35).

The profit from stockholders' initial capital, created through the work of the corporate employees (whose own income has to be kept at a minimum) thus becomes similar in its logic to the aristocracy's collecting fees and dues from the commoners who work on their land. Such profits are not earned. They are justified exclusively through the "divine" privilege of initial prop-erty rights, since no other social or economic form of rational justification can be offered. The legal fiction of corporate law supports this prejudice by conceiving of the corporation today not as a thing to be owned but as a "nexus of contract." This legal fiction, however, privileges the stockhold-er's "contract" over that of other parties on the basis of an assumption that stockholder rights are rules that "people would have negotiated," if only they could have done so. "Perhaps the corporate contract," Kelly quotes Fischel and Easterbrook in *Economic Structure of Corporate Law*, "is not more than a rhetorical device" (Kelly, *Divine Right of Capital*, 71). The language of con-tract fulfills an important function: it obfuscates the fact that corporations are created by the state, Kelly points out, and thus logically should be sub-ordinated to state regulations and accountable to the community of citizens.

To show the remnant of premodern sensibility which blocks the way of such accountability in the modern American context, Kelly refers to the research of Ernst Kantorowicz. In his book *The King's Two Bodies*, Kantorowicz showed how the concept of incorporation had been developed on the basis of the ecclesiastical concept of the body of Christ and then transferred by early modern lawyers to the king's body in order to legally justify the fictional political construct of absolute monarchy as an immortal, continuous formation. The king's body as a "corporation sole" was conceptually divided into the "body natural" and the "body politic." The former was mortal, the latter was immortal and coextensive with the kingdom's land, so that upon the king's death the body politic could be reincarnated instantly in the body of his heir. This kind of "man-made irreality," Kantorowicz wrote, "indeed, that strange construction of a human mind which finally becomes slave to its own fictions—we are normally more ready to find in the religious sphere than in the allegedly sober and realistic realms of law."[61]

The quasi-religious royal logic of the corporate body, at once human and divine, still informs the fiction of corporate personhood. In Kelly's analysis, this is what allows a big modern corporation to enjoy all the rights of a citizen while avoiding a citizen's duties and responsibilities. Like the medieval king, the corporate person is ubiquitous and enjoys perpetual life. Like him, it has two bodies: its buildings and employees (its body natural), and its body of stockholders (its body politic). The body politic practices "migration of the soul" regularly, whenever shares trade hands. And due to the doctrine of limited liability, stockholders bear no responsibility for the transgressions of the corporation.

The stockholder body politic "is not only incapable of *doing* wrong, but even of *thinking* wrong. Like fictions about the king, corporate fictions serve a single purpose: to protect current arrangements of power" (Kelly, *Divine Right of Capital*, 91; emphasis in original). The corporate system in its present form, Kelly concludes, shares the impenetrability of the pre-democratic, closed tribal societies analyzed in Karl Popper's *The Open Society and Its Enemies*: "These ancient civilizations equated the fate of society with the fate of the ruling class, just as we equate the fate of corporations with the fate of stockholders" (Kelly, *Divine Right of Capital*, 61). Such an aristocratic tribal logic, expressed in the "organic" political theories of antiquity, survives, according to Popper, in the societies based on totalitarian ideologies.[62]

Novak's legitimation of corporate sovereignty, advanced in his 1996 Pfizer Lecture "The Future of the Corporation," was in fact thoroughly in line with Kantorowicz's and Popper's findings:

> The laws governing corporations appear to go back in their origin to ancient Egyptian burial societies and, in the Christian West, to religious monasteries, towns, and universities. Such legally constituted societies possessed an independence recognized by successive political regimes. Their independence from the state had a legitimacy implicitly founded in primeval rights of association and common

respect for the sacred. Such institutions were constituted to endure
beyond the lifetimes of their founding generation.[63]

The AEI-sponsored project suggested such reorientation toward ancient
tribalism. The remodeling of the American political system upon the corporate pattern was to start with giving the corporations access to full political
participation. In 2010 the Supreme Court decision in *Citizens United v. Federal Election Commission* made a successful step toward realization of this
plan. It endorsed the notion of corporate personhood and allowed under the
pretext of the First Amendment's protection of the freedom of speech direct
corporate participation in the political process through unlimited spending.[64]

In administrative terms, however, the fusion of the corporation with
the state, envisioned by the theocons, would restore the United States to
its colonial past. The first American colonies were corporations (the Virginia Company of London, the Massachusetts Bay Company, and the like)
chartered by the British crown to manage the state and its trade. From the
end of the seventeenth century, the British king revoked their charters and
turned these commercial domains into royal colonies, which were later taken
from him and made into an independent federal republic by the American
Revolution.

Considering this historical background, one could say that the foundation of the independent United States was based not just on a separation
from the British Empire but also on their de-corporatization. Accordingly,
it is hardly a surprise that the founding fathers of the United States were on
guard against the corporate threat to political power.[65] For example, take
Thomas Jefferson's letter to Tom Logan (November 12, 1816), quoted in
Citizens United by dissenting Justice Stevens against Justice Scalia's alleged
"originalism": "I hope we shall . . . crush in [its] birth the aristocracy of our
monied corporations which dare already to challenge our government to a
trial of strength and bid defiance to the laws of our country."[66] Throughout
most of the nineteenth century, the states and the federal government chartered public corporations for limited amounts of time for purposes of public
benefit, such as building roads, canals, or bridges.

Remodeling the United States' political system upon the corporate structure would mean not just a subversion of the principles of liberal democracy
but a de facto subordination of the national interest, this time not to the
British crown but to the financial interests of a multinational group of
shareholders.[67] In this system, according to corporate logic, non-propertied
Americans would become outsiders in their own country, just as employees
are outsiders in corporate governance. The economic and political sovereignty which the modern corporation claims from the state raises it to
the status of a dangerous competitor of the state. John Kenneth Galbraith
observed already in 1972: "When the modern corporation acquires power
over markets, power in the community, power over the state, power over

belief, it is a political instrument, different in form and degree but not in kind from the state itself."[68]

After the fiasco of the *First Things* symposium in 1996, Neuhaus had no choice but to concede to Novak's project of endowing the corporation with Christian ideology. Whereas Neuhaus complained that the church was excluded from participation in politics through the laws controlling its tax-exempt status,[69] the successful advancement of corporate participation in the political process could make the corporation into a political instrument equaling the state and even superseding it as a moral authority.

By 1996 Novak, in his turn, wrote yet more boldly about the corporation's "essential role in the future of self-governing republics, and its central position in the building of the chief alternative to government: civil society."[70] His understanding of "civil society" as equivalent to the church suggests that by this time his and Neuhaus's views had indeed substantially merged:

> When St. Ambrose of Milan (340–397) forbade the soldiers of Emperor Theodosius to enter his cathedral, and they obeyed, he was marking off the boundaries of civil society, in this case, the church—across which the state dared not intrude. In an analogous way, other corporations of civil society appealed to legal precedents, traditions, and principles to defend their own independence from soldiers of the regime, tyrants, and armed bullies who coveted their goods. Often rights were lost, injustices were done, and right had to be revindicated by force of arms or after the passage of evil times. But a sense of the limits of the state gradually took hold, and with it, the preeminence of the institutions of civil society over those of the state.[71]

By the time of the presidential elections of 2000, the eclectic proto-Christian ideological construct aiming at the subversion of the American state had acquired its full and systematic form. The theocon vision of a Christian state accountable to the authority of the Catholic Church and the neocon vision of a state subservient to the sovereign corporate interest happily coincided in the project of a valorized political system based on the corporate body of Christ. In the person of the American president who famously claimed: "I trust God speaks through me. Without that, I couldn't do my job,"[72] the theoconservative discourse apart found, all of a sudden, its supreme subject of enunciation and a legal executive.

Theory into Practice: Enunciating Christ's Body

The radical endeavor of the symposium "End of Democracy?" paid off in unexpected ways: George W. Bush, who decided to run for the presidency on the pro-life platform articulated in *First Things*, contacted Neuhaus in May

1998 seeking his help in establishing connections to the religious right in the Northeast. Linker pointed out that the liberal critics "fail to appreciate the extent to which the theocons and their supporters genuinely believe that cultural and moral questions are the core of politics, rightly understood."[73] The rhetoric of protecting "the most vulnerable" (Neuhaus, *The Naked Public Square*, 118) indeed implies that Catholic antiabortion law should bind all American citizens and thus aims at a subversion of the political foundations of the United States in secular liberal democracy. Neuhaus's political aspiration, driven by this rhetoric, was as far-reaching as a revival of "Eusebius' vision of a providential convergence between church and empire under the lordship of Christ" (ibid., 172).

Already in 1984, Father Neuhaus presented his strategy in dealing with the American empire (as Karl Rove, Michael Hardt, and Antonio Negri call the American state) as a modern version of "Constantinianism" (Neuhaus, *The Naked Public Square*, 172). He called his fellow Christians to the "commitment to the moment that is ours" (ibid., 12), wagering boldly, even fanatically, that the enterprise that had failed in the Roman Empire toward the end of the fourth century A.D. would have another chance to succeed, this time through the global power of the United States at the turn of the twenty-first century.

When Neuhaus became Bush's unofficial advisor on issues of cultural and religious policy, and *First Things*—a major publication of the theoconservative movement—was read in the White House, this vision came to a near-realization. Michael Gerson, the evangelical speechwriter hired by Bush's political advisor Karl Rove, perused Neuhaus's and Novak's texts, folding their idiom into the country's official language, dressing American public discourse in heavy religious symbolism. Accordingly, from his very first weeks in office, Bush began implementing their program of the religious body politic and the promotion of corporate interests.[74]

The logic of top-down, non-transparent, for-profit corporate governance informing the religiously inspired Bush administration was backed up by the discursive and legal positionality of the president, advanced in the theory of the "unitary executive."[75] This theory had already been developed in 1996 by the legal scholar John Yoo, who argued in a 125-page article in the *California Law Review* that the U.S. Constitution did not reject but maintained the structure of the British monarchy by investing the crown's powers into the office of the president and transferring Parliament's duties to Congress. "In the 1990s, Yoo had been an eccentric figure at the periphery of legal thought. Now, his views became binding authority within the United States government."[76] Now claiming the enunciative power of the new presidential role as a lawgiver in the name of a higher truth, the president's orders could focalize such formerly marginal discourses as those of Novak, Neuhaus, and Yoo. "Bush's fusion of a religious outlook with administration policy is a striking shift in rhetoric. Other presidents petitioned for blessings and guidance. Bush positions himself as a prophet, speaking for God."[77]

The trends of fusing church with state and state with corporation were epitomized in the White House's first two major initiatives, both launched by executive order: the White House Office of Faith-Based and Community Initiatives, which awarded annual federal grants to churches and religious organizations, and the National Energy Policy Development Group, which worked in close and secretive collaboration with representatives of the oil, natural gas, and coal industries, securing their unconstrained access to national and global energy resources.[78] The invasion of Iraq in 2003, prepared for by the Group's "National Energy Policy," was celebrated by the religious right as a long-desired Christian missionary war and praised by the theocon ideologues as a "just war" against "evil."[79] As Neuhaus had theorized in *The Naked Public Square*, American military power would be justified in the humble goal of being God's tool (55–77), if driven not by a nationalistic hubris of imperial domination but by the country's redefined mission to spread the gospel.

The emblematic takeover of Iraq's Oil Ministry by U.S. troops on the first day of the occupation of Baghdad, indeed, went hand in hand with a rapid spread of Christian missions and churches throughout Iraq. In *American Theocracy* Kevin Phillips reports:

> A year after the military took Baghdad, a survey by the *Los Angeles Times* found thirty evangelical missions in the city. Kyle Fisk, executive administrator of the National Association of Evangelicals, told the newspaper that "Iraq will become the center for spreading the gospel of Jesus Christ to Iran, Libya and throughout the Middle East." John Brady, head of operations of the Southern Baptist Convention International Missions Board in the Middle East and North Africa, said in a fund-raising letter that events in Iraq represented a "war for souls." Within two years seven new evangelical Christian churches had been launched in Baghdad alone.[80]

Not coincidentally, the American state's new status as a tool for spreading the gospel to the Muslim world while privatizing Iraq's natural resources relied heavily on the corporate body of the Christian mercenary army Blackwater.[81] The notorious anti-Muslim speeches made in 2003 by the Army lieutenant general William Boykin, then the deputy undersecretary of defense for intelligence, gave public confirmation that the American military and government saw the wars in Iraq and Afghanistan as Christian crusades. Boykin's loud praise of George W. Bush's having assumed office through the performative utterance of the Supreme Court, and not through the popular vote, attested to the religious right's sense of triumph: "Why is this man in the White House? The majority of Americans did not vote for him. Why is he there? And I tell you this morning that he's in the White House because God put him there for a time such as this."[82]

The soft-spoken Neuhaus, who advised Christian fundamentalists in 1984 that successful subversion happens not through a fanatic confrontation but "over a long period of time by subtle transformations that largely escap[e] the notice of those who lived through them" (Neuhaus, *The Naked Public Square*, 12), was more savvy than the boisterous Boykin about the political workings of the divine: he described the Supreme Court's decision in *Bush v. Gore* (2000) succinctly as "the right one."[83]

The executive Christianization of the American state emboldened religious groups and organizations, which had already been quietly pursuing the fusion of church and state. Their activities immediately embroiled hundreds of local communities in religious conflicts. The Enfield Schools case in Connecticut, one of many across the country, offers a microcosmic example of what religious attempts to reclaim "the naked public square" looked like in practice.[84]

In May 2010 two senior students and their parents from the small town of Enfield filed a complaint with the District Court of Connecticut about the decision of the Enfield Board of Education to hold their public high-school graduations at First Baptist Cathedral of Hartford, a Christian fundamentalist mega-church with an explicitly missionary agenda "to win souls, make disciples and create an environment where everyone will experience God's love." Graduating Enfield seniors were expected to receive their diplomas in the cathedral's sanctuary underneath a large Christian cross and banners proclaiming "Jesus Christ is Lord" and "I am GOD."

The plaintiffs—one Jewish and one agnostic student, with their families—felt that the municipal Board of Education was attempting to coerce them, through this graduation arrangement, to enter a place of Christian worship and expose themselves to heavy Christian symbolism as the price of attending the event. Moreover, they maintained that the choice of a religious location over many other secular options available to the Enfield Public Schools strongly conveyed governmental favoritism toward Christianity. The Board of Education's choice also entailed the use of public funds to support religiously themed graduations and entangled the public schools with a religious institution.

The conflict about the Enfield graduations did not have to lead to litigation. United States and Connecticut constitutional law on the matter was unambiguous: the practice of holding public school graduations in a religious environment violated the Establishment Clause of the First Amendment to the U.S. Constitution as well as Article Seven of the Connecticut Constitution, which provides that "no person shall by law be compelled to . . . support, nor be . . . associated with, any congregation, church or religious association." However, as the ensuing legal investigation would show, the violation of this law turned out to be not a matter of legal ignorance but the very purpose of the board. After several vote reversals, the board had decided to defy the objections of non-Christian students and defend its choice of a religious location in court.

Discovery proceedings conducted by the ACLU, Americans United for Separation of Church and State (AU), and the ACLU Program on Freedom of Religion and Belief, acting as counsels for the plaintiffs, brought to light that the practice of celebrating public school graduations at First Cathedral coincided with the arrival of a "faith-based" administration in the White House. The practice began in 2001 and had already spread to five Hartford-area school districts by the time two public high schools under the board's control, Enrico Fermi and Enfield High, joined the trend in 2007 and 2008 respectively.[85]

The board made the decision to move the festivities to First Cathedral in 2006, while the athletic fields where the graduations habitually took place were under construction. In defiance of repeated warnings from the ACLU and AU, the board continued the practice after the construction work had been finished. In 2010 the board also ignored a survey showing that Enfield High seniors favored returning graduations to the school grounds, where they could scream, laugh, and throw beach balls, silly string, and mortar-boards up in the air. In the solemn and dignified venue of the cathedral, they were reminded by a minister to abstain from this kind of behavior.

The board's choice of First Cathedral as a celebration site, as well as the board's decision to engage in a lawsuit over the issue, were prompted by the aggressive lobbying of the Family Institute of Connecticut (FIC), a socially conservative pro-life and antigay religious organization, which according to its website advocates for "traditional Judeo-Christian family values"; seeks to see "Judeo-Christian principles . . . re-employed in our society and its public policy"; and struggles for "[a] society committed to helping family, church, synagogue and community meet the needs of its members without undue dependence upon government."

The FIC, which identifies itself as "the one group leading the fight for the religious liberty of ALL Connecticut's churches," is one of those mediating structures between church and state theorized by Neuhaus and Novak in the 1980s. Established in 1989 as an ideological and political counterforce to the advancement of women's and LGBT rights, it had become especially aggressive under the Bush administration. In 2004 it created a Political Action Committee in order to lobby state officials and legislators directly about its religious platform.

The FIC brought in contact several radical religious actors (First Cathedral's Archbishop LeRoy Bailey, the Board of Education chairman Greg Stokes, and the American Center for Law and Justice [ACLJ]) and coordinated their ardent pursuit of the Christianization of the state. Bailey, a vocal opponent of same-sex marriage in Connecticut, served on the FIC Clergy Advisory Council. He had brought his message to the Northeast from Tennessee. Under his guidance the cathedral he helped design had served as an ideological center of what some observers have described as "the southernization of America."[86] The chairman of the Board of Education, Greg

Stokes, was a pastor of Cornerstone Bible Church, an evangelical church in East Windsor, Connecticut. He wrote on his blog that his "first love and responsibility is the fast growing congregation of Cornerstone Church" and his "second responsibility is to the Enfield Board of Education." Indeed, he used his elected public office to prioritize the interests of the church.[87]

The ACLJ, founded in 1990 by the evangelical pastor Pat Robertson in imitation of the ACLU, has, according to its website, "'led the way' in Christian legal advocacy." The ACLJ pursues the goal of legalizing the fusion of church and state by reinterpreting the Establishment Clause of the First Amendment to the U.S. Constitution in Neuhaus's terms as guaranteeing the liberty of the church to proselytize in and through public institutions. The Family Institute of Connecticut assured Chairman Stokes that ACLJ lawyers would represent the Enfield Schools pro bono if the board voted to continue holding graduations in First Cathedral in defiance of the non-Christians' complaints. To the ACLJ, the Enfield litigation offered another chance at subverting well-established constitutional law through a precedent in a federal court. With luck, they hoped, a practice previously considered unconstitutional might be legalized.

The FIC's executive director, Peter Wolfgang, urged the organization's members to lobby the Enfield Board of Education as concerned citizens. His e-mail alerts sounded a menacing note: "In Enfield, A Call to Arms!"—"This is our only opportunity to ensure that religious liberty is not trampled by default!" Failure to assure the graduations in the cathedral, he wrote, "will increase the power of aggressive secularism and cause further harm to the proper role of faith communities in our state," meaning the communities of fundamentalist faith. Wolfgang announced that "the secular left wants to punish Christian churches for their prophetic voice" and that "the battle over graduations"—a battle designed and chosen by the FIC—"is simply the newest front in a war to silence and marginalize churches."[88] Wolfgang did as Neuhaus taught: "Only the church militant can be the servant church" (Neuhaus, *The Naked Public Square*, 225). After the board rescinded under pressure its initial decision to return the graduations to the schools' athletic fields, the FIC publicly proclaimed the triumph of its efforts and thanked "Chairman Greg Stokes, whose steady support made victory possible."[89]

For all its political importance, this fight against secularism was also not without profit. Bailey, Stokes, and the FIC looked not only to establish "a symbolic link between the church and state," as the District Court of Connecticut would note, but also to perform the very pragmatic appropriation of the state's money for religious political action, undermining the state's constitutional foundations and ideological independence. In 2010 the cathedral charged a rent of $8,200 per school for each two-hour graduation. In 2009 it added to Enfield High's bill $1,000 for the use of the handicap ramp and $1,600 for the receptions. The money, paid to the cathedral, came from the local real estate and motor vehicle taxes paid by Enfield residents, including the plaintiffs. In response to a media inquiry whether First Cathedral, as a nonprofit corporation, paid taxes on the rental fees it received (as it must on any income that is unrelated to its mission), a cathedral official stated that the cathedral did not pay tax because the rental of the sanctuary—like everything else First Cathedral did—related to the cathedral's mission.[90] Nevertheless, the board's defense strategy in the lawsuit was to deny this mission as well as the religious motivation behind the board's choice of the graduation venue.

The board argued that the religious symbolism of First Cathedral would be neutralized by removing the banners with religious quotations and by covering the religious art. However, besides the fact that no such modifications had ever been undertaken, the church building itself was shaped like a dove, crowned with a gigantic cross, decorated with stained glass windows displaying religious scenes, and adorned with five big crosses on its façade. Nevertheless, in his deposition Archbishop Bailey denied the religious symbolism of his church, which he characterized evasively not as Christian but as "eclectic."

The court thus had to call on expert testimony about the cathedral's Christian representation. As an expert witness, the Reverend Dr. Frank Kirkpatrick differed from Bailey in his understanding of First Cathedral's religious imagery:

> Reverend Kirkpatrick believes the fountain in the lobby represented a baptismal font, but Bailey does not; Kirkpatrick believes Jesus Christ is represented by the dove, but Bailey does not; Kirkpatrick believes the fish depicted in the carpet represents one of the most important symbols in the Christian tradition, but Bailey does not; Kirkpatrick believes the image of the chalice embodies the blood of Jesus which Christians believe he shed for humankind at his crucifixion, but Bailey believes it represents "community."[91]

The denial of the sacred meaning of the Christian representation and places of worship became a common strategy among clergy pursuing the cause of the fusion of church and state. To be sure, not all evangelicals shared this attitude. Mark Galli, the senior managing editor of the evangelical magazine *Christianity Today*, took exception to the quiet proselytizing in the Enfield affair as follows: "But does it strike anyone else as odd how reticent many churches are to make it plain to visitors that when they enter the church, they are entering a sovereign state where someone besides the State is Lord?"[92]

However, the openly competitive, separatist evangelical stance toward the state asserted by Galli was precisely the one that Neuhaus criticized as politically inadvisable. In order not to frighten many sensible people, he urged, fundamentalists should dim down in public their talk about the Christian will and not "equate our programs with the purposes of God." "Fanaticism is contagious" and would result in the fanaticism of the opponents (Neuhaus,

The Naked Public Square, 8). An insidious use of the democratic political and legal process is more effective for the goals of politicized Christianity than an open, militant confrontation. For "what passes as a full-blooded and aggressive assertion of the truth is a denial of the greater truth" (Neuhaus, *The Naked Public Square*, 123).

The counsels for the plaintiffs specifically addressed this strategy of secular camouflage in the pursuit of religious goals: "Even when no formal religious worship service is underway, a church (and especially its sanctuary) remains an inherently religious setting—the physical embodiment of the faith community it shelters. To many faiths, a house of worship and all its constituent parts are objects of veneration."[93] Rich support for this self-evident claim was assembled from many contemporary religious websites, Catholic, Greek Orthodox, Anglican, Hindu, and Jewish, all of which alerted their believers to the worship character of religious art and architecture.[94] But there is also legal consensus as to the significance of religious symbolism. The Supreme Court of the United States has recognized that

> symbolism is a primitive but effective way of communicating ideas. The use of an emblem or flag to symbolize some system, idea, institution, or personality, is a short cut from mind to mind. Causes and nations, political parties, lodges and ecclesiastical groups seek to knit the loyalty of their followings to a flag or banner, a color or design. . . . The church speaks through the Cross, the Crucifix, the altar and shrine, and clerical raiment.[95]

Just as religious symbolism projected into public space unavoidably turns this space into a place of religious worship, the mere entering of the place of religious worship draws a visitor into participation in a religious act. Under American constitutional law, both experiences, if imposed on nonbelievers or representatives of different religious persuasions, interfere with the individual's religious freedom, and even the briefest suspension of constitutional rights is regarded as an irreparable injury to the individual. On these grounds, the District Court of Connecticut granted the plaintiffs' request for injunctive relief. The Schools were ultimately prohibited from holding graduations at the church by a settlement agreement reached in July 2012.

Notwithstanding this decision, from 2001 to 2010, the state of Connecticut had been repeatedly induced to pay for the subversion of its constitution through the vehicle of public school graduations. By 2010 this "sacred enterprise" had advanced so far that Jewish and agnostic citizens protecting their constitutional rights against the Christian pressure of exclusion or conversion in the relatively progressive state of Connecticut had to bring their action under pseudonyms "to protect themselves from social ostracism, economic injury, governmental retaliation, and even physical harm," dangers that are "routinely faced by plaintiffs who bring Establishment Clause challenges to religious activities in public schools."[96] Such subversive attempts to bind citizens into the body of Christ demonstrated the political reality behind the 1984 claims that the "'new Christian right,' even though it demands conformity to its beliefs, may help restore real democracy to a public arena shorn of moral values."[97]

Christianizing Public Space—Marketing Christ's Body

On the national scale, the theoconservative consolidation of the American citizenry into the militant body of Christ was advanced by means of Mel Gibson's programmatic film *The Passion of the Christ*, strategically released during the Bush reelection campaign of 2004. The film dwelt for two hours on the "painful, protracted, and agonizing death"[98] of Jesus, excruciatingly tortured from the moment of his arrest in Gethsemane to his death on the cross. Jesus's teaching, limited to several truncated flashbacks, only briefly interrupted the brutalization of his body. Michael Novak, who saw the film on July 21, 2003, when Gibson brought a rough cut of the film to Washington "for a few commentators and interested writers to see," wrote an ecstatic review in the *Weekly Standard*, calling it "the most powerful movie I have ever seen," "a meditation and a prayer."[99]

Neuhaus, who watched the film at one of the advanced promotional screenings several weeks before its official release on Ash Wednesday 2004, praised it in his *First Things* column: "It is a gross understatement to say that it is an extraordinary film. It is certainly the best cinematic treatment of the passion or, indeed, of any biblical subject that I have ever seen."[100] Russell Hittinger and Elizabeth Lev characterized the film in their review for *First Things* as "the best movie ever made about Jesus Christ," the film that is "bound to change our estimation of how a film can portray the life of Christ."[101]

The Christian right's fascination with this rendition of the life of Christ, according to Hittinger and Lev, stemmed from their sense that "from the agony in the garden, where Gibson begins, to the pietà at the foot of the cross, Jesus does what he teaches."[102] Nonetheless, a group of four Catholic and three Jewish scholars reviewing the script on behalf of the U.S. Conference of Catholic Bishops and the Anti-Defamation League issued a judgment to the contrary.

The group found that the "cross is so much the focus that the significance of Jesus' life is obscured" and "viewers learn virtually nothing about the ministry of Jesus, of his preaching and teaching about God's reign, his distinctive table companionship, his mediation of God's gracious mercy." Instead, they are "presented only with a body to be tormented. . . . Without some understanding of the meaning of Jesus' entire life," the scholars wrote, "the [film's] inventive cruelty produces a theology of pain: the more Jesus is tortured the greater is his love and, by implication, the more the Father's desires are being obeyed."[103] In light of this evaluation, it appears that the theocons welcomed Gibson's Jesus so fervently because he did what they taught.[104]

When in his *First Things* column Neuhaus promoted the film and urged everyone to see it, adding: "(No, of course I don't get a cut)," he was not entirely truthful. Even though the film was allegedly a visual transcription of the Gospels, it would be more accurate to say that the document for which it provided the dramatized counterpart was rather Neuhaus's and Colson's 1994 manifesto "Evangelicals and Catholics Together: The Christian Mission in the Third Millennium."[105] Following the vision laid out in Neuhaus's 1984 book, this political manifesto of theoconservatism, cosigned by many leading representatives of both faiths, announced their stern commitment to the global mission of spreading Christianity, including the Christianization of the American state.

The signers of the document declared, in Pauline idiom, war on "all that opposes Christ and his cause" ("Evangelicals and Catholics Together," 18) and called on Christians to reconcile their differences in doctrine, worship, practice, and piety on the basis of their shared missionary goals justified by their faith in Christ: "As Evangelicals and Catholics, we dare not by needless and loveless conflict between ourselves give aid and comfort to the enemies of the cause of Christ" (ibid., 16). Gibson's reduction of Jesus's teaching to Christ's passion successfully offered the theocons a long-desired common denominator for the Catholic and evangelical faiths.[106] The bloody imagination of Catholic coinage, stemming from the practice of meditation on the wounds of Christ, and the message "Christ died for our sins" resonated well with the evangelical emphasis on the atonement.[107]

Conceived and self-produced on the margins of Hollywood, Gibson's glorification of a theology of pain turned into an outright theoconservative political campaign in the hands of a Dallas-based Christian public relations and marketing firm, A. Larry Ross Communications, that the director engaged along with many other Christian firms to handle the film's distribution.[108] Ross, president of the company, started his career as a public relations agent for General Motors but with Reagan's election switched to Christian marketing, with the evangelist Billy Graham a client of his since 1981.

According to its website, Ross's firm was "founded in 1994 to 'restore faith in media,' provide 'value-added P.R. that defines values' and give Christian messages relevance and meaning in mainstream media."[109] Ross's task was to manage the crisis of communication with the film's critics by changing the terms of public debate while doing nothing to alter the film's many historical and scriptural blunders and offensive aggression. "We were working to reframe the picture about the issues and show that it was a film meant to inspire, not to offend," Ross wrote.[110]

Under his supervision, the faith-based marketing campaign for the film adopted the strategies of the faith-based electoral campaigns of George W.

Bush. With Ross's support, Gibson targeted conservative religious groups long in advance of the film's release, offering them previews of rough cuts and telling his personal story of sin and conversion: "I fell to my knees, and God saved me. The wounds of Jesus healed my wounds."[111] In a display of contrition, Gibson narrated how he filmed his own hand driving the first nail into Christ's palm. He claimed divine inspiration behind his endeavors.

Ross's promotion of Gibson, whose financial success he attributed to Gibson's personal "authenticity" equal only to that of Billy Graham,[112] uncannily echoed Lieutenant General Boykin's celebration of George W. Bush: "It is as if God has blessed him and his career for such a time as this, to tell a story that had affected him so deeply he felt he had to share it with the world."[113] The action hero's halting confessions, accompanied by self-conscious body language, indeed helped create an air of sincerity for evangelical audiences and swiftly turned into profit. One instance of faith-based marketing, reported by the Associated Press, can stand for many:

> Senior Minister Derek Duncan didn't blanch at the $23,000 cost [of the screening], which the church picked up: He saw a unique opportunity to spread the message of Jesus. "I believe our society is so visual, so if you can see it—present it in that way—it might move you in a deeper way," Duncan said.
>
> Other evangelicals have had the same idea, encouraged by the proliferation of testimonials, Web sites and books plugging the movie. Some pastors and Christian radio stations contracted with theaters for private screenings—many aimed specifically at conversion—well before the release date.
>
> They're getting sneak peeks while interest builds in the $25-million film, which Gibson co-wrote, directed and financed. His Icon Productions and distributor Newmarket Films said this week they've added 800 additional theaters to the original 2,000 to meet demand for advance tickets.
>
> Merchandising deals are helping to stoke the fervor.
>
> Bob Siemon Designs, producer of millions of WWJD (What Would Jesus Do?) bracelets, is selling "Passion" lapel pins, key rings and inch-long nail pendants. Already, it has distributed 1 million "Passion" witness cards, inscribed with scriptural verses, said Dwight Robinson, a spokesman for the Santa Ana, California-based company.[114]

Such exploits made the film into an unprecedented national blockbuster by the time of its release.[115] Cast as a doppelgänger of the president, Gibson was expected to boost the national leader's prestige and affirm the truth and popularity of the White House's chosen ideology. In an open letter to Gibson published in the *National Review*, Ross urged the director to make further movies on biblical themes. He hoped that Gibson had "created a wave that others in Hollywood will follow—based on either a spiritual or a financial incentive."[116]

In April 2004 Ross posted an exclusive submission to Beliefnet.com, entitled "A Modern Public Relations Practitioner Looks at the Apostle Paul—The World's Greatest Communicator: Beyond Information and Education to Transformation." In the piece he concluded that the famous founder of the Christian Church should be the model for modern public relations. Ross listed twenty PR principles which he analogized to the features of Pauline discourse. For example, "strengthen the brand" referred to Paul's refashioning of his public image from persecutor to supporter of the church, and "practice reputation management" referred to Paul's claim of divine inspiration behind his mission.[117] The article made clear that Ross understood his advocacy on behalf of *The Passion of the Christ* as an integral part of transforming American civil society into a church.

The Christian PR firms construed their task unambiguously: the believers gave their money for tickets, and they would give votes.[118] However, whereas Ross quoted Bruce Davey, Gibson's partner at Icon Productions, who celebrated the film's high-grossing opening as the triumph of the will of the people over the "pundits" ("The people have spoken; they wanted it"),[119] Gibson himself bragged that such attention to his film required "an extraordinary sleight of hand."[120] He meant the strategy of "controlled marketing," which ruled out interviews for the collaborating distribution firms, including any discussion of technical elements of the film's production, ahead of the film's release.

The film's major selling point consisted indeed in Gibson's enunciation of the divine truth of his vision of the passion.[121] This provocative claim, putting his subjective treatment above the historical fact and the witness of the New Testament, capitalized on the advanced technology of visual illusionism. Digital enhancement of moving images became Hollywood's major gimmick around 2000, giving a new boost to the "cinema of attractions" by mesmerizing viewers with more intensive and naturalistic visual performances and simulations of traumatic events. As *American Cinematographer* reported in March 2004, Gibson used 135 digital effects to intensify the representation of violence,[122] hoping, as he claimed, "to profoundly change people" by pushing "viewers over the edge."[123]

The gory late-medieval passion iconography in the spirit of Matthias Grünewald looked even more eerie when digitally animated and cast in three-dimensional parameters. This forced return to archaic sensibility by means of the newest technology echoed the ideological imagination of Novak's collaborators at the AEI about the revival of the medieval monastery and archaic governmental forms via the Christianized body of the modern multinational corporation.

Gibson's great predecessor in the art of politically potent visual illusionism, the Soviet propaganda filmmaker Sergei Eisenstein, speculated in the late 1940s about the then-utopian possibilities of *stereokino* (stereoscopic cinema), which would be experienced as real three-dimensionality. In his 1947 essay "About Stereoscopic Cinema," he imagined how the palpably three-dimensional moving image, enhanced by stereo sound, "'pours' out of the screen into the auditorium" and "suddenly 'swallows' us into a formerly invisible distance beyond the screen, or 'pierces' into us, with a drive never before so powerfully experienced."[124]

Eisenstein celebrated the ability of this technological innovation to provide the spectators with a "compelling illusion of their vitality," thus aptly satisfying some of mankind's "deep needs" and "latent urges" to experience the mimetic as real, to fuse with the spectacle (Eisenstein, "About Stereoscopic Cinema," 37, 41). Eisenstein expected the new and vital medium of the stereoscopic cinema to be able to amalgamate the diegetic space of the film and the non-diegetic space of the screening room so as to unite image and spectator in a psychologically simulated unity. In his vision, this technological capacity would take to a new level the longing for a ritual union of actors and audiences and exemplified a revived archaic drive to reconcile the spectacle and spectators into an organic whole (Eisenstein, "About Stereoscopic Cinema," 42).

The art historian Oliver Grau, who places Eisenstein's essay among the conceptual and historical predecessors of contemporary virtual art, emphasizes the political nature of Eisenstein's aesthetic and technological speculations and points to his will to engage this powerful medium of the future as a means of exercising control over the audience's emotions and perceptions for the sake of advancing socialist ideology.[125]

Gibson's three-dimensional simulation of the passion was designed to advance a political goal of consolidating the cross-denominational populist religious forces into "an organic whole." It was forcefully extending the body of Christ via the medium of mass entertainment into the secular spaces of the IMAX cinemas of American malls. Many of these were block-booked by the churches throughout the opening weekend, becoming locales of religious pilgrimage and sacred worship, with praying and preaching sessions before and after the film showings.[126] Thus Gibson's film helped realize the symbolic construction of the Christianized public space that Neuhaus theorized twenty years earlier:

> The theological and sociological views are not mutually exclusive. God's revelation in Christ is, in sociological language, the "system of symbols" by which Christians construct a world that is "uniquely realistic." As Christians, we want immediately to add that it is uniquely realistic because it is uniquely real, that is to say, uniquely true. But that assertion is beyond the competence of social science either to affirm or deny.[127]

This unaccountability of the religious model of symbolic construction and performative enunciation of truth, which is rooted in belief alone, was characteristic of both Gibson's faith-based marketing campaign and the worldview of the Bush administration. In a famous interview, an administration official (later identified as Karl Rove) claimed the power of an ideology to define reality itself:

> Judicious study of discernible reality. That's not the way the world really works anymore. We're an empire now, and when we act, we create our own reality. And while you're studying that reality— judiciously, as you will—we'll act again, creating other new realities, which you can study too, and that's how things will sort out. We're history's actors . . . and you, all of you, will be left to just study what we do.[128]

Gibson's postulation of reality on the basis of his enunciated belief proved, in fact, powerful enough to triumph even over the authority of the Catholic Church. Pope John Paul II was reported to endorse the film, saying about Gibson's representation of Christ's passion: "It is as it was,"[129] despite the film's distortion of the scriptures and historical fact. And the U.S. Conference of Catholic Bishops put the film on their 2004 list of films recommended for families, despite the fact that the report commissioned by the conference's own Office for Ecumenical and Interreligious Affairs found that the film violates many magisterial Catholic documents on Jewish-Christian relations, including several Vatican instructions for the representation of the passion, published on the organization's own website.[130]

The truth of theoconservative political reality which Gibson's film helped to create was combative. The Ad Hoc Scholars warned that "the film takes every opportunity to embellish the violence of the Passion, thereby increasing the likelihood of an audience to be filled with outrage at those who perpetrated such a horrendous crime" against Jesus.[131] Although Gibson's film immediately sparked fears of the potential inflammatory anti-Semitism historically associated with the passion plays, the film allowed for a much broader and inclusive category of enemy.

The reduction of Jesus's role to suffering, deprived of a religious or historical context, resulted in his character being, in the words of a critic, "strangely remote, almost a cypher."[132] It invited the viewer's identification with suffering as such while pointing indexically to an equally open positionality of persecutors to be targeted depending on the context. The uses of the suffering Christ were indeed many.

For Novak in 1981, for example, the description "a man of sorrows, and acquainted with grief" applied to the sufferings of the big modern business corporation, "a much despised incarnation of God's presence in this world," at the hands of governmental agencies.[133] For Neuhaus in 1984, the persecuted were the politicized evangelicals who could no longer bear their exclusion (guaranteed by the American Constitution) from worldly power over their fellow citizens. By 2004, a whole army of religiously justified "makers of history" could not wait to shake off the constraints imposed on them by the secular state and return with great glory and unlimited power.

The incendiary character of the film was not lost on its critics, many of whom characterized it as "a war movie"[134] with a strong message of "revenge,"[135] creating "a quick and easy moral contrast of 'us' and 'them.' "[136] Reportedly, at one of the screenings Gibson was asked about this evident divide: "Who opposes Jesus?" His answer was cautiously evasive: "They are either satanic or the dupes of Satan."[137] But the theoconservative manifesto had designated the "spiritual hosts of wickedness" much more concretely. It was "Islam, which in many instances denies the freedom to witness to the Gospel" and therefore "must be of increasing concern to those who care about religious freedom and the Christian mission," along with "a widespread secularization" which "increasingly descends into a moral, intellectual, and spiritual nihilism that denies not only the One who is the Truth but the very idea of truth itself" ("Evangelicals and Catholics Together," 16).

The terrorist attacks on the World Trade Center offered a concrete opportunity for cultivating the religious image of both enemies. Gibson's cinematic dramatization of the Christian sacrifice was well calculated to coincide with the faith-based administration's speedy preparation and launching of wars in Afghanistan and Iraq sold to the public as wars of retribution. Even though Gibson himself, allegedly, did not support the war in Iraq, the Christian PR firms he engaged and the right-wing religious audiences to which he pitched the film did so fervently and expressly.

The aggressive sensibility of the time was best epitomized in the words of Paul Bremer, a Catholic convert who would become proconsul of the U.S. occupation of Iraq. Two days after the September 11 attacks, Bremer wrote in the *Wall Street Journal*:

> Our retribution must move beyond the limp-wristed attacks of the past decade, action that seemed designed to "signal" our seriousness to the terrorists without inflicting real damage. Naturally, their feebleness demonstrated the opposite. This time the terrorists and their supporters must be crushed. This will mean war with one or more countries. And it will be a long war, not of the "Made for TV" variety. As in all wars, there will be civilian casualties. We will win some battles and lose some. More Americans will die. In the end America can and will prevail, as we always do.[138]

Bremer's statement made it clear that the theocons fully shared Jean Baudrillard's contempt for the Gulf War of George H. W. Bush as "the dead war," "the unfrozen cold war," "the corpse of war."[139] "The limp-wristed attacks of the past decade" had met a pop-cultural parody in the Coen Brothers' *The Big Lebowski*, where George H. W. Bush's halting declaration of war on Iraq

("This aggression will not stand") was appropriated by the lethargic pacifist Lebowski, The Dude.

Counterpointed to the elder Bush's "line in the sand" was the ultimatum screamed by the alleged queer pedophile and bowling-alley bully Jesús Quintana: "Nobody fucks with the Jesus!"[140] In their 1998 production, the Coen Brothers discerned the magic of empowerment through the divine name in the utterance of a declaration of war. Ironically, they pinned down Neuhaus's maxim that "when it is the Lord's battle you are fighting, politics takes on an aura of deadly earnestness" (Neuhaus, *The Naked Public Square*, 8). Gibson's film reflected this "deadly earnestness" of the theocons' call for a crushing retribution.[141] When, after the terrorist attacks, George W. Bush addressed the nation from Washington's National Cathedral, proclaiming in thick Christian idiom that America's duty was not just to "answer these attacks," but also to "rid the world of evil," the role of the nation was officially identified with that of the Redeemer[142]—entirely in accord with theoconservative aspirations for a meaningful religious war.[143]

Since in the worldview adopted by the White House, the United States of America is and should be the body of Christ, the president's characterization of "the war against terrorism" as a "crusade," soon the focus of controversy, was neither an unfortunate metaphor nor an impolitic historical analogy, nor even a "dog whistle" directed to a select public.[144] Metaphors and analogies can be disputed on the grounds of accuracy. The call to a crusade was rather an illocutionary act, a performative statement conveying the administration's determination that the injury of September 11 had been inflicted not on the American state or its citizens but on the embodiment of the divine itself, and accordingly was to be answered not with police action or diplomacy but with a holy war.

The concept of the body of Christ underlying George W. Bush's language provided the ideological framework for resurrecting "the corpse of war" and postulating a metaphysical notion of the enemy as intrinsic evil, the combat with which would justify the most horrendous forms of cruelty.[145] The contemplation of the wounds of Christ and identification with his martyrdom had been a traditional topos of the medieval Crusade songs, composed with the explicit purpose of mobilizing the Christian armies in their fight with Islam. For example, the twelfth-century song "Crucifigat omnes / Domini crux altera / nova Christi vulnera!" ("May a second cross of the Lord, the new wounds of Christ, crucify them all!") denounced the conquest of Jerusalem by the Muslims as an injury to the sacred Christian sites—and thus to the body of Christ—and called for the infidels' total annihilation.[146]

In an article entitled "Mel Gibson's reply to 9/11," the actor Michael Moriarty offered a twenty-first-century expression of this sensibility:

> Osama bin Laden's assault on the Twin Towers was also a declaration
> of spiritual war. With his hijacked planes, he was basically saying that

we English-speaking peoples don't believe in anything except money
and our own greed for power. In other words, we wouldn't know
true religious fervor any more than we would know how to speak
Arabic. The Islamists hadn't counted on the courage and selflessness
of Gibson's faith. Nor do they know the depth to which a worldwide
spiritual armada will gather to confront bin Laden and his minions
and defend our 2,000-year-old message. . . . Do I object to that act
of killing by the God of love and forgiveness? The Catholic Church
declared unequivocally that there is such a thing as a "just war." . . .
To that extent, perhaps Gibson is a contemporary prophet. Seemingly
unafraid of anything, the director took the implications of human
history and added an Old Testament warning: Yahweh is not known
to be all-forgiving.[147]

This religiously animated stance happily compensated for the criticism of
modern warfare once offered on the left. "There is a profound scorn in the
kind of 'clean' war which renders the other powerless without destroying its
flesh, which makes it a point of honor to disarm and neutralize but not to
kill," Baudrillard wrote in 1995. "In a sense, it is worse than the other kind
of war because it spared life. It is like humiliation: by taking less than life it
is worse than taking life."

As if in response to Baudrillard's observation that the virtual reality of TV
culture has overtaken actuality and blocks "any passage to action,"[148] "Saint
Mel"[149] Gibson offered a full-blooded religiously postulated virtual reality
that was more real than real. Lacking any political or economic uncertainty,
moral relativism, or humor, it expressed precisely that "passage to action," to
religiously justified real bloodshed in the Middle East that Baudrillard had
found so wanting a decade earlier.

Gibson's *The Passion of the Christ* sprang from the same phenomenon of
religious infiltration into the country's mainstream politics and public life as
the American abuse of Iraqi prisoners in Abu Ghraib.[150] The torture photographs published in April 2004, about a month after the release of Gibson's
film, revealed to the world what the notion of a Christian "just war" looked
like in the minds of the average American soldiers and contractors engaged
in Iraq. The passion iconography which they projected onto their Muslim
victims uncannily merged with that of the Ku Klux Klan.[151] The torturers,
having loyally responded to their government's call for the war of retribution,
naively cast its spectacle in terms that had been familiar to them before only
from the domestic retributive culture of capital punishment, the hallmark
of American exceptionalism among twenty-first-century Western nations.[152]

The legal scholar David Garland has shown a strong continuity between
the American phenomenon of the death penalty and the Southern tradition
of lynching in that both phenomena exemplify local communities' religiously
motivated defiance of the federal government (Garland, *Peculiar Institution,*

35). Lynching shared the Christian sensibility of the gory dramatizations and moralistic symbolizations of medieval public executions, often staged as processions imitating the passion of Christ. When in 1972 the Supreme Court in the Furman decision temporarily suspended the death penalty, the *Los Angeles Times* quoted a fundamentalist preacher, Dr. Carl McIntire, as saying: "The Supreme Court is taking the country further away from the moral law and the teachings of God." At the same time, letters from readers complained: "Without the death penalty we are changing our society from Christian to atheist," or "The death penalty may no longer be man's law but it still is God's law."[153]

In the contemporary United States, the continuity of lynching in the death penalty is perceptible, according to Garland, not just in notorious and well-documented racial profiling of convicts but above all in the popular imagination itself. To make up for the official procedure of execution, the performance of which today is sterile, bureaucratic, and closed to the public, the populace in death-penalty states often gathers in prison parking lots on execution day to vent their desire for more tangible retribution and stage the brutal spectacle of lynching in effigy (Garland, *Peculiar Institution*, 58). "From the mass media's point of view," Garland writes, the American secular state's official prohibition on videotaping and photographing executions makes the carrying out of the sentence into "a lost opportunity, a story deliberately spoiled" (Garland, *Peculiar Institution*, 53–54, 297). The amateur photographs from Abu Ghraib compensated for this lost opportunity, offering a spectacle of revenge. So did Gibson's film.

Capitalizing on the religious right's fixation on the retributive symbolism of death (Garland, *Peculiar Institution*, 179–80), Gibson's simulation of the wounds of Christ catered to the populist desire for the justified spectacle of violence while suggesting what a commensurate Christian retribution would look like. The film's "R" rating, warning of the film's extreme violence, as it happened, did not dissuade Christian audiences but only drew the masses to the spectacle.[154] One Christian leader claimed that "R" in this case stood for "redemption."[155]

Instructively, the Canadian-British coproduction *The Gospel of John*, directed by Philip Saville and released on September 26, 2003, five months before Gibson's film, went unnoticed by the American public precisely because of its exact adherence to the text of the Gospel, its reliance on an advisory board of biblical scholars, and its historically accurate interpretation of Jesus's conflict with the Jewish religious establishment. Saville's nonviolent film, centered on Jesus's teaching, incurred the contempt of the Christian right. The film treated religion as a cultural tradition, not a "fantasy-space"[156] asserted by the subjective upsurge of ideological urgency.

The American state's adoption of the notion of religious warfare promoted populist fantasies of retributive cruelty from the status of local aberrations in the context of the secular government to that of mainstream official policy. At

Senate hearings in May 2004 investigating the abuse of Iraqi prisoners that had been made public through the Abu Ghraib photographs, Senator James Inhofe of Oklahoma, a member of the Senate Armed Services Committee, stated:

> As I watch this outrage, this outrage everyone seems to have about the treatment of these prisoners, I was, I have to say—and I'm probably not the only one up at this table that is more outraged by the outrage than we are by the treatment . . . I am also outraged that we have so many humanitarian do-gooders right now crawling all over these prisons looking for human-rights violations while our troops, our heroes, are fighting and dying.[157]

Gibson's transfiguration of the message of the Gospels into the message of Christ's torn body equally supported the theocons' warfare on the home front against another "spiritual host of wickedness"—the secular state. Not coincidentally, his film changed the Gospels' witness to the content and dynamic of Jesus's political and religious conflict with the Roman and Jewish establishments. Gibson reinterpreted this conflict in terms of the populist tradition of medieval morality and mystery plays which foregrounded Jesus's competition with Satan, absent from the biblical passion narratives.

Satan appears at the very opening of the film to challenge Jesus right before his arrest in Gethsemane: "Nobody can bear such a burden of sin!" In response, everything that follows screams from the screen: "Look, I can!" Since Satan is soon revealed to be in league with the Romans and their local allies, the Pharisees, the demonstration of Jesus's superior divine powers (a temptation explicitly rejected in the Gospels) targets directly those non-Christian adversaries.

In the Gospels, when Pontius Pilate, the Roman governor of Judea, asks Jesus whether he is the king of the Jews, the latter's response is explicitly noncompetitive in regard to the worldly power: "My kingdom is not of this world." And indeed, his kingdom might be above or beneath the Roman state, but it is not on the same plane and therefore not in rivalry with it. Precisely this understanding of the relation between worldly and divine powers underlies the Establishment Clause of the First Amendment of the U.S. Constitution. "Its first and most immediate purpose," the U.S. Supreme Court declared, quoting James Madison's "Memorial and Remonstrance Against Religious Assessments," "rested on the belief that a union of government and religion tends to destroy government and to degrade religion . . . [as] religion is too personal, too sacred, too holy, to permit its 'unhallowed perversion' by a civil magistrate."[158]

"My kingdom is not of this world. If it were not, would they have delivered me?" Jesus continues his train of thought. In response to these mysterious and evasive words, the civil magistrate Pilate reasserts: "Then you are the king."

Figure 6.1. Jesus and Pontius Pilate facing each other as equals. Mel Gibson, *The Passion of the Christ.*

This construal of Jesus's words by a pagan ruler who projects into them the worldly dynamics of power familiar to him also informs Gibson's theo-conservative interpretation of Jesus's relation to the Roman state as one of symmetrical competition. In fact, theocons put much effort into channeling the public debate about the film away from the question of its anti-Semitism toward the issue of Jesus's prosecution by the Roman state, a topic more in line with their ideology. For example, Novak:

> Most important, Gibson's narrative shows that Pilate alone has the power to put Jesus to death, and the film's full narrative weight assigns responsibility to Rome and the Roman soldiers. The Anti-Defamation League is wrong to assert that the Jewish authorities are "forcing the decision" and that the Jewish high priest is "controlling" Pontius Pilate.[159]

Despite the severe beatings that he has already undergone, Jesus, all covered with blood, one eye swollen, stands firmly upright with a steady, clear gaze fixed on Pilate, who paces uncertainly back and forth in front of him. Jesus ignores the Roman's offer of a drink and doesn't move even slightly when Pilate comes within inches of him to ask, "not cynically dismissive" but "earnestly inquiring":[160] "What is truth?" Jesus gives no answer, but Gibson's response is inscribed in the mise-en-scène: so they stand, symmetrically face to face, a worldly and a divine ruler, of the same size and posture. Jesus facing Pilate and the camera, the governor's bald head turned with its back to the viewer as if signifying a void. (See fig. 6.1.)

That their confrontation is a contest of powers becomes most transparent in the scourging scene, seventeen minutes long. A high-angle establishing shot opens a view onto the courtyard of the Roman prison. This well-lit space represents the stronghold of Roman law. Its power is embodied not only in the massive stone construction but also in an impressive escort of armed soldiers that forcefully breaks into this space, dragging the small stumbling figure of the chained Jesus toward his place of torture. An empty block in the middle of the courtyard already marks the future centrality of this victim.

The bird's-eye perspective overwhelms with a sense of the inequality of forces in confrontation here. On one side are the Romans, represented by a lethargically indifferent clerk in charge of overseeing the scourging procedure and the imbecile-looking executioners who parade their terrifying torture tools with sadistic anticipation. On the other side, the Jewish Pharisees, subsidiaries of the Roman state. Strong attributes of both groups' status are expressed through their meticulous costumes and firm positioning in the mise-en-scène. They are contrasted with Jesus in his torn formless robe and disheveled hair being dragged here and there by his chains. Both establishment groups represent the two types of law, Jewish and Roman, to which Jesus's sacrifice would soon put an end.

The scourging starts with evocative shots. Images of the executioners pulling out their barbed iron whips are followed by the evocative sound of invisible strokes synchronized with reaction shots of Jesus's face. Soon, however, digital effects begin to simulate the naturalistic wounds and splashes of blood. The most striking feature of this scene and of the film as a whole, as many critics observed, is Jesus's defiance of pain.

His dispassionate, restrained moaning and steady unperturbed expression convey a sense of masculine heroic stoicism. The Romans are so astonished, challenged, and provoked by his supernatural composure that they only intensify their efforts, as if to verify whether the victim is indeed the embodiment of the divine. Even the lethargic clerk ends up jumping to his feet like the referee of a boxing match, in the grip of utter curiosity, excitement, and agitation.

After Jesus finally slides behind the scourging block and the executioners seem to be about to stop, he gathers his strength and pulls himself up, as if asking for more. And more comes. Provoked by this challenge, the clerk orders the guards to continue scourging, this time on the front of the body. When Jesus is turned over, his face becomes suddenly visible in a revealing close-up. His unperturbed gleaming glance is still discernible through his half-closed eyelids, but his features are disfigured into a pattern of blue, purple, and red, which repeats the color scheme of the courtyard's ground.

His face stands out against the stony background only through the intensity of color. Fusing with stone, his bruised flesh appears more stony than stone. Sanctified by his blood, the locale of Roman law enforcement slowly transforms into a place of Christian worship. The stronghold of Roman authority starts to fuse with the body of Christ. Accordingly, in the second part of the scourging scene, the viewer is presented with shots from Jesus's point of view, which pull the spectators into the mise-en-scène. The audience

Figure 6.2. Jesus's reversed point of view shot of the Roman courtyard. Mel Gibson, *The Passion of the Christ.*

comes to identify with the savior and his wounds while being reassured by his astonishing presence of mind. For example, Jesus's point of view at his torturer's foot introduces a brief flashback to the scene of the last supper, where he had introduced the sacrament of the Eucharist and predicted his destiny while washing John's feet and encouraging his disciples not to fear because all comes from the Father.

At a certain moment, when the intensified brutalization seems unending, Mary exclaims: "My son—when, where, how will you choose to be delivered of this . . ." Her words indicate that the spectacle is a consequence of Jesus's will. Despite his victimization, he is ultimately in control over events, since he is on his Father's mission. It takes an extra-narrative device to break up the deadlock of this sadomasochistic competition. A Roman official who was not present at the scourging suddenly enters the courtyard and commands a stop to the unholy display of powers, since the executioners have visibly lost control. Only the embodiment of the divine, the scene asserts, could withstand such an onslaught of brutality.

To finally pull him away, the Romans turn Jesus over again, and here the major ideological shot of the film suddenly inverts the mise-en-scène. The bloody ground becomes the ceiling. Heaven comes down upon the earth. This shot is a meta-subjective point of view of Christ's body which pulls the viewer into the scheme of the providential convergence of church and state through a reversal of values and constellations of power. (See fig. 6.2.) Another high-angle shot follows, opening a view onto the same courtyard after the sacrificial bloodshed. The Romans are gone. The empty space washed in Christ's blood adumbrates a church with the scourging pillar as a future altar, at which, Gibson hints, the sacrifice of Christ's body would be commemorated from mass to mass through the elevation of the host and the drinking of wine.

Figure 6.3. After flagellation: Roman courtyard as the church. Mel Gibson, *The Passion of the Christ.*

Mary and Maria Magdalene come with white cloths to gather blood. The blood-soaked textiles and the torture tools on display will be relics in the future Catholic Church. (See fig. 6.3.) They suggest that the mystery of Christ's sacrifice has advanced one more stage toward its fulfillment, and some attributes of Roman authority have already been transformed into those of the Christian Church. This sacrifice would culminate in the crucifixion, which would, in its turn, transform the tool of Roman execution into the major Christian symbol. According to historians of Christian art, the instruments of the passion (*arma Christi*) in medieval performances of the passion plays and devotional images were supposed to shift "the man of sorrows context . . . from that of the Passion to that of the Eucharist, from a past event to . . . present and future."[161]

The Christian Church in Gibson's interpretation is based not on the belief in Christ's resurrection but on the commemoration and repetition of the trauma of his passion. Undeniably, there is something powerfully traumatic in this condensation of a historic event of Jesus's execution with the 2,000-year-long ecclesiastical mythology that has sprung from it. Gibson made visceral the notion of the unforgiving church, the church that is not and cannot be reconciled with the state, the church that still remembers why it must always be antagonistic and mistrustful toward worldly power. In the middle of the scourging, Gibson offers a close-up of Jesus's chained hands balled into two bloody fists: an ambiguous image of agony and menace, all too reminiscent of the symbols favored by resistance fighters who are determined to wreak revenge on their oppressors and come back in triumph. In its cinematic emulation of the "Bible of the poor" (*Biblia pauperum*), Gibson's film endorsed the theocons' declared commitment to absorbing the state into the Christian mission, at whatever cost and by whatever means, even if this state is no longer the Roman Empire but American liberal democracy.

Figure 6.4. Cildo Meireles, *Missão/Missões* (*How to Build Cathedrals*), 1987. Composed of 600,000 coins, 800 communion wafers, 2,000 cattle bones, 80 paving stones, and black cloth. 11 ft. 9 in. × 11 ft. 9 in. × 8 ft. 7½ in. Copyright © Blanton Museum of Art, the University of Texas at Austin, Gift of the Peter Norton Family Foundation, 1998 (1998.76). Photo: Rick Hall.

How to Build Cathedrals

At the Blanton Museum of Art at the University of Texas at Austin, one can see an installation representing another dimension of the body of Christ, entitled *Missão/Missões* (*How to Build Cathedrals*, 1987) by the Brazilian conceptual artist Cildo Meireles. It features a cubical space enveloped in a black veil. The ceiling, hung thickly with suspended cattle bones, emits light. The floor, covered with a mass of red copper coins, reflects this light from below. A pendant column of communion wafers connects them in the middle. (See fig. 6.4.)

The veil highlights the mystery of the holy sacrament while allowing an insight into the fusion of religious and colonial interests in the Jesuit missions in southern Brazil, Paraguay, and northern Argentina in the seventeenth and eighteenth centuries. The ecclesiastical drive for wealth through agricultural exploitation, Meireles suggests, was an integral part of the missionary agenda and can be seen as an allegory of the neoliberal recolonization of Latin America in the 1980s.

Meireles's *Cathedrals* tells us that Christ's body is always an ideological construct and a device. The installation represents a metonymical overlap of the sacramental body of Christ, which holds a community together in a chain of wafers, with this community's voluminous body and its manufactured makeup. The body of Christ partakes of the social space of culture, economics, and politics, even if it seems to be separated from that world by a dark membrane. Its sacred and profane dimensions are concurrently differentiated, pitted against each other, interlocked, shifted, fused, or replaced with one another, and ultimately transcended when the heavenly light and glitter of coins meet in midair. The veil's porous fabric hides and exposes the seductive attraction of the sacred canopy. Its capacity to sanctify the most profane drives draws the viewers in as well as repels them from the sacred space.

The most striking feature of Meireles's piece is, however, that its critical dimension does not negate the aura of sublime serenity and mystery his arrangement conveys. The metaphysics of belief is not compromised by what Meireles exposes as the ecclesiastical hypocrisy of the colonial enterprise; rather, belief only mystifies and strengthens the sense of impregnability of the sacred body. Anyone who dares can enter it and operate in its name. The sacred name's performative force anchors manipulation and (self-)deception in the sincerity of belief.

All the religious adventurers featured in this book who turn to the medial and discursive potential of Christ's body move within the same rhetorical paradigm of subversion, seeking via a Pauline enunciation of truth the illocutionary uptake for their perlocutionary ideological construct which constitutes the thought-practice capable of changing the world according to their vision. Their examples teach us that historical potentialities are multiple and multidirectional. Every instantiation of the discourse apart nestles in a juncture at which the progression of events could have unfolded otherwise. The failed projects of history are instructive in that their echoes still reverberate through cultural transmission.

The early church claimed power over the imperial realm via the giving of political counsel to the emperors and the Christianization of the law. I show that Epiphanius's subversive argument about the necessity of iconoclastic legislation de facto took as its target the representation of imperial power. The logic of this conflict would come to historical prominence only in later instances of European iconoclasm but also uncannily reiterated in the contemporary United States. So Dostoevsky's rejection of institutionalized Christianity, the religious symbolism of which he wanted to replace with an ethically differentiated public consciousness, can be heard in Harvey Cox's vision of the "secular city" with its civil ethics of internalized Judeo-Christian values.[162]

Lavater's project of countering the Enlightenment with a religiously inspired vision of the corporeal unity of a transparent mankind was placed, with a certain respect for reality, into the utopian space of the afterlife. In other cases, similar fantasies of incorporation were played out in the political space of modern constitutional governance and economy. Richard Neuhaus and his followers relied on the ambiguous identification of church and empire when advocating that Catholic law should bind all American citizens into the body of Christ. In continuity with that aim, Mel Gibson helped transport the sacramental power of Christian symbolism beyond ecclesiastical confines. His transformation of the torture imagery of Christ's passion into a technologically mediated sacrament of the Eucharist echoes, albeit on different historical and technological premises, the late-medieval sensibility instantiated in the *Book of the Holy Trinity*. That book's verbal alchemy similarly staged the sacrament of Christ's blood for a desired public effect, but in the *corpus libri*.

Pasolini conceived of the camera as the body of Christ in his new cinematic gospel that upheld his social vision of Christianity as a revolutionary religion of the poor. His film is dedicated to the memory of Pope John XXIII in gratitude for the liberalizing reforms of the Second Vatican Council (1962–65). But the body of Christ was also used in the following decades to challenge these reforms, incarnating an ideology that aimed at shoring up a sacrificial economy, justification of warfare, and glorification of pain among the socially weak—the antithesis of the social gospel, achieved through sacramental rhetoric. If nothing else, through their very diversity of goals and interests, these instances of the discourse apart should make it clear, once again, that Christ's body has held such a powerfully persistent grip over human minds because it has provided not a system of values but a means of communication.

Foreword

1. See Christiane Frémont, *L'Être et la relation: Lettres de Leibniz à Des Bosses* (Paris: Vrin, 1999), esp. 72–73.

2. "*Unum autem necessarium*," that is, the 1 as differentiated from 0, as Leibniz put it in his New Year's letter on binary arithmetic to Duke Rudolf August of Braunschweig-Wolfenbüttel, January 2, 1697. See Gottfried Wilhelm Leibniz, *Sämtliche Schriften und Briefe*, First Series, *Allgemeiner politischer und historischer Briefwechsel*, vol. 13 (Berlin: Akademie Verlag, 1987), 120.

3. Tertullian, *De praescriptione haereticorum*, chaps. 38–39; ed. and trans. by R. F. Refoulé as *Traité de la prescription contre les hérétiques* (Paris: Éditions du Cerf, 1957), 141–43. Similar arguments are found in Irenaeus and Jerome. Isidore of Seville borrows the passage for his *Etymologiae*. Tertullian alludes to 1 Corinthians 11:19, "For there must be also heresies among you, that they which are approved may be made manifest among you." On heresy and writing, see also Brian Stock, *The Implications of Literacy: Written Language and Models of Interpretation in the Eleventh and Twelfth Centuries* (Princeton, N.J.: Princeton University Press, 1983), 92–151.

4. Jorge Luis Borges, "Tlön, Uqbar, Orbis Tertius," in *Labyrinths: Selected Stories and Other Writings*, trans. James E. Irby (New York: New Directions, 1964), 13.

5. Erich Auerbach, "Figura," in *Scenes from the Drama of European Literature* (Minneapolis: University of Minnesota Press, 1984), 11–76.

6. Erich Auerbach, *Mimesis: The Representation of Reality in Western Literature*, trans. Willard R. Trask (Princeton, N.J.: Princeton University Press, 1953), 40–49.

7. Theodor W. Adorno, "Parataxis: On Hölderlin's Late Poetry," in *Notes to Literature*, vol. 2, ed. Rolf Tiedemann, trans. Shierry Weber Nicholsen (New York: Columbia University Press, 1991–92), 109–49. "By shattering the symbolic unity of the work of art, [Hölderlin] pointed up the untruth in any reconciliation of the general and the particular within an unreconciled reality. . . . The parataxes [in Hölderlin's late poetry] are striking—artificial disturbances that evade the logical hierarchy of a subordinating syntax. . . . Dispensing with predicative assertion causes the rhythm to approach musical development, just as it softens the identity claims of speculative thought, which undertakes to dissolve history into its identity with spirit" (Adorno, "Parataxis," 127, 130, 132).

Introduction

1. See Daniel Giralt-Miracle, ed., *Gaudí: Exploring Form: Space, Geometry, Structure and Construction* (Barcelona: Lunwerg Editores, 2002), 17–25.

2. René Nouailhat, "L'Opérateur christologique: Dix thèses pour une problématique," in *Dialogues d'Histoire Ancienne* 11 (1985): 611–12. Quotation trans. Haun Saussy.

3. Alain Badiou, *Saint Paul: The Foundation of Universalism*, trans. Ray Brassier (Stanford, Calif.: Stanford University Press, 2003), 35.

4. Dale Martin, *The Corinthian Body* (New Haven, Conn.: Yale University Press, 1995), xv. Emphasis in original.

5. Badiou, *Saint Paul*, 2.

6. J. L. Austin, *How to Do Things with Words*, ed. J. O. Urmson and Marina Sbisà (Cambridge, Mass.: Harvard University Press, 1975), 8.

7. Martin, *Corinthian Body*, 56–57.

8. Pier Paolo Pasolini, "To Carlo Betocchi, November 17, 1954," in Nico Naldini, ed., *The Letters of Pier Paolo Pasolini: 1940–1954*, vol. 1, trans. Stuart Hood (London: Quartet Books, 1992), 499.

9. See Martin, *Corinthian Body*, 3–25.

10. See Marcel Mauss on a linkage of magic with a system of jural obligations, on the one hand, and religious rites, on the other in *A General Theory of Magic*, trans. Robert Brain (London: Routledge, 2001), 23–25.

11. Badiou, *Saint Paul*, 17.

12. Austin, *How to Do Things*, 22. Emphasis in original.

13. Jacques Derrida, "Signature Event Context," in *Margins of Philosophy*, trans. Alan Bass (Chicago: University of Chicago Press, 1982), 325–27.

14. Derrida, "Signature," 324–27.

15. J. Hillis Miller, *Speech Acts in Literature* (Stanford, Calif.: Stanford University Press, 2001), 103.

16. Haun Saussy, "Comparisons, World Literature, and the Common Denominator," in *A Companion to Comparative Literature*, ed. Ali Behdad and Dominic Thomas (New York: Wiley-Blackwell, 2011), 60.

17. Erich Auerbach, "Philology and *Weltliteratur*," trans. Maire and Edward Said, *Centennial Review* 3, no. 1 (1969): 14–15.

18. Michael Warner, *Publics and Counterpublics* (New York: Zone Books, 2002), 120.

19. Sheldon Pollock, "Cosmopolitan Comparison," American Comparative Literature Association keynote address, New Orleans 2010, 14–15. Unpublished manuscript.

20. The trajectory of this ideology is meticulously laid out in Damon Linker's book *The Theocons: Secular America under Siege* (New York: Doubleday, 2006). Linker himself once belonged to the movement which he calls theoconservatism, but dissented from its ranks after discerning that the ideologues who insisted on the admission of religion to public life aimed at nothing less than a subversion of the American political system of liberal democracy. He wrote his book "to alert Americans—and especially those who cherish our nation's tradition of secular politics—to the threat that the theocons pose to the country" (Linker, *Theocons*, xiii.) Ever since its publication his book has become a handbook for lawyers working to defend the constitutional mandate of the separation of church and state.

21. Régis Debray, *Cours de médiologie générale* (Paris: Gallimard, 1991), 92. Italics in original. Debray writes further: "The Christian revolution can be defined

as the intrusion of a strong mediology into a cultural milieu (that of Judaism or of Hellenism) where the mediations were weak" (103).

Chapter 1

1. Margaret R. Miles, "'The Evidence of Our Eyes': Patristic Studies and Popular Christianity in the Fourth Century," *Studia Patristica* 18, no. 1 (1983): 59–63.

2. "Letter from Epiphanius, Bishop of Salamis, in Cyprus, to John, Bishop of Jerusalem," trans. W. H. Fremantle, G. Lewis, and W. G. Martley, in *Nicene and Post-Nicene Fathers*, Second Series, vol. 6, ed. Philip Schaff and Henry Wace (Buffalo, N.Y.: Christian Literature, 1893). The letter may be found at http://www.newadvent.org. Further citations from the "Letter to John" will refer to the same source, 1–9.

3. Adèle Coulin Weibel, *Two Thousand Years of Textiles: The Figured Textiles of Europe and the Near East* (New York: Pantheon Books, 1952), 81.

4. Felicity Harley, "Christianity and the Transformation of Classical Art," in *A Companion to Late Antiquity*, ed. Philip Rousseau (New York: Wiley-Blackwell, 2012), 311.

5. Gerhard B. Ladner, "The Concept of the Image in the Greek Fathers and the Byzantine Iconoclastic Controversy," *Dumbarton Oaks Papers* 7 (1953): 1–34.

6. André Grabar, *Christian Iconography: A Study of Its Origins*, trans. Terry Grabar (Princeton, N.J.: Princeton University Press, 1968), 83–86; see also Robin M. Jensen, *Face to Face: Portraits of the Divine in Early Christianity* (Minneapolis, Minn.: Fortress, 2005).

7. Paul Maas, "Die ikonoklastische Episode in dem Brief des Epiphanios an Johannes," *Byzantinische Zeitschrift* 30 (1929/30): 279–86.

8. Karl Holl, "Die Schriften des Epiphanius gegen die Bilderverehrung," *Gesammelte Aufsätze zur Kirchengeschichte, II: Der Osten* (Tübingen: Mohr, 1928–32), 351–87. First published in *Sitzungsbericht der Berliner Akademie* (Berlin, 1916).

9. Ernst Kitzinger, "The Cult of Images before Iconoclasm," *Dumbarton Oaks Papers* 8 (1954): 93. The major Christian dictionaries, for example *Dictionary of Christian Biography*, *Dictionary of Christian Antiquities*, and *Christliche Ikonographie*, refer to Epiphanius's iconoclasm as a puzzling individual outburst, remarkably out of place in his epoch.

10. Bruno Latour, "What Is Iconoclash? Or Is There a World beyond the Image Wars?" in *Iconoclash*, ed. Bruno Latour and Peter Weibel (Cambridge, Mass.: MIT Press, 2002), 15.

11. *Dictionary of Christian Antiquities*, vol. 1 (1875), s.v. "Idolatry."

12. See Elizabeth A. Clark, *The Origenist Controversy: The Cultural Construction of an Early Christian Debate* (Princeton, N.J.: Princeton University Press, 1992), 54.

13. Karl Baus, *From the Apostolic Community to Constantine*, vol. 1 of *Handbook of Church History*, ed. Hubert Jedin and John Dolan (New York: Herder and Herder, 1965), 398.

14. Baus, *From the Apostolic Community*, 405–32; and Noël Q. King, *The Emperor Theodosius and the Establishment of Christianity* (London: SCM, 1961), 32–36.

15. Peter Brown, *Power and Persuasion in Late Antiquity: Towards a Christian Empire* (Madison: University of Wisconsin Press, 1992), 65–73.

16. Claudia Rapp, *Holy Bishops in Late Antiquity: The Nature of Christian Leadership in an Age of Transition* (Berkeley: University of California Press, 2005), 202.

17. John G. Gager, "Body-Symbols and Social Reality: Resurrection, Incarnation and Asceticism in Early Christianity," *Religion* 12 (1982): 356–59.

18. Brown, *Power and Persuasion*, 65–73.

19. Gager, "Body-Symbols," 347.

20. Ibid., 357.

21. On the tension and fusion of the roles of monk and bishop in the early Christian East, see Andrea Sterk, *Renouncing the World Yet Leading the Church: The Monk-Bishop in Late Antiquity* (Cambridge, Mass.: Harvard University Press, 2004).

22. Thomas F. Torrance, "The Triunity of God in the Nicene Theology of the Fourth Century," in *Theological Dialogue between Orthodox and Reformed Churches*, vol. 2, ed. Thomas F. Torrance (Edinburgh: Scottish Academic, 1993), 33.

23. Thomas F. Torrance, "Epiphanius and the Council of Constantinople," in *The Trinitarian Faith: The Evangelical Theology of the Ancient Catholic Church* (Edinburgh: Clark, 1993), 326–40.

24. Jon F. Dechow, *Dogma and Mysticism in Early Christianity: Epiphanius of Cyprus and the Legacy of Origen* (Macon, Ga.: Mercer University Press, 1988), 311–12.

25. Frank Williams, introduction to *The Panarion of Epiphanius of Salamis*, trans. Frank Williams (Leiden: Brill, 1987–94), xvii.

26. Epiphanius, *Ancoratus*, cited in Torrance, "The Triunity of God," 25. My emphasis.

27. Auerbach, "Figura," 34.

28. Robert V. Hotchkiss, ed. and trans., *A Pseudo-Epiphanius Testimony Book* (Missoula: Scholars' Press, University of Montana, 1974).

29. Epiphanius, *Ancoratus* 118, here quoted after Torrance, "The Triunity of God," 28.

30. Robert W. Dyson, ed. and trans., *Augustine: The City of God against the Pagans* (Cambridge: Cambridge University Press, 1998), xiii.

31. Brown, *Power and Persuasion*, 4.

32. See F. Homes Dudden, *The Life and Times of St. Ambrose*, vol. 2 (Oxford: Clarendon, 1935), 371–92.

33. Brown, *Power and Persuasion*, 4.

34. On the topos of forced ordination, see Sterk, *Renouncing the World*, 1–9.

35. On Epiphanius's polemics with Evagrius and on the latter's conception of "passionlessness" and "pure prayer," see Elizabeth A. Clark, "New Perspectives on the Origenist Controversy: Human Embodiment and Ascetic Strategies," *Church History* 59, no. 2 (1989): 154.

36. Sterk, *Renouncing the World*, 32.

37. Rapp, *Holy Bishops*, 64–65.

38. Ibid., 141–42.

39. Clark, *The Origenist Controversy*, 22.

40. Auerbach, "Figura," 36.

41. Ibid., 30.

42. Ibid., 53.

43. Clark, "New Perspectives," 150.

44. Tertullian, *De idololatria*, 16, in *Patrologia Cursus Completus: Series Latina*, ed. J.-P. Migne (Paris: Migne, 1844), 1:1, col. 686; and Tertullian, *De corona*, 13, in Migne, 1:2, cols. 95–97.

45. On Epiphanius's understanding of the resurrection of the body, see Caroline Walker Bynum, *The Resurrection of the Body in Western Christianity, 200–1336* (New York: Columbia University Press, 1995), 68–69.

46. Dechow, *Dogma and Mysticism*, 311–12.

47. Tertullian, *Adversus Marcionem*, 4:40, here quoted after Auerbach, "Figura," 31.

48. Coulin Weibel, *Two Thousand Years of Textiles*, 81.

49. Auerbach, "Figura," 26–27.

50. Clark, *Origenist Controversy*, 102.

51. Gager, "Body-Symbols," 356.

52. Maas, "Die ikonoklastische Episode," 284–85.

53. This fragment and those that follow are translated by Haun Saussy from the restored Greek text established by Hans Georg Thümmel, "Die bilderfeindlichen Schriften des Epiphanios von Salamis," *Byzantinoslavica* 47 (1986): 169–88. References are keyed to this text.

54. See Erik Peterson, "Christus als Imperator," *Catholica* 5 (1936): 64–72; Simon R. F. Price, *Rituals and Power: The Roman Imperial Cult in Asia Minor* (Cambridge: Cambridge University Press, 1984), 170–206.

55. Jensen, *Face to Face*, 35–68.

56. See Eva M. Lassen, "The Use of the Father Image in Imperial Propaganda and 1 Corinthians 4:14–21," *Tyndale Bulletin* 42 (1991): 127–36.

57. Francis Dvorník, *Early Christian and Byzantine Political Philosophy: Origins and Background*, vol. 2 (Washington D.C.: Dumbarton Oaks Center for Byzantine Studies, trustees for Harvard University, 1966), 679.

58. Jensen, *Face to Face*, 166.

59. Grabar, *Christian Iconography*, 38.

60. Dvorník, *Early Christian and Byzantine Political Philosophy*, 652.

61. See Erich Becker, "Protest gegen den Kaiserkult und Verherrlichung des Sieges am Pons Milvius in der christlichen Kunst der konstantinischen Zeit," in *Konstantin der Große und seine Zeit: Gesammelte Studien: Festgabe Zum Konstantinsjubiläum 1913 und Zum Goldenen Priesterjubiläum von Mgr. Dr. A. De Waal*, ed. F. J. Dölger (Freiburg: Herder'sche Verlagshandlung, 1913), 186; Dvorník, *Early Christian and Byzantine Political Philosophy*, 630–43.

62. Grabar, *Christian Iconography*, 6.

63. Eusebius, "Epistula ad Constantiam Augustam," in *Patrologia Cursus Completus: Series Graeca*, ed. J.-P. Migne (Paris: Migne, 1857), 20:1545–49.

64. Harley, "Christianity and the Transformation," 319–20.

65. Matt. 6:24; Luke 16:13, RSV.

66. Brown, *Power and Persuasion*, 105.

67. Gager, "Body-Symbols," 356.

68. James A. Francis, "Visual and Verbal Representation: Image, Text, Person, Power," in *A Companion to Late Antiquity*, ed. Philip Rousseau (New York: Wiley-Blackwell, 2012), 301–4.

69. Andrew Louth, "The Body in Western Catholic Christianity," in *Religion and the Body*, ed. S. Coakley (Cambridge: Cambridge University Press, 1997), 121.

70. Eusebius, *The History of the Church from Christ to Constantine*, trans. G. A. Williamson (New York: New York University Press, 1966), 400.

71. Richard Krautheimer, *Early Christian and Byzantine Architecture* (New York: Viking Penguin, 1986), 106.

72. See A. H. S. Megaw, "Byzantine Architecture and Decoration in Cyprus," *Dumbarton Oaks Papers* 28 (1974), 61–64; and A.H.S. Megaw, "Discussion: Architecture, Liturgy, and Chronology," in *Kourion: Excavations in the Episcopal Precinct* (Washington, D.C.: Dumbarton Oaks, 2007), 157–76.

73. Dechow, *Dogma and Mysticism*, 395.

74. Grabar, *Christian Iconography*, 41.

75. Sebastian Brock, "Iconoclasm and the Monophysites," in *Iconoclasm*, ed. Anthony Bryer and Judith Herrin (Birmingham: Center for Byzantine Studies, University of Birmingham, 1975), 53–58.

76. M. J. Mondzain, *Image, Icône, Économie* (Paris: Seuil, 1996), 13–21.

Chapter 2

1. Das *Buch der heyligen Dreyualdekeit*, manuscript KdZ 78 A 11, Kupferstichkabinett, Staatliche Museen zu Berlin—Preußischer Kulturbesitz.

2. Ioannes XXII, "Titulus VI: De Crimine Falsi," in *Corpus Iuris Canonici*, ed. Emil Friedberg and Aemilius Ludwig Richter (Leipzig: Tauchnitz, 1879), col. 1295–96.

3. Gustav Lewinstein, *Die Alchemie und die Alchemisten* (Berlin: Lüderitz, 1870), 20.

4. Wilhelm Ganzenmüller, "Das 'Buch der Heiligen Dreifaltigkeit': Eine deutsche Alchemie aus dem Anfang des 15. Jahrhunderts," in *Beiträge zur Geschichte der Technologie und der Alchemie* (Weinheim: Verlag Chemie, 1956; reprint of 1939 article), 239.

5. See Ganzenmüller, "Das 'Buch der Heiligen Dreifaltigkeit,' " 260.

6. Hans-Werner Schütt, *Auf der Suche nach dem Stein der Weisen: Die Geschichte der Alchemie* (Munich: Beck, 2000), 370.

7. *Lapidarium*, cited in Ganzenmüller, "Das 'Buch der Heiligen Dreifaltigkeit,' " 260. Quotation trans. Haun Saussy.

8. Cited from the first Berlin version. See note 1. All translations from German here and further are mine.

9. Uwe Junker, *Das "Buch der Heiligen Dreifaltigkeit" in seiner zweiten, alchemistischen Fassung (Kadolzburg 1433)* (Cologne: Institut für Geschichte der Medizin der Universität, 1986), 259. Further quotations will refer to this text.

10. Renate Blumenfeld-Kosinski, "The Conceptualization and Imagery of the Great Schism," in *A Companion to the Great Western Schism (1378–1417)*, ed. Joëlle Rollo-Koster and Thomas M. Izbicki (Leiden: Brill, 2009), 143–49.

11. See Christopher M. Bellitto, "The Reform Context of the Great Western Schism," in *A Companion to the Great Western Schism (1378–1417)*, ed. Joëlle Rollo-Koster and Thomas M. Izbicki (Leiden: Brill, 2009), 330–32.

12. Rainer A. Muller, ed., *Deutsche Geschichte in Quellen und Darstellung: Spätmittelalter 1250–1495*, vol. 2 (Stuttgart: Reclam, 2000).

13. Phillip H. Stump, "The Council of Constance (1414–18) and the End of the Schism," in *A Companion to the Great Western Schism (1378–1417)*, ed. Joëlle Rollo-Koster and Thomas M. Izbicki (Leiden: Brill, 2009), 395–442.

14. Jürgen Miethke, "Die Konzilien als Forum der öffentlichen Meinung im 15. Jahrhundert," *Deutsches Archiv für Erforschung des Mittelalters* 37, no. 2 (1981): 736–73. Further references to this document will be given parenthetically in the text.

15. On this topic see Paul Lehmann, "Konstanz und Basel als Büchermärkte während der großen Kirchenversammlungen," in *Erforschung der Mittelalters: Ausgewählte Abhandlungen und Aufsätze*, vol. 1 (Stuttgart: Hiersemann, 1959), 253–79.

16. On the social effectiveness of magical practices, including performative language, see Marcel Mauss, *A General Theory of Magic*, trans. Robert Brain (London: Routledge), 120–33.

17. Marshall McLuhan, *Understanding Media: The Extensions of Man* (New York: McGraw-Hill, 1964), 7.

18. Helmut Birkhan, "Das Alchemische Zeichen: Allgemeines zur wissenschaftlichen Axiomatik der Alchemie und Spezielles zum *Buch der heiligen Dreifaltigkeit*," in *The Presence*, ed. Keith Griffiths and Siegfried Zielinski (Salzburg: Blimp, 1999), 40–53.

19. Pope John XXII, "Bull against the Deceiving Alchemists," quoted in Curt Hunnius, *Dämonen, Ärzte, Alchemisten* (Stuttgart: Wissenschaftliche Verlagsgesellschaft, 1962), 294. My translation into English.

20. Lewinstein, *Die Alchemie*, 19.

21. Jacqueline Cerquiglini-Toulet, *The Color of Melancholy: The Uses of Books in the Fourteenth Century*, trans. Lydia G. Cochrane (Baltimore: Johns Hopkins University Press, 1997), xiii–xvi and 156.

22. Thomas M. Izbicki, "The Authority of Peter and Paul: The Use of Biblical Authority during the Great Schism," in *A Companion to the Great Western Schism (1378–1417)*, ed. Joëlle Rollo-Koster and Thomas M. Izbicki (Leiden: Brill, 2009), 376.

23. Izbicki, "The Authority of Peter and Paul," 376–77.

24. Ann W. Astell, *Eating Beauty: The Eucharist and the Spiritual Arts of the Middle Ages* (Ithaca, N.Y.: Cornell University Press, 2006), 4–5.

25. For a discussion of the *Book*'s alchemical symbolism, see Gustav Friedrich Hartlaub, "Signa Hermetis (Zwei Alte Alchemische Bilderhandschriften)," *Zeitschrift des Deutschen Vereins für Kunstwissenschaft* 4 (1937): 93–112.

26. Ganzenmüller, "Das 'Buch der Heiligen Dreifaltigkeit,'" 237.

27. See Bernhard Töpfer, "Hoffnungen auf Erneuerung des paradiesischen Zustands (*status innocentiae*)—ein Beitrag zur Vorgeschichte des hussitischen Adamitentums," in *Eschatologie und Hussitismus*, ed. Alexander Patschovsky and František Šmahel (Prague: Historisches Institut, 1996), 169–84.

28. Ganzenmüller, "Das 'Buch der Heiligen Dreifaltigkeit,'" 237.

29. Ferdinand Seibt, "Jan Hus—zwischen Zeiten, Völkern, Konfessionen," in *Jan Hus: Zwischen Zeiten, Völkern, Konfessionen*, ed. Ferdinand Seibt (Munich: Oldenbourg, 1997), 23; Peter Segl, "Schisma, Krise, Häresie und Schwarzer Tod: Signaturen der 'Welt vor Hus,'" in *Jan Hus*, 27; Ferdinand Seibt, "Geistige Reformbewegungen zur Zeit des Konstanzer Konzils," in *Hussitenstudien:*

Personen, Ereignisse, Ideen einer frühen Revolution (Munich: Oldenbourg, 1987), 97–111.

30. See Alexander Patschovsky, "Beginen, Begarden and Terziaren im 14. und 15. Jahrhundert: Das Beispiel des Basler Beginenstreits (1400/04–1411)," in *Ketzer, Juden, Antichrist: Gesammelte Aufsätze zum 60. Geburtstag von Alexander Patschovsky*, ed. Matthias Kaup (Göttingen: Niedersächsische Staats- und Universitätsbibliothek, 2001), 406. The essay may be found at http://webdoc.sub.gwdg.de.

31. Katharina Biegger, *"De Invocatione Beatae Mariae Virginis": Paracelsus und die Marienverehrung* (Stuttgart: Franz Steiner, 1990), 63.

32. Ibid., 65.

33. See Seibt, "Geistige Reformbewegungen," 98.

34. Bellitto, "Reform Context," 317.

35. Suzannah Biernoff, *Sight and Embodiment in the Middle Ages* (New York: Palgrave Macmillan, 2002), 133. Further references to this source will be given parenthetically in the text.

36. See Ganzenmüller, "Das 'Buch der Heiligen Dreifaltigkeit,' " 235–36.

37. See Sarah Beckwith, *Christ's Body: Identity, Culture and Society in Late Medieval Writings* (London: Routledge, 1996), 3.

38. Töpfer, "Hoffnungen auf Erneuerung," 179.

39. See Robert Peter Ebert, Oskar Reichmann, and Klaus-Peter Wegera, eds., *Frühneuhochdeutsche Grammatik*, § 598 (Tübingen: Niemeyer, 1993).

40. Fritz Pradel, *Griechische und süditalienische Gebete, Beschwörungen und Rezepte des Mittelalters*, vol. 3.3 of *Religionsgeschichtliche Versuche und Vorarbeiten*, ed. Albrecht Dieterich and Richard Wünsch (Giessen: Töpelmann, 1907), 381.

41. Laurel Amtower, *Engaging Words: The Culture of Reading in the Later Middle Ages* (New York: Palgrave, 2000), 79.

42. Ibid., 82.

43. William Brashear, "Magical Papyri: Magic in Bookform," in *Das Buch als magisches und als Repräsentationsobjekt*, ed. Peter Ganz (Wiesbaden: Harrassowitz, 1992), 29.

44. Ibid., 29.

45. For a discussion of a bilingual circulation of books in the German Late Middle Ages, see Ernst Hellgardt, "Latin and the Vernacular: Mechthild of Magdeburg—Mechthild of Hackeborn—Gertrude of Helfta," in *A Companion to Mysticism and Devotion in Northern Germany in the Late Middle Ages*, ed. Elizabeth Andersen, Henrike Lähnemann, and Anne Simon (Leiden: Brill, 2014), 131–45.

46. Junker, *Das "Buch der Heiligen Dreifaltigkeit,"* 72–76.

47. Hartlaub, "Signa Hermetis," 152, 157.

48. Ibid., 152–54.

49. See Rainald Grosshans, *Maerten van Heemskerck: Die Gemälde* (Berlin: Horst Boetticher Verlag, 1980), 163.

50. See Franz Joseph Dölger, *Heidnische und christliche Brotstempel mit religiösen Zeichen: Zur Geschichte des Hostienstempels*, in *Antike und Christentum: Kultur- und religionsgeschichtliche Studien*, vol. 1 (Münster: Aschendorff, 1974; reprint of 1929 edition), 44–46.

51. Berent Schwineköper, "Christus-Reliquien-Verehrung und Politik," *Blätter für deutsche Landesgeschichte* 117 (1981): 183–281.

52. Quoted in Miethke, "Die Konzilien als Forum," 770. Quotation trans. Haun Saussy.

53. Ibid., 763.

54. Marshall McLuhan, *The Gutenberg Galaxy: The Making of Typographic Man* (Toronto: University of Toronto Press, 1962), 8. On print and nation formation, see also Benedict Anderson, *Imagined Communities* (London: Verso, 1995).

55. Michel Camille, *Image on the Edge: The Margins of Medieval Art* (Cambridge, Mass.: Harvard University Press, 1992).

56. Jürgen Bärsch, "Liturgy and Reform: Northern German Convents in the Late Middle Ages," in *A Companion to Mysticism and Devotion in Northern Germany in the Late Middle Ages*, ed. Elizabeth Andersen, Henrike Lähnemann, and Anne Simon (Leiden: Brill, 2014), 23.

57. Lola Badia, "The *Arbor Scientiae*: A 'New' Encyclopedia in the Thirteenth-Century Occitan-Catalan Cultural Context," in *Arbor Scientiae: Der Baum des Wissens von Ramon Lull*, ed. Fernando Domínguez Reboiras, Pere Villalba Varneda, and Peter Walter (Turnhout: Brepols, 2002), 2.

58. Gerald Strauss, introduction to *Pre-Reformation Germany*, ed. Gerald Strauss (London: Macmillan, 1972), 10.

59. See Heinrich Koller, "Zur Reformpolitik Kaiser Sigmunds," in *Sigismund von Luxemburg: Kaiser und König in Mitteleuropa, 1387–1437: Beiträge zur Herrschaft Kaiser Sigismunds und der europäischen Geschichte um 1400*, ed. Josef Macek, Ernö Marosi, and Ferdinand Seibt (Warendorf: Fahlbusch, 1994), 15–25.

60. Junker, *Das "Buch der Heiligen Dreifaltigkeit*," 178.

Chapter 3

1. Badiou, *Saint Paul*, 2.

2. Richard T. Gray, *About Face: German Physiognomic Thought from Lavater to Auschwitz* (Detroit, Mich.: Wayne State University Press, 2004).

3. Horst Weigelt, *Johann Kaspar Lavater: Leben, Werk und Wirkung* (Göttingen: Vandenhoeck & Ruprecht, 1991), 74.

4. Ibid., 50.

5. Ibid., 75.

6. Johan Caspar Lavater, *Brüderliche Schreiben an verschiedene Jünglinge*, here quoted in Horst Weigelt, *Lavater*, 78.

7. Lavater, quoted in Weigelt, *Lavater*, 79.

8. Weigelt, *Lavater*, 32–49.

9. Johann Caspar Lavater, *Aussichten in die Ewigkeit: 1768–1773/78*, ed. Ursula Caflisch-Schnetzler, vol. 2 of *Ausgewählte Werke in Historisch-Kritischer Ausgabe* (Zurich: Verlag Neue Züricher Zeitung, 2001), 6. All translations into English are mine. Further references to this work will be given parenthetically in text.

10. See Ursula Caflisch-Schnetzler, introduction to *Aussichtein in die Ewigkeit*, xviii.

11. Stephen Jay Gould, *Ontogeny and Phylogeny* (Cambridge, Mass.: Belknap Press of Harvard University Press, 1977), 22.

12. See Caflisch-Schnetzler, introduction, xx–xxi; Karl Pestalozzi, "Lavater's Utopie," in *Literaturwissenschaft und Geschichtsphilosophie: Festschrift für Wilhelm Emrich*, ed. Hermut Arntzen et al. (Berlin: de Gruyter, 1975), 283–89.

13. Badiou, *Saint Paul*, 28.

14. Weigelt, *Lavater*, 73.

15. Lavater, quoted in Weigelt, *Lavater*, 20.

16. Weigelt, *Lavater*, 19–22.

17. Johann Caspar Lavater, *Aussichten in die Ewigkeit: Gemeinnütziger Auszug aus dem größeren Werke dieses Namens* (Zürich, 1781).

18. Jürgen Habermas, *Strukturwandel der Öffentlichkeit: Untersuchungen zu einer Kategorie der bürgerlichen Gesellschaft* (Neuwied, Berlin: Luchterhand, 1965), 36.

19. See Pestalozzi, "Lavater's Utopie," 295–97.

20. Badiou, *Saint Paul*, 44.

21. Frederick Beiser, *The Fate of Reason* (Cambridge, Mass.: Harvard University Press, 1993), 1. This work will be cited parenthetically in the text.

22. The word *gleichförmig*, which I have translated somewhat unidiomatically as "con-form," is of considerable technical importance to Lavater. It allows the projection of the temporal into the eternal which is his main objective.

23. Badiou, *Saint Paul*, 45.

24. David Wellbery, *Lessing's Laocoon: Semiotics and Aesthetics in the Age of Reason* (Cambridge: Cambridge University Press, 1984), 5.

25. Badiou, *Saint Paul*, 41.

26. Goethe, quoted in Weigelt, *Lavater*, 48.

27. Weigelt, *Lavater*, 5.

28. Frédéric Barbier, "The German Language and Book Trade in Europe," in *Literary Cultures and the Material Book*, ed. Simon Eliot, Andrew Nash, and Ian Willison (London: British Library, 2007), 253–67.

29. Ibid., 258.

30. Bernhard Fabian, "Friedrich Nicolai: Creator of the German Republic of Letters," in *Literary Cultures and the Material Book*, ed. Simon Eliot, Andrew Nash, and Ian Willison (London: British Library, 2007), 241–52.

31. Max Wehrli, "Lavater und das geistige Zürich," in *Das Antlitz Gottes im Antlitz des Menschen: Zugänge zu Johann Kaspar Lavater*, ed. Karl Pestalozzi and Horst Weigelt (Göttingen: Vandenhoeck & Ruprecht, 1994), 14.

32. Lavater, quoted in introduction to *Aussichtein in die Ewigkeit*, by Caflisch-Schnetzler, xviii.

33. Weigelt, *Lavater*, 14.

34. See Weigelt, *Lavater*, 15; and Pestalozzi, "Lavater's Utopie," 299.

35. Lavater, quoted in Gerhard Ebeling, "Genie des Herzens unter dem *genius saeculi*—Johann Caspar Lavater als Theologe," in *Das Antlitz Gottes*, 31.

36. Lavater, quoted in Ebeling, "Genie des Herzens," 35.

37. Charles Bonnet, *Contemplation of Nature* (London: Longman, Becket and Hondt, 1766), 21.

38. Francis Bacon, *De Augmentis Scientiarum*, quoted in Arthur Schopenhauer, *The World as Will and Representation*, vol. 1, trans. E. F. J. Payne (New York: Dover, 1969), 83.

39. Badiou, *Saint Paul*, 2.

40. Johan Caspar Lavater, "Worte Jesu," quoted in Weigelt, *Lavater*, 89. My translation.

41. Ibid.,34. Emphasis added.

42. Hans Wysling, "Die Literatur," in *Zürich im 18. Jahrhundert: Zum 150. Jahrestag der Universität Zürich*, ed. Hans Wysling (Zurich: Berichthaus, 1983), 188.

43. Ernst Benz, "Swedenborg und Lavater: Über die religiösen Grundlagen der Physiognomik," *Zeitschrift für Kirchengeschichte* 57 (1938): 157.

44. Immanuel Kant, *Dreams of a Spirit-Seer: Illustrated by Dreams of Metaphysics*, ed. with an introduction and notes by Frank Sewall, trans. Emanuel F. Goerwitz (London and New York: Sonnenschein, Macmillan, 1900), 122.

45. Kant, *Dreams of a Spirit-Seer*, 45. Further references to this text will be given parenthetically.

46. Johann Caspar Lavater, "Von der Geringheit meiner physiognomischen Kenntnisse," in *Physiognomische Fragmente zur Beförderung der Menschenkenntnis und Menschenliebe*, ed. Christoph Siegrist (Stuttgart: Reclam, 1999), 15–21.

47. Emanuel Swedenborg, *Arcana Caelestia*, quoted in Benz, "Swedenborg und Lavater," 164. My translation.

48. Benz, "Swedenborg and Lavater," 163–89.

49. Lavater refers to the necessity of a "physiognomic genius" for the successful reading of people in "Die Physiognomik, eine Wissenschaft," in *Physiognomische Fragmente zur Beförderung der Menschenkenntnis und Menschenliebe*, ed. Christoph Siegrist (Stuttgart: Reclam, 1999), 40.

50. Johann Caspar Lavater, "Über Christusbilder," in *Physiognomische Fragmente zur Beförderung der Menschenkenntnis und Menschenliebe*, vol. 4 (Winterthur: In der Heinr. Steiner'schen Buchhandlung, 1830). Further references to this text will be given in parentheses.

51. Henry Home of Kames, *Elements of Criticism*, vol. 1 (London: Printed for Vernor and Hood . . . by Alex Lawrie, Edinburgh, 1805), 287.

52. On Winckelmann's standard-setting classical aesthetics, see Jeffrey Morrison, *Winckelmann and the Notion of Aesthetic Education* (Oxford: Clarendon, 1996).

53. Weigelt, *Lavater*, 83.

54. Gerhard Wolf, "'. . . sed ne taceatur': Lavaters 'Grille mit den Christusköpfen' und die Tradition der authentischen Bilder," in *Der exzentrische Blick: Gespräch über Physiognomik*, ed. Claudia Schmölders (Berlin: Akademie Verlag, 1996), 43–76.

55. Ernst Kitzinger and Elizabeth Senior, *Portraits of Christ* (Middlesex, Eng.: Penguin Books, 1940), 19–20.

56. See Gager, "Body-Symbols," 345–63.

57. For a historical and political background on the public sphere in which Lavater acted, see Rold Graber, *Bürgerliche Öffentlichkeit und Spätabsolutistischer Staat: Sozietätenbewegung und Konfliktkonjunktur in Zürich 1746–1780* (Zurich: Chronos Verlag, 1993); and Rudolf Braun, *Das ausgehende Ancien Régime in der Schweiz: Aufriß einer Sozial- und Wirtschaftsgeschichte des 18. Jahrhunderts* (Göttingen: Vandenhoeck & Ruprecht, 1984).

58. Weigelt, *Lavater*, 22.

59. Arthur Schopenhauer, "Criticism of the Kantian Philosophy," in *The World as Will and Representation*, vol. 1, trans. E. F. J. Payne (New York: Dover, 1969), 428.

60. Schopenhauer, "Criticism," 419.

61. Schopenhauer, *The World as Will*, 241.

62. On the history of this vignette, see Georg Gessner, *Johann Kaspar Lavaters Lebensbeschreibung* (Winterthur: Steiner, 1802), 2:149–50.

Chapter 4

1. Anna Dostoevskaia, *Dostoevsky: Reminiscences*, ed. and trans. Beatrice Stillman (New York: Liveright, 1975), 393.

2. Updated information on the provenance and history of this painting may be found at http://sammlungonline.kunstmuseumbasel.ch/.

3. Dostoevskaia, *Dostoevsky*, 134.

4. Fyodor Dostoevsky, *The Idiot*, trans. Richard Pevear and Larissa Volokhonsky (New York: Vintage Classics, 2003) 408. This work will be hereafter cited in parentheses in the text.

5. See Leo Steinberg, *The Sexuality of Christ in Renaissance Art and in Modern Oblivion* (Chicago: University of Chicago Press, 1996).

6. Mark Roskill, introduction to *Hans Holbein: Paintings, Prints, and Reception*, ed. Mark Roskill and John Oliver Hand (Washington, D.C.: National Gallery of Art, 2001), 9–10.

7. See Derek Wilson, *Hans Holbein: Portrait of an Unknown Man* (London: Weidenfeld and Nicolson, 1996), 94; Nigel Spivey, *Enduring Creation: Art, Pain, and Fortitude* (Berkeley: University of California Press, 2001), 101–11.

8. Dostoevsky, *The Idiot*, 408–9.

9. Richard Pevear, introduction to *The Idiot*, viii.

10. Steven Cassedy, *Dostoevsky's Religion* (Stanford, Calif.: Stanford University Press, 2005), 27.

11. Anna Dostoevsky, quoted in Pevear, introduction to *The Idiot*, ix.

12. Dostoevsky, *The Idiot*, 23.

13. Andrew Wachtel, "Dostoevsky's *The Idiot*: The Novel as Photograph," *History of Photography* 26, no. 3 (2002): 213.

14. Badiou, *Saint Paul*, 30.

15. Rowan Williams, *Dostoevsky: Language, Faith, and Fiction* (Waco, Tex.: Baylor University Press, 2008), 46. Italics in original.

16. Badiou, *Saint Paul*, 28.

17. Cassedy, *Dostoevsky's Religion*, 159–62.

18. Vladimir Soloviev, "A Note in Defense of Dostoevsky against the Charge of a 'New Christianity,'" in *The Heart of Reality: Essays on Beauty, Love, and Ethics*, ed. and trans. Vladimir Wozniuk (Notre Dame, Ind.: University of Notre Dame Press, 2003), 201.

19. Soloviev, "A Note in Defense," 201.

20. Ibid., 204.

21. Ibid., 202.

22. Vladimir Soloviev, "Three Addresses in Memory of Dostoevsky," in *The Heart of Reality: Essays on Beauty, Love, and Ethics*, ed. and trans. Vladimir Wozniuk (Notre Dame, Ind.: University of Notre Dame Press, 2003), 11.

23. See Marina Kostalevsky, *Dostoevsky and Soloviev: The Art of Integral Vision* (New Haven, Conn.: Yale University Press, 1997), 112–44.

24. See Nancy Ruttenburg, *Dostoevsky's Democracy* (Princeton, N.J.: Princeton University Press, 2008).

25. Cassedy, *Dostoevsky's Religion*, 26–63.

26. See, for example, the Durkheimian social anthropologist Mary Douglas, "Effects of Modernization on Religious Change," *Daedalus* 111, no. 1 (1982): 1–19.

27. Friedrich Schleiermacher, *On Religion: Speeches to Its Cultured Despisers*, trans. John Oman (Louisville, Ky.: Westminster/John Knox, 1994), 39.

28. Friedrich Schleiermacher, *The Christian Faith* (Edinburgh: Bloomsbury, 1999), 481.

29. Ibid., 476.

30. G. W. F. Hegel, *Phenomenology of Spirit*, trans. A. V. Miller (Oxford: Clarendon, 1977), 461.

31. Ibid., 462.

32. Ibid., 473.

33. Richard Kroner, introduction to *Early Theological Writings*, by G.W. F. Hegel (Philadelphia: University of Pennsylvania Press, 1979), 5–6.

34. David Friedrich Strauss, letter to Christian Märklin (February 6, 1832), quoted in Werner Zager, introduction to *Das Leben Jesu, kritisch bearbeitet, by David Friedrich Strauß*, ed. Werner Zager (Waltrop: Spenner, 2003), xix.

35. Zager, introduction, xxi.

36. Charles-Augustin Sainte-Beuve, quoted in John Haynes Holmes, introduction to *The Life of Jesus*, by Ernest Renan (New York: Modern Library, 1927), 23.

37. Strauss, letter to Christian Märklin, xxi.

38. Sainte-Beuve, quoted in Holmes, introduction to *The Life of Jesus*, 23.

39. Friedrich Nietzsche, *Thoughts Out of Season*, in *The Complete Works of Friedrich Nietzsche*, vol. 4, ed. Oscar Levy, trans. Anthony M. Ludovici (London: Foulis, 1914), 51.

40. Nietzsche, *Thoughts Out of Season*, 56.

41. See, for example, Robert Gooding-Williams, *Zarathustra's Dionysian Modernism* (Stanford, Calif.: Stanford University Press, 2001).

42. For the discussion of modern time constructs, which go back to Nietzsche, see, for example, Bruno Hillebrand, *Ästhetik des Augenblicks: Der Dichter als Überwinder der Zeit—von Goethe bis heute* (Göttingen: Vandenhoeck & Ruprecht, 1999); or see Karl Heinz Bohrer, *Plötzlichkeit: Zum Augenblick des ästhetischen Scheins* (Frankfurt am Main: Suhrkamp, 1981).

43. Friedrich Nietzsche, *Thus Spake Zarathustra*, in *The Complete Works of Friedrich Nietzsche*, vol. 11, ed. Oscar Levy, trans. Thomas Common (London: Foulis, 1914), 351.

44. Lev Shestov, "Dostoevsky and Nietzsche: The Philosophy of Tragedy," in *Essays in Russian Literature: The Conservative View: Leontiev, Rozanov, Shestov*, ed. Spencer E. Roberts (Athens: Ohio University Press, 1968), 99.

45. Shestov, "Dostoevsky and Nietzsche," 99.

46. Exemplary of such a traditional understanding of Dostoevsky within the Nietzschean paradigm is Alex de Jonge's book *Dostoevsky and the Age of Intensity* (London: Secker and Warburg, 1975): "Dostoevsky in particular probes into the deep-structure of his age. He does not seek realistic representation, he depicts the psyche of his world. He writes not the history of the nineteenth century, but its mythology. . . . His Russia is . . . a Russia of the mind" (2).

And further: Dostoevsky "provides a unique account of the traumas and dislocations which civilization had wrought upon the psyche of nineteenth-century man" (3).

47. Thomas Mann, "Dostojevskij—mit Maßen," in *Essays*, vol. 1, ed. Michael Mann (Frankfurt am Main: Fischer, 1977), 167–82. Further references to this document will be given parenthetically in the text. English translation is mine.

48. These conceptions indeed came to inform utopian visions of time in the modernist literature of consciousness. See Bohrer, *Plötzlichkeit*, 180–218.

49. See Dostoevsky's discussion of the dynamics and philosophical implications of the epileptic experience in *The Idiot*, 226.

50. Mann, "Dostojevskij—mit Maßen," 173.

51. See my article "Polyphonie und Karneval: Spuren Dostoevskijs in Thomas Manns Roman *Doktor Faustus*," *Poetica* 3/4 (2005): 463–94.

52. Georg Lukács, *Der russische Realismus in der Weltliteratur* (Berlin: Aufbau-Verlag, 1952), 9.

53. Bakhtin, quoted in Caryl Emerson, "The Tolstoy Connection in Bakhtin," *Rethinking Bakhtin*, ed. Gary Saul Morson, Caryl Emerson (Stanford, Calif.: Stanford University Press, 1989), 282.

54. Mann, "Dostojevskij—mit Maßen," 170.

55. Williams, *Dostoevsky*, 46.

56. Pavel Florensky, "Reversed Perspective," in *Beyond Vision: Essays on the Perception of Art*, ed. Nicoletta Misler, trans. Wendy Salmond (London: Reaktion Books, 2002), 201–72.

57. Florensky, "Reversed Perspective," 272.

58. Fyodor Dostoevsky, *The Brothers Karamazov: A Novel in Four Parts with Epilogue*, trans. and annot. Richard Pevear and Larissa Volokhonsky (New York: Farrar, Straus and Giroux, 2002), 63. Obviously, the present discussion does not endorse the recent nationalist instrumentalization of the supposed uniqueness of Russian culture and orthodoxy. This novel is parenthetically cited in text by page number.

59. Pevear, introduction to *The Idiot*, x.

60. Charles Lock, "Carnival and Incarnation: Bakhtin and Orthodox Theology," in *Critical Essays on Mikhail Bakhtin*, ed. Caryl Emerson (New York: Hall, 1999), 286.

61. In *Dostoevsky: Language, Faith, and Fiction* (2011), Rowan Williams rearticulated a Bakhtinian reading of Dostoevsky from a specifically religious point of view. In this way Williams brought out the latently religious character of Bakhtin's approach to Dostoevsky.

62. Mikhail Bakhtin, *Problems of Dostoevsky's Poetics*, ed. and trans. Caryl Emerson (Minneapolis: University of Minnesota Press, 1984), 58.

63. Ibid., 64–65.

64. Ibid., 62.

65. See Joseph Frank, *Dostoevsky: A Writer in His Time* (Princeton, N.J.: Princeton University Press, 2010).

66. Dostoevsky, *Brothers Karamazov*, 60.

67. Joseph Frank, *The Idea of Spatial Form* (New Brunswick, N.J.: Rutgers University Press, 1991), 10.

68. Konrad Onasch, "Der Kirchenraum als 'sakrale Schaubühne,'" in *Die Ikonenmalerei: Grundzüge einer systematischen Darstellung* (Leipzig: Koehler Amelang, 1968), 34–35.

69. Dostoevsky, *Brothers Karamazov*, 39.

70. Ibid., 42.

71. See Ruttenburg, *Dostoevsky's Democracy*.

72. See César Domínguez, Haun Saussy, and Darío Villanueva, *Introducing Comparative Literature: New Trends and Applications* (New York: Routledge, 2014): "If the novel organizes verbal reality, and film effects the same organization with visual reality, one could advance the argument that in *El Quixote* there is a deliberate verbal predetermination of the visual, not only in those elements that have to do with purely aesthetic, pictorial, or descriptive elements, but also in terms of those that are dynamic, relational, and cinematic. This verbal predetermination of the visual facilitates screenwriters' and film-makers' adaptations of Cervantes's work, but also allows us to speak of a 'pre-cinematography' in *El Quixote*" (121).

73. Fyodor Dostoevsky, *The Adolescent*, trans. Andrew R. MacAndrew (Garden City, N.Y.: Doubleday, 1971), 454–55.

74. Jonge, *Dostoevsky and the Age of Intensity*, 4.

75. Dostoevsky, *Adolescent*, 456.

76. Amtower, *Engaging Words*, 43.

77. See Abram Reitblat and Christine Thomas, "From Literary Almanacs to 'Thick Journals': The Emergence of a Readership for Russian Literature, 1820s–1840s," in *Literary Cultures and the Material Book*, ed. Simon Eliot, Andrew Nash, and Ian Willison (London: British Library, 2007), 191–205.

78. Soloviev, "Three Addresses," 11.

79. Ibid., 11–12.

80. Konrad Onasch, "Dionysios vom Areopag," in *Die Ikonenmalerei*, 18–28.

81. Onasch, "Der Kirchenraum als 'sakrale Schaubühne,'" 32–36.

82. Pavel Florenskiĭ, *Izbrannye trudy po iskusstvu* (Moscow: Izobrazitel'noe Iskusstvo, 1996), 98. Translation is mine. See Pavel Florensky, *Iconostasis*, trans. Donald Sheehan and Olga Andrejev (Crestwood, N.Y.: St. Vladimir's Seminary Press, 1996), 62.

83. Fyodor Dostoevsky, *Crime and Punishment*, trans. Richard Pevear and Larissa Volokhonsky (New York: Vintage, 1993), 103.

84. Ibid., 104.

85. Dostoevsky, *Brothers Karamazov*, 75.

86. Dostoevsky, *The Idiot*, 477.

87. Ibid., 476.

88. See Jacques Catteau, *Dostoyevsky and the Process of Literary Creation*, trans. Audrey Littlewood (Cambridge: Cambridge University Press, 1989), 23.

89. Fyodor Dostoevsky, *Letters of Fyodor Michailovitch Dostoevsky to His Family and Friends*, trans. Ethel Mayne (London: Chatto Windus, 1914), 175.

90. Bakhtin, *Problems*, 48–49.

91. Dostoevsky, *The Idiot*, 234–35.

92. A. G. Dostoyevskaya, *Vospominaniya A. G. Dostoyevskoy*, ed. L. P. Grossman (Moscow-Leningrad, 1925), 112.

93. Dostoevsky, *The Idiot*, 475–76.

94. On the social phenomenon of the performative usage of language for the sake of creating a utopia, see Alexei Yurchak, *Everything Was Forever, Until It Was No More: The Last Soviet Generation* (Princeton, N.J.: Princeton University Press, 2005).

95. Gustave Flaubert, *Bouvard et Pécuchet*, in Flaubert, *Oeuvres*, vol. 2, ed. Albert Thibaudet and René Dumesnil (Paris: Gallimard, 1952), 953. On a flood of parodistic literature of this kind, see Anne Herschberg-Pierrot, *Dictionnaire des idées reçues de Flaubert* (Lille: Presses Universitaires de Lille, 1988), 130.

96. On the origin of the word in the typographic practice of the time, see Herschberg-Pierrot, *Dictionnaire des idées reçues de Flaubert*, 22.

97. Fyodor Dostoevsky, *A Writer's Diary*, trans. and anno. Kenneth Lantz, intro. Gary Saul Morson, vol. 1 (Evanston, Ill.: Northwestern University Press, 1993–94), 648.

98. Joseph Frank, *Dostoevsky: The Seeds of Revolt, 1821–1849* (Princeton, N.J.: Princeton University Press, 1976), 184.

99. Dostoevsky, quoted in Mikhail Bakhtin, *Problems of Dostoevsky's Poetics*, trans. R. W. Rotsel (Ann Arbor, Mich.: Ardis, 1973), 80.

100. Frank, *Dostoevsky: The Seeds*, 71. Claude Bernard's *Introduction à l'étude de la médecine expérimentale* (1865) was one of the sacred texts of positivism.

101. See Fyodor Dostoevsky, "Letter to Mme. N.D. Fonvisin, March 1854," in *Letters*, 69–73. See also Ruttenberg, *Dostoevsky's Democracy*.

102. Belinksy, quoted in Joseph Frank, *Dostoevsky: The Seeds*, 194.

103. Walter Benjamin, *The Origin of German Tragic Drama*, trans. John Osborne (London: Verso, 1994), 183.

104. Dostoevsky, *The Idiot*, 225–26. Truncated quotation.

105. "National consciousness is our weak spot; it lacks more than anything else," writes Dostoevsky in his letter to Apollon Nikolayevich Maikov on October 7, 1868, in *Letters*, 152.

106. Jacques Lacan, "On the Possible Treatment of Psychosis," in *Écrits: A Selection*, trans. Alan Sheridan (New York: Norton, 1977), 217–20.

107. See such writings by Jacques Lacan as "On a Question Preliminary to Any Possible Treatment of Psychosis" and "The Signification of the Phallus" in *Écrits*, 179–225; 281–91.

108. Elisabeth Roudinesco, *Jacques Lacan*, trans. Barbara Bay (New York: Columbia University Press, 1997), 205.

109. Julia Kristeva, "Holbein's Dead Christ," in *Fragments for a History of the Human Body*, vol. 1, ed. Michel Feher (New York: Zone, 1990), 239–69.

110. Kristeva, "Holbein's Dead Christ," 261.

111. Dostoevsky, *The Idiot*, 476–77.

Chapter 5

1. Fabio Mauri, Carolyn Christov-Bakargiev, and Marcella Cossu, *Fabio Mauri: Opere e Azioni, 1954–1994* (Rome: Carte segrete, 1994), 164–66.

2. Giacomo Manzoli, "La pellicola, la telecamera, il corpo e la realtà: Su una performance bolognese di Pier Paolo Pasolini," *Cineteca Online*, February 2002. The essay may be found at http://www.pierpaolopasolini.eu.

3. Mauri, Christov-Bakargiev, and Cossu, *Fabio Mauri*, 164.

4. On Pasolini's complicated relationship to Gramsci, see Joseph Francese, "Pasolini: Between Passion and 'Ideology,'" in *Pier Paolo Pasolini: In Living Memory*, ed. Ben Lawton and Maura Bergonzoni (Washington, D.C.: New Academia, 2009), 21–32.

5. Oswald Stack and Pier Paolo Pasolini, *Pasolini on Pasolini: Interviews with Oswald Stack* (London: Thames and Hudson, 1969), 78.

6. Mauri, Christov-Bakargiev, and Cossu, *Fabio Mauri*, 164.

7. See the discussion of this performance in Marco F. Senaldi, "The Director Who Became the Screen: Fabio Mauri, Pier Paolo Pasolini, and *Intellettuale*," in *Cinéma, critique des images*, ed. Claudia d'Alonzo and Ken Slock (Pasian di Prato: Campanotto Editore, 2012), 269–74.

8. Russell Williams, "Pasolini's Ideology in His Cultural Essays of the Fifties," *The Italianist* 5 (1985): 39–40; Michael Caesar, "Outside the Palace: Pasolini's Journalism (1973–75)," *The Italianist* 5 (1985): 60–61.

9. Badiou, *Saint Paul*, 17.

10. Teresa De Lauretis, "Language, Representation, Practice: Re-reading Pasolini's Essays on Cinema," *Italian Quarterly* 1 (1980): 159–66; Teresa De Lauretis, *Alice Doesn't: Feminism, Semiotics and Cinema* (London: Macmillan, 1984), 40–53.

11. Quoted in Nico Naldini, introduction to Pier Paolo Pasolini, *The Letters of Pier Paolo Pasolini: 1940–1954*, vol. 1, ed. Nico Naldini (London: Quartet Books, 1992), 7.

12. Badiou, *Saint Paul*, 72.

13. See Steinberg, *The Sexuality of Christ*.

14. Lacan, "On the Possible Treatment of Psychosis," 198.

15. Lacan, "The Signification of the Phallus," 288.

16. Lacan, "On the Possible Treatment of Psychosis," 217. On Lacan's claim that his teaching possessed a religious dimension, see Elisabeth Roudinesco, *Jacques Lacan*, trans. Barbara Bay (New York: Columbia University Press, 1997), 205.

17. Badiou, *Saint Paul*, 73.

18. Pier Paolo Pasolini, "To Carlo Betocchi, November 17, 1954," in *The Letters*, 499.

19. Badiou, *Saint Paul*, 89–90.

20. Ibid., 90.

21. For a theoretical elaboration of this concept, see Leo Bersani, *The Culture of Redemption* (Cambridge, Mass.: Harvard University Press, 1990), 7–126.

22. Pier Paolo Pasolini, "Teorema," *Cineforum* 9 (May 1969): 85.

23. Theodor W. Adorno, "Cultural Criticism and Society," in *Prisms*, trans. Samuel Weber and Shierry Weber (Cambridge, Mass.: MIT Press, 1981), 19–34.

24. Enzo Siciliano, *Pasolini: A Biography*, trans. John Shepley (New York: Random House, 1982), 57. Further references to this document will be given parenthetically in the text.

25. Pasolini, quoted in Siciliano, *Pasolini*, 74.

26. See Bill Nichols, introduction to Pier Paolo Pasolini, "The Cinema of Poetry," in *Movies and Methods: An Anthology*, ed. Bill Nichols (Berkeley: University of California Press, 1976), 542–43.

27. Alexandre Astruc, "The Birth of a New Avant-Garde: Le Caméra-Stylo," in *The New Wave: Critical Landmarks Selected by Peter Graham,* by Peter Graham (Garden City, N.Y.: Doubleday, 1968), 17–23.

28. Pasolini, "Cinema of Poetry," 544.

29. See William C. Stokoe, *Sign Language Structure: An Outline of the Visual Communication Systems of the American Deaf* (Buffalo, N.Y.: Department of Anthropology and Linguistics, University of Buffalo, 1960).

30. Ibid., 10.

31. Pier Paolo Pasolini, *Pasolini rilegge Pasolini: Intervista con Giuseppe Cardillo,* ed. Luigi Fontanella (Milan: Archinto, 2005), 50.

32. Giuliana Bruno, "The Body of Pasolini's Semiotics: A Sequel Twenty Years Later," in *Pier Paolo Pasolini: Contemporary Perspectives,* ed. Patrick Rumble and Bart Testa (Toronto: University of Toronto Press, 1994), 93.

33. For an exhaustive study of the history and theory of sign language and its notation systems, especially in the German context, see Ulrike Bergermann, *Ein Bild von einer Sprache: Konzepte von Bild und Schrift und das Hamburger Notationssystem für Gebärdensprachen* (Munich: Fink, 2001).

34. Humphrey-Dirksen L. Bauman, "Toward a Poetics of Vision, Space, and the Body: Sign Language and Literary Theory," in *The Disability Studies Reader,* ed. Lennard J. Davis (New York: Routledge, 1997), 317.

35. Pasolini, "Cinema of Poetry," 544. Emphasis added.

36. Gilles Deleuze, *Cinema 1: The Movement-Image,* trans. Hugh Tomlinson and Barbara Habberjam (Minneapolis: University of Minnesota Press, 1997), 73.

37. Pasolini, "Cinema of Poetry," 545.

38. Haun Saussy, "So Natural, It's Automatic: Humanistic Studies and Culture Machines," *Southern African Journal of Folklore Studies* 15 (2005): 5–12.

39. Stokoe, *Sign Language Structure,* 7.

40. Bauman, "Toward a Poetics of Vision," 317.

41. Oskar Schlemmer, *The Letters and Diaries of Oskar Schlemmer,* ed. Tut Schlemmer, trans. Krishna Winston (Middletown, Conn.: Wesleyan University Press, 1972), 50.

42. Lea Vergine, *Body Art and Performance: The Body as Language* (Milan: Skira, 2000), 8.

43. Ibid., 110–13.

44. Noa Steimatsky, "Pasolini on Terra Sancta: Towards a Theology of Film," *Yale Journal of Criticism* 11, no. 1 (1998): 247.

45. Robert J. Miller, ed., *The Complete Gospels: Annotated Scholars Version* (Sonoma, Calif.: Polebridge, 1994), 60.

46. Miller, *Complete Gospels,* 60.

47. Béla Balázs, *Theory of the Film: Character and Growth of a New Art* (London: Dobson, 1952), 54–55.

48. Stokoe, *Sign Language Structure,* 10.

49. Bauman, "Toward a Poetics of Vision," 322.

50. Ibid., 323.

51. Maurice Merleau-Ponty, *Phenomenology of Perception,* trans. Colin Smith (London and New York: Routledge and Paul; Humanities Press, 1962), 72.

52. Mauri, Christov-Bakargiev, and Cossu, *Fabio Mauri,* 312.

53. Fabio Mauri, "The Gospel by/about Pasolini," in *Pier Paolo Pasolini: A Future Life* (Italy: Associazione "Fondo Pier Paolo Pasolini," 1988), 268.

54. Vergine, *Body Art and Performance*, 9.

55. Ibid., 7.

56. See Marquis de Sade, *The 120 Days of Sodom & Other Writings*, comp. and trans. Austryn Wainhouse and Richard Seaver (New York: Grove, 1987), 191–241.

57. Richard Balzer, *Peepshows: A Visual History* (New York: Abrams, 1998), 10–43.

58. Ibid., 20.

59. Simone de Beauvoir, "Must We Burn Sade?" trans. Annette Michelson, in *The Marquis de Sade: An Essay by Simone de Beauvoir; with Selections from His Writings*, comp. and trans. Paul Dinnage (New York: Grove, 1953), 12. Further references to this document will be given parenthetically in the text.

60. Comte de Lautréamont, *Maldoror & the Complete Works of the Comte de Lautréamont*, trans. Alexis Lykiard (Cambridge, Mass.: Exact Change, 1994), 112.

61. Pier Paolo Pasolini, *Salò, or 120 Days of Sodom*, VHS, MGM Distribution Company, 1998.

62. Bersani, *Culture of Redemption*, 1.

63. David Wood, *Body Probe: Mutating Physical Boundaries* (London: Creation, 1999), 98–99.

64. See Abel Ferrara, *Pasolini* (2014), film.

65. Steimatsky, "Pasolini on *Terra Sancta*," 239–40.

66. "Dante and Virgil in Front of Lucifer," Dante, *Divine Comedy*, MS. Holkham misc. 48, p. 53, Bodleian Library, Oxford University. This and other illuminations may be found at http://www.bodley.ox.ac.uk/.

67. Vergine, *Body Art and Performance*, 153–54.

68. Henri Hubert and Marcel Mauss, *Sacrifice: Its Nature and Function*, trans. W. D. Halls (Chicago: University of Chicago Press, 1964), 9.

69. John Freccero, *Dante: The Poetics of Conversion* (Cambridge, Mass.: Harvard University Press, 1986), 168.

70. Ibid., 169.

71. Ibid.

72. Fabio Mauri, "*Intellettuale*," in *Pier Paolo Pasolini: Una vita futura: La forma dello sguardo, Roma, 15 Ottobre—15 Dicembre 1985* (Rome: Graf Roma, 1985), 34.

73. Dante, *The Divine Comedy of Dante Alighieri: Hell, Purgatory, Paradise*, trans. Henry F. Cary (New York: Collier, 1909), 146.

74. Pier Paolo Pasolini, "The Unpopular Cinema," in *Heretical Empiricism*, ed. Louise K. Barnett, trans. Ben Lawton and Louise K. Barnett (Bloomington: Indiana University Press, 1988), 274–75.

75. Bersani, *Culture of Redemption*, 1–2.

76. Hans Magnus Enzensberger, "Constituents of a Theory of the Media," in Hans Magnus Enzensberger, *The Consciousness Industry: On Literature, Politics and the Media*, selected by Michael Roloff (New York: Seabury, 1974), 97.

77. Enzensberger, "Constituents of a Theory of the Media," 110.

78. Antonio Gramsci, "The Intellectuals," in *Selections from the Prison Note-books*, ed. and trans. Quintin Hoare and Geoffrey Nowell-Smith (New York: International, 1972), 9.

79. Ibid.

80. Ibid.

81. Pier Paolo Pasolini, *Theorem*, trans. Stuart Hood (London: Quartet Books, 1992), 175–76.

82. Ibid., 175.

83. Stack and Pasolini, *Pasolini on Pasolini*, 157.

84. Bersani, *Culture of Redemption*, 1.

85. Stack and Pasolini, *Pasolini on Pasolini*, 79.

86. See Eric Santner, *Stranded Objects: Mourning, Memory, and Film in Postwar Germany* (Ithaca, N.Y.: Cornell University Press, 1990), 1–57.

Chapter 6

1. Jacob Heilbrunn, "Neocon v. Theocon," *The New Republic*, December 30, 1996, 20–21.

2. The appeal, *Washington v. Glucksberg*, was granted *certiorari* by the Supreme Court and Reinhardt's decision was overturned in June 1997.

3. Editorial, "The Ninth Circuit's Fatal Overreach," *First Things*, May 1996, 12–13.

4. Removal of life-sustaining support from patients in a vegetative condition and the acceptance of treatment refusal were already commonly practiced in the United States. Such practices differed from the physician-assisted suicide discussed in *Compassion in Dying* only in minor technical respects. See *Compassion in Dying v. Washington*, 850 F. Supp. 1454 (W.D. Wash. 1994), affirmed en banc, 79 F.3d 790, 817–24 (9th Cir. 1996).

5. *Compassion in Dying*, 79 F.3d at 839 (9th Cir. 1996) (paragraphing modified).

6. Richard John Neuhaus, *The Naked Public Square: Religion and Democracy in America* (Grand Rapids, Mich.: Eerdmans, 1984), 133. Further references to this document will be given parenthetically in the text.

7. "The End of Democracy? The Judicial Usurpation of Politics," *First Things*, November 1996, 18–42. Further references to this document will be given parenthetically in the text.

8. Alexis de Tocqueville, *Democracy in America and Two Essays on America*, trans. Gerald E. Bevan (London: Penguin Books, 2003), 342.

9. On the reality of this threat at the time, see Jeremy Scahill, *Blackwater: The Rise of the World's Most Powerful Mercenary Army* (New York: Nation Books, 2008), 80–88.

10. Germain Grisez, *Christian Moral Principles*, vol. 1 of *The Way of the Lord Jesus* (Chicago: Franciscan Herald, 1983), 10.

11. Germain Grisez, *Living a Christian Life*, vol. 2 of *The Way of the Lord Jesus* (Quincy, Ill.: Franciscan Herald, 1993), 884.

12. Sara Dubow, *Ourselves Unborn* (Oxford: Oxford University Press, 2011), 2.

13. Grisez, *Living a Christian Life*, 885.

14. *Compassion in Dying*, 79 F.3d at 805; quoting *Planned Parenthood v. Casey*, 505 U.S. 833, 852 (1992) (emphasis by Reinhardt).

15. Grisez, *Christian Moral Principles*, 12.

16. Ibid. As an instance, consider Grisez's participation in removing Charles Curran from his tenured position as a theology professor at the Catholic University of America for his approval of contraception.

17. Grisez, *Christian Moral Principles*, 25.

18. Antonin Scalia, quoted in "End of Democracy?" *First Things*, November 1996, 20.

19. Grisez, *Christian Moral Principles*, 26.

20. See Robert P. George, ed., *Natural Law and Moral Inquiry: Ethics, Metaphysics and Politics in the Work of Germain Grisez* (Washington, D.C.: Georgetown University Press, 1998).

21. John Paul II, *Evangelium Vitae*, quoted in "The End of Democracy?" 39.

22. Grisez, *Christian Moral Principles*, 27.

23. See the follow-up to the symposium "The End of Democracy? A Discussion Continued," *First Things*, January 1997, 19–24.

24. See Heilbrunn, "Neocon v. Theocon," 20–24; Linker, *The Theocons*, 102–10.

25. Grisez, *Christian Moral Principles*, 25.

26. Gertrude Himmelfarb, "Correspondence," *First Things*, January 1997, 2.

27. On the early history of politically engaged fundamentalism in the 1950s and 1960s represented by the right-wing propagandist preacher Carl McIntire and his fight against the FCC's Fairness Doctrine, see Heather Hendershot, "God's Angriest Man: Carl McIntire, Cold War Fundamentalism, and Right-Wing Broadcasting," *American Quarterly* 59, no. 2 (2007): 373–96.

28. John Herbers, "Political and Religious Shifts Rekindle Church-State Issue," review of *The Naked Public Square* by Richard John Neuhaus, *The New York Times*, September 2, 1984, 1.

29. Neuhaus, *The Naked Public Square*, 42. All further references to this source will be given parenthetically in the text.

30. J. M. Cameron, "Meeting the Lord in the Air," review of *The Naked Public Square* by Richard John Neuhaus, *The New York Review of Books*, October 11, 1984, 40.

31. These words were allegedly Michigan Senator Arthur Vandenberg's advice to President Truman at a secret meeting in the White House on February 27, 1947, regarding rhetorical strategies for inaugurating the Cold War policy of containment toward the Soviet Union (the Truman Doctrine) on the outbreak of the Greek Civil War. See Arnold A. Offner, *Another Such Victory: President Truman and the Cold War, 1945–1953* (Stanford, Calif.: Stanford University Press, 2002), 198–99.

32. In the mid-1970s the American Enterprise Institute initiated a debate on "mediating structures" as a part of its initiative to combat New Deal policies and to break up "big government" and "the welfare state." See Peter L. Berger and Richard John Neuhaus, *To Empower People: The Role of Mediating Structures in Public Policy* (Washington, D.C.: American Enterprise Institute, 1977); and Michael Novak, ed., *Democracy and Mediating Structures: A Theological Inquiry* (Washington, D.C.: American Enterprise Institute, 1980).

33. Paul Tillich, *Systematic Theology* (Chicago: University of Chicago Press, 1967), 3:249–50.

34. Ibid.

35. Ibid., 1:149.

36. Neuhaus went on to elaborate on this proposition in his next book, *The Catholic Moment: The Paradox of the Church in the Postmodern World* (San Francisco: Harper and Row, 1987). In 1990 he converted to Catholicism and a year later was ordained a Catholic priest.

37. On the divine monarchies of Russia, Germany, and China see, for example, Reinhard Bendix, *Kings or People: Power and the Mandate to Rule* (Berkeley: University of California Press, 1978).

38. In "Political and Religious Shifts," Herbers reported that Neuhaus's book "has within a few weeks become a rallying point for those who agree with Mr. Reagan" (20).

39. Neuhaus complained that "in all our institutions, including churches, there is pervasive confusion about what is meant by references such as 'liberal democracy,' 'pluralism,' and 'freedom' " (*The Naked Public Square*, 9). For his redefinition of these concepts on Christian premises, including the meaning of the Establishment Clause of the First Amendment, see *The Naked Public Square*, 9–19, 78–93, 144–55.

40. Harvey Cox, "Putting God Back in Politics," review of *The Naked Public Square* by Richard John Neuhaus, *The New York Times Book Review,* August 26, 1984, 11.

41. Ibid.

42. Michel Foucault, "What Are the Iranians Dreaming About?" in *Foucault and the Iranian Revolution: Gender and the Seductions of Islamism,* by Janet Afary and Kevin B. Anderson (Chicago: University of Chicago Press, 2005), 203–9.

43. Ibid.

44. Slavoj Žižek, "Formal Democracy and Its Discontents: Violations of the Fantasy-Space," *American Imago* 48, no. 2 (1991): 191.

45. *Compassion in Dying*, 79 F.3d at 813 (1996).

46. On the occasion of the book's twenty-fifth anniversary, a number of Neuhaus's partisans reaffirmed their adherence to his views in *The Naked Public Square Reconsidered: Religion and Politics in the Twenty-First Century*, ed. Christopher Wolfe (Wilmington, Del.: ISI Books, 2009).

47. For representative, generally positive reviews, see Michael Scully, "Finding a Place for Religion in Public Life," *Wall Street Journal*, July 30, 1984, 14; Cox, "Putting God Back in Politics"; Cameron, "Meeting the Lord in the Air."

48. See Linker's discussion of Novak's ideological career in *The Theocons*, 34–41.

49. Richard J. Barnet, *The Crisis of the Corporation* (New York: AMACOM, 1975), 8.

50. Michael Novak, "Changing the Paradigms: The Cultural Deficiencies of Capitalism," in *Democracy and Mediating Structures: A Theological Inquiry*, ed. Michael Novak (Washington, D.C.: American Enterprise Institute, 1980), 181–82.

51. Linker, *The Theocons*, 38.

52. Irving Kristol, *Two Cheers for Capitalism* (New York: Basic Books, 1978), x.

53. Michael Novak, *The Spirit of Democratic Capitalism* (New York: American Enterprise Institute/Simon and Schuster, 1982), 335. Emphasis in original.

54. Novak, "A Theology of the Corporation," in *The Corporation: A Theological Inquiry*, ed. Michael Novak and John W. Cooper (Washington, D.C.: American Enterprise Institute, 1981), 199.

55. See Novak, *The Spirit of Democratic Capitalism*, 337–58; or Novak, "A Theology of the Corporation," 207–13.

56. Novak, *The Spirit of Democratic Capitalism*, 337, 339.

57. Novak, "A Theology of the Corporation," 219.

58. Novak, *The Spirit of Democratic Capitalism*, 343. Further references to this source will be given parenthetically in the text.

59. See Bernard Murchland, "The Socialist Critique of the Corporation," in Novak, *The Corporation: A Theological Inquiry*, 169, 172–73. Further references to the latter source will be given parenthetically in the text.

60. See Marjorie Kelly, *The Divine Right of Capital: Dethroning the Corporate Aristocracy* (San Francisco: Berrett-Koehler, 2001), 21. Further references to this source will be given parenthetically in the text.

61. Ernst H. Kantorowicz, *The King's Two Bodies: A Study in Mediaeval Political Theology* (Princeton, N.J.: Princeton University Press, 1957), 5.

62. Karl Popper, *The Spell of Plato*, vol. 1 of *The Open Society and Its Enemies* (London: Routledge and Kegan Paul, 1949), 74–75.

63. Michael Novak, *The Future of the Corporation* (Washington, D.C.: American Enterprise Institute, 1996), 5–6.

64. For a genealogy of this legal development, see Glenn Greenwald, *With Liberty and Justice for Some: How the Law Is Used to Destroy Equality and Protect the Powerful* (New York: Holt, 2011).

65. See the discussion of these issues in the dissenting opinion of Justice Stevens and concurring dissenting justices in *Citizens United*, 130 S.Ct. 876, 948–952 (2010).

66. *Citizens United*, 130 S.Ct. at 949. See also the discussion of the early American corporate law subordinating the design of corporations to the purpose of the public good and its erosion in betrayal of the founding principles in Kelly, *The Divine Right of Capital*, 129-132.

67. See Teachout about the framers' "obsession with foreign influence derived from a fear that foreign powers and individuals had no basic investment in the well-being of the country" in "The Anti-Corruption Principle," 94 *Cornell Law Review* 341, 393, n. 245 (2009), cited in *Citizens United*, 130 S.Ct. at 948.

68. John Kenneth Galbraith, from an address delivered in Toronto, December 29, 1972, and published in *American Economic Review*, March 1973. Quoted in Barnet, *The Crisis of the Corporation*, 6.

69. Neuhaus, *The Naked Public Square*, 117.

70. Novak, *The Future of the Corporation*, 26.

71. Ibid., 7–8.

72. "Bush Quietly Meets with Amish Here," *Lancaster New Era*, July 16, 2004.

73. Linker, *The Theocons*, 179.

74. For a detailed discussion of theoconservative legislation concerning the body politic under the Bush administration, see Linker, *The Theocons*, 147–75.

The Bush administration's service to corporate interests was explored in detail by Robert Scheer, John Nichols, Ari Berman, and other investigative journalists writing for *The Nation* between 2000 and 2008. For a meticulous exploration of the alliance among the Christian and economic interest groups, see Kevin Phillips, *American Theocracy: The Peril and Politics of Radical Religion, Oil, and Borrowed Money in the 21st Century* (New York: Penguin Books, 2007), 171–262.

75. On the political and legal genealogy of the theory of the "unitary executive," see Jess Bravin, *The Terror Courts: Rough Justice at Guantanamo Bay* (New Haven, Conn.: Yale University Press, 2013), 21–35.

76. Ibid., 31.

77. David S. Domke, *God Willing? Political Fundamentalism in the White House* (2004), quoted in Phillips, *American Theocracy*, 207.

78. The work of the National Energy Policy Development Group, established by Bush in his second week in office and chaired by Vice-President Dick Cheney, has remained inaccessible to public scrutiny. The report produced by this group, "National Energy Policy," is regarded as the foundation for controversial U.S. military actions in foreign countries, including the invasion of Iraq. See the discussion of the report in Michael Klare, "Bush-Cheney Energy Strategy: Procuring the Rest of the World's Oil," *Foreign Policy in Focus* (January 2004), at www.commondreams.org. See also John Nichols, *Dick: The Man Who Is President* (New York: New, 2004).

79. For example, the evangelical missionary organization Christian Freedom International, founded and run by veterans of the Reagan administration, passionately supported Bush's war on terror. See Scahill, *Blackwater*, 213; and Phillips, *American Theocracy*, 258–62.

80. Phillips, *American Theocracy*, 260.

81. Scahill, *Blackwater*, 133. The company was renamed as XE Services in 2009 and as Academi in 2011.

82. Ibid., 376.

83. Quoted in Linker, *The Theocons*, 115.

84. See *Does v. Enfield Public Schools*, 716 F.Supp.2d 172 (D.Conn. 2010).

85. See *Does v. Enfield Public Schools*, "Complaint," 11, may be found at http://www.acluct.org.

86. Phillips, *American Theocracy*, 132.

87. Quoted in *Does v. Enfield Public Schools*, "Complaint," 15.

88. *Does v. Enfield Public Schools*, 716 F.Supp.2d at 193–194, and "Complaint," 15.

89. "Complaint," 16.

90. "Complaint," 11.

91. *Does v. Enfield Public Schools*, 716 F.Supp.2d at 197–198.

92. Mark Galli, "The Lord Who Acts Like It," *Christianity Today*, December 12, 2011, 2.

93. *Does v. Enfield Public Schools*, "Plaintiffs-Appellees' Opposition to Emergency Motion for Expedited Appeal and for Stay of Injunction Pending Appeal," 21.

94. See "Plaintiffs-Appellees' Opposition," 21–23.

95. *W. Va. State Board of Education v. Barnette*, 319 U.S. 624, 632 (1943), quoted in "Plaintiffs-Appellees' Opposition," 24.

96. "Complaint," 3.

97. Herbers, "Political and Religious Shifts," 20.

98. Quoting Reinhardt in *Compassion in Dying*; see above, note 5.

99. Michael Novak, "Passion Play," *The Weekly Standard*, August 25, 2003, 31–34.

100. Richard John Neuhaus, "The Passion of Christ," *First Things*, February 2004, 62.

101. Russell Hittinger and Elizabeth Lev, "Gibson's Passion," *First Things*, March 2004, 7.

102. Ibid.

103. "Report of the Ad Hoc Scholars Group: Reviewing the Script of *The Passion*," in *Perspectives on "The Passion of the Christ": Religious Thinkers and Writers Explore the Issues Raised by the Controversial Movie,* ed. Jonathan Burnham (New York: Miramax Books, 2004), 233.

104. On the Catholic traditionalism reflected in the film and Gibson's own involvement with the neoconservative and traditionalist program, see Mary C. Boys, "Seeing Different Movies, Talking Past Each Other," in *Perspectives on "The Passion of the Christ,"* 147–63.

105. "Evangelicals and Catholics Together: The Christian Mission in the Third Millennium," *First Things*, May 1994, 15–22. Further references to this document are given parenthetically in the text.

106. Anita Chabria, "'Passion' Campaign Aims to Overcome Christian Rifts," *PRWeek* 8, March 2004, may be found at http://www.alarryross.com.

107. Ken Kusmer, "Faithful Get Sneak Peek at 'Passion,'" Associated Press, February 20, 2004, may be found at http://www.alarryross.com.

108. The other firms are listed in Jane Sumner, "Gibson Set Stage for 'Passion' with Controlled Marketing: The Greatest Story Ever Sold?" *The Dallas Morning News*, February 17, 2004, may be found at http://www.alarryross.com.

109. A. Larry Ross Communications, http://www.alarryross.com. See Ann Vargas, "When Your Client Is God," *PRWeek*, March 13, 2000, may be found at http://www.alarryross.com.

110. Quoted in Deborah Caldwell, "Selling Passion," in *Perspectives on "The Passion of the Christ,"* 212.

111. Gibson, quoted in Caldwell, "Selling Passion," 216.

112. Compare the French semiotician Roland Barthes's discussion of Graham's prosody and rhetoric, likening him to a salesman, in "Billy Graham au Vel' d'Hiv'," in *Mythologies* (Paris: Éditions du Seuil, 1957), 99–102.

113. A. Larry Ross, "Mel Gibson, We Thought We Knew Ye," *Religious News Service* 2004, may be found at http://www.alarryross.com.

114. Kusmer, "Faithful Get Sneak Peek at 'Passion.'"

115. The film made $126.2 million the first weekend in over 3,000 theaters on the first weekend and became the year's highest-grossing film worldwide, earning over $608 million.

116. A. Larry Ross, "Passionate Encounter: At the Intersection of Faith and Culture," *National Review Online*, March 10, 2004, may be found at http://www.nationalreview.com. Compare Ross's calculation with Slavoj Žižek's discussion of the film's failure to convey "any authentic Christian experience" and thereby paying the "dialectical price" of relapsing into the paradigm of Hollywood

entertainment. See Žižek, *The Parallax View* (Cambridge, Mass.: MIT Press, 2006), 357–59.

117. See A. Larry Ross, "The World's Greatest Communicator: Beyond Information and Education to Transformation," at http://www.alarryross.com.

118. See, for example, Caldwell, "Selling Passion," 220. See also Phillips on the political mobilization of the churches for Bush's 2004 reelection campaign in *American Theocracy*, 211.

119. Ross, "Mel Gibson, We Thought We Knew Ye."

120. Quoted in Sumner, "Gibson Set Stage for 'Passion' with Controlled Marketing."

121. See Gibson's widely reported claims that the Holy Ghost worked through him, whereas he was "just conducting traffic." See Caldwell, "Selling Passion," 216.

122. Ron Magid, "Adding Agony to the Passion," *American Cinematographer* 85, no. 3 (2004): 57. See also Stephen Prince, "Beholding Blood Sacrifice in *The Passion of the Christ*: How Real Is Movie Violence?" *Film Quarterly* 56, no. 4 (2006): 11–22.

123. Gibson, quoted in Alison Griffiths, "The Revered Gaze: The Medieval Imagery in Mel Gibson's *The Passion of the Christ*," *Cinema Journal* 46, no. 2 (2007): 23.

124. See Sergei Eisenstein, "About Stereoscopic Cinema," in *The Penguin Film Review 1946–1949*, vol. 2 (Totowa, N.J.: Rowman and Littlefield, 1978), 35–45. Here, 38, 39. Further references are given parenthetically in the text.

125. See Oliver Grau's discussion of Eisenstein's essay in *Virtual Art: From Illusion to Immersion*, trans. Gloria Custance (Cambridge, Mass.: MIT Press, 2003), 153–55.

126. Griffiths, "The Revered Gaze," 11. See also Caldwell, "Selling Passion," 221.

127. Neuhaus, *The Naked Public Square*, 132.

128. Quoted in Ron Suskind, "Faith, Certainty and the Presidency of George W. Bush," *The New York Times Magazine*, October 17, 2004, may be found at http://www.nytimes.com.

129. Peggy Noonan, "It Is as It Was: Mel Gibson's 'The Passion' Gets a Thumbs-Up from the Pope," *The Wall Street Journal*, December 17, 2003, may be found at http://online.wsj.com. This statement was allegedly soon retracted by Vatican officials.

130. "Report of the Ad Hoc Scholars Group," in *Perspectives on "The Passion of the Christ*," 235.

131. Ibid., 233.

132. James Martin, "The Last Station: A Catholic Reflection on *The Passion*," in *Perspectives on "The Passion of the Christ*," 108.

133. Novak, "A Theology of the Corporation," 203.

134. See Susan Thistlethwaite, "Mel Makes a War Movie," in *Perspectives on "The Passion of the Christ*," 127–45.

135. Jim Wallis, "*The Passion* and the Message," in *Perspectives on "The Passion of the Christ*," 123–24.

136. Paula Fredriksen, "Gospel Truths: Hollywood, History, and Christianity," in *Perspectives on "The Passion of the Christ*," 47.

137. Jon Meacham, "Who Really Killed Jesus?" in *Perspectives on "The Passion of the Christ,"* 13.

138. L. Paul Bremer, "What Now? Crush Them; Let Us Wage Total War on Our Foes," *Wall Street Journal*, September 13, 2001.

139. Jean Baudrillard, "The Gulf War Did Not Take Place," in *Selected Writings*, ed. and intro. Mark Poster (Stanford, Calif.: Stanford University Press, 2001), 231.

140. On Quintana's parody of Jesus, see J. M. Tyree and Ben Walters, *The Big Lebowski* (London: British Film Institute, 2007), 80. On the Coens' pop-cultural treatment of violence, war, and heroism at the time of the Gulf War, see Todd A. Comer, "'This Aggression Will Not Stand': Myth, War, and Ethics in *The Big Lebowski*," *SubStance* 34, no. 2 (2005): 98–117.

141. Gibson's filmic response to this call was not unique. Even such a secular cinematic chronicler of American presidential history as Oliver Stone relied on the same logic of contemplating the injury as a call for revenge in his three-hour-long film *The World Trade Center* (2006).

142. One of the historical predecessors among such national identifications with Christ is Germany of the 1920s and 1930s. See the exploration of this topic in Susannah Heschel's *Aryan Jesus: Christian Theologians and the Bible in Nazi Germany* (Princeton, N.J.: Princeton University Press, 2008).

143. Quoted in Linker, *The Theocons*, xii. On the theoconservative exploitation of the Catholic concept of "just war," see Linker, *The Theocons*, 128–46.

144. On the practice of "dog-whistling," see David D. Kirkpatrick, "Speaking in the Tongue of Evangelicals," *The New York Times*, October 17, 2004. On the religious rhetoric of Bush after 9/11, see Phillips, *American Theocracy*, 204–8.

145. See, for example, Alissa J. Rubin, "Photos Stoke Tension over the Afghan Civilian Deaths," *The New York Times*, March 1, 2011, at http://www.nytimes.com. Unlike the Abu Ghraib photographs, the bulk of the *Spiegel* photographs of the atrocities performed by the American soldiers in Afghanistan were found too graphic to be published.

146. Quoted in Thomas B. Payne, "Philip the Chancellor and the Conductus Prosula: 'Motetish' Works from the School of Notre-Dame," in *Music in Medieval Europe: Studies in Honour of Bryan Gillingham*, ed. Terence Bailey and Alma Santosuosso (Aldershot, Eng.: Ashgate, 2007), 220–38.

147. Michael Moriarty, "Mel Gibson's Reply to 9/11," *Free Republic*, March 9, 2004, at http://www.freerepublic.com. Moriarty was not alone. A viewer from North Carolina reportedly compared watching the film to viewing television news footage of the burning Twin Towers of the World Trade Center, whereas the critic Jack Miles described Gibson's Satan as "a gray-faced, hollow-eyed terrorist . . . the most insinuatingly sinister Satan ever seen on screen." Quoted in Griffiths, "The Revered Gaze," 25–26, 33.

148. Baudrillard, "The Gulf War," 241, 233.

149. Boys, "Seeing Different Movies," 153.

150. This well-documented development seems to have escaped Douglas V. Porpora, Alexander G. Nikolaev, Julia Hagemann May, and Alexander Jenkins, coauthors of *Post-Ethical Society: The Iraq War, Abu Ghraib, and the Moral Failure of the Secular* (Chicago: University of Chicago Press, 2013).

151. See the detailed discussion of the Abu Ghraib imagery in W. J. T. Mitchell, *Cloning Terror: The War of Images, 9/11 to the Present* (Chicago: University of Chicago Press, 2011), 113–27 and 137–59. The visual revelations were soon complemented by audio recordings which on August 4, 2004, captured contractors of Erik Prince's Christian army massacring the civilians in Najaf while screaming "Fuckin' niggers!" (see Scahill, *Blackwater*, 189).

152. David Garland, *Peculiar Institution: America's Death Penalty in an Age of Abolition* (Cambridge, Mass.: Harvard University Press, 2010), 20. Further references will be given parenthetically in the text.

153. Quoted in Garland, *Peculiar Institution*, 252.

154. See the review by Richard N. Ostling, "Another Jesus Film Raises the Jewish Issue," Associated Press, September 4, 2003, may be found at http://www .beliefnet.com.

155. See Ross, "Passionate Encounter."

156. Žižek, "Formal Democracy and Its Discontents."

157. James Inhofe, response to "Allegations of Mistreatment of Iraqi Prisoners," May 11, 2004, in *United States Senate Committee on Armed Services, Review of Department of Defense Detention and Interrogation Operations* (Washington, D.C.: U.S. Government Printing Office, 2005), 297, 331.

158. *Engel v. Vitale*, 370 U.S. 421, 431–32 (1962), paragraphing modified.

159. Novak, "Passion Play," 3, may be found at http://www.weeklystandard .com.

160. Neuhaus, "The Passion of Christ," 62.

161. Griffiths, "The Revered Gaze," 28.

162. See Harvey Cox, *The Secular City: Secularization and Urbanization in Theological Perspective* (New York: Macmillan, 1965).

Adorno, Theodor W. "Cultural Criticism and Society." In *Prisms*, translated by Samuel Weber and Shierry Weber, 19–34. Cambridge, Mass.: MIT Press, 1981.

———. "Parataxis: On Hölderlin's Late Poetry." In *Notes to Literature*, vol. 2, edited by Rolf Tiedemann, translated by Shierry Weber Nicholsen, 109–49. New York: Columbia University Press, 1991–92.

Agamben, Giorgio. *Homo Sacer: Sovereign Power and Bare Life*. Translated by Daniel Heller-Roazen. Stanford, Calif.: Stanford University Press, 1998.

Amtower, Laurel. *Engaging Words: The Culture of Reading in the Later Middle Ages*. New York: Palgrave, 2000.

Anderson, Benedict. *Imagined Communities*. London: Verso, 1995.

Astell, Ann W. *Eating Beauty: The Eucharist and the Spiritual Arts of the Middle Ages*. Ithaca, N.Y.: Cornell University Press, 2006.

Astruc, Alexandre. "The Birth of a New Avant-Garde: Le Caméra-Stylo." In *The New Wave: Critical Landmarks*, selected by Peter Graham, 17–23. Garden City, N.Y.: Doubleday, 1968.

Auerbach, Erich. "Figura." In *Scenes from the Drama of European Literature*, 11–76. Minneapolis: University of Minnesota Press, 1984.

———. *Mimesis: The Representation of Reality in Western Literature*. Translated by Willard R. Trask. Princeton, N.J.: Princeton University Press, 1953.

———. "Philology and *Weltliteratur*." Translated by Maire Said and Edward Said. *Centennial Review* 3, no. 1 (1969): 1–17.

Austin, J. L. *How to Do Things with Words*. Edited by J. O. Urmson and Marina Sbisà. Cambridge, Mass.: Harvard University Press, 1975.

Badia, Lola. "The Arbor Scientiae: A 'New' Encyclopedia in the Thirteenth-Century Occitan-Catalan Cultural Context." In *Arbor Scientiae: Der Baum des Wissens von Ramon Lull*, edited by Fernando Domínguez Reboiras, Pere Villalba Varneda, and Peter Walter, 1–19. Turnhout: Brepols, 2002.

Badiou, Alain. *Saint Paul: The Foundation of Universalism*. Translated by Ray Brassier. Stanford, Calif.: Stanford University Press, 2003.

Bakhtin, Mikhail. *The Dialogic Imagination*. Edited by Michael Holquist, translated by Caryl Emerson and Michael Holquist. Austin: University of Texas Press, 1981.

———. *Problems of Dostoevksy's Poetics*. Translated by R. W. Rotsel. Ann Arbor, Mich.: Ardis, 1973.

Balázs, Béla. *Theory of the Film: Character and Growth of a New Art*. London: Dobson, 1952.

Balzer, Richard. *Peepshows: A Visual History*. New York: Abrams, 1998.

Barbier, Frédéric. "The German Language and Book Trade in Europe." In *Literary Cultures and the Material Book*, edited by Simon Eliot, Andrew Nash, and Ian Willison, 253–67. London: British Library, 2007.

Barnet, Richard J. *The Crisis of the Corporation*. New York: AMACOM, 1975.

Bärsch, Jürgen. "Liturgy and Reform: Northern German Convents in the Late Middle Ages." In *A Companion to Mysticism and Devotion in Northern Germany in the Late Middle Ages*, edited by Elizabeth Andersen, Henrike Lähnemann, and Anne Simon, 21–46. Leiden: Brill, 2014.

Barthes, Roland. *Mythologies*. Paris: Éditions du Seuil, 1957.

Baudrillard, Jean. *Selected Writings*. Edited and introduced by Mark Poster. Stanford, Calif.: Stanford University Press, 2001.

Bauman, Humphrey-Dirksen L. "Toward a Poetics of Vision, Space, and the Body: Sign Language and Literary Theory." In *The Disability Studies Reader*, edited by Lennard J. Davis, 315–31. New York: Routledge, 1997.

Baus, Karl. *From the Apostolic Community to Constantine*. Vol. 1 of *Handbook of Church History*. New York: Herder and Herder, 1965.

Beauvoir, Simone de. "Must We Burn Sade?" In *The Marquis de Sade: An Essay by Simone de Beauvoir, with Selections from His Writings*, compiled by Paul Dinnage, translated by Annette Michelson, 9–82. New York: Grove, 1953.

Becker, Erich. "Protest gegen den Kaiserkult und Verherrlichung des Sieges am Pons Milvius in der christlichen Kunst der konstantinischen Zeit." In *Konstantin der Große und seine Zeit: Gesammelte Studien: Festgabe Zum Konstantinsjubiläum 1913 und Zum Goldenen Priesterjubiläum von Mgr. Dr. A. De Waal*, edited by F. J. Dölger, 155–90. Freiburg: Herder'sche Verlagshandlung, 1913.

Beckwith, Sarah. *Christ's Body: Identity, Culture and Society in Late Medieval Writings*. London: Routledge, 1996.

Beiser, Frederick. *The Fate of Reason*. Cambridge, Mass.: Harvard University Press, 1993.

Bellitto, Christopher M. "The Reform Context of the Great Western Schism." In *A Companion to the Great Western Schism (1378–1417)*, edited by Joëlle Rollo-Koster and Thomas M. Izbicki, 303–32. Leiden: Brill, 2009.

Bendix, Reinhard. *Kings or People: Power and the Mandate to Rule*. Berkeley: University of California Press, 1978.

Benjamin, Walter. *The Origin of German Tragic Drama*. Translated by John Osborne. London: Verso, 1994.

Benz, Ernst. "Swedenborg und Lavater: Über die religiösen Grundlagen der Physiognomik." *Zeitschrift für Kirchengeschichte* 57 (1938): 153–216.

Berger, Peter L., and Richard John Neuhaus. *To Empower People: The Role of Mediating Structures in Public Policy*. Washington, D.C.: American Enterprise Institute, 1977.

Bergermann, Ulrike. *Ein Bild von einer Sprache: Konzepte von Bild und Schrift und das Hamburger Notationssystem für Gebärdensprachen*. Munich: Fink, 2001.

Bersani, Leo. *The Culture of Redemption*. Cambridge, Mass.: Harvard University Press, 1990.

Biegger, Katharina. *"De Invocatione Beatae Mariae Virginis": Paracelsus und die Marienverehrung*. Stuttgart: Franz Steiner, 1990.

Biernoff, Suzannah. *Sight and Embodiment in the Middle Ages.* New York: Palgrave Macmillan, 2002.

Birkhan, Helmut. "Das alchemistische Zeichen: Allgemeines zur wissenschaftlichen Axiomatik der Alchemie und Spezielles zum *Buch der Heiligen Dreifaltigkeit.*" In *The Presence,* edited by Keith Griffiths and Siegfried Zielinski, 40–53. Salzburg: Blimp, 1999.

Blumenfeld-Kosinski, Renate. "The Conceptualization and Imagery of the Great Schism." In *A Companion to the Great Western Schism (1378–1417),* edited by Joëlle Rollo-Koster and Thomas M. Izbicki, 123–58. Leiden: Brill, 2009.

Bohrer, Karl Heinz. *Plötzlichkeit: Zum Augenblick des ästhetischen Scheins.* Frankfurt am Main: Suhrkamp, 1981.

Bonnet, Charles. *The Contemplation of Nature.* London: Longman, 1766.

———. *La Palingénésie Philosophique, ou, Idées sur l'état passé et l'état futur des êtres vivants.* Geneva: Philibert & Chirol, 1770.

Borges, Jorge Luis. "Tlön, Uqbar, Orbis Tertius." In *Labyrinths: Selected Stories and Other Writings,* edited by Donald A. Yates, James East Irby, and André Maurois, 3–18. New York: New Directions, 1964.

Brashear, William. "Magical Papyri: Magic in Bookform." In *Das Buch als magisches und als Repräsentationsobjekt,* edited by Peter Ganz, 25–57. Wiesbaden: Harrassowitz, 1992.

Braun, Rudolf. *Das ausgehende Ancien Régime in der Schweiz: Aufriß einer Sozial- und Wirtschaftsgeschichte des 18. Jahrhunderts.* Göttingen: Vandenhoeck & Ruprecht, 1984.

Bremer, L. Paul. "What Now? Crush Them; Let Us Wage Total War on Our Foes." *Wall Street Journal,* September 13, 2001.

Brock, Sebastian. "Iconoclasm and the Monophysites." In *Iconoclasm, Papers Given at the Ninth Spring Symposium of Byzantine Studies, University of Birmingham, March 1975,* edited by Anthony Bryer and Judith Herrin, 53–58. Birmingham, Eng.: Center for Byzantine Studies, University of Birmingham, 1975.

Brown, Peter. *Power and Persuasion in Late Antiquity: Towards a Christian Empire.* Madison: University of Wisconsin Press, 1992.

Bruno, Giuliana. "The Body of Pasolini's Semiotics: A Sequel Twenty Years Later." In *Pier Paolo Pasolini: Contemporary Perspectives,* edited by Patrick Rumble and Bart Testa, 88–105. Toronto: University of Toronto Press, 1994.

Buch der Heiligen Dreifaltigkeit. Manuscript KdZ 78 A 11, Kupferstichkabinett. Staatliche Museen zu Berlin—Preußischer Kulturbesitz.

Burnham, Jonathan, ed. *Perspectives on "The Passion of the Christ": Religious Thinkers and Writers Explore the Issues Raised by the Controversial Movie.* New York: Miramax Books, 2004.

"Bush Quietly Meets with Amish Here." *Lancaster New Era,* July 16, 2004.

Bynum, Caroline Walker. *The Resurrection of the Body in Western Christianity, 200–1336.* New York: Columbia University Press, 1995.

Caesar, Michael. "Outside the Palace: Pasolini's Journalism (1973–75)." *The Italianist* 5 (1985): 60–61.

Cameron, J. M. "Meeting the Lord in the Air." Review of *The Naked Public Square* by Richard John Neuhaus. *The New York Review of Books,* October 11, 1984.

Camille, Michel. *Image on the Edge: The Margins of Medieval Art.* Cambridge, Mass.: Harvard University Press, 1992.

Campe, Rüdiger, and Manfred Schneider, eds. *Geschichten der Physiognomik.* Freiburg im Breisgau: Rombach, 1996.

Cary, Henry F., trans. *The Divine Comedy of Dante Alighieri: Hell, Purgatory, Paradise.* New York: Collier, 1909.

Cassedy, Steven. *Dostoevsky's Religion.* Stanford, Calif.: Stanford University Press, 2005.

Catteau, Jacques. *Dostoyevsky and the Process of Literary Creation.* Translated by Audrey Littlewood. Cambridge: Cambridge University Press, 1989.

Cerquiglini-Toulet, Jacqueline. *The Color of Melancholy: The Uses of Books in the Fourteenth Century.* Translated by Lydia G. Cochrane. Baltimore: Johns Hopkins University Press, 1997.

Chabria, Anita. "'Passion' Campaign Aims to Overcome Christian Rifts." *PRWeek*, March 8, 2004, may be found at http://www.alarryross.com.

Citizens United v. Federal Election Commission. 130 S. Ct. 876 (2010).

Clark, Elizabeth A. "New Perspectives on the Origenist Controversy: Human Embodiment and Ascetic Strategies." *Church History* 59, no. 2 (1989): 145–62.

———. *The Origenist Controversy: The Cultural Construction of an Early Christian Debate.* Princeton, N.J.: Princeton University Press, 1992.

Comer, Todd A. "'This Aggression Will Not Stand': Myth, War, and Ethics in *The Big Lebowski.*" *SubStance* 34, no. 2 (2005): 98–117.

Compassion in Dying v. Washington. 850 F. Supp. 1454 (W.D. Wash. 1994), affirmed en banc, 79 F.3d 790 (9th Cir. 1996).

Coulin Weibel, Adèle. *Two Thousands Years of Textiles: The Figured Textiles of Europe and the Near East.* New York: Pantheon Books, 1952.

Cox, Harvey. "Putting God Back in Politics." Review of *The Naked Public Square* by Richard John Neuhaus. *The New York Times Book Review*, August 26, 1984.

———. *The Secular City: Secularization and Urbanization in Theological Perspective.* New York: Macmillan, 1965.

Debray, Régis. *Cours de médiologie générale.* Paris: Gallimard, 1991.

Dechow, Jon F. *Dogma and Mysticism in Early Christianity: Epiphanius of Cyprus and the Legacy of Origen.* Macon, Ga.: Mercer University Press, 1988.

Deleuze, Gilles. *Cinema 1: The Movement-Image.* Translated by Hugh Tomlinson and Barbara Habberjam. Minneapolis: University of Minnesota Press, 1997.

Delli Colli, Tonino. "Interview with Tonino Delli Colli." DVD *Mamma Roma.*

Derrida, Jacques. *Limited Inc.* Evanston, Ill.: Northwestern University Press, 1988.

———. "Signature Event Context." In *Margins of Philosophy*, translated by Alan Bass, 307–30. Chicago: University of Chicago Press, 1982.

Does v. Enfield Public Schools. 716 F.Supp.2d 172 (D. Conn. 2010).

Dölger, Franz Joseph. *Heidnische und christliche Brotstempel mit religiösen Zeichen: Zur Geschichte des Hostienstempels.* In *Antike und Christentum: Kultur- und religionsgeschichtliche Studien*, vol. 1. Münster: Aschendorff, 1974; reprint of 1929 edition.

Domínguez, César, Haun Saussy, and Darío Villanueva. *Introducing Comparative Literature: New Trends and Applications.* New York: Routledge, 2014.

Dostoevskaia, Anna. *Dostoevsky: Reminiscences.* Edited and translated by Beatrice Stillman. New York: Liveright, 1975.

———. *Vospominaniya A. G. Dostoyevskoy.* Edited by L. P. Grossman. Moscow-Leningrad, 1925.

Dostoevsky, Fyodor. *The Adolescent.* Translated by Andrew R. MacAndrew. Garden City, N.Y.: Doubleday, 1971.

———. *The Brothers Karamazov: A Novel in Four Parts with Epilogue.* Translated and annotated by Richard Pevear and Larissa Volokhonsky. New York: Farrar, Straus and Giroux, 2002.

———. *Crime and Punishment.* Translated by Richard Pevear and Larissa Volokhonsky. New York: Vintage, 1993.

———. *The Idiot.* Translated by Richard Pevear and Larissa Volokhonsky. New York: Vintage Classics, 2003.

———. *Letters of Fyodor Michailovitch Dostoevsky to His Family and Friends.* Translated by Ethel Mayne. London: Chatto and Windus, 1914.

———. *A Writer's Diary.* Translated and annotated by Kenneth Lantz, with an introductory study by Gary Saul Morson. Vol. 1. Evanston, Ill.: Northwestern University Press, 1993–94.

Douglas, Mary. "Effects of Modernization on Religious Change." *Daedalus* 111, no. 1 (1982): 1–19.

Dubow, Sara. *Ourselves Unborn.* Oxford: Oxford University Press, 2011.

Dudden, D. D., and F. Homes. *The Life and Times of St. Ambrose.* Vol. 2. Oxford: Clarendon, 1935.

Dvornik, Francis. *Early Christian and Byzantine Political Philosophy: Origins and Background.* Vol. 2. Washington, D.C.: Dumbarton Oaks Center for Byzantine Studies, Trustees for Harvard University, 1966.

Dyson, R. W. Introduction to *The City of God Against the Pagans*, by Augustine, edited and translated by R. W. Dyson, x–xxix. Cambridge: Cambridge University Press, 1998.

Ebeling, Gerhard. "Genie des Herzens unter dem *genius saeculi*—Johann Caspar Lavater als Theologe." In *Das Antlitz Gottes im Antlitz des Menschen: Zugänge zu Johann Kaspar Lavater*, edited by Karl Pestalozzi and Horst Weigelt, 23–60. Göttingen: Vandenhoeck & Ruprecht, 1994.

Ebert, Robert Peter, Oskar Reichmann, and Klaus-Peter Wegera. *Frühneuhochdeutsche Grammatik.* Tübingen: Niemeyer, 1993.

Eisenstein, Sergei. "About Stereoscopic Cinema." In *The Penguin Film Review 1946–1949.* Vol. 2: 35–45. Totowa, N.J.: Rowman and Littlefield, 1978.

Emerson, Caryl. "The Tolstoy Connection in Bakhtin." In *Rethinking Bakhtin*, edited by Gary Saul Morson and Caryl Emerson, 149–170. Stanford, Calif.: Stanford University Press, 1989.

"The End of Democracy? A Discussion Continued." *First Things*, January 1997.

Enzensberger, Hans Magnus. "Constituents of a Theory of the Media." In *The Consciousness Industry: On Literature, Politics and the Media*, selected by Michael Roloff, translated by Stuart Hood, 95–128. New York: Seabury, 1974.

Epiphanius. *Ancoratus und Panarion haer. 1–33.* Edited by Karl Holl. Leipzig: Hinrichs, 1915.

———. "Letter from Epiphanius, Bishop of Salamis, in Cyprus, to John, Bishop of Jerusalem." Translated by W. H. Fremantle, G. Lewis, and W. G. Martley.

In *Nicene and Post-Nicene Fathers*, Second Series, edited by Philip Schaff and Henry Wace. Vol. 6. Buffalo, N.Y.: Christian Literature, 1893. The letter may be found at http://www.newadvent.org.

Eusebius. *The History of the Church from Christ to Constantine*. Translated by G. A. Williamson. New York: New York University Press, 1966.

———. "Epistula ad Constantiam Augustam." In *Patrologia Cursus Completus: Series Graeca*, edited by J.-P. Migne. Paris: Migne, 1857.

"Evangelicals and Catholics Together: The Christian Mission in the Third Millennium." *First Things*, May 1994.

Fabian, Bernhard. "Friedrich Nicolai: Creator of the German Republic of Letters." In *Literary Cultures and the Material Book*, edited by Simon Eliot, Andrew Nash, and Ian Willison, 241–52. London: British Library, 2007.

Falls, Thomas B., ed. and trans. *Writings of Saint Justin Martyr*. New York: Christian Heritage, 1948.

Ferrara, Abel. *Pasolini*. 2014. Film.

Flaubert, Gustave. *Bouvard et Pécuchet*. In *Oeuvres*, vol. 2, edited by Albert Thibaudet and René Dumesnil. Paris: Gallimard, 1952.

Florensky, Pavel. *Iconostasis*. Translated by Donald Sheehan and Olga Andrejev. Crestwood, N.Y.: St. Vladimir's Seminary Press, 1996.

———. *Izbrannye trudy po iskusstvu*. Moscow: Izobrazitel'noe Iskusstvo, 1996.

———. "Reversed Perspective." In *Beyond Vision: Essays on the Perception of Art*, edited by Nicoletta Misler, translated by Wendy Salmond, 201–72. London: Reaktion Books, 2002.

Foucault, Michel. "What Are the Iranians Dreaming About?" In *Foucault and the Iranian Revolution: Gender and the Seductions of Islamism*, by Janet Afary and Kevin B. Anderson, 203–9. Chicago: University of Chicago Press, 2005.

Francese, Joseph. "Pasolini: Between Passion and 'Ideology.'" In *Pier Paolo Pasolini: In Living Memory*, edited by Ben Lawton and Maura Bergonzoni, 21–32. Washington, D.C.: New Academia, 2009.

Francis, James A. "Visual and Verbal Representation: Image, Text, Person, Power." In *A Companion to Late Antiquity*, edited by Philip Rousseau, 285–305. New York: Wiley-Blackwell, 2012.

Frank, Joseph. *Dostoevsky: The Seeds of Revolt 1821–1849*. Princeton, N.J.: Princeton University Press, 1976.

———. *Dostoevsky: A Writer in His Time*. Princeton, N.J.: Princeton University Press, 2010.

———. *The Idea of Spatial Form*. New Brunswick, N.J.: Rutgers University Press, 1991.

Freccero, John. *Dante: The Poetics of Conversion*. Cambridge, Mass.: Harvard University Press, 1986.

Frémont, Christiane. *L'Être et la relation: Lettres de Leibniz à Des Bosses*. Paris: Vrin, 1999.

Gager, John G. "Body-Symbols and Social Reality: Resurrection, Incarnation and Asceticism in Early Christianity." *Religion* 12 (1982): 345–63.

Galli, Mark. "The Lord Who Acts Like It." *Christianity Today*, December 12, 2011.

Ganzenmüller, Wilhelm. "Das 'Buch der Heiligen Dreifaltigkeit.' Eine deutsche Alchemie aus dem Anfang des 15. Jahrhunderts." In *Beiträge zur Geschichte der Technologie und der Alchemie*, 231–71. Weinheim: Verlag Chemie, 1956; reprint of 1939 article.

Garland, David. *Peculiar Institution: America's Death Penalty in an Age of Abolition.* Cambridge, Mass.: Harvard University Press, 2010.

George, Robert P., ed. *Natural Law and Moral Inquiry: Ethics, Metaphysics and Politics in the Work of Germain Grisez.* Washington, D.C.: Georgetown University Press, 1998.

Gessner, Georg. *Johann Kaspar Lavaters Lebensbeschreibung.* Winterthur: Steiner, 1802.

Gibson, Mel. *The Passion of the Christ.* DVD.

Giralt-Miracle, Daniel, ed. *Gaudí: Exploring Form: Space, Geometry, Structure and Construction.* Barcelona: Lunwerg Editores, 2002.

Gooding-Williams, Robert. *Zarathustra's Dionysian Modernism.* Stanford, Calif.: Stanford University Press, 2001.

Gould, Stephen Jay. *Ontogeny and Phylogeny.* Cambridge, Mass.: Belknap Press, Harvard University Press, 1977.

Grabar, André. *Christian Iconography: A Study of Its Origins.* Princeton, N.J.: Princeton University Press, 1968.

Graber, Rolf. *Bürgerliche Öffentlichkeit und Spätabsolutistischer Staat: Sozietätenbewegung und Konfliktkonjunktur in Zürich 1746–1780.* Zurich: Chronos Verlag, 1993.

Gramsci, Antonio. "The Intellectuals." In *Selections from the Prison Notebooks,* edited and translated by Quintin Hoare and Geoffrey Nowell-Smith, 2–23. New York: International, 1972.

Grau, Oliver. *Virtual Art: From Illusion to Immersion.* Translated by Gloria Custance. Cambridge, Mass.: MIT Press, 2003.

Gray, Richard T. *About Face: German Physiognomic Thought from Lavater to Auschwitz.* Detroit, Mich.: Wayne State University Press, 2004.

Greenwald, Glenn. *With Liberty and Justice for Some: How the Law Is Used to Destroy Equality and Protect the Powerful.* New York: Holt, 2011.

Griffiths, Alison. "The Revered Gaze: The Medieval Imagery in Mel Gibson's *The Passion of the Christ.*" *Cinema Journal* 46, no. 2 (2007): 3–39.

Grisez, Germain. *The Way of the Lord Jesus.* Vol. 1: *Christian Moral Principles.* Chicago: Franciscan Herald, 1983.

———. *The Way of the Lord Jesus.* Vol. 2: *Living a Christian Life.* Quincy, Ill.: Franciscan, 1993.

Grosshaus, Rainald. *Maerten van Heemskerck: Die Gemälde.* Berlin: Horst Boetticher Verlag, 1980.

Habermas, Jürgen. *Strukturwandel der Öffentlichkeit: Untersuchungen zu einer Kategorie der bürgerlichen Gesellschaft.* Neuwied, Berlin: Luchterhand, 1965.

Harley, Felicity. "Christianity and the Transformation of Classical Art." In *A Companion to Late Antiquity,* edited by Philip Rousseau, 306–26. New York: Wiley-Blackwell, 2012.

Hartlaub, Gustav Friedrich. "Signa Hermetis: Zwei Alte Alchemische Bilderhandschriften." *Zeitschrift des Deutschen Vereins für Kunstwissenschaft* 4 (1937), part 1: 93–112 and part 2: 144–62.

Hegel, G. W. F. *Phenomenology of Spirit.* Translated by A. V. Miller. Oxford: Clarendon, 1977.

Heilbrunn, Jacob. "Neocon v. Theocon." *The New Republic*, December 30, 1996.

Hellgardt, Ernst. "Latin and the Vernacular: Mechthild of Magdeburg—Mechthild of Hackeborn—Gertrude of Helfta." In *A Companion to Mysticism and Devotion in Northern Germany in the Late Middle Ages*, edited by Elizabeth Andersen, Henrike Lähnemann, and Anne Simon, 131–55. Leiden: Brill, 2014.

Hendershot, Heather. "God's Angriest Man: Carl McIntire, Cold War Fundamentalism, and Right-Wing Broadcasting." *American Quarterly* 59, no. 2 (2007): 373–96.

Herbers, John. "Political and Religious Shifts Rekindle Church-State Issue." Review of *The Naked Public Square* by Richard John Neuhaus. *The New York Times*, September 2, 1984.

Herschberg-Pierrot, Anne. *Dictionnaire des idées reçues de Flaubert*. Lille: Presses Universitaires de Lille, 1988.

Heschel, Susannah. *Aryan Jesus: Christian Theologians and the Bible in Nazi Germany*. Princeton, N.J.: Princeton University Press, 2008.

Hillebrand, Bruno. *Ästhetik des Augenblicks: Der Dichter als Überwinder der Zeit—von Goethe bis heute*. Göttingen: Vandenhoeck & Ruprecht, 1999.

Himmelfarb, Gertrude. "Correspondence." *First Things*, January 1997.

Hittinger, Russell, and Elizabeth Lev. "Gibson's Passion." *First Things*, March 2004.

Holl, Karl. *Gesammelte Aufsätze zur Kirchengeschichte, II: Der Osten*, 351–87. Tübingen: Mohr (Paul Siebeck), 1916.

Holmes, John Haynes. Introduction to *The Life of Jesus*, by Ernest Renan, 15–23. New York: Modern Library, 1927.

Hotchkiss, Robert V., ed. and trans. *A Pseudo-Epiphanius Testimony Book*. Missoula: Scholars' Press, University of Montana, 1974.

Hubert, Henri, and Marcel Mauss. *Sacrifice: Its Nature and Function*. Translated by W. D. Halls. Chicago: University of Chicago Press, 1964.

Hunnius, Curt. *Dämonen, Ärzte, Alchemisten*. Stuttgart: Wissenschaftliche Verlagsgesellschaft, 1962.

Inhofe, James. Response to "Allegations of Mistreatment of Iraqi Prisoners," May 11, 2004. In *United States Senate Committee on Armed Services, Review of Department of Defense Detention and Interrogation Operations*. Washington, D.C.: U.S. Government Printing Office, 2005.

Ioannes XXII [Pope John XXII]. *Titulus VI: De Crimine Falsi*, in *Corpus Iuris Canonici*, ed. Emil Friedberg and Aemilius Ludwig Richter, col. 1295–96. Leipzig: Tauchnitz, 1879.

Izbicki, Thomas M. "The Authority of Peter and Paul: The Use of Biblical Authority during the Great Schism." In *A Companion to the Great Western Schism (1378–1417)*, edited by Joëlle Rollo-Koster and Thomas M. Izbicki, 375–94. Leiden: Brill, 2009.

Jensen, Robin M. *Face to Face: Portraits of the Divine in Early Christianity*. Minneapolis, Minn.: Fortress, 2005.

Jonge, Alex de. *Dostoevsky and the Age of Intensity*. New York: St. Martin's, 1975.

Junker, Uwe. *Das "Buch der Heiligen Dreifaltigkeit" in seiner zweiten, alchemistischen Fassung (Kadolzburg 1433)*. Cologne: Institut für Geschichte der Medizin der Universität, 1986.

Kames, Henry Home. *Elements of Criticism*. Vol. 1. London: Printed for Vernor and Hood . . . by Alex Lawrie, Edinburgh, 1805.

Kant, Immanuel. *Dreams of a Spirit-Seer: Illustrated by Dreams of Metaphysics*, edited by Frank Sewall, translated by Emanuel F. Goerwitz. London: Sonnenschein; New York: Macmillan, 1900.

Kantorowicz, Ernst H. *The King's Two Bodies: A Study in Mediaeval Political Theology*. Princeton, N.J.: Princeton University Press, 1957.

Kelly, Marjorie. *The Divine Right of Capital: Dethroning the Corporate Aristocracy*. San Francisco: Berrett-Koehler, 2001.

King, Noël Q. *The Emperor Theodosius and the Establishment of Christianity*. London: SCM, 1961.

Kirkpatrick, David D. "Speaking in the Tongue of Evangelicals." *The New York Times*, October 17, 2004.

Kitzinger, Ernst, and Elizabeth Senior. *Portraits of Christ*. Middlesex, Eng.: Penguin Books, 1940.

Klare, Michael. "Bush-Cheney Energy Strategy: Procuring the Rest of the World's Oil." *Foreign Policy in Focus*, January 2004, may be found at www.common dreams.org.

Koller, Heinrich. "Zur Reformpolitik Kaiser Sigmunds." In *Sigismund von Luxemburg: Kaiser und König in Mitteleuropa, 1387–1437: Beiträge zur Herrschaft Kaiser Sigismunds und der europäischen Geschichte um 1400*, edited by Josef Macek, Ernö Marosi, and Ferdinand Seibt, 15–25. Warendorf: Fahlbusch, 1994.

Kostalevsky, Marina. *Dostoevsky and Soloviev: The Art of Integral Vision*. New Haven, Conn.: Yale University Press, 1997.

Krautheimer, Richard. *Early Christian and Byzantine Architecture*. New York: Penguin, 1986.

Kristeva, Julia. "Holbein's Dead Christ." In *Fragments for a History of the Human Body*. Vol. 1, edited by Michel Feher, Ramona Naddaff, and Nadia Tazi, 239–69. New York: Zone, 1989.

Kristol, Irving. *Two Cheers for Capitalism*. New York: Basic Books, 1978.

Kroner, Richard. Introduction to *Early Theological Writings*, by G. W. F. Hegel, 1–66. Philadelphia: University of Pennsylvania Press, 1979.

Kusmer, Ken. "Faithful Get Sneak Peek at 'Passion.'" Associated Press, February 20, 2004, may be found at http://www.alarryross.com.

Lacan, Jacques. *Écrits: A Selection*. Translated by Alan Sheridan. New York: Norton, 1977.

Ladner, Gerhard B. "The Concept of the Image in the Greek Fathers and the Byzantine Iconoclastic Controversy." *Dumbarton Oaks Papers* 7 (1953): 1–34.

Lassen, Eva M. "The Use of the Father Image in Imperial Propaganda and 1 Corinthians 4:14–21." *Tyndale Bulletin* 42 (1991): 127–36.

Latour, Bruno. "What Is Iconoclash? Or Is There a World Beyond the Image Wars?" In *Iconoclash*, edited by Bruno Latour and Peter Weibel, 14–37. Cambridge, Mass.: MIT Press, 2002.

Lauretis, Teresa De. *Alice Doesn't: Feminism, Semiotics and Cinema*. London: Macmillan, 1984.

———. "Language, Representation, Practice: Re-reading Pasolini's Essays on Cinema." *Italian Quarterly* 1 (1980): 159–66.

Lautréamont, Comte de. *Maldoror & the Complete Works of the Comte de Lau-tréamont*. Translated by Alexis Lykiard. Cambridge, Mass.: Exact Change, 1994.

Lavater, Johann Caspar. *Aussichten in die Ewigkeit: 1768–1773/78*, edited by Ursula Caflisch-Schnetzler. Vol. 2 of *Ausgewählte Werke in Historisch-Kritischer Ausgabe*. Zurich: Verlag Neue Züricher Zeitung, 2001.

———. *Physiognomische Fragmente zur Beförderung der Menschenkenntnis und Menschenliebe*. Edited by Christoph Siegrist. Stuttgart: Reclam, 1999.

———. "Über Christusbilder." In *Physiognomische Fragmente zur Beförderung der Menschenkenntnis und Menschenliebe*, vol. 4, edited by Johann Michael Armbruster, 101–12. Winterthur: In der Heinr. Steiner'schen Buchhandlung, 1830.

———. *Werke 1769–1771*. Edited by Martin Ernst Hirzel. Vol. 3 of *Ausgewählte Werke in Historisch-Kritischer Ausgabe*. Zurich: Verlag Neue Züricher Zeitung, 2002.

Lehmann, Paul. "Konstanz und Basel als Büchermärkte während der großen Kirchenversammlungen." In *Erforschung des Mittelalters: Ausgewählte Abhandlungen und Aufsätze*, vol. 1: 253–79. Stuttgart: Hiersemann, 1959.

Leibniz, Gottfried Wilhelm. *Sämtliche Schriften und Briefe*. First Series. *Allgemeiner politischer und historischer Briefwechsel*, vol. 13. Berlin: Akademie Verlag, 1987.

Lewinstein, Gustav. *Die Alchemie und die Alchemisten*. Berlin: Lüderitz, 1870.

Linker, Damon. *The Theocons: Secular America under Siege*. New York: Doubleday, 2006.

Lock, Charles. "Carnival and Incarnation: Bakhtin and Orthodox Theology." In *Critical Essays on Mikhail Bakhtin*, edited by Caryl Emerson, 285–99. New York: Hall, 1999.

Louth, Andrew. "The Body in Western Catholic Christianity." In *Religion and the Body*, edited by Sarah Coakley, 111–30. Cambridge: Cambridge University Press, 1997.

Lukács, Georg. *Der russische Realismus in der Weltliteratur*. Berlin: Aufbau-Verlag, 1952.

Maas, Paul. "Die ikonoklastische Episode in dem Brief des Epiphanios an Johannes." *Byzantinische Zeitschrift* 30 (1929/30): 279–86.

Magid, Ron. "Adding Agony to the Passion." *American Cinematographer* 85, no. 3 (2004): 56–57.

Mann, Thomas. "Dostojevskij—mit Maßen." In *Essays*, vol. 1, edited by Michael Mann, 167–82. Frankfurt am Main: Fischer, 1977.

Manzoli, Giacomo. "La pellicola, la telecamera, il corpo e la realtà: Su una performance bolognese di Pier Paolo Pasolini." *Cineteca Online*. February 2002. The essay may be found at http://www.pierpaolopasolini.eu.

Martin, Dale. *The Corinthian Body*. New Haven, Conn.: Yale University Press, 1995.

Mauri, Fabio. "The Gospel by/about Pasolini." In *Pier Paolo Pasolini: A Future Life*, 268. [Italy]: Associazione "Fondo Pier Paolo Pasolini," 1988.

———. "Intellettuale." In Mauri, Fabio, and Pier Paolo Pasolini, *Pier Paolo Pasolini: Una vita futura: La forma dello sguardo: Roma, 15 ottobre–15 dicembre 1985*, 34. [Rome]: Graf Roma, 1985.

Mauri, Fabio, Carolyn Christov-Bakargiev, and Marcella Cossu. *Fabio Mauri: Opere e azioni 1954–1994*. Rome: Carte segrete, 1994.

Mauss, Marcel. *A General Theory of Magic*. Translated by Robert Brain. London: Routledge.

McLuhan, Marshall. *The Gutenberg Galaxy: The Making of Typographic Man*. Toronto: University of Toronto Press, 1962.

———. *Understanding Media: The Extensions of Man*. New York: McGraw-Hill, 1964.

Megaw, A. H. S. *Byzantine Architecture and Decoration in Cyprus*. Dumbarton Oaks Papers 28 (1974).

———. "Discussion: Architecture, Liturgy, and Chronology." In *Kourion: Excavations in the Episcopal Precinct*, 157–76. Washington, D.C.: Dumbarton Oaks, 2007.

Merleau-Ponty, Maurice. *Phenomenology of Perception*. Translated by Colin Smith. London, New York: Routledge and Paul, Humanities Press, 1962.

Miethke, Jürgen. "Die Konzilien als Forum der öffentlichen Meinung im 15. Jahrhundert." *Deutsches Archiv für Erforschung des Mittelalters* 37, no. 2 (1981): 736–73.

Miles, Margaret R. "'The Evidence of Our Eyes': Patristic Studies and Popular Christianity in the Fourth Century." *Studia Patristica* 18 (1983): 59–63.

Miller, Hillis J. *Speech Acts in Literature*. Stanford, Calif.: Stanford University Press, 2001.

Miller, Robert J., ed. *The Complete Gospels: Annotated Scholars Version*. Sonoma, Calif.: Polebridge, 1994.

Mitchell, W. J. T. *Cloning Terror: The War of Images, 9/11 to the Present*. Chicago: University of Chicago Press, 2011.

Mitscherlich, Alexander, and Margarete Mitscherlich. *The Inability to Mourn: The Principles of Collective Behavior*. Translated by Beverly R. Placzek. New York: Grove, 1975.

Mondzain, Marie-José. *Image, icône, économie: Les sources byzantines de l'imaginaire contemporain*. Paris: Éditions du Seuil, 1996.

———. *L'Image naturelle*. Paris: Le Nouveau Commerce, 1995.

Moriarty, Michael. "Mel Gibson's Reply to 9/11." *Free Republic*, March 9, 2004, http://www.freerepublic.com.

Morrison, Jeffrey. *Winckelmann and the Notion of Aesthetic Education*. Oxford: Clarendon, 1996.

Muller, Rainer A., ed. *Deutsche Geschichte in Quellen und Darstellung: Spätmittelalter 1250–1495*. Vol. 2. Stuttgart: Reclam, 2000.

Murchland, Bernard. "The Socialist Critique of the Corporation." In *The Corporation: A Theological Inquiry*, edited by Michael Novak and John W. Cooper, 156-180. Washington, D.C.: American Enterprise Institute, 1981.

Neuhaus, Richard John. *The Catholic Moment: The Paradox of the Church in the Postmodern World*. San Francisco: Harper and Row, 1987.

———. *The Naked Public Square: Religion and Democracy in America*. Grand Rapids, Mich.: Eerdmans, 1984.

———. Review of *The Passion of the Christ*. *First Things*, February 2004.

Nichols, Bill. Introduction to "The Cinema of Poetry," by Pier Paolo Pasolini. In *Movies and Methods: An Anthology*, edited by Bill Nichols, 542–43. Berkeley: University of California Press, 1976.

Nichols, John. *Dick: The Man Who Is President*. New York: New Press, 2004.

Nietzsche, Friedrich. *Thoughts Out of Season*. In *The Complete Works of Friedrich Nietzsche*, vol. 4, edited by Oscar Levy, translated by Anthony M. Ludovici. London: Foulis, 1914.

———. *Thus Spake Zarathustra*. In *The Complete Works of Friedrich Nietzsche*, vol. 11, edited by Oscar Levy, translated by Thomas Common. London: Foulis, 1914.

"The Ninth Circuit's Fatal Overreach." *First Things*, May 1996.

Noonan, Peggy. "It Is as It Was: Mel Gibson's 'The Passion' Gets a Thumbs-Up from the Pope." *The Wall Street Journal*, December 17, 2003, at http://online.wsj.com.

Nouailhat, René. "L'Opérateur christologique: Dix thèses pour une problématique." *Dialogues d'Histoire Ancienne* 11 (1985): 607–35.

Novak, Michael, ed. *Democracy and Mediating Structures: A Theological Inquiry*. Washington, D.C.: American Enterprise Institute, 1980.

———. *The Future of the Corporation*. Washington, D.C.: American Enterprise Institute, 1996.

———. "Passion Play." *The Weekly Standard*, August 25, 2003.

———. *The Spirit of Democratic Capitalism*. New York: American Enterprise Institute, Simon and Schuster, 1982.

———. "A Theology of the Corporation." In *The Corporation: A Theological Inquiry*, edited by Michael Novak and John W. Cooper, 203- 230. Washington, D.C.: American Enterprise Institute, 1981.

Offner, Arnold A. *Another Such Victory: President Truman and the Cold War, 1945–1953*. Stanford, Calif.: Stanford University Press, 2002.

Onasch, Konrad. *Die Ikonenmalerei: Grundzüge einer systematischen Darstellung*. Leipzig: Koehler & Amelang, 1968.

Ostling, Richard N. "Another Jesus Film Raises the Jewish Issue." Associated Press, September 4, 2003, may be found at http://www.beliefnet.com.

Ostrogorsky, Georg. *Studien zur Geschichte des byzantinischen Bilderstreits*. Amsterdam: Hakkert, 1964, reprint; Breslau: Marcus, 1929.

Pasolini, Pier Paolo. "The Cinema of Poetry." In *Movies and Methods: An Anthology*, edited by Bill Nichols, 542–58. Berkeley: University of California Press, 1976.

———. *Il Vangelo secondo Matteo*. DVD.

———. *The Letters of Pier Paolo Pasolini: 1940–1954*. Vol. 1, edited by Nico Naldini, translated by Stuart Hood. London: Quartet Books, 1992.

———. *Pasolini rilegge Pasolini: Intervista con Giuseppe Cardillo*. Edited by Luigi Fontanella. Milan: Archinto, 2005.

———. *Salò, or 120 Days of Sodom*. VHS. MGM Distribution Company, 1998.

———. *Theorem*. Translated by Stuart Hood. London: Quartet Books, 1992.

———. "Teorema." *Cineforum* 9 (May 1969): 85.

———. "The Unpopular Cinema." In *Heretical Empiricism*, edited by Louise K. Barnett, translated by Ben Lawton and Louise K. Barnett, 267–75. Bloomington: Indiana University Press, 1988.

Patschovsky, Alexander. "Beginen, Begarden and Terziaren im 14. und 15. Jahrhundert: Das Beispiel des Basler Beginenstreits (1400/04–1411)." In *Patschovsky, Alexander: Ketzer, Juden, Antichrist: Gesammelte Aufsätze zum*

60. *Geburtstag von Alexander Patschovsky*, edited by Matthias Kaup, 403–18. Göttingen: Niedersächsische Staats- und Universitätsbibliothek, 2001. May be found at http://webdoc.sub.gwdg.de.

Pattison, George, and Diane Oenning Thompson, eds. *Dostoevsky and the Christian Tradition*. New York: Cambridge University Press, 2000.

Payne, Thomas B. "Philip the Chancellor and the Conductus Prosula: 'Motetish' Works from the School of Notre-Dame." In *Music in Medieval Europe: Studies in Honour of Bryan Gillingham*, edited by Terence Bailey and Alma Santo-suosso, 220–38. Aldershot, Eng.: Ashgate, 2007.

Pestalozzi, Karl. "Lavater's Utopie." In *Literaturwissenschaft und Geschichtsphilosophie: Festschrift für Wilhelm Emrich*, edited by Hermut Arntzen, Bernd Balzer, Karl Pestalozzi, and Rainer Wagner, 283–301. Berlin: de Gruyter, 1975.

Pestalozzi, Karl, and Horst Weigelt, eds. *Das Antlitz Gottes im Antlitz des Menschen: Zugänge zu Johann Kaspar Lavater*. Göttingen: Vandenhoeck & Ruprecht, 1994.

Peterson, Erik. "Christus als Imperator." *Catholica* 5 (1970; reprint of 1936): 64–72.

Pevear, Richard. Introduction to *The Idiot*, by Fyodor Dostoevsky. Translated by Richard Pevear and Larissa Volokhonsky, vii–xix. New York: Vintage Classics, 2003.

Phillips, Kevin. *American Theocracy: The Peril and Politics of Radical Religion, Oil, and Borrowed Money in the 21st Century*. New York: Penguin Books, 2007.

Pollock, Sheldon. "Cosmopolitan Comparison." American Comparative Literature Association keynote address. New Orleans, 2010. Unpublished manuscript.

Popper, Karl. *The Open Society and Its Enemies*. Vol. 1: *The Spell of Plato*. London: Routledge and Paul, 1949.

Porpora, Douglas V., Alexander G. Nikolaev, Julia Hagemann May, and Alexander Jenkins. *Post-Ethical Society: The Iraq War, Abu Ghraib, and the Moral Failure of the Secular*. Chicago: University of Chicago Press, 2013.

Pradel, Fritz. *Griechische und süditalienische Gebete, Beschwörungen und Rezepte des Mittelalters*. Vol. 3:3 of *Religionsgeschichtliche Versuche und Vorarbeiten*, edited by Albrecht Dieterich and Richard Wünsch. Giessen: Töpelmann, 1907.

Price, Simon R. F. *Rituals and Power: The Roman Imperial Cult in Asia Minor*. Cambridge: Cambridge University Press, 1984.

Prince, Stephen. "Beholding Blood Sacrifice in *The Passion of the Christ*: How Real Is Movie Violence?" *Film Quarterly* 56, no. 4 (2006): 11–22.

Rapp, Claudia. *Holy Bishops in Late Antiquity: The Nature of Christian Leadership in an Age of Transition*. Berkeley: University of California Press, 2005.

Refoulé, R. F. *Traité de la prescription contre les hérétiques*. Paris: Éditions du Cerf, 1957.

Reitblat, Abram, and Christine Thomas. "From Literary Almanacs to 'Thick Journals': The Emergence of a Readership for Russian Literature, 1820s–1840s." In *Literary Cultures and the Material Book*, edited by Simon Eliot, Andrew Nash, and Ian Willison, 191–205. London: British Library, 2007.

Renan, Ernest. *The Life of Jesus*. Edited by John Haynes Holmes. New York: Modern Library, 1927.

Roskill, Mark. Introduction to *Hans Holbein: Paintings, Prints, and Reception*, edited by Mark Roskill and John Oliver Hand, 9–15. Washington, D.C.: National Gallery of Art, 2001.

Ross, A. Larry. "Mel Gibson, We Thought We Knew Ye." *Religious News Service*, 2004, may be found at http://www.alarryross.com.

———. "Passionate Encounter: At the Intersection of Faith and Culture." *National Review Online*, March 10, 2004, at http://www.nationalreview.com.

———. "The World's Greatest Communicator: Beyond Information and Education to Transformation," may be found at http://www.alarryross.com.

Roudinesco, Elisabeth. *Jacques Lacan*. Translated by Barbara Bay. New York: Columbia University Press, 1997.

Rubin, Alissa J. "Photos Stoke Tension Over the Afghan Civilian Deaths." *The New York Times*, March 11, 2011, at http://www.nytimes.com.

Ruttenburg, Nancy. *Dostoevsky's Democracy*. Princeton, N.J.: Princeton University Press, 2008.

Sade, Marquis de. *The 120 Days of Sodom & Other Writings*. Compiled and translated by Austryn Wainhouse and Richard Seaver. New York: Grove, 1987.

Santner, Eric. *Stranded Objects: Mourning, Memory, and Film in Postwar Germany*. Ithaca, N.Y.: Cornell University Press, 1990.

Saussy, Haun. "Comparisons, World Literature, and the Common Denominator." In *A Companion to Comparative Literature*, edited by Ali Behdad and Dominic Thomas, 60–64. New York: Wiley-Blackwell, 2011.

———. "So Natural, It's Automatic: Humanistic Studies and Culture Machines." *Southern African Journal of Folklore Studies* 15 (2005): 5–12.

Scahill, Jeremy. *Blackwater: The Rise of the World's Most Powerful Mercenary Army*. New York: Nation Books, 2008.

Schleiermacher, Friedrich. *The Christian Faith*. Edinburgh: Bloomsbury, 1999.

———. *On Religion: Speeches to Its Cultured Despisers*. Translated by John Oman. Louisville, Ky.: Westminster, John Knox Press, 1994.

Schlemmer, Oskar. *The Letters and Diaries of Oskar Schlemmer*. Edited by Tut Schlemmer, translated by Krishna Winston. Middletown, Conn.: Wesleyan University Press, 1972.

Schopenhauer, Arthur. *The World as Will and Representation*. Vol. 1. Translated by E. F. J. Payne. New York: Dover, 1969.

Schütt, Hans-Werner. *Auf der Suche nach dem Stein der Weisen: Die Geschichte der Alchemie*. Munich: Beck, 2000.

Schwineköper, Berent. "Christus-Reliquien-Verehrung und Politik." *Blätter für deutsche Landesgeschichte* 117 (1981): 183–281.

Scully, Michael. "Finding a Place for Religion in Public Life." *Wall Street Journal*, July 30, 1984.

Segl, Peter. "Schisma, Krise, Häresie und Schwarzer Tod: Signaturen der Welt vor Hus." In *Jan Hus: Zwischen Zeiten, Völkern, Konfessionen: Vorträge des internationalen Symposions in Bayreuth vom 22. bis 26. September 1993*, edited by Ferdinand Seibt and Zdenek Radslav Dittrich, 27–38. Munich: R. Oldenbourg, 1997.

Seibt, Ferdinand. "Geistige Reformbewegungen zur Zeit des Konstanzer Konzils." In *Hussitenstudien: Personen, Ereignisse, Ideen einer frühen Revolution*, 97–111. Munich: R. Oldenbourg, 1987.

———. "Jan Hus—zwischen Zeiten, Völkern, Konfessionen." In *Jan Hus: Zwischen Zeiten, Völkern, Konfessionen: Vorträge des internationalen Symposions in Bayreuth vom 22. bis 26. September 1993*, edited by Ferdinand Seibt and Zdenek Radslav Dittrich, 11–26. Munich: R. Oldenbourg, 1997.

Senaldi, Marco F. "The Director Who Became the Screen: Fabio Mauri, Pier Paolo Pasolini, and *Intellettuale*." In *Cinéma, critique des images*, edited by Claudia d'Alonzo and Ken Slock, 269–74. Pasian di Prato: Campanotto Editore, 2012.

Shestov, Lev. "Dostoevsky and Nietzsche: The Philosophy of Tragedy." In *Essays in Russian Literature: The Conservative View: Leontiev, Rozanov, Shestov*, edited by Spencer E. Roberts, 3–183. Athens: Ohio University Press, 1968.

Shookman, Ellis, ed. *The Faces of Physiognomy: Interdisciplinary Approaches to Johann Caspar Lavater*. Columbia, S.C.: Camden House, 1993.

Siciliano, Enzo. *Pasolini: A Biography*. Translated by John Shepley. New York: Random House, 1982.

Soloviev, Vladimir. "A Note in Defense of Dostoevsky against the Charge of a 'New Christianity.'" In *The Heart of Reality: Essays on Beauty, Love, and Ethics*, edited and translated by Vladimir Wozniuk, 199–204. Notre Dame, Ind.: University of Notre Dame Press, 2003.

———. "Three Addresses in Memory of Dostoevsky." In *The Heart of Reality: Essays on Beauty, Love, and Ethics*, edited and translated by Vladimir Wozniuk, 1–28. Notre Dame, Ind.: University of Notre Dame Press, 2003.

Solovieva, Olga. "Polyphonie und Karneval: Spuren Dostoevskijs in Thomas Manns Roman *Doktor Faustus*." *Poetica* 3, no. 4 (2005): 463–94.

Spivey, Nigel. *Enduring Creation: Art, Pain, and Fortitude*. Berkeley: University of California Press, 2001.

Stack, Oswald, and Pier Paolo Pasolini. *Pasolini on Pasolini: Interviews with Oswald Stack*. London: Thames and Hudson, 1969.

Steimatsky, Noa. "Pasolini on *Terra Sancta*: Towards a Theology of Film." *Yale Journal of Criticism* 11, no. 1 (1998): 239–57.

Steinberg, Leo. *The Sexuality of Christ in Renaissance Art and in Modern Oblivion*. Chicago: University of Chicago Press, 1996.

Sterk, Andrea. *Renouncing the World Yet Leading the Church: The Monk-Bishop in Late Antiquity*. Cambridge, Mass.: Harvard University Press, 2004.

Stock, Brian. *The Implications of Literacy: Written Language and Models of Interpretation in the Eleventh and Twelfth Centuries*. Princeton, N.J.: Princeton University Press, 1983.

Stokoe, William C. *Sign Language Structure: An Outline of the Visual Communication Systems of the American Deaf*. Buffalo, N.Y.: Department of Anthropology and Linguistics, University of Buffalo, 1960.

Strauss, David Friedrich. *Das Leben Jesu, kritisch bearbeitet*. Edited by Werner Zager. Waltrop: Hartmut Spenner, 2003.

Strauss, Gerald. Introduction to *Pre-Reformation Germany*, edited by Gerald Strauss, 9–12. London: Macmillan, 1972.

Stump, Phillip H. "The Council of Constance (1414–18) and the End of the Schism." In *A Companion to the Great Western Schism (1378–1417)*, edited by Joëlle Rollo-Koster and Thomas M. Izbicki, 395–442. Leiden: Brill, 2009.

Sumner, Jane. "Gibson Set Stage for 'Passion' with Controlled Marketing: The Greatest Story Ever Sold?" *The Dallas Morning News*, February 17, 2004, may be found at http://www.alarryross.com.

Suskind, Ron. "Faith, Certainty and the Presidency of George W. Bush." *The New York Times Magazine*, October 17, 2004, at http://www.nytimes.com.

Tertullian. *De corona*. In *Patrologia Cursus Completus*, Series Latina, 1:2, edited by J.-P. Migne. Paris: Migne, 1844.

——. *De idololatria*. In *Patrologia Cursus Completus*, Series Latina, 1:1, edited by J.-P. Migne. Paris: Migne, 1844.

Thümmel, Hans Georg. "Die bilderfeindlichen Schriften des Epiphanius von Salamis." *Byzantinoslavica* 47, no. 2 (1986): 181–88.

Tillich, Paul. *Systematic Theology*. Vols. 1–3. Chicago: University of Chicago Press, 1967.

Tocqueville, Alexis de. *Democracy in America and Two Essays on America*. Translated by Gerald E. Bevan. London: Penguin Books, 2003.

Töpfer, Bernhard. "Hoffnungen auf Erneuerung des paradiesischen Zustands (status innocentiae)—ein Beitrag zur Vorgeschichte des hussitischen Adamitentums." In *Eschatologie und Hussitismus*, edited by Alexander Patschovsky and František Šmahel, 169–84. Prague: Historisches Institut, 1996.

Torrance, Thomas F. *The Trinitarian Faith: The Evangelical Theology of the Ancient Catholic Church*. Edinburgh: T & T Clark, 1988.

——. "The Triunity of God in the Nicene Theology of the Fourth Century." In *Theological Dialogue between Orthodox and Reformed Churches*, vol. 2, edited by Thomas F. Torrance, 3–37. Edinburgh: Scottish Academic, 1993.

Vargas, Ann. "When Your Client Is God." *PRWeek*, March 13, 2000.

Vergine, Lea. *Body Art and Performance: The Body as Language*. Milan: Skira Editore, 2000.

Wachtel, Andrew. "Dostoevsky's *The Idiot*: The Novel as Photograph." *History of Photography* 26, no. 3 (2002): 205–15.

Warner, Michael. *Publics and Counterpublics*. New York: Zone Books, 2002.

Wehrli, Max. "Lavater und das geistige Zürich." In *Das Antlitz Gottes im Antlitz des Menschen: Zugänge zu Johann Kaspar Lavater*, edited by Karl Pestalozzi and Horst Weigelt, 9–22. Göttingen: Vandenhoeck & Ruprecht, 1994.

Weigelt, Horst. *Johann Kaspar Lavater: Leben, Werk und Wirkung*. Göttingen: Vandenhoeck & Ruprecht, 1991.

Wellbery, David. *Lessing's Laocoon: Semiotics and Aesthetics in the Age of Reason*. Cambridge: Cambridge University Press, 1984.

Williams, Frank. Introduction to *The Panarion of Epiphanius of Salamis*, edited and translated by Frank Williams, ix–xxvii. Leiden: Brill, 1987–94.

Williams, Rowan. *Dostoevsky: Language, Faith, and Fiction*. Waco, Tex.: Baylor University Press, 2008.

Williams, Russell. "Pasolini's Ideology in His Cultural Essays of the Fifties." *The Italianist* 5 (1985): 39–40.

Wilson, Derek. *Hans Holbein: Portrait of an Unknown Man*. London: Weidenfeld and Nicolson, 1996.

Wolf, Gerhard. "'. . . sed ne taceatur.' Lavaters 'Grille mit den Christusköpfen' und die Tradition der authentischen Bilder." In *Der exzentrische Blick:*

Gespräch über Physiognomik, edited by Claudia Schmölders, 43–76. Berlin: Akademie Verlag, 1996.

Wolfe, Christopher, ed. *The Naked Public Square Reconsidered: Religion and Politics in the Twenty-First Century*. Wilmington, Del.: ISI Books, 2009.

Wood, David. *Body Probe: Mutating Physical Boundaries*. London: Creation, 1999.

Wysling, Hans. "Die Literatur." In *Zürich im 18. Jahrhundert: Zum 150. Jahrestag der Universität Zürich*, edited by Hans Wysling, 131–88. Zurich: Berichthaus, 1983.

Yurchak, Alexei. *Everything Was Forever, Until It Was No More: The Last Soviet Generation*. Princeton, N.J.: Princeton University Press, 2005.

Zager, Werner. Introduction to *Das Leben Jesu, kritisch bearbeitet*, by David Friedrich Strauss, edited by Werner Zager, i–xlv. Waltrop: Spenner, 2003.

Žižek, Slavoj. "Formal Democracy and Its Discontents: Violations of the Fantasy-Space." *American Imago* 48, no. 2 (1991): 181–98.

———. *The Parallax View*. Cambridge, Mass.: MIT Press, 2006.

Page numbers in **boldface** refer to illustrations.